GOVERNMENT BEYOND THE CENTRE

SERIES EDITOR: GERRY STOKER

The world of sub-central government and administration – including local authorities, quasi-governmental bodies and the agencies of public-private partnerships – has seen massive changes in recent years and is at the heart of the current restructuring of government in the United Kingdom and other Western democracies.

The intention of the *Government Beyond the Centre* series is to bring the study of this often-neglected world into the mainstream of social science research, applying the spotlight of critical analysis to what has traditionally been the preserve of institutional public administration approaches.

Its focus is on the agenda of change currently being faced by sub-central government, the economic, political and ideological forces that underlie it, and the structures of power and influence that are emerging. Its objective is to provide up-to-date and informative accounts of the new forms of government, management and administration that are emerging.

The series will be of interest to students and practitioners of politics, public and social administration, and all those interested in the reshaping of the governmental institutions which have a daily and major impact on our lives.

GOVERNMENT BEYOND THE CENTRE

SERIES EDITOR: GERRY STOKER

Published

Wendy Ball and John Solomos (eds)
Race and Local Politics

Richard Batley and Gerry Stoker (eds)
Local Government in Europe

John Gyford
Citizens, Consumers and Councils

Yvonne Rydin
The British Planning System

John Stewart and Gerry Stoker (eds)
The Future of Local Government

Forthcoming

Clive Gray
Government Beyond the Centre

Richard Kerley
Managing in Local Government

Steve Leach, John Stewart and Kieron Walsh
The Changing Organisation and Management of Local Government

David Wilson and Chris Game
An Introduction to Local Government

Series Standing Order
If you would like to receive future titles in this series as they are published,
you can make use of our standing order facility. To place a standing order
please contact your bookseller or, in case of difficulty, write to us at the
address below with your name and address and the name of the series.
Please state with which title you wish to begin your standing order.
(If you live outside the UK we may not have the rights for your area,
in which case we will forward your order to the publisher concerned.)

Standing Order Service, Macmillan Distribution Ltd,
Houndmills, Basingstoke, Hampshire, RG21 2XS, England

THE BRITISH PLANNING SYSTEM

An Introduction

Yvonne Rydin

MACMILLAN

First published 1993 by
THE MACMILLAN PRESS LTD
Houndmills, Basingstoke, Hampshire RG21 2XS
and London
Companies and representatives
throughout the world

Copy-edited and typeset by Povey–Edmondson
Okehampton and Rochdale, England

ISBN 0–333–52740–2 hardcover
ISBN 0–333–52741–0 paperback

A catalogue record for this book is available
from the British Library.

Reprinted 1994

Printed in Great Britain by
Mackays of Chatham PLC
Chatham, Kent

Dedicated to
George, Simon and Rita

Contents

PART 3   *THE POLITICS OF PLANNING*

List of Tables, Figures, Maps, Exhibits and Summary Boxes

■ Tables

■ Figures

■ Maps

■ Exhibits

■ Summary Boxes

Glossary

AAI	Area of Archeological Importance
ACC	Association of County Councils
ADAS	Agricultural Development Advisory Service
ADC	Association of District Councils
ALARP	As Low As Reasonably Practicable
AMA	Association of Metropolitan Authorities
AONB	Area of Outstanding Natural Beauty
BATNEEC	Best Available Technology Not Entailing Excessive Cost
BNF	British Nuclear Fuels
BPEO	Best Practicable Environmental Option
BPM	Best Practicable Means
CADW	Welsh Historic Monuments
CAP	Common Agricultural Policy (EC)
CBI	Confederation of British Industry
CC	Countryside Commission
CDP	Community Development Project
CEC	Commission of European Communities
CEGB	Central Electricity Generating Board
CIoTr	Chartered Institute of Transport
CLD	Certificate of Lawful Development
CLU	Certificate of Lawful Use
COPA	Control of Pollution Act
COSLA	Convention of Scottish Local Authorities
DCPN	Development Control Policy Note
DES	Department of Education and Science
DLG	Derelict Land Grant
DoE	Department of the Environment
DoEm	Department of Employment
DoEn	Department of Energy
DoTr	Department of Transport
EA	Environmental Assessment
EC	European Community
EEA	European Environmental Agency
EIA	Environmental Impact Assessment
EIP	Examination in Public
EPA	Environment Protection Agency
ESA	Environmentally Sensitive Area
EZ	Enterprise Zone

GDO	General Development Order
GEAR	Glasgow Eastern Area Renewal Project
GIA	General Improvement Area
GLC	Greater London Council
HAT	Housing Action Trust
HIP	Housing Investment Programme
HMIP	Her Majesty's Inspectorate of Pollution
HMIPI	Her Majesty's Industrial Pollution Inspectorate
IAP	Inner Area Programme
IPC	Integrated Pollution Control
LAW	Land Authority for Wales
LBA	London Boroughs Association
LDDC	London Docklands Development Corporation
LEA	Local Enterprise Agency
LEC	Local Enterprise Council
LEGUP	Local Enterprise Grant for Urban Projects
LENTA	London Enterprise and Training Agency
LGPLA	Local Government Planning and Land Act
MAFF	Ministry of Agriculture Fisheries and Food
MPG	Minerals Planning Guidelines
NCC	Nature Conservancy Council
NGO	Non-governmental organisation
NPG	National Planning Guideline
NPPG	National Planning Policy Guidelines
NRA	National Rivers Authority
NSA	Nitrate Sensitive Area
ODP	Office Development Permit
PLI	Public Local Inquiry
PAN	Planning Advisory Note
PPG	Planning Policy Guidance Note
PTA	Passenger Transport Authority
PTE	Passenger Transport Executive
PTP	Passenger Transport Plan
RCEP	Royal Commission on Environmental Pollution
RDC	Rural Development Commission
RIBA	Royal Institute of British Architects
RICS	Royal Institution of Chartered Surveyors
RPG	Regional Planning Guidelines
RSNC	Royal Society for Nature Conservation
RTPI	Royal Town Planning Institute
RWA	Regional Water Authority
SDA	Scottish Development Agency
SDD	Scottish Development Department

SDP	Social Democratic Party
SE	Scottish Enterprise
SERPLAN	Standing Conference of London and South East Regional Planning
SPNR	Society for the Protection of Nature Reserves
SPZ	Simplified Planning Zone
SSSI	Site of Special Scientific Interest
TEC	Training and Enterprise Council
TPO	Tree Preservation Order
TPP	Transport Policies and Programmes
UCO	Use Classes Order
UDC	Urban Development Corporation
UDG	Urban Development Grant
UDP	Unitary Development Plan
UKAEA	United Kingdom Atomic Energy Authority
UNEP	United Nations Environment Programme
WDA	Waste Disposal Authority
WDA	Welsh Development Agency
WO	Welsh Office
WRA	Waste Regulating Authority

Acknowledgements

The idea for this book was first suggested to me by Gerry Stoker in the summer of 1988 so the first thanks should go to him for setting me on the road of several years' work amongst the nether reaches of the planning system. I admit that there were times when I wished I had not started but I am unreservedly glad to have arrived. My totally unqualified thanks go to Gerry for his encouragement, advice and detailed reading of several drafts in his capacity of academic editor. My thanks also to my publisher, Steven Kennedy, for his care of the book and his enthusiasm for the project. Several people generously read parts of the text and offered helpful comments. I would particularly like to thank Erling Berge, Keith Hayton, George Myerson, Phil Pinch and Simon Zadek and the publisher's reviewers. Jo Little kindly provided some reference material.

I wish to acknowledge the supportive environment provided by my colleagues at the London School of Economics, both within the Department of Geography and outside. In particular I should mention Jutta Muller, who helped with the preparation of the text in the most careful manner possible. Mike Scorer, in the Drawing Office, did some beautiful work with the various diagrams, under quite inexcusable pressure of time. Alison Grieg and Shirley Maclean helped with some vital references at the last minute.

Finally my thanks must go to my (extended) family for all their belief and help, not least with childcare! The book is dedicated to the three most important people in my life, to whom I owe the greatest thanks for making everything so worthwhile.

Needless to say, I accept full responsibility for any errors and misintepretations in the text.

YVONNE RYDIN

Introduction

■ What is planning?

Planning, as discussed in this book, has three key characteristics. First, it is a future oriented activity. Planning seeks to devise strategies which will lead to desired end states. Many dictionary definitions of the word planning begin with this idea of decision making to achieve a given goal and it is at the heart of an influential theory of planning known as procedural planning theory (discussed in Chapter 2). Second, planning is primarily a public sector activity. It describes a process by which the public sector, at central, regional and local levels, seeks to influence the activities of firms and households through guidance, regulation and incentives. This is not to suggest that the decision making that occurs within the private sector is not of interest. On the contrary, one of the main arguments of this book is the need to understand these private sector processes in order to understand how the public sector conducts its planning activities. However, the starting point for a review of the planning system is an analysis of the policies, procedures and institutions of the public sector. Third, the particular type of planning covered by this book is focused on the physical environment, whereas in other contexts planning may refer to economic or social planning. This draws on another sense of the dictionary definition of planning, the association with drawings and layouts for buildings, sites and urban areas. The urban design aspects of planning have a history stretching back to Grecian and Roman times and many planning courses still emphasise drawing board training for would-be planners. However most planning activity is now concerned with the physical environment without focusing on these design skills. Planning is about devising strategies for reshaping the built and natural environment. These strategies may take a variety of forms and their implementation need not necessarily be guided by a design blueprint. The aesthetic quality of the urban environment need not be the main goal. The goals may cover: the redistribution of resources to disadvantaged inner city groups; the longevity of the built stock; the conservation of wildlife; or the encouragement of urban development. The common strand is the focus on the use of the built and natural environment, and on strategies which can alter that use.

1

Such a definition is still, of course, very broad in scope. Planning activity describes a range of concerns, expressed through many specific policies. Accepting that planning is an umbrella term carries several implications. There is bound to be confusion over the boundaries of the planning system. Not all policies considered to lie within the boundaries will carry the label 'planning'. With an expanding range of state activities more and more policy concerns have come within the compass of planning textbooks: transport, housing, inner cities, pollution to name but a few. Since these concerns are the subject of policy specialisms of their own, planning will overlap with several other policy areas and, indeed, claim to include them. The scope of planning at any particular time will relate to the currently accepted limits to the public sector's role in devising strategies for the physical environment. It is important to recognise that as social and economic change occurs, the area shaded by the planning umbrella will alter. New (or old) problems will come (back) to the fore and new (or old) issues become politically salient (again). At times the emphasis will closely relate to the physical character of development, at other times to the social, economic or broader environmental implications of that development. The areas that a planning textbook should focus on will alter in line with current problems and political concerns.

The starting point in examining the planning umbrella is the planning legislation passed by Parliament, the concerns of the Department of the Environment, the activities of planning departments in local authorities and other related organisations, and the range of work undertaken by planners and related professionals. In the period immediately after the Second World War the main point of reference for anyone interested in the planning system would have been the 1947 Town and Country Planning Act. This piece of land use planning legislation was significant in that it instituted an almost comprehensive regime for control of development, supplemented by plans setting out intentions in relation to the broad pattern of development. In the context of war damage, rapid population growth and economic prosperity, the concern with managing substantial urban construction was at the centre of the planning system. Economic prosperity brought with it higher expectations for the quality of life and of the physical environment. But the processes of economic development continued to leave substantial areas and social groups relatively, or even absolutely, disadvantaged: inner city poverty; urban dereliction; poor housing standards; increasing pollution. Planning policies spread into new concerns. The nature of the planning response to these concerns was shaped by the institutional and political context at the time. Growth of local government and professionalisation of local government officers was an important context in the late 1960s and early 1970s. Similarly the planning response to the economic cycles of the late 1970s and 1980s was framed by the programme for rolling back the state instituted by the government of Margaret Thatcher.

So any useful definition of planning must be capable of coping with the changing scope of such activity. And a planning textbook should be relevant to the concerns and range of public sector policies currently constituting planning activity in the 1990s. For this reason, the policy areas covered by this book, and the relative depth in which they are covered, reflect my perception of the most significant areas within the planning system. Particular emphasis is given to two areas: land use planning which remains at the core of British planning, with the implementation of many other policy goals dependant on land use planning procedures; and environmental planning which has become steadily more important within all public and private sector decision making since the late 1980s. Recognition is also given to the place that countryside policy holds in the policy culture of Britain, despite (or perhaps because of) our high levels of urbanisation. Within urban policy, the current concerns with urban regeneration are reflected in a greater emphasis on promoting urban development than on, say, aspects of housing policy which would have been more prominent in the 1970s. Similarly in transport policy, only a fairly brief overview is attempted since the implications of new environmental concerns for transport policy are likely to call forth major changes in orientation.

A further justification for the emphasis in the book is that the concern is with the planning system, as a set of procedures and institutions for devising and implementing strategies. This is distinct from a primary concern with the content and detail of policy, where the experience of implementing policies in different situations is more relevant than the mechanisms for formulating and ensuring implementation. A hard and fast distinction cannot, of course, be made between planning systems and policies. Policies are, in a sense, the output of the systems. And any evaluation of the planning system will require knowledge of the policies in practice. But there is a difference of focus which justifies the choice of the areas emphasised in this book. The resulting survey should be appropriate to the needs of planning students and planners today.

■ The relevance of British planning

The British planning system clearly has certain specific characteristics. It represents a response to the environmental problems of the first industrial nation, both in the 19th century and then through the changes of the 20th century. It has been shaped by uniquely British versions of two of the major political ideologies of the postwar period. First, there is the commitment to the welfare state following the Second World War, seeking to redress inequalities of income but within a mixed economy framework which fell short of the social democracy of, say, Sweden. Second, there is the impact of Thatcherism, a term widely given to the political project of the British government headed by Margaret Thatcher from 1979–90, which sought to free the market from state control and interference. The detail of British policy, procedures and institutions reflects these specific British contexts.

However, there are cross-cultural dimensions to British planning. Many concepts have been borrowed from other countries experience: Prussian land policy and urban design was influential on early conceptions of British land use planning; the environmental impact assessment is taken from the United States National Environmental Policy Act of 1969; national parks also have their North American precedents. In return the model of British planning has been transplanted to many other countries, both under colonial policy and by selective imitation. Thus knowledge of how the British system actually works in practice is of relevance to analysts from many countries trying to understand their own national systems and make proposals for policy innovations. The impact of Thatcherism may have been most pronounced in its home base, but similar political trends have been felt through many parts of the world. The detail of change in the planning system and the way in which it worked through to environmental change are relevant wherever Thatcherism was paralleled.

Across Europe the spread of new concepts and ideas in planning has been accelerated by the role of the EC. Britain has had to change procedures and institutions at the European Commission's behest and found itself subject to the rulings of the European Courts. Greater contact between policy makers and professionals across the continent has also led to a diffusion of ideas at the same time that contact between economic actors is making the integrated market more of a reality. Knowledge of policy practice in the various nation states of our common European home is becoming more and more necessary for the student and practitioner alike. It is only lack of space and time that prevents a more directly comparative dimension in the book as it stands.

However, the relevance of knowledge of the British planning system does not lie only in the detail of procedures and institutions and their cross-national dimension. The British planning system is a long running case study of public sector activity operating within a market or capitalist economy. As such, it can tell us much about the possibilities and constraints of such activity. There are many similarities in the environmental problems that countries based on a market economy face: in patterns of urbanisation and counterurbanisation; in pollution generation; in inner city decay; and in demands on rural areas. The relationship between public and private sectors in market economies is a key element in explaining these problems and determining the nature of responses by the planning system. Analysis of the dynamic interrelation between public and private sector over the physical environment in Britain can raise questions and make suggestions for how that analysis could proceed in other national arenas, even if it will not directly provide knowledge of that relationship in other countries.

■ Studying the planning system

How should we approach the study of planning to enable us to understand both the detail of the British planning system and, more generally how planning for the physical environment operates in practice? Two themes in relation to this question run throughout the book. First, to understand planning it is necessary to see planning in context, as a social, political and economic activity. An account which concentrates purely on the procedures of the planning system is, therefore, insufficient since it tries to divorce the planning system from those processes of which it is an integral part and which are essential to any understanding of planning in practice. Second, there is considerable dispute over the analysis of these socioeconomic processes and, therefore, over the role of planning in relation to them. This dispute is not to be regretted, in my view. Vigorous debate is the indicator of a healthy and vital community in planning studies. It promotes new understanding of the role of planning, helps to prevent complacency among professionals and can engender new programmes for political action. This book does not propose a single view of the relation of planning to socioeconomic processes (see Figure I.1). It consciously takes on board a variety of disputing approaches and organises them to help the reader find the way around an otherwise confusing debate.

□ *Providing a historical context*

Both the planning system and the debate about planning have changed over time and Part 1 of the book, *The Development of Planning Policy and Theory*, examines this development. Here the changing economic and social conditions are set alongside the emerging policies and institutions of planning. As new socioeconomic conditions are created, new problems are brought to the attention of policy makers

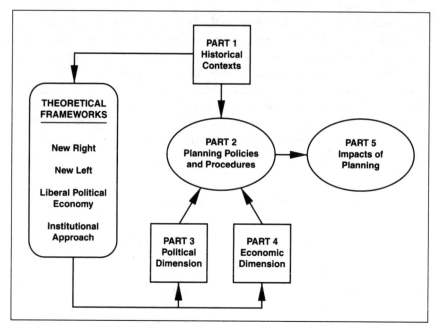

Figure I.1   *The structure of the book*

and some of these the planning system tries to address. At the same time, the development of the system has been associated with the growing professionalisation of planners and the increased sophistication of academic discussion about planning as planning organisations and their educational counterparts have matured in organisational terms. Thus the general socioeconomic context and the more specific institutional context for planning frame the detail of new and changing policies.

Key trends and discontinuities are emphasised, rather than attempting to provide a comprehensive and detailed historical narrative. A fairly rough and ready periodisation is used, suggesting links not only between specific forms of socioeconomic change and particular policy developments but also with the implicit or explicit theoretical positions adopted. The fit is not watertight but the coincidences are intriguing. It is possible, indeed common, to derive a history of planning policy in which change occurs naturally in response to the passage of time and the appearance of problems associated with environmental change. But at any time, there is a theoretical view implicit in the prevailing policy framework. As that framework changes, conflicts between theories can develop, with the theoretical debate becoming an element of policy change itself. Indeed the legitimating role of much planning theory can be clearly seen if theoretical developments are laid alongside the evolution of the planning professions and related academy. As Cooke argues, planning theory is stubbornly normative (1983, p.25).

Chapter 1, *Establishing the Planning System*, looks at the 19th century origins of British planning and the tentative early planning legislation of the interwar period. In the period up to the start of the First World War, planning focused on the public health and housing concerns arising from the consequences of industrialisation and rapid urbanisation. Also ever present was the threat of social unrest arising from the appalling social conditions. Planning developed as an urban design response to these problems. Implicit in the resulting planning action was the notion of environmental determinism, that changing the physical environment would alter peoples nature and behaviour. In the interwar period, the world economic recession put unemployment and regional disparities arising from economic restructuring high on the political agenda, while the Second World War prompted a more wholesale movement for social and physical reconstruction. Planning began to develop a separate identity, focused around land use and espousing a theory of problem-free public adminstration in which the public sector would direct resource allocation.

After the Second World War the main framework of the planning system was established. Chapter 2 tells of *Experience and Change in the Postwar Period*. In the 1950s and 1960s planning extended its range of policies in the context of relative economic prosperity and political consensus. Planners consolidated their professional position and conceived of themselves as generic decision makers, able to tackle any area of policy concerned directly, or indirectly, with the physical environment. The theoretical development of procedural planning theory bolstered the extension of the planning system and planners' remit. However, the 1970s ended the postwar boom with an economic crisis. Deprivation within urban areas had again became a relevant political issue, pointing to the inability of planning to resolve this enduring problem. At the same time concern with the excesses of the preceding period of growth were also increasingly making themselves felt. The result was a crisis of confidence for the planning profession and a fracturing of the debate about planning. Critiques of planning practice from a variety of standpoints abounded, some suggesting marginal improvements but others questioning the whole approach and function of planners. These critiques came from organisation theory, from radical and liberal political economy, and from political sociology, terms which will be explained in Chapter 2.

The crisis of the 1970s bore fruit in the political project of Thatcherism discussed in Chapter 3, *The Decade of Thatcherism and After*. The

1980s were another period of intense restructuring with recovery following recession and rapid investment in new technology. Political restructuring also occurred as the New Right ideology of the Thatcher government challenged established viewpoints and reoriented both policy practice and political campaigning. The planning profession found itself under attack and sought to established new rationales within both the public and the private sectors. The theoretical debate reflected these features, with a New Right perspective on planning being, rather gently, challenged by a New Left perspective, and the academic community seeking to combine a theoretical understanding of planning practice with a less stringently critical stance, in the form of the institutional approach. Again these various approaches are discussed in Chapter 3.

The period after the departure of Margaret Thatcher as Prime Minister brings us into the 1990s and the present day. World economic recession again prevails with environmental crises, closer integration within the EC, and political disintegration across the broader European continent also on the agenda. It is in this context and with a view to developments over the next decade that the analysis of planning in the rest of the book proceeds. To guide that analysis, and open up the various dimensions of debate about planning, four theoretical perspectives are selected as most pertinent to the conditions of the 1990s. These are the New Right which remains a potent ideological position, the New Left which is struggling to re-establish itself, the institutional approach which continues to consolidate in academic arenas, and liberal political economy which is enjoying a renaissance in the guise of environmental economics. These positions are reviewed at the end of Chapter 3 and structure the discussion later in the book.

□ *Describing the planning system*

A description of the details of the planning system is a necessary precursor to more in-depth analysis of planning in practice. Therefore Part 2, *Planning Today*, provides an account of the core elements of the planning system. Chapter 4 looks at *Land Use Planning and Conservation*. Land use planning remains at the heart of the planning system, providing the key tool of comprehensive development control and the flexibility of broad brush and detailed development plans. Conservation policy is closely linked to land use planning through the designation of conservation areas and the more rigorous application of development control to highly valued elements in the physical environment. In Chapter 5, *Countryside Policy*, the package of policies for rural Britain are examined, with their often contradictory attempts to provide for access to the countryside, protection of rural areas from development, nature conservation, rural economic development and resource exploitation. The growing importance placed on environmental protection is reflected in the burgeoning area of *Environmental Planning*, covered in Chapter 6. Following a brief survey of water management, more emphasis is placed on pollution control, waste management and the integration of environmental concerns into land use planning, including the introduction of environmental impact assessment. Finally, in Chapter 7, *Urban Policy and Transport*, are considered with particular emphasis on urban grant and subsidy systems and on measures to transfer land to private sector developers: relatively less emphasis is given to transport planning. It is inevitable that any survey of the broad ranging planning system will be selective. The intention in Part 2 is to provide a survey that addresses the concerns of the 1990s and places particular stress on what are seen as key areas for the future.

While the aim is to introduce readers to the British planning system, the starting point is the operation of that system in England. Thus most of the references to legislation and other policy documents are restricted to those applicable within England. However, at the end of each section the significant variations that exist between the English situation and that prevailing in Wales or Scotland are identified. The imposition of direct rule in Northern Ireland renders the situation there even more distinct from that in England. It has not proved possible to provide parallel details for Northern Ireland in every policy area, but where points of particular interest arise, this has been noted.

☐ *Analysing the politics of planning*

By the end of Part 2 the planning system has been described, set in a historical frame, and the alternative ways of analysing the operation of that system introduced. In Parts 3 and 4, greater use is made of these alternative theoretical approaches to examine planning in practice. Parts 3 and 4 consider the political and economic dimensions to the operation of planning respectively. In Part 3, *The Politics of Planning*, a central place is given to the argument, so strongly put by urban sociologists in the 1970s, that planning is fundamentally a political process. There are three dimensions to this argument.

First, planning involves decisions about the allocation of resources. Land use planning will alter land values and the spatial pattern of those land values by development control decisions which grant or deny planning permission. For decades, countryside policy has had to deal with the demands from the farming industry for continued economic support, support which has had widely recognised adverse consequences on various groups. Pollution control can transfer costs from those affected by polluting emissions, whether in health or direct economic terms, to the polluter, making the polluter pay. And in urban areas planning has frequently focused on the struggle between different groups over the control of scarce land and the values it represents for direct use and exchange in the market place. Through its influence on the allocation of resources, planning, therefore, has a distributive impact. This would be enough to earn the planning system the description political. But such distributive consequences can also stimulate collective action to engage in political campaigning.

This second sense of the term political refers to the quantity of activity generated by the planning system in which one group tries to influence the decisions and actions of another. In some cases this will involve non-governmental organisations (NGOs) or pressure groups trying to influence a government organisation, as when a local amenity society presses for a refusal of planning permission for a particular site. In other cases, the interaction will be between governmental organisations: a local authority negotiating with central government over grant allocations; conflicts between local authorities over green belt designations; disputes between various quangos, say between English Nature, English Heritage and the National Rivers Authority (NRA) over the future of a riverside site of special scientific interest or SSSI owned by English Heritage. These examples also highlight the fact that the form of interaction between organisations will vary. A spectrum of such political action can be conceived with outright conflict at the one end, forms of campaigning and negotiation in the middle, and routine consultation and liaison at the other end. Organisations are more likely to engage in conflictual relations when two conditions are met: that the distributive consequences of the decision are severe and adverse for one group; and that there is an ideological conflict underlying the specific circumstances of the issue at hand.

The third sense of political planning concerns this ideological dimension. There are left and right wing approaches to planning the physical environment. There are also views of planning incorporated in other political ideologies which may lay outside the left–right spectrum, as with green ideologies. The ideologies engage with each other in the debate over planning policy and its future direction. This debate concerns both means and ends in planning. The scope given to market forces in the urban regeneration, the extent to which local community groups should be involved in land use planning, and the extent of public expenditure on pollution control are all examples of differences over the detail of the planning system which may arise between adherents of different ideological positions. But there will also be differences in the criteria by which planning activity is judged to be successful. Generation of private wealth and profit will be a major goal for the Right, but not for the Left or Greens. Employment generation will by encouraged by the Right and the Left but not by Greens. Minimising the scale of public sector control over local decisions may be welcomed by the Right and Greens, but not necessarily by the Left. These issues of debate over principle and detail provide another political dimension to the planning system.

In Part 3, these political dimensions are dealt with under three headings. In Chapter 8, *The State*, the various governmental organisations involved in the planning system are described and their interaction discussed. This includes British central and local government, the role of quangos and the increasing importance of the EC. Chapter 9, on *The Planners*, takes the professionalisation of planners as the key theme and explores the nature of occupational control within the planning system and the relation of planners to the public in different kinds of planning organisation. Finally, Chapter 10 looks at *The Public*, considering their interaction with the planning system through various kinds of pressure group, the use of political parties and the underlying structure of public attitudes to planning concerns.

Brief Exhibits are provided throughout Part 3 to help link this discussion to questions of planning. These give detail to the more general political analysis and also help to amplify the description of policies and procedures given in Part 2. These Exhibits range from the role of the EC in introducing environmental assessment, to the attitude of professionals within the water industry, to the potential of public local inquiries as a vehicle for public participation. Throughout the main text of Part 3 and these Exhibits the relative value of the different theoretical perspectives – the New Right, liberal political economy, New Left and institutional approach – are assessed. Each perspective has its own view of the state, planners and the public (see Figure 3.2). For example, the New Right has developed a critique of the state which emphasises its tendency towards bureaucracy and unnecessary red tape. On the other hand, the institutional approach has found, through detailed empirical work, repeated evidence of the ways in which planners mediate between interests and use networking and negotiation skills. These different insights of the competing perspectives are applied, both to explore further the theoretical perspectives themselves, but also for the greater understanding they can give us of the planning system in practice.

☐ *Analysing planning and the market*

Planning is a political process but it is also essential for planners to understand the nature of economic processes. Indeed, it is because planning is engaged in resource allocation and has distributive consequences, that knowledge of the market is so necessary. For British planning, like most examples across the world, operates in the context of capitalism based on market processes. As a public sector activity, planning constantly engages with these market processes, trying to regulate, stimulate and impose order and structure on them. In Britain's advanced capitalist economy, the state is so closely involved with the economy that it can be difficult to separate them in any analysis of a detailed planning situation. These are the issues tackled in Part 4, *Planning and the Market*

There is a tendency in general parlance and media presentations to assume that there is one correct view of how the economy operates, with marginal, often highly technical, disputes between economists over, say, the best indicator for the money supply. However, there are well developed alternative models of the economy and state–economy relations. The four theoretical perspectives I selected towards the end of Part 1 provide four different economic models. The New Right perspective draws on an idealised account of the market model, operating within the assumptions of perfect competition. Liberal political economy uses the tools of welfare economics to provide a critique of this ideal market model based on the concept of market failure. Underpinning the New Left approach remains the influential marxist model, placing its analysis of capital accumulation at the heart of all economic, social and political action. Finally, the institutional approach to planning is paralleled by an institutional approach to economics which provides a distinctive multi-disciplinary analysis of market processes.

In Chapter 11, *Alternative Approaches*, these four perspectives are outlined. This is amplified in Chapters 12–15 which provide case studies of planning issues. Chapter 12 looks at the vexed problem of providing *Land for Housing*, Chapter 13 considers *Minerals Exploitation*, focusing particularly on coal, Chapter 14 tackles *Pollution: Emission and Control* and Chapter 15 analyses *The Inner City Problem*. In each case the issue is analysed from the points of view of the four alternative approaches, with the emphasis on getting that particular approach over rather than criticising it. The contrast between the four approaches provides a continual, implicit critique by each approach of the other three.

☐ *Assessing planning*

Part 5 provides a overview, *Assessing Planning*. This consists of two chapters. In Chapter 16 the assessment focuses on *The Impacts of British Planning*. This chapter draws together statistical material and published research results to consider what the effects of the planning system has been. This is an ambitious task and it is in the nature of such a review that a comprehensive and conclusive judgement cannot be made: there are too many gaps in the research literature and space constrains review of what is available. But some clear trends are apparent, in many cases the research and data is fairly conclusive and a consequent critique of the planning system can be developed. Finally, Chapter 17 asks the question *Why Plan?*, and probes the necessity of a planning system, looking back at the general nature of the relationship between the planning system and economic change. It considers the potential planning offers for securing social change and the implications this has for political action surrounding planning issues. Finally, it assesses the extent to which the potential for change is currently dissipated and wasted and argues for continued debate as a way forward to change.

■ *PART 1* ■

THE DEVELOPMENT OF PLANNING POLICY AND THEORY

Part 1 of the book begins with a review of the development of planning policy over time. Alongside this I discuss the changing nature of planning theory. The theoretical debate is interwoven with the historical review of the scope of planning policies and both elements are seen as relating to the changing nature of social and economic processes. Each historical period under discussion is thus considered in relation to: economic and social change; emerging problems and policies; and theory.

■ *Chapter 1* ■

Establishing the Planning System

■ The 19th and early 20th century origins of planning

☐ *Economic and social change*

While histories of planning may trace its origins right back to the urban design practices of the Greeks and link its development to the town designs of the medieval and Renaissance periods, it is generally accepted that the impetus to modern planning activity came from the massive industrialisation of the 19th century (see Table 1.1). For this industrialisation brought with it large scale population growth and, more important, population movement. Between 1801 and 1901 the population of England and Wales grew from 8.9 million to 32.5 million. The towns and cities grew at an unprecedented rate as people moved from rural to urban areas. Between 1821 and 1851 alone some 4 million people migrated to the towns and by 1851 some 50 per cent of the population was urban in residence. The resultant urban squalor is well documented, most famously in Engels' *Conditions of the English Working Class* (1845 German edn, 1892 English edn). Conditions for the average family were cramped, damp and insanitary. Along with an inadequate diet, this resulted in high mortality rates and a weak and unhealthy working class population. Furthermore the conditions produced a general public health risk through the inadequate water and sewerage systems for the dense urban population. The resulting epidemics, particularly of cholera in the 1840s, spread the consequences of inadequate housing beyond the occupants themselves.

Urbanisation and industrialisation went along with rapid economic growth. This economic growth was underpinned by the creation of a labour force in the form of a proletariat, unfettered by links to land or craft and dependent on wage labour for meeting essential living costs. The factory system of production controlled the workforce with economic and organisational discipline. But such discipline could never be complete in its effectiveness. Resistance to the exploitation involved

17

Table 1.1 *Chronology of key planning policy documents*

	Up to 1919	1920–49	1950–69	1970s	1980s	1990–2
REGIONAL POLICY		Distribution of Industry Act New Towns Act Barlow Report	Industrial Development Act Local Government Act Town Development Act	Local Employment Act Industry Act		Planning and Compensation Act
LAND USE PLANNING	Housing, Town Planning, etc. Act Housing, Town Planning Act	Town and Country Planning Acts	Civic Amenities Act Town and Country Planning Act Skeffington Report	Local Government Act Community Land Scheme	White Paper: *Lifting the Burden* Circular 22/80 Housing and Planning Act Local Government Planning and Land Act	
COUNTRYSIDE POLICY		Agriculture Act National Parks and Access to the Countryside Act	Protection of Birds Act Countryside Acts Green Belt Pamphlet	Entry to Common Agricultural Policy	Wildlife and Countryside Acts Agriculture Act Reform of Common Agricultural Policy	Reform of Common Agricultural Policy
ENVIRONMENTAL PLANNING	Public Health Acts Alkali Acts		River Acts Clear Air Acts Noise Abatement Acts	Control of Pollution Act Royal Commission on Environmental Pollution established Water Act	Circular 15/88 on Environmental Assessment	Environmental Protection Act Water Act White Papers
HOUSING, URBAN AND TRANSPORT POLICY	Shaftesbury, Torrens and Cross Acts		Housing Act Buchanan Report	Housing Act Inner Urban Areas Act	Local Government Planning and Land Act Housing and Planning Act	

in such wage labour and to the squalid urban conditions increasingly took the form of class-based politics as the labour movement slowly developed. In doing so, it had the examples of more revolutionary movements on the Continent to look to. The pressure from domestic and overseas labour movements created another impetus for reform to improve working class living standards. The threat of revolution in Britain seems to have been most imminent just after the First World War with the mass demobilisation of soldiers into a collapsing economy. In 1909 Lloyd George had proclaimed a People's Budget and the postwar Homes Fit For Heroes budget promised a further programme of reform to stem the feared revolutionary tide. Summary Box 1.1 sets out the key developments of the period in the economic/social, political and planning spheres.

Summary Box 1.1 *19th and early 20th centuries*

Economic and social change:	Industrialisation
	Urbanisation
	War
Salient political issues:	Public health
	Social unrest
Key planning activities:	Housing
	Public sanitation
Planning profession:	Architects
	Engineers
Conceptualisation of planning:	Urban design
Theoretical framework:	Environmental determinism

☐ *Problems and policies*

The key concern arising from 19th century industrialisation was with housing for the mass of the working population, and in particular with the public health aspects of that housing. In 1840 the Select Committee on the Health of Towns reported, followed by the Royal Commission on the State of Large Towns in 1845. The result was the Public Health Act of 1848 which created a Central Board of Health and local boards with responsibility for local sanitary conditions. The next three decades saw three acts enabling the clearance of unfit housing: the Shaftesbury Act of 1851, the Torrens Act of 1868 and the Cross Act of 1875. 1875 also saw the passage of a new consolidating Public Health Act which paved the way for urban and rural sanitary district bye-laws specifying minimum new housing standards in terms of street width, dwelling design and construction. The appalling air pollution caused by emissions from factories was also recognised to be a public health hazard. Attention particularly focused on the alkali works, emitting corrosive hydrogen chloride gases, resulting in the introduction of the first of a series of Alkali Acts in 1863.

These series of measures had little effect by the end of the 19th century. This was made clear in Chadwick's 1884 *Report on the Sanitary Conditions of the Labouring Poor* and the effects were beginning to concern a number of industrialists, either for philanthropic reasons or because of the assumed link between quality of environment and labour productivity. Certain notable individuals assumed responsibility for improving living conditions for their workforce through the development of model towns, for example, Salt at Saltaire (1853), Lever at Port Sunlight (1887), and Cadbury at Bournville (1878). In each case considerable emphasis was given to providing housing which promoted clean, sanitary and healthy living. The idea of a pleasant, self-contained environment providing for work and leisure proved a powerful one.

By the end of the century, this idea had been given its fullest expression in the 1898 tract by Ebenezer Howard, *A Peaceful Path to Social Reform*, whose title told of the perceived link between the threat of revolutionary change and planning activity. The tract propounded the idea of garden cities, which would combine the best elements of urban and rural life and provide a blueprint for urban growth. It was also a response to the suburbanisation that was beginning to occur with the building boom of the 1890s, linked to electrification of tramways and workers' concessionary rail fares. This concept of garden cities was discussed further by the Committee on Unhealthy Areas, which reported in 1900, and given organisational support in the Garden City Association (later to become the Town and Country Planning Association) formed in 1899. In 1902 the Garden City Pioneer Company began trading, followed the next year by First Garden City Ltd which developed Letchworth. The development of Welwyn Garden City was begun after the conclusion of the First World War, in 1919.

The housing and public health concerns of the 19th century legislation and the comprehensive management of new urban areas implied by the garden city movement both influenced the first piece of legislation to bear the word 'planning'. Also influential was the example of German planning, used by both the National Housing Reform Council and the Association of Municipal Corporations to press for planning legislation (Hague, 1984, p. 55). The Housing, Town Planning, etc. Act of 1909 created permissive powers for local authorities or landowners to prepare schemes regulating suburban growth. The plan preparation procedures were, however, cumbersome, and of 172 authorised schemes, only 13 were submitted by 1919.

The 1919 Housing and Town Planning Act sought to streamline the administrative procedures while extending the scope of planning control. Borough and urban districts with a population of over 20 000 were now required to prepare planning schemes for areas of new development and developers were advised to obtain interim development orders before undertaking development in scheme areas otherwise they risked losing potentially valuable compensation. It also contained various provisions for building 'Homes Fit For Heroes' and, indeed, the land use planning provisions were curtailed in order to give the housing drive the fullest opportunities (Hague, 1984, p. 59).

It was early recognised that the extension of state activity through planning would enhance certain land values and attempts were made to claw back these increments through a variety of taxation measures. In 1895 a specific ad hoc scheme, the Tower Bridge Southern Approach Act, had sought to reclaim the betterment due to a road improvement scheme, and in 1910 the Finance Act contained no fewer than four duties for land taxation. None of these schemes proved successful, with the four duties being abandoned in 1920. The plan preparation powers of the 1909 Planning Act were also repealed, along with cumbersome compensation and taxation provisions to deal with the resulting changes in land values. The main success in this area was in clarifying the rules for compensation of land compulsorily purchased by the state: the 'Six Rules' of the Acquisition of Land (Assessment of Compensation) Act 1919 largely stand to this day.

By the late 19th century, it was becoming increasingly apparent that urbanisation posed a threat to existing valued features of urban and rural areas. Financial support for the agricultural industry had been proposed by the Selborne Committee in 1917 and the 1920 Agriculture Act instituted a first attempt at a support scheme, only to be repealed the following year because of the cost. The rural despoliation resulting from tree-felling during the First World War was addressed by the establishment of the Forestry Commission in 1919, though the primary concern of this body has always been with timber production rather than rural amenity. More general public concern with the countryside was evidenced in the number of societies formed around these issues: the Commons, Footpaths and Open Space Society in 1865, the Society for the Protection of Ancient Buildings in 1877, the Royal Society for the Protection of Birds in 1889 and the National Trust for Places of Historic Interest or Natural Beauty in 1895. Urban conservation concerns were given central government recognition in the 1882 and 1913 Ancient

Monuments Acts and the 1880 Royal Commission on Historic Monuments.

The effect on amenity of increased roadbuilding and traffic, albeit modest by postwar standards, led to the 1925 Roads Improvement Act, which empowered local authorities to purchase land alongside highways for planting and amenity purposes. The Road Beautification Association, a voluntary body, was formed in 1928 to promote the use of these powers. A more specific area of planning activity, the 1907 Advertisements Regulations Act, also reflected an early concern with general urban amenity.

☐ *Theory*

Planning activity during this period had a clear focus and, albeit implicit, analytic framework. Planning focused on physical aspects of urban design. This fitted with the sanitary engineering concerns that prompted the early planning legislation and with the consequent identification of planners with the engineering and architectural professions. In 1909 there were only four men practising in the United Kingdom as professional planners (Hague, 1984, p. 97). Conferences held by the Royal Institute of British Architects in 1910 and the Institute of Municipal and County Engineers in 1911 discussed the development of planning and confirmed the urban design orientation. This approach was carried through when the Town Planning Institute was founded in 1914, setting its first examinations in 1920. Admission was on the basis of a professional qualification in architecture, engineering or surveying, the Town Planning Institute providing post-professional training.

This fitted with the analytic approach underlying much planning activity: environmental determinism. Through careful and expert design of the physical fabric of urban areas, an environment could be created which not only improved living standards but also improved the inhabitants themselves, physically, morally and socially (Pepper, 1984, pp. 110–13). The link with creating reformed urban residents and avoiding anti-social or, indeed, revolutionary behaviour was clear. Hague (op. cit., p. 54) also argues that planning activity at this time was linked with a concern over the physical well-being of the British race in the context of competition between imperialist nations, notably Britain and Germany, and in the face of evidence of the poor physical health of recruits to the 1899 Boer War, as revealed in the 1904 report of the Inter-Departmental Committee on Physical Deterioration and, again, during the call-up for the First World War.

This is perhaps best expressed in the debate on the 1909 Housing, Town Planning, etc. Act itself, in which the Act's purpose was described as: to provide a domestic condition for the people in which their physical health, their morals, their character and their whole social condition can be improved (*Parliamentary Debates,* May 1908). These sentiments were echoed in the 1919 Housing and Town Planning Act, whose housing provisions followed on from a number of official reports drawing a link between poor housing and industrial unrest, such as the 1917 Report of the Royal Commission on Industrial Unrest and the Report of the Royal Commission on Housing of the Industrial Population of Scotland of the same year.

This theory saw planning activity as essentially a technical process of design and drawing, unrelated in its operation to economic or political processes. The success of such activity thus depended on the technical ability of the planner, who could be considered an applied engineer. The main challenge to this approach came from Geddes, a biologist who published a book in 1915 arguing for planning policies aimed at adapting the physical environment to the changing needs of modern society and proposing an appropriate methodology: survey, analysis, plan. These ideas were developed further in the next decades and have continued to underpin much planning thought and activity to this day. Summary Box 1.2 sets out the key features of environmental determinism as a theoretical framework

Summary Box 1.2 *Environmental determinism*

Definition of planning:	Urban design
View of planners:	Technical experts in built form
Process involved:	Design; mapmaking; technical drawing
Relation to economy:	Nil
Relation to politics:	Nil
Outcomes:	Dependent on planner's skill
Research focus:	Areas of (re)development
Theoretical antecedents:	–

■ The 1920s to 1940s: towards the 1947 Town and Country Planning Act

□ *Economic and social change*

With the collapse of the inflated wartime economy upon demobilisation in 1918, Britain entered three decades of severe economic and social upheaval. A world recession in demand created mass unemployment, aggravated by the industrial restructuring that occurred. The resultant effects in the depressed regions are well known: long-term unemployment, idle and abandoned plant, severe poverty, the urban dereliction of disinvestment. But this was also a period of rapid economic growth for the South East and Midlands. New industries located in greenfield sites on the urban periphery, using electric power from the new National Grid rather than coal. In 1937–8 alone 372 factories opened in the London area.

A speculative housebuilding industry and burgeoning building society movement translated this into large scale residential developments for a new generation of owner-occupiers, with government encouragement in the form of tax relief on mortgage interest payments under the 1923 Housing Act. Some 2.7 million dwellings were built in England and Wales during 1930–40. At the outbreak of World War Two one-third of all dwellings had been built since 1918. Operating at much lower densities than 19th century urban development, these residential, industrial and associated commercial areas spread over large parts of rural England, encouraged by the developments in energy supply and transport technology.

The housebuilding boom was just beginning to lift Britain out of recession when rearmament propelled society once more into a wartime economy. This was a very different experience to that of the First World War, though. Whereas the war of 1914–18 had been supplied by entrepreneurs operating in a relatively free market, the war of 1939–45 was public sector directed. The level of government involvement in the details of civil and military preparation for war was unprecedented. At the same time, mobilisation, evacuation of the cities and other population movement placed different social groups from different parts of the country in contact with each other, often for the first time. The effect was politically radicalising, preparing the way for a new form of public sector activity once peace was declared (see Summary Box 1.3).

☐ Problems and policies

The severe unemployment of the interwar years, concentrated as it was in particular regions in the North, created the impetus for regionally-based incentives to industrial activity. The earliest policies were property-based, providing new factory space in trading estates under the Board of Trade. Grants for industrial building and employment were also an early and enduring feature.

Summary Box 1.3 *1920s, 1930s and 1940s*

Economic and social change:	Recession and restructuring
	War and reconstruction
Salient political issues:	Regional unemployment
	Suburban growth
Key planning activities:	Regional planning
Planning profession:	Growth of separate identity
Conceptualisation of planning:	Public sector direction of land use
Theoretical framework:	Naive public administration

At the other end of the country, in the more prosperous southern and midland regions, attempts were being made to cope with the rapid suburbanisation. From 1927 to 1939 there was an average annual loss of open land of 25 000 ha. In 1925 the Town Planning Act, although largely a consolidating act, for the first time separated planning from housing as an area of public concern. The 1932 Town and Country Planning Act introduced the power to prepare planning schemes for any land, including built up areas and land unlikely to be developed in the near future. Once approved, development in the plan area was subject to local authority control and, prior to plan approval, the provisions for interim development control were extended. Ministerial approval was required for the plans and some scope for modification and amendment introduced. The minister responsible at that time was the Minister of Health. Policy makers were also building on the model town and garden city concepts of the 19th and early 20th centuries with the 1935 Parliamentary Committee on Garden Cities and Satellite Towns.

Alongside this planning activity for areas of growth went a concern with protecting rural areas from unplanned growth. The 1920s and 1930s saw a further increase in the number of societies based on such concern, the most notable example being the Council for the Preservation of Rural England (later the Council for the Protection of Rural England) set up in 1926, who soon pressed for a Rural Amenities Bill. Much of this concern focused around leisure use of the countryside, increasingly by urban residents. In 1929–31 Addison chaired a committee on National Parks and in 1932, following the mass trespass on Kinder Scout, the Rights of Way Act provided some access rights for the leisure users of the countryside. The Youth Hostels Association was set up in 1921 and in 1935 the Ramblers Association was formed. The latter pressed for further extension of access rights, lobbying hard for the 1939 Access to Mountains Act. However, the final legislation was much weaker than had been hoped for, reflecting the power of rural land-owners and the other dominant thread of countryside policy – the support of the farming industry. The 1929 and 1931 Agricultural Marketing Acts re-established a system of financial support for the industry.

Much of this work on national parks, garden cities and regional development was sidelined when the international crisis brought down the Labour Government in 1931 leading to a period of expenditure cuts. It was only after the declaration of World War Two and the formation of a wartime coalition government that these issues were seriously examined again. A batch of major wartime reports under the auspices of the 1943 Cabinet Committee on Reconstruction and the resulting postwar legislation provided the main basis for the planning system.

In 1943, the Ministry of Town and Country Planning Act established a separate and specific ministerial responsibility for planning, taking over from the short lived Ministry of Works and Planning (1942–3). The same year saw interim development control extended to all land in England and Wales not already under an operative planning scheme. Essentially permission was needed for all development if compensation rights were to be protected. This set the scene for the 1947 Act.

The crowning piece of comprehensive planning legislation was this 1947 Town and Country Planning Act, heralded by the 1944 White Paper *The Control of Land Use*. This imposed a compulsory planning duty on all local authorities for the first time. By 1 July 1951 all areas were to have development plans indicating the areas allocated to the main uses, the main transport routes, minerals areas, woodlands, green belts, reservoirs, and means of water supply and sewage disposal. Town maps supplemented such county maps and provided the detail for urban areas including any designated comprehensive development areas (CDAs) where major urban redevelopment was proposed. Some of these focused on war damaged town centres, others on areas of slum clearance. These CDAs instituted a prolonged programme of clearance and redevelopment for reshaping and improving urban areas, taking the lead of the 1930 Greenwood Housing Act. Programme maps showed the stages by which development was to occur, given that development plans were to cover a 20 year period. The preparatory work for the development plans included an extensive report of survey which focused on physical land use issues.

All development, broadly defined in the 1947 Act but excluding agricultural development, was to be subject to development control, the need to obtain prior planning permission from the local planning authority. The 1947 Act thus introduced comprehensive and compulsory planning in the form of drawing up area-based plans and controlling development, case by case. This was a departure from the prewar planning system which was essentially a form of zoning in which the development plan itself created development rights.

These planning provisions were underpinned by two other policy changes. First, there was a degree of local government reorganisation of responsibilities. The 1947 Act identified county councils and county boroughs as the local planning authorities, rather than the county districts, thus reducing the total number of local planning authorities from 1441 to 145. The growing importance of the county councils had been anticipated since the 1929 Local Government Act had given them highway responsibilities and the power to prepare planning schemes in default of the districts.

Secondly, arising out of the 1942 Uthwatt Report of the Expert Committee on Compensation and Betterment, there was greater recognition of the role that public landownership and land taxation policies could play. The 1944 Town and Country Planning Act gave local authorities the power to compulsorily purchase land for planning purposes if it had been 'blitzed', that is war damaged, or 'blighted', that is suffered from poor layout or obsolete development. The 1932 Town and Country Planning Act had already raised the betterment levy payable on increases in land values to 75 per cent but the 1947 Town and Country Planning Act went further. It compulsorily purchased all development rights, through the development control provisions. A global fund of £300 million, administered by the Central Land Board, was provided for once-and-for-all compensation and, on grant of any planning permission, a betterment levy, set at 100 per cent of the increase in land values, was applied. As a result, all land was supposed to exchange hands at existing use value only, taking no account of the increase in value associated with the proposed development.

In the field of regional policy, development areas were designated under the 1945 Distribution of Industry Act, with grants to encourage industrial relocation. This followed through the arguments of the 1940 Barlow Report of the Royal Commission on the Distribution of the Industrial Population (see below), and the commitment to maintaining full employment contained in the 1944 White Paper on employment policy. In addition, incentives in development areas were supplemented by restrictions on new industrial development in more prosperous areas. This took the form of the need to obtain an industrial development certificate (IDC) prior to undertaking such development activity, under the provisions of the Town and Country Planning Act 1947.

The garden city or model town idea was transformed into the new town concept. The 1946 Reith Report from the New Towns Committee and the 1946 New Towns Act effected the transformation. From this legislation, plans for 32 new towns would eventually be drawn up and implemented. In each case a master plan would design a town from scratch, with the public sector compulsorily purchasing the land and directing development to ensure the provision of facilities and limit the involvement of the private sector.

In 1942 the Scott Report of the Committee on Land Utilisation in Rural Areas was published, enshrining the principle of protecting rural land and agricultural areas, to be followed by the Dower Report of 1945 and the Hobhouse Report of 1947. These reports proposed national parks in England and Wales overseen by a National Parks Commission. The purpose of national park designation included: landscape beauty, public access, wildlife conservation, and conservation of buildings or places of architectural or historic interest, as well as agricultural protection. The 1949 National Parks and Access to the Countryside Act established such national parks together with areas of outstanding natural beauty (AONBs) and nature reserves. However, the proposal for a powerful overseeing organisation, the National Parks Commission, was rejected. Instead local planning authorities took on these functions. The National Parks Commission was set up but with only an advisory role. A Countryside Commission was also formed. In Scotland the 1945 Ramsay Committee recommended five national parks but their proposals were not implemented. The 1949 Act did not apply to Scotland.

The Nature Conservancy was also established in 1949 by Royal Charter, following the 1945 Special Committee on Wildlife Conservation and the 1947 Haseley Committee on Conservation of Nature in England and Wales. This latter Committee, while arguing for nature conservation measures, concluded that there was no fundamental conflict between access for amenity considerations and wildlife interests and the promotion of both aspects was encouraged. Provision was made under the 1949 Act for mapping rights of way. This followed on the report of the 1948 Sub-committee on Footpaths and Access to the Countryside, an offshoot of the Hobhouse Committee. Meanwhile, the Nature Conservancy's role was to provide scientific advice, establish and manage nature reserves and develop research.

While providing a framework for meeting leisure, amenity and wildlife concerns over rural areas, this entire countryside policy rested on the primary principle of conserving rural areas for agricultural activity. The 1947 Agriculture Act explicitly set out the commitment to the British farming industry and established a new system of financial support based on guaranteed prices for agricultural products. Failure to farm productively could lead to censure by the country council and, eventually, to notice to quit.

Meanwhile in urban areas, the burgeoning planning system took on the enhanced protection of urban heritage. During the interwar period, several amenity societies had been founded: for example, the Ancient Monuments Society in 1924 and the Georgian Society in 1937. The 1932 Town and Country Planning Act had given local authorities powers to enforce the retention of significant trees in urban locations while the 1944 Act introduced the important power of listing buildings of architectural or historic interest.

□ *Theory*

During the interwar period the planning profession gained confidence in its separate identity and specialist perspective, as more and more local authorities employed planners. The growing quantity of planning legislation was effectively creating a public sector profession. From 1931 the Town Planning Institute provided a town planning qualification rather than post-professional training and during the 1930s the first 'recognised' schools of planning operated. Planning-related pressure groups also became more influential in promoting and developing planning policy. Early in the 1930s the Town Planning Institute and other professional and environmental bodies wrote to the Prime Minister regretting the apparent demise of active planning policy and pressing for new legislation. The Town and Country Planning Association is credited with being particularly important in shaping the 1947 Town and Country Planning Act through its general activities and the involvement of influential planners and members such as Frederick Osborne, an active Labour Party member.

While the town planning educational syllabi still focused heavily on urban design, a more general vision of planning activity was gaining ascendancy. This can be described as a vision of comprehensive, integrated allocation of land uses. The public sector, through its planning functions, sought to provide and implement a general framework for resource allocation which would ensure the best use of resources throughout the country. Both underutilisation and over-exploitation would be avoided. A variety of tools would be available to ensure the implementation of this plan, emphasising the many dimensions to the problem of optimal land use. The key element of this vision was the need to provide a comprehensive strategy for tackling these many dimensions, which was also integrated in terms of recognising the interrelations between these dimensions. Thus the 1943 Ministry of Town and Country Planning Act could state the objective of the

Ministry as: to secure consistency and continuity in the framing and execution of a National Policy with regard to the use and development of land.

Of great significance in developing this view of planning was the Barlow Report of 1940. For this argued that the problems of the depressed northern regions, with their high levels of industrial disinvestment, and the rapidly growing southern and midland regions, with their substantial suburban development, were two faces of the same coin. The problems were interrelated so that successful resolution of one problem depended on tackling the other. Also important was H. Warren and W. R. Davidge's book *Decentralisation of Population and Industry: a new principle in town planning*, which argued for planning as part of national economic and social planning (Cullingworth, 1988, p. 5). Documents such as these provided the intellectual support for comprehensive, integrated planning, covering numerous dimensions of land use in relation to each other throughout the country.

The logic of this approach could propose quite radical planning solutions. The Uthwatt Expert Committee argued that the key to securing the proper pattern of land use lay in solving the problems of compensation and betterment, that is the recompense for downward and upward movements in land prices resulting from new patterns of land use. Following a comprehensive integrated planning approach, the committee recommended extending public sector activity to include land taxation and, logically, land nationalisation measures. Political considerations, however, meant that only land taxation measures were considered realistic policy options.

The essence of this approach was the public sector direction of resource allocation, mainly through controlling land use in a variety of ways. The role of economic processes through the land market in hindering 'proper planning' was recognised, through the pioneering work of the Uthwatt Expert Committee, but planning was seen as capable of externally directing those processes. While the whole programme of building up a planning system reflected the growing public acceptance of a socialist solution to interwar and wartime problems, the resulting planning activity was not seen as essentially political. Rather, planners were public sector urban managers in a technical, apolitical role. This was in line with the growing professionalisation of planning activity. The process of planning was seen as relatively problem-free in that it involved devising appropriate policies and then implementing them. As Cullingworth (1988, p. 14) points out, what was new was the belief that the problems could be tackled in the same way as a military operation. Given the requisite powers this should be fairly straightforward, and little thought was given to potentially unsuccessful outcomes from this process. A 'naive' view of socialist centralised planning dominated, closely related to the views propounded by the Labour Government of the time. As Hague (1984, p. 64) says, the significance of the new legislation was that the idea of town planning could convey important symbols of a new social order.

The political pressures of the postwar period were to curtail this vision of planning, limiting the directive role of the public sector and returning much control over resource allocation to the private sector. This division of responsibilities undercut the comprehensive, integrated nature of planning. Within the new mixed economy consensus, a new model of planning activity had to be devised (see Summary Box 1.4).

Summary Box 1.4 *Naive public administration*

Definition of planning:	Public sector direction of land use
View of planners:	Public sector urban managers
Process involved:	Policy formulation and implementation
Relation to economy:	External direction of economy
Relation to politics:	Implementation of socialist programme
Outcomes:	Naive view of success
Research focus:	Particular policies
Theoretical antecedents:	–

■ The story so far

During the period from the 19th century through to the 1947 Town and Country Planning Act, the planning system evolved from an ad hoc concern with issues of public health and urban social unrest to a comprehensive attempt to instil order into the management of land use. This reflects the tremendous shift in the organisation of society and in political attitudes that occurred in this period. Changes in production methods, growth in the scale of society and a new emphasis on the state as the means of solving social and economic problems, all underpinned the development of the planning system. This, in turn, was reflected in the growth of a separate planning profession and the emergence of a new planning theory to justify their actions, replacing older, simpler ideas about environmental determinism.

Further reading

There are numerous histories of the origins of planning. Hague (1984) is particularly interesting. Other useful texts are: Ashworth (1954), Cherry (1972) and Sutcliffe (1981). Cherry (1974) covers the period 1914–74 but includes discussion of the RTPI. For detailed study there is the four-volume official history of the planning system by Cullingworth (1975a, 1975b, 1979, 1980 – see the end of Chapter 2 for more details). Volume 1 particularly focuses on the war years. Countryside policy is well served by Sheail's history of the interwar years (1981).

■ *Chapter 2* ■

Experience and Change in the Postwar Period

■ The 1950s and 1960s: economic growth and the mixed economy consensus

□ *Economic and social change*

Immediately after the war, the incoming Labour government faced serious economic problems, with a public sector deficit of £443 million in 1947 which severely limited their plans for a public sector-led economy. However, by the end of the 1950s, Britain was entering a long period of economic growth which brought with it an increase in and spread of living standards. National output rose, unemployment fell and the economy bumped along at the constraints of full resource use and productive capacity. With the replacement of the postwar 1945 Labour government, which had embodied the naive socialist public administration ideal, the state came firmly under the sway of the mixed economy consensus. Whether Labour or Conservative governments were in power, their view on economic management was broadly similar. Butskellism (an amalgam of the economic policies of the Labour Chancellor Gaitskell and the Conservative Butler) ruled the day. Both were riding along on the economic wave of increasing national output based on the 'white heat of new technology', as the early stages of the electronic industrial revolution were termed, together with increased concentration of capital and the culmination of Taylorism in production processes, whereby assembly lines organised a rigid division of labour.

Alongside economic growth went a variety of social changes. Population grew, largely from indigenous growth as family formation took off after the long interrupted war years. Near full employment also encouraged immigration from Britain's former Empire, now the Commonwealth. The increased living standards of the growing population stimulated many new forms of development: residential, industrial, office and shopping areas. The form of these areas were influenced by the greatly more mobile nature of the population as car ownership increased. This, together with the strains that growth placed on already dense urban areas, precipitated the decentralisation of population and then employment that was to shape much of the postwar urban experience.

The major focus of these decades was, therefore, on the scale of and problems arising from economic growth. Even the need to deal with the war damage of bombed town centres, residential and industrial areas was seen as much as a profitable development opportunity as a reconstruction task. But towards the end of the period it began to be acknowledged that the mixed economy approach did not sweep away problems of inequality and deprivation. The 'rediscovery' of poverty at home and the example of the American 'race riots' as a response to ethnically concentrated deprivation both raised questions about the future direction of public policy in Britain (see Summary Box 2.1).

Summary Box 2.1   *1950s and 1960s*

Economic and social change:	Postwar boom
	Mixed economy
	Consensus politics
Salient political issues:	Increasing living standards
	Rapid development
Key planning activities:	New Towns
	Redevelopment
Planning profession:	Corporate planners
Conceptualisation of planning:	Generic decision making
Theoretical framework:	Procedural planning theory

☐ *Problems and policies*

During this period a number of initiatives were undertaken in a variety of policy areas: new towns, regional policy, countryside protection, pollution control, urban poverty, housing, and transport. The land use planning system was also restructured. This variety indicates the growth that was occurring in the range of planning activity and also the implementation of many policy ideas merely discussed during the formative years of the planning system.

The implementation of the new towns programme showed how a simple idea could involve substantial resources. 13 new towns were designated from 1947 to 1950: 8 round London – Basildon, Bracknell,

Crawley, Harlow, Hatfield, Hemel Hempstead, Stevenage and Welwyn Garden City; 2 in the North East – Peterlee and Newton Aycliffe; 2 in Scotland – Glenrothes and East Kilbride; and 1 in Wales – Cwmbran. Within these new town areas, a development corporation directed the planning and building of the new settlement, working to a master plan. In an extension of the concept, the 1952 Town Development Act paved the way for expanded towns whereby population could be decanted from overcrowded urban areas in the major conurbations, into newly developed areas adjoining existing small settlements. During the 1950s the policy focus shifted from new towns to expanded towns and only one further new town was designated in this decade – Cumbernauld in 1956.

Then in 1959 another New Towns Act instituted the next generation of towns and set up a Commission for New Towns to oversee their operation. This second wave of new towns comprised: Skelmersdale, Livingstone, Telford, Redditch, Runcorn, Washington and Irvine. In addition Peterborough, Northampton and Warrington were designated for development under new town powers but on a partnership basis between the local development corporations and the local authorities.

Meanwhile regional planning took on new forms. The definition of areas, within which grants to encourage industrial development and employment applied, changed several times. The 1960 Employment Act introduced development areas defined by exceeding a benchmark unemployment level of 4 per cent; the 1966 Industrial Development Act returned to regionally-based areas; in 1967 Special Development Areas were introduced where a higher level of incentive operated; and in 1969 Intermediate Areas were defined following the recommendations of the Hunt Commission. The Hunt Commission had noted a particular problem of dereliction in intermediate areas. Derelict land within these areas was made eligible for grants under the 1966 Local Government Act but the proposals from the Hunt Commission for a national programme and a derelict land reclamation agency were never implemented.

Regional planning was also extended to offices as well as industry, in recognition of the growing importance of this sector and the pressure it was placing on the major cities, particularly London and Birmingham. The Location of Offices Bureau (LOB) was established in 1963 to encourage the decentralisation of commercial activities and in 1965 the Control of Offices and Industrial Development Act introduced the need to obtain an office development permit (ODP) before undertaking any major commercial development in designated areas.

These incentives and controls of regional planning were further placed within a framework of indicative planning documents, intended to guide the private and public sectors. In 1965 regional economic planning councils and boards of local but non-elected representatives and civil servants respectively were set up for the eight English planning regions, Northern Ireland, Wales and Scotland. These provided a mechanism for preparing regional plans such as those for the South East: the South East Study of 1964, the Strategy for the South East of 1967 and the Strategic Plan for the South East of 1970. Briefly they were overseen by the Department of Economic Affairs, which issued its National Plan in 1965 before being promptly disbanded. Regional plans were supposed to provide a stage in the detailed implementation of this Plan.

The development plans of the land use planning system were to be the lowest tiers in this hierarchy of strategic planning. Significant changes were made to the development plan regime towards the end of the 1960s. Concerned at the extent to which urban and rural development was running ahead of the rather inflexible development plans of the 1947 Act, the Planning Advisory Group was set up in 1964, to report a year later on *The Future of Development Plans*. Under the strong influence of the increasingly professionalised planning body, the Royal Town Planning Institute, the group recommended a two-tier system of development plans: broad brush structure plans and more detailed local plans. This was put into effect through the 1968 Town and Country Planning Act.

Structure plans consisted of a written statement and a key diagram, supported by an explanatory memorandum and a statement of public participation and other consultations. Structure plans were subject to continuous review rather than on a five yearly cycle as with the old-style development plans. The ongoing survey which prompted review was broadly based, looking at social and economic forces and not just the physical land use matters of the 1947 plans. Local plans consisted of a written statement, maps and other descriptive matter as relevant. Three types of local plan were proposed: district plans covering all or part of a district; subject or topic plans looking at a particular issue; and action area plans effectively replacing plans for comprehensive development areas.

The 1968 Town and Country Planning Act also strengthened the implementation of the policies contained in these various plans through development control. An implied five year time limit on planning permissions was introduced along with provision for local authorities to issue a stop notice if it believed that development was occurring without the benefit of planning permission. At the same time, public concern at the rate of development and the changes it was bringing led to calls for more public involvement in planning. The 1969 report of the Skeffington Committee on public participation, entitled *People and*

Plans, encouraged local authorities to involve communities in plan making at every stage (Gyford, 1991, pp. 72–9).

The betterment levy provisions of the Town and Country Planning Act 1947 were abolished, along with the global fund for compensation, in the Town and Country Planning Acts of 1953 and 1954. This re-established market value for most land market transactions but existing use value continued to determine compensation on compulsory purchase until 1959, when a further Town and Country Planning Act re-established open market value as the basis for all transactions. This confirmed the shift from a naive public adminstration approach, where the public sector directed the allocation of land, to a mixed economy approach, where the state pursued its policies in the context of and within the constraints of market processes. Indeed provisions were introduced to compensate private landowners for some of the adverse effects of planning activity. The 1959 Act introduced the purchase notice, later termed a blight notice, whereby the local authority was forced to buy land which had been rendered incapable of reasonable beneficial use by a planning decision. For example, this covered the 'blighting' of houses on land allocated for roadbuilding at some time in the future.

The late 1960s saw an attempt by a Labour Government to take development land out of the influence of market processes again through the Land Commission of 1967. This instituted a form of land nationalisation but lack of sufficient financial backing rendered it largely ineffective. It was revoked in 1971 and landowners who had been holding their land off the market during the Commission's operation could now trade freely again. Capital Gains Tax, which was introduced in the Finance Act of 1967, proved more long lasting. This taxed increases in the value of capital assets, including property and land, from a 1965 base date. Once inflation rates warranted it, the increased values were compared with the general level of inflation and only increases above the general level taxed.

Protecting urban heritage remained a popular planning goal, with a wider range of architectural periods finding their supporters. In 1958 the Victorian Society was founded and in 1967 the Civic Trust scored a notable triumph when the Private Members Bill it had sponsored became the Civic Amenities Act. This introduced the concept of conservation areas within which special planning protection operated. The Act also set out the principle that all planning decisions should consider the preservation and enhancement of an area's character and appearance. Listed buildings also gained greater protection with the provision of grants for maintenance and repair under the 1962 Local Authorities (Historic Buildings) Act. The first list of such historic buildings was completed in 1968 with 170 000 properties on it. The standard of amenities in new developments was protected through the use of standards, such as those for daylighting (Planning Bulletin No. 5, 1964), and through general design advice, as in the 1953 Ministerial booklet on *Design in Towns and Villages*.

Countryside protection was extended in several ways. Countryside Acts for England and Wales (1968) and Scotland (1967) introduced a general duty to consider the desirability of conserving areas of natural beauty and amenity. The functions of the National Parks Advisory Committee were taken over by an enlarged Countryside Commission. In Scotland a separate Countryside Commission was established by the 1967 Countryside (Scotland) Act and in Northern Ireland, the Ulster Countryside Commission was established in 1965 with a largely advisory role. A degree of planning control was introduced for unusually large or tall agricultural buildings in 1960 and 1967. Coastal areas were given special attention. Two Ministerial circulars (56/63 and 7/66) provided advice on the preservation of such areas and requested local authorities to prepare special policy statements. Nine regional conferences on coastal planning were held during 1966 and 1967. This culminated in two 1970 Countryside Commission reports on *The Planning of the Coastline* and *The Coastal Heritage*. The concept of the heritage coastline was proposed for designation in development plans after consultation with the Countryside Commission.

Leisure use of the countryside was a major policy concern. Under the Countryside Acts of 1967 and 1968, country parks were introduced, to be designated and maintained by local authorities. This picked up on the 1966 White Paper on *Leisure in the Countryside*. A special park was set up under separate legislation in 1967 in the Lee Valley managed by the Lee Valley Regional Park Authority. The leisure aspect was also highlighted in the reassessment of waterways that occurred in the late 1960s. Following a 1966 British Waterways Board report and a 1967 White Paper, the Transport Act of 1968 set out a Charter for Waterways which identified certain canals and rivers for cruising. It also established the Inland Waterways Amenity Council. Access to the countryside was specially considered in the 1968 Countryside Act and Town and Country Planning Act. Following on the 1967 Gosling Committee on Footpaths, the legislation allowed for the maintenance of paths, sign-posting and finance for access.

Perhaps of greatest significance, the Ministry of Housing and Local Government issued a pamphlet in 1962 on designating green belts, which provided support and guidance on their widespread application. This followed the 1957 circular which established the purposes and procedures of green belt policy. As a result many local planning authorities took up the invitation to designate such belts around towns and cities. While such designation does not provide for public access nor landscape maintenance, the protection afforded from the main forms of urban development made green belts very popular with many suburban communities. As Elson (1986) has analysed, as a policy tool green belts had many attractions for planners, since they combined an element of simplicity and clarity with local discretion.

The underlying rationale of countryside policy in supporting agriculture was not effected by these extensions of planning activity. In the 1950s, financial support took the form of minimum support prices for goods and deficiency payments for farmers. The 1957 Agriculture Act gave legislative basis to a system which, by its operation, encouraged increases in agricultural productivity and capital investment. The contradiction between this and other goals of countryside policy were to become clear in the following decades.

Pollution control also came back onto the policy agenda. The famed 1952 London Smog claimed 4 000 lives leading to the appointment of the Beaver Committee to investigate air pollution. This committee estimated the economic cost of pollution at £350 million per annum due to corrosion, lost production in agriculture, industry and transport and inefficiencies in fuel burning. Following the Beaver Report, emissions into the atmosphere were controlled by the 1956 and 1968 Clean Air Acts. These prohibited dark smoke emissions, controlled grit and dust emissions, set standards for chimney heights and designated smoke control areas where smokeless fuels had to be used for domestic purposes. Discharges into rivers came under local authority control through the 1951 and 1961 River Acts, the latter following the Pippard Committee on Discharges into the Thames. In Scotland a Scottish Rivers Purification Advisory Committee and a network of river purification authorities were established to tackle water quality.

A number of government committees examined a whole range of environmental issues during these years. In 1961 the Key Committee considered Household Refuse Disposal; in 1967 the Browne Committee looked at Refuse Storage and Collection; and in 1970 the Jaeger Committee studied Sewage Disposal. Noise pollution was examined by the Wilson Committee in 1963, having already received consideration in the 1960 Noise Abatement Act. In 1968 statutory control of vehicle noise was introduced by the Ministry of Transport under Motor Vehicles (Construction and Use) Amendment Regulations. The 1968 Transport Act further controlled local amenities through giving local authorities the power to prohibit vehicles in certain areas at certain times of day. The specific problem of aircraft noise was tackled in the 1965 Airports Authority Act and 1968 Civil Aviation Act.

Housing was one area where a strong continuity of concern was evident. The 19th century solution of slum clearance carried through with major programmes of demolition and new build. Central government subsidies encouraged rapid high rise building. However by the end of this period, the problems of this approach were being recognised in terms of the high economic cost, the unsatisfactory nature of the resulting housing and the destruction of existing communities involved. The legislative framework for a housing policy based on improvement and rehabilitation already existed. Discretionary grants for housing improvement had been introduced in the 1949 Housing Act. Standard grants for installing amenities were covered by the 1959 Housing Purchase and Housing Act, and the 1964 Housing Act provided for the designation of general improvement areas, but without linking them to any specific grant provision.

It was in 1966 that the Deeplish Study on *Improvement Possibilities in a District of Rochdale* demonstrated the practical potential of a shift from clearance and rebuild to rehabilitation in housing policy. The Dennington Committee produced a report into *Our Older Homes* in 1967: in the same year the Scottish Housing Advisory Committee produced a parallel report into *Scotland's Older Homes*. The 1968 White Paper *Old Houses into New Homes* heralded the 1969 Housing Act with its proposals for grant-aided general improvement areas (GIAs). The equivalent legislation for Scotland, the 1968 Housing (Scotland) Act, adopted a similar basic approach but in its espousal of 'tolerable' housing standards as opposed to 'unfit' housing standards it was ahead of English policy by 18 years.

The consideration of housing problems merged into a more general concern with urban problems and laid the foundations for the inner city policy of the 1970s. The 1966 Local Government Act and the 1969 Local Government (Social Need) Act set up the Education Priority Area Scheme, where additional resources were channelled into state education in areas of need, and also the Urban Programme, which consisted of grants to local authorities to finance expenditure arising from their location in an urban area of special social need. The Urban Programme was a flexible policy tool. Under its provisions, a variety of local authority projects could be funded by central government at rates up to 75 per cent of costs. By the end of the decade, the Home Office became more concerned with inner city conditions, largely because of the law and order implications. This resulted in the 12 community development projects (CDPs) being set up. Under this initiative, teams in deprived areas studied the root causes of deprivation and sought to remedy it through community participation. The radical analyses and recommendations of the various CDPs found little favour with the

Home Office, and the programme was officially disbanded within a few years of its inception. The Home Office had assumed the root cause of the problem was lack of local coordination; the CDPs tended to favour an analysis in terms of the uneven investment of capital in a market-based economy.

The rapid increase in car ownership and road freight traffic was also posing severe urban problems, examined in the Buchanan report of 1963 *Traffic in Towns*. This highlighted the conflict between enhancing accessibility within, through and to urban areas and maintaining residential and historic amenities within those areas. As a result it was proposed that planning authorities should clearly distinguish environmentally sensitive and hence protected areas from areas where enhanced road provision was to be made. These ideas were never fully taken account of in road and land use planning. Following the 1967 White Paper on *Public Transport and Traffic*, the 1968 Transport Act introduced passenger transport areas in the six major conurbations, within which passenger transport executives operated and passenger transport authorities planned public transport. Transport plans were formally considered part of the development plan under the 1968 Town and Country Planning Act (see above). The intention of the 1968 Act was to strengthen the transport role of local government and grants were provided to support this: capital grants for public transport infrastructure, a bus grant and fuel subsidies for rural areas. But in 1969 a Green Paper *Roads for the Future* set out plans for a new inter-urban network and this continued and expanded the substantial public funding of major trunk road construction programmes, which has dominated transport planning throughout the postwar period.

Finally, the process of reviewing the organisational structure of local government began in this period. Major reforms were to come early in the 1970s but in London these were already taking effect. London had always raised particular concerns generating a range of special reports in the interwar period, including that from the 1921–31 Royal Commission on the Local Government of Greater London. In 1963, following the Herbert Committee's report, London's local government was reorganised resulting in the establishment of the Greater London Council (GLC), coordinating the work of 32 London boroughs. Change for the rest of local government was to follow shortly.

□ *Theory*

This growth of planning activity in response to the many problems thrown up by economic, population and urban growth was underpinned by the development of procedural planning theory. The planning profession was, by now, well established as a separate profession. The Royal Town Planning Institute, having acquired a Royal Charter in 1959, had developed strong vertical links with its growing membership at central and local government levels. New city planning departments had been set up in many local authorities, Cardiff, Leicester, Newcastle and Liverpool being among the first. Meanwhile central government were employing professional planners in relevant departments. The first full-time undergraduate planning schools were also established during the 1950s.

As the scope of the planning system had grown, with more and more issues seen as having a land use dimension, planning professionals were considered to be much more than urban designers. In 1950s the Schuster Report of the Committee on the Qualifications of Planners was published. This recommended widening the entrants to the profession from mainly architectural, engineering and surveying backgrounds to include economists, geographers and sociologists. The syllabi of planning courses were correspondingly broadened to include these social sciences. However this redefinition of the planning profession created some problems in specifying the specialist expertise of the planner. The result was a move beyond the physical, spatial conception of the planner towards a generalist planner with extended responsibilities. Planners claimed to have the capacity to deal with location decisions, population movements, urban growth, the use of land, slum clearance, city centre redevelopment, transport proposals, the design of new towns and rehabilitation.

As the scope of public sector activity expanded, particularly at the local authority level, so planners seemed well placed to advise on many of the new activities. Furthermore, within local government these activities were seen in the context of corporate planning, an approach whereby the interrelation between different local authority departments' work was considered important and in need of central coordination. Again planners saw themselves as well placed to fulfil such a coordinating role through the medium of an appropriate development plan or other planning strategy. Land use was the map on which all public sector activities could be coordinated.

The theoretical rationalisation for this central role of professional planners was found by recasting planning as a general form of decision making (see Faludi, 1973 and Faludi's edited volume, 1973, for a review). Procedural planning theory proposed optimal ways of taking decisions so as to devise solutions to predefined goals. The most idealist of these decision making prescriptions was the rational comprehensive model in which the planner collected all necessary information and data, and rationally devised a policy that would achieve the desired goal by selecting between alternative policies. The chosen policy was then implemented and feedback or monitoring ensured that decision making could only improve over time. This approach was criticised for its unrealistic assumptions concerning the planner's ability to collect the necessary data and foresee all the problems of implementation. More realistic modes of decision making were recommended. Principal among these was disjointed incrementalism (Braybrooke and Lindblom, 1963) whereby the existing situation was taken as the starting point from which policy could promote change, rather than suggesting that planners had a clean sheet on which to impose their optimal plans. The constraints of available data and committable resources were recognised as limiting the extent of possible change so that planning policies edged forward, step by step, to desired goals rather than trying to achieve them in one leap.

In whatever form it took, procedural planning theory saw planners as generalist experts in decision making, collating the necessary information and formulating policy solutions. As Faludi says, in a footnote on p. 1 of his seminal 1973 book on *Planning Theory:*

> Definitions given to systems analysis . . . and operations research . . . are the same as that of planning given above. This underlies one of the points to be made about planning theory, i.e. the generality of the phenomenon planning, and hence its wide applicability.

The dynamics of economic processes which might hinder or enable the implementation of these solutions were hardly considered. Similarly the political system was seen as setting the goals for planning but, thereafter, planners operated in an essentially apolitical manner. The quality of information collection, plan formulation and monitoring processes, all aspects of the decision making process itself, determined whether planning achieved satisfactory outcomes. This theory proved quite unable to cope with the problems arising both from two decades of growth and its eventual collapse in the 1970s (see Summary Box 2.2).

■ The 1970s: coping with growth and its collapse

□ *Economic and social change*

The decade of the 1970s saw the economic boom of the postwar period peak and collapse. The property boom of the early 1970s saw a tremendous increase in development values and activities, accompanied by substantial infrastructure investment, particularly in roads. The

Summary Box 2.2   *Procedural planning theory*

Definition of planning:	Generic decision making
View of planners:	Rational decision makers
Process involved:	Decision making
Relation to economy:	Nil
Relation to politics:	Goals set by political process
Outcomes:	Dependent on information, monitoring and feedback
Research focus:	Profession planners
Theoretical antecedents:	Generalisation of **Naive Public Administration**

collapse of the boom in 1973–4, as oil prices and interest rates rose, proved no easier to deal with. Suddenly the pressure which had driven a largely reactive planning system was taken away, and it became clear the extent to which economic growth had been assumed in devising public policy. Thus the 1975 Pilcher Report on Commercial Property Development could argue that a healthy property market was vital to achieving social and economic policy objectives.

Even before this collapse the problems of substantial growth were becoming apparent, as was its inability to eradicate inequality. Existing public sector policies for managing growth were increasingly being criticised. Environmentalists were beginning to make their voice heard where issues of pollution and traffic generation were concerned. Providing adequate housing for the burgeoning population became a more politically vexed problem as the inadequacies of the previously adopted solution of public and private mass housing were highlighted. The procedures of the planning system were strained by the number and scale of the issues it was trying to tackle.

But the problems of the decade were not just ones of the scale of growth. The end of the 1960s saw the beginning of recognition that severe poverty was still a feature of many people's way of life. The social and economic policies of the postwar period had not successfully spread the increase in standard of living to all sectors of the population. In particular the migrants from the Commonwealth and their British-born families were facing severe deprivation as a result of working class poverty and racist discrimination. These features provided one facet of the 'inner city' problem increasingly recognised in the 1970s. The other facet was provided by the changing patterns of population and employment location. Over the years 1971–7 Merseyside lost 6 per cent of its population; London lost 0.5 million residents. Yet in 1976 the seven

Summary Box 2.3   *1970s*

Economic and social change:	Turning point in economic growth
	Urban–rural shift
	Inner city decline
Salient political issues:	Racism and urban disorder
	Excesses of economic growth
Key planning activities:	Inner city policy
	Rehabilitation and conservation
	Pollution control
Planning profession:	Crisis of competence
Conceptualisation of planning:	A – Policy implementation
	B – State intervention
	C – Local politics
Theoretical Framework	A – Organisation theory
	B – Political economy I and II
	C – Political sociology

metropolitan areas amounted for 40 per cent of all registered unemployment. The suburbanisation of the 1960s had turned into a flight from the cities, as offices and industry moved premises and households who were able joined them. This trend was accelerated by the housing redevelopment policies of local authorities, the new towns programme, regional policies such as office development permits and the mobility afforded by roadbuilding programmes. By the end of the decade, the urban–rural shift in British society was well established.

The problems of the inner city and persistent poverty were made worse by the downturn in the economy which followed the 1973–4 oil crisis and the resulting inflationary spiral. Unemployment rose, economic growth fell back and, under the conditions of a loan from the International Monetary Fund to cover Britain's balance of payments deficit after the oil price rise, the public sector was cut back. The conditions for the Thatcherism of the 1980s were set. The entry of the UK into the EC also set in train the long, slow process of europeanisation of British policy, an issue which was to contribute to Margaret Thatcher's downfall and dominate the 1990s (see Summary Box 2.3).

□ Problems and policies

A few themes in planning policy were brought to a conclusion in this decade. The new towns programme was effectively wound up with

380 000 being cut from the population targets for new towns in 1977. This particularly affected the most recently designated new towns, such as Milton Keynes and Central Lancashire. In 1976 the New Towns Act made provision for the assets of the New Towns Commission to be transferred to local authorities as each town building programme was completed. Regional planning in its then-current form was rapidly wound down with a greater emphasis placed on inner city problems within regions. But other themes were continued and new ones were added. The planning system could now be categorised under the headings used in Part 2; land use planning and conservation; countryside policy; environmental planning; urban policy and transport.

Within land use planning, the procedures of the system were again under scrutiny. This time most attention was focused on development control rather than development planning. An important tool was made available to local authorities in their negotiations on planning applications in the form of Section 52 agreements contained in the 1971 Town and Country Planning Act. Three years later the Housing Act enabled positive covenants made under Section 126 to be enforced against subsequent purchasers of land, adding a further tool for controlling land use: generally only negative covenants, prohibiting an action, are enforceable. In newly developed areas, development control was assisted by the advice given in the influential Essex County Council *Design Guide for Residential Areas* of 1973.

Considerable discussion centred on two analyses of development control procedures and practice. The first analysis was that carried out by the Dobry Committee. The Dobry Committee was appointed in 1973 and published its interim and final reports on *The Review of the Development Control System* in 1974 and 1975, together with a separate report on the control of demolition. While pinpointing many complaints of the system, its recommendations for expediting development control were not taken up by central government. These recommendations included separating two classes of planning application: A – minor and uncontroversial; and B – major and/or controversial. Time limits for consultation were to be set. For Type A applications, permission was deemed to be granted after 42 days. Extensive delegation of Type A applications to planners and/or small committees of councillors was proposed. For Type B applications, negotiation between planner and applicant was encouraged. A variety of other measures were also recommended: planning fees, use of design guides and development briefs, strong control in special environmental areas, and setting up information and planning advice centres. Overall the reports argued that efficient and effective development control was linked to speedy development plan preparation, ensuring up-to-date strategic guidance.

The second analysis came from the House of Commons Expenditure Committee's 1976–7 investigation of planning procedures. Gathering together a variety of opinions and data, the committee repeated concern with inefficiencies and delays in the development control process.

As far as development planning was concerned, local government was coming to terms with the new requirements of the 1968 Town and Country Planning Act. Structure plans in particular consumed large amounts of local authority planning resources with many district councils continuing to rely on the old-style development plans rather than preparing new local plans, although in Scotland the preparation of statutory local plans was obligatory. The particular circumstances created in Scotland by the exploitation of North Sea oil and gas resulted in an addition to the range of planning documents guiding development control. In 1974 the Scottish Development Department (SDD) issued the first of a series of National Planning Guidelines, setting out national (Scottish) policy on *Oil or Gas-related Coastal Development*. The usefulness of this guideline led to the introduction of a number of others on key planning issues. The guidelines not only influenced subsidiary development planning but also required the local authority to notify the SDD if they planned to grant planning permission contrary to the advice contained in a guideline.

Development planning in Scotland was also supplemented by the preparation, during the 1970s of regional reports, prepared by regional councils (see below) for the whole or part of their area. This reflected the fact that structure plans were generally being prepared for sub-regional areas and a framework was needed to mesh the different plans together. Such reports were slim documents without formal procedures for preparation. They were quickly prepared to fulfil a need prior to the first round of structure plans being prepared. As such they were a one-off event.

The context for land use planning was particularly affected by a series of institutional reorganisations. The 1972 Local Government Act, following but acting against the advice of the Redcliffe-Maud Committee, instituted the current two-tier system of local government in England and Wales. As from 1974 county and district councils across the country split planning functions. This reform cut across the changes made in the 1968 Town and Country Planning Act, which had assumed unitary local authorities preparing both structure and local plans under one roof. Now county councils prepared structure plans and district councils most local plans, opening up the opportunity for conflict and dispute. To coordinate the preparation of the various plans the 1972 Local Government Act established development plan schemes, setting out within each county who should do what and when. The 1972 Act also clarified those planning applications for which county councils as opposed to district councils were responsible, primarily minerals workings and applications in conflict with declared county council intentions.

In 1975 local government in Scotland was reorganised along similar lines with region councils operating as the tier above district councils, following the recommendations of the 1969 Wheatley Report and the 1973 Local Government (Scotland) Act. In Glasgow, however, the region not the metropolitan authority was the relevant transport planning body. Whereas in England and Wales, more and more local authority functions were being moved away to quangos, local authorities in Scotland continued to perform many of these functions. For example, in 1973 the Water Act created 10 regional water authorities in England and Wales each charged with producing 20 year long-term programmes of development, 7 year medium-term programmes and 5 year rolling programmes of investment. In Scotland, however, water management remained a local government affair.

The 1970s also saw the most recent attempt to tackle the issues of land value, compensation and betterment by nationalising development land. The 1974 White Paper Land was followed by the Community Land Act of 1975 and the Development Land Tax Act of 1976. The former provided for development land to pass through the ownership of local authorities or the Land Authority for Wales (LAW), thereby ensuring that the land was being used in the public interest. The latter taxed increments in land value arising from the grant of planning permission so that the land was sold on by the local authority (or LAW) at close to existing use value. Development Gains Tax had already been introduced in 1973 in an attempt to curb the substantial profits being made by landowners in the property boom of the early 1970s. Cumbersome procedures, substantial exemptions and exceptions and the hope of repeal once again undermined the effectiveness of the overall policy package, resulting in the legislation being used to channel land to developers rather than capture the development profit for the community and influence the nature of development in any meaningful way (Massey and Catalano, 1978). The failure of the Community Land Scheme was widely acknowledged and there have been no attempts at comprehensive land nationalisation since. Rather than integrating policies for land ownership and land taxation into the land use planning system, attention has shifted since the 1970s towards ad hoc measures of land ownership transfer concerned to promote urban regeneration.

Urban conservation continued to be an important subsidiary theme within land use planning with conservation areas granted statutory status by the 1972 Town and Country Planning (Amendment) Act. Powers for enhancing such areas were included, along with measures on advertisement control and tree surgery, in the 1974 Town and Country Amenities Act. Demolition of most listed buildings in conservation areas now came under development control. The National Heritage Fund, administered by the Civic Trust, was set up in 1975 to give grants for maintaining and restoring historic buildings.

At the end of the decade, in 1979, an Ancient Monuments Act was passed. This broadened the definition of an ancient monument and required that any works to any such ancient monument had to be approved by the Secretary of State. The Act also created the designation of areas of archaeological importance (AAIs) which provided for grants and restrictions on development to allow archaeological excavation. Grants for building preservation were also expanded.

Countryside policy in this decade debated the two, potentially conflicting aspects of leisure access and natural amenity. A number of reports contributed to the debate. In 1971 the Sandford Committee was appointed to consider national parks policy. It reported in 1974 concluding that in cases of conflict natural beauty should prevail over public enjoyment of the countryside. The 1975–6 House of Commons Expenditure Committee reconsidered these issues in its own inquiry into National Parks and Access to the Countryside. In Scotland a 1974 Parks Strategy was developed which proposed a hierarchy of parks for public access: urban parks, country parks, regional parks, and special parks. Meanwhile the 1973 Nugent Committee on Defence Lands was considering the potential conflicts with access and amenity created by military training.

Towards the end of the decade the need for extra protection for areas of the countryside was emphasised. A 1977 Countryside Commission report on *New Agricultural Landscapes* and a 1979 paper from a Countryside Review Committee of civil servants were raising concern with the effects of agriculture on lowland landscapes. A two-tier system of protection was proposed but not implemented. In 1978 the Countryside Commission for Scotland produced a report on Scotland's Scenic Heritage and also proposed identifying areas for special protection. The particular needs of the Norfolk Broads, under pressure from agriculture and the leisure industry, led to a voluntary consortium of local authorities setting up the Broads Authority to protect the special landscape qualities and ecosystem of these Norfolk waterways. The authority was grant aided under the 1972 Local Government Act and from Exchequer funds. This reflected a growing international concern with water-dependent areas as evidenced in the 1976 Ramsar Convention on Wetlands.

Following the reorganisation of local government, national park functions had to be redistributed. County council national park committees took on the main role although the Peak District and the Lake District had their own planning boards. District councils continued to undertake certain functions in conjunction with the planning committees or boards, or on an agency basis: tree preservation, derelict land reclamation and country park management in particular.

Environmental planning was extended and significantly developed in this period, particularly with regard to pollution control. This was in response to the continuing growth of the environmental movement during this period and the evident problems of past growth. In 1970 a White Paper *The Protection of the Environment: The Fight Against Pollution* was published. The Royal Commission on Environmental Pollution was established and produced a series of reports during 1972–9. Its remit was to 'advise on matters, both national and international, concerning the pollution of the environment, on the adequacy of research in this field, and the future possibility of danger to the environment'.

In 1974 the Government issued a report on monitoring the environment and put forward the Control of Pollution Act covering waste disposal, water pollution, noise and atmospheric pollution. It also introduced the need for a disposal licence for tipping minerals. This was supplemented by the 1974 Health and Safety at Work Act which provided for scheduled industrial processes to be covered by the Industrial Air Pollution Inspectorate of the Health and Safety Executive. With regard to noise pollution, the Noise Advisory Council was set up in 1970 and the 1974 Control of Pollution Act allowed for the designation of noise abatement zones. The issue of aircraft noise was again tackled by an Air Navigation (Noise Certification) Order of 1970 which set noise standards for aircraft following the recommendations of an international conference.

While roadbuilding continued, environmental concerns were also beginning to have an impact on transport policy. In 1972 the Urban Motorways Committee reported on *New Roads in Towns*. This proposed that road planning should be integral to urban planning and include consideration of all the costs and benefits of construction. In 1977 the Leitch Report on *Trunk Road Assessment* was published which included discussion of the methods of valuing the environmental impact of road construction. The report also led to changes in the procedures whereby road schemes were assessed to accommodate the increasingly vociferous objections to major road proposals. The Sandford Committee (see above) further established that new road routes through

National Parks should be avoided. The decade also began with the Report of the Roskill Commission on the Third London Airport in which environmental concerns had featured largely. The shift towards more environmentally conscious public policy was becoming evident at the European level. As Part 3 will detail, environmental policy has been one of the key areas where the EC has had a direct impact on the British planning system. The Treaty of Rome contained no reference to environmental protection. However, 1970 was designated European Conservation Year and in 1972 the Commission launched an environmental policy. The first Environment Action Programme was launched in following year.

The major policy initiative of the 1970s, though, centred around the inner city problem. While the key mover in the 1960s had been the Home Office, in the 1970s it was the newly-created Department of the Environment (although the DoE did not officially take over the Urban Programme until 1977). Two early initiatives of the decade were the 1972 Shelter Neighbourhood Project and the 1974 Comprehensive Community Programme for areas of intense deprivation. The major action came in 1973 when the Department commissioned the Six Towns Study which, during 1975–7, produced six major reports: three Inner Area Studies discussed the causes and dynamics of urban problems; and three Urban Guideline Programmes suggested policy management strategies for remedying the problems. There was some conflict between the consultants and the DoE as the latter favoured an analysis in terms of improved intragovernmental coordination, a managerialist approach, while the consultants studies tended to favour an emphasis on the lack of resources in the local economies. This echoed the dispute between the Home Office and the CDPs in the late 1960s.

The DoE line dominated and the resulting White Paper *Policy for the Inner City* was published in 1977, followed in 1978 by the Inner Urban Areas Act. This gave powers to local authorities to support the creation of employment opportunities and improve the environment of industrial areas by designating industrial improvement areas. Grant aid for derelict land reclamation was also provided. This supplemented the grant aid applicable in Derelict Land Clearance Areas within Intermediate Areas under the 1970 Local Employment Act and, more generally, under the 1972 Local Government Act.

Seven partnership authorities were also funded to make grants over a two year period for subsidising industrial and commercial rents. These were: Birmingham, Liverpool, Manchester/Salford, Newcastle/Gateshead and three London boroughs, Hackney, Islington, Lambeth. Lesser funding went to 23 programme authorities and 16 other designated districts. The partnerships differed from the other arrangements in that a joint committee managed the programme, chaired by a DoE minister and with representatives of local authorities, central government departments and agencies. This committee produced an annual inner area programme (IAP) setting out the strategy for each partnership authority. Within these partnership areas, public authorities were to prepare schedules of void sites for reclamation and development.

In Scotland, the Scottish Development Agency (SDA) was set up to promote local economic development, following the example of the Highlands and Islands Development Board set up in 1965. One of the SDAs main tasks was to act as the lead organisation for the GEAR project, seeking to renew Glasgow's East End.

Meanwhile the shift towards rehabilitation within housing policy continued. The Housing Act of 1971 increased the financial support for housing improvement in areas of stress unemployment. The 1974 Housing Act introduced housing action areas, areas of the worst housing conditions where grants and a public sector-led programme of improvement would operate. The aim was to prevent the ripple effect of deterioration spreading from one housing area to another. 1977 saw the publication of a substantial and important White Paper, *Housing Policy: A Consultative Document*, which undertook a comprehensive review of the adequacy of the housing stock and the effectiveness of housing policy. The same year saw the introduction of housing investment programmes (HIPs), in which local authorities set out their strategies for capital investment in local housing. In Scotland, Housing Plans were introduced in 1978, paralleling HIPs. By the end of the decade there was increasing recognition of the problems of public sector housing with the Department of the Environment setting up its Priority Estates Project in 1979.

In the area of transport policy, the emphasis on roadbuilding, supplemented by public transport subsidy, continued but more formal plans were being developed at national and local level. National level plans focused on the issue of trunk roads and motorways. 1976–8 saw Green and White Papers on transport culminating in the 1978 Transport Act. National policy on roads would now be presented in annual White Papers and subjected to parliamentary debate. Meanwhile the 1972 Local Government (England and Wales) Act required county councils, from 1975 onwards, to produce annual transport policies and programmes (TPPs), non-statutory comprehensive statements of objectives and policies together with expenditure programmes. These focused mainly on road provision, so in 1978 the Transport Act introduced annual rolling passenger transport plans (PTPs) prepared by the country council as passenger transport authority, which looked at public transport over five year periods. The package of transport policy documents at the local level, therefore, consisted of the passenger transport plan, the transport policy and programme and the transport sections of the structure plan.

☐ *Theory*

The 1970s were a period of crisis for the planning profession. During the previous two decades, a variety of activities had been added to the repertoire of the planning system and planners had come to claim an expertise in all sorts of policy areas. But the period of economic growth saw the planning system showing signs of strain even before the economic collapse in 1974. Planning had not been able to fulfil its promise of balancing growth across the country and spreading its benefits widely within society. Excesses of development coexisted with areas of dereliction, severe deprivation with massive windfall development profits, and the environmental problems of growth were becoming increasingly apparent. The procedural changes in the planning system and institutional reorganisation were not leading to any apparent increase in efficiency and two successive attempts to increase the role of the public sector in directing development through land nationalisation had been spectacular failures. There was a pressing need for a re-examination by professional planners of their activities and for a renewed intellectual justification for planning. The result was a critique on several fronts of the dominant procedural planning theory of the time, drawing on the new social science disciplines at the core of much planning education by now. As Healey, McDougall and Thomas (1982, p. 5) point out: 'A distinctive characteristic of the urban and regional planning tradition has always been the readiness to adopt uncritically and often unwittingly the tenets of intellectual and ideological waves which sweep through the academic and para-academic world.'

One strand turned to organisation theory to explain the problems facing the planning system in terms of its internal limitations. Planning was seen from the point of view of policy formulation and implementation. The problems of implementation became the focus for attention (Child, 1977; Pollit *et al.*, 1979; Barrett and Fudge, 1981). Rather than concentrating on methods for devising the ideal plan, the key issue became the constraints on achieving policy goals and hence the best way to put policy into practice. Identifying resource availability and enhancing monitoring mechanisms was one variation of procedural planning theory but theoretical developments mainly occurred in reconceptualising the formulation-implementation linkages. The policy process became viewed as continual renegotiation between policy actors, redefining the policy goals as part of implementation. Networking and bargaining were seen as valuable skills for planners to aid the realistic achievement of plan aims. This theoretical development reasserted the important role planners played, not only in drawing up plans and policies but in achieving the policy goals and, in the process, redefining these goals. Planners were seen as potentially political actors in that they engaged in negotiation over resource allocation but they were seen to do so in a relatively impartial manner, loyal to the goals of policy rather than any particular sectional interest group. On the other hand, while resource constraints were perceived as the key factor determining plan implementation and changing the nature of planners' activities, the relationship between planning and economic processes was left largely unexplored (see Summary Box 2.4).

Summary Box 2.4   *Organisation theory*

Definition of planning:	Policy implementation
View of planners:	Networkers
Process involved:	Negotiation
Relation to economy:	Nil
Relation to politics:	Planners bargain with interested parties
Outcomes:	Dependent on skill in handling resource constraints
Research focus:	Local authorities and quangos
Theoretical antecedents:	Critique of **Procedural Planning Theory**

The second strand of planning theory in the 1970s tackled this issue of the relationship between planning and economic processes head on. The strand contained 'liberal' (I) and 'radical' (II) variants of what was termed the political economy approach. Liberal political economy drew on the more accessible aspects of welfare economics to derive concepts of market failure applicable to urban and environmental problems (Evans, 1973; Harrison, 1977; Baumol and Oates, 1975). This suggested a number of justifications for public sector activity to redress such market failure and achieve more efficient or equitable market outcomes. Using a variety of economic techniques, exemplified by the cost benefit analysis, planners could act as expert assessors of the impact of environmental change. Their ability to achieve an optimal balance in resource allocation depended on how these assessment methods were operationalised. A number of assumptions were involved in any such assessment, explicitly or implicitly, and the nature of such assumptions could greatly influence the decisions recommended and hence the outcomes of the planning process. However, many of the most important assumptions, such as those concerning the weighting given to any distributional outcome, often remained implicit or were made in an apparently objective way by the planner. Thus planners were involved in taking political decisions in the guise of objective assessment. Within this theoretical approach, the relation of planners' activities to the broader political process remained unexplored, planners being presented as objective experts (see Summary Box 2.5).

Summary Box 2.5 *Liberal political economy*

Definition of planning:	Redressing market failure
View of planners:	Assessors of impact of environmental change
Process involved:	Economic assessment
Relation to economy:	Intervention based on quasi-market valuations
Relation to politics:	Nil
Outcomes:	Dependent on assumptions used in assessments
Research focus:	Social markets
Theoretical antecedents:	Contextualising development of **Procedural Planning Theory**

In contrast, the second, radical strand of political economy explicitly tackled the political nature of the planner's role alongside its economic nature. Using a marxist model of society, radical political economy explored the ways in which the state influenced the flow of capital within the economy, its rate of turnover and accumulation (Harvey, 1973; Broadbent, 1977). While there is a large body of marxist literature disputing the degree to which state actions are functional for capital accumulation, this approach inevitably involved consideration of functionality, particularly as it drew heavily on the work of French marxists inspired by the functionalist philosophy of Althusser (Castells, 1977; Pickvance, 1976). It searched for the ways in which planning policy could serve the interests of capitalists, either in general or in specific fractions. Planners were not seen as apolitical professionals but as agents of an essentially capitalist state, continually responding to the drive for profit within a capitalist economy. Planning was, therefore, a political process and deeply implicated in the workings of a capitalist economy. In so far as planning was an example of state activity which was functional for capitalism, the outcomes of planning supported profit levels, maintained the class system and staved off economic crisis. Variants of radical political economy, which recognised the existence of disfunctional state activity, usually explained this in terms of conflict between fractions of capital over the direction of state policy. In such situations there would be losers as well as winners amongst the capitalist class and there was, therefore, the potential for working class victories over capitalist interests. It became a matter of empirical research to determine the exact outcomes in each case (see Summary Box 2.6).

Summary Box 2.6   *Radical political economy*

Definition of planning:	Supporting capital accumulation
View of planners:	Agents of a capitalist state
Process involved:	Influencing circuits of capital
Relation to economy:	Responding to profit drive
Relation to politics:	Example of functional role of state
Outcomes:	Dependent on conflict between capitals and classes
Research focus:	Production and collective consumption processes
Theoretical antecedents:	Radical Critique of **Naive Public Administration** and **Procedural Planning Theory**

A final critique of procedural planning theory was provided by political scientists and sociologists who studied local planning as an example of urban politics. Numerous empirical case studies documented the way in which planners interacted with local politicians, pressure groups and representatives of local business in generating various decisions concerning the local environment (Davies, 1972; Dennis, 1972; Dearlove, 1973; Elkin, 1974; Wates, 1976). The local economic structure provided the rationale for certain local actors to become involved in planning decisions, but planning was essentially seen as a political activity. The generation of inequitable outcomes was thus central to an understanding of the planning process. Planners were seen as having a degree of control over the generation of these outcomes through allocation of certain resources, that is planners were seen as urban gatekeepers (Pahl, 1975). As with radical political economy, this provided a newly critical account of the planning system, with a much less sanguine view of the potential for improving the system's operation (see Summary Box 2.7).

Summary Box 2.7 *Political sociology*

Definition of planning	Local politics
View of planners	Urban gatekeepers
Process involved	Allocation of scarce resources
Relation to economy	Economics as source of conflicts
Relation to politics	"Planning *is* political"
Outcomes	Inequality in distribution
Research focus	Political groupings
Theoretical antecedents	Critique of **Procedural Planning Theory**

■ The story so far

The postwar period up to 1979 saw the planning system blossom as it grew in scope and importance, and then wilt under the pressures of a collapsing economy and the political legacy of unfulfilled promises. The rational management of the environment promised by the planning system in the 1950s and 1960s was never a realistic option and planners, having spent almost three decades establishing themselves as central public sector professionals, were faced with a barrage of criticism by the late 1970s. Many environmental problems demanded policy action but the resource base for the planning system was increasingly constrained and the intellectual support for the planning profession was fragmenting and turning instead to an exposure of planning's weaknesses and inadequacies.

Further reading

Cullingworth's official history of the planning system covers the period 1939–69 in four volumes which look at: Reconstruction and Land Use Planning (1975a); National Parks and Recreation in the Countryside (1975b); New Town Policies (1979); and Land Values, Compensation and Betterment

(1980). Other useful texts for this period are Hall *et al.*'s study of the land use planning system (1973), the MacEwan's history of National Parks (1987), Johnson's environmentalist account of planning, including a study of the DoE (1973), and Ambrose and Colenutt (1975), Fraser (1984) or Marriott (1969) for a flavour of urban development after the war. Given current concerns, the land nationalisation debate is covered briefly here and more detail can be found in Cox (1984). Theoretical references can be found in Faludi's edited volume (1973) and Healey *et al.* (1982).

■ *Chapter 3* ■

The Decade of Thatcherism and After

■ The decade of Thatcherism

□ *Economic and social change*

The 1980s were the decade of Thatcherism, a political response to the economic and social conditions of the time which has had its own profound social and economic consequences. The decade began with the deepening and eventual bottoming of the economic recession that followed the 1973–4 oil crisis, accentuated by a tight monetarist budget in 1981. It was characterised by the worst unemployment and industrial disinvestment since the interwar period. Long-term unemployment among the young and those approaching retirement became a common occurrence. The effects of a cyclical recession were reinforced by the introduction of new technology based on computer microprocessors. As a result of recession and restructuring, industrial employment fell. However industrial output was also falling as the longer-term trend away from manufacturing towards service industries had an ever greater impact. By the end of the decade, the application of new technology and a spate of reinvestment following the devaluation of capital in preceding years was beginning to have an effect as economic growth went up again. This was a fragile recovery though and, by the end of the decade, the signs of a further downward spiral for the following decade were becoming clear.

Urban decentralisation continued to affect the location of economic activity. New technology often required new locations particularly as it went with a shift to new patterns of production, often labelled post-Fordist or flexible specialisation, in which greater use was made of sub-contracting together with part-time and often female labour. The search for appropriate labour pools and new industrial locations, and the continuing push and pull pressures for residential decentralisation maintained the urban–rural shift. The inner city problem thus became ever worse as selective outmigration from the cities by the mobile and better-off was combined with the loss of working class employment opportunities within urban areas. Large sections of the remaining population faced dependency on state benefits given the lack of available jobs. This was highlighted by the inner city riots of 1980–1 which the Scarman Inquiry analysed as having their roots in the economic deprivation of the areas, engendering alienation particularly among the young. By the end of the decade, however, evidence was coming forward that the process may have reached its peak at least as far as the residential sector was concerned, with selective re-urbanisation.

These economic changes underpinned the growth of Thatcherism during the decade, as success in the 1979 General Election was succeeded by success in 1983 and 1987. Thatcherism represented a significant ideological shift in British politics and, possibly, public opinion. The mixed economy consensus was breaking up in response to the apparent inability of Keynesian economic management and welfare state social policies to deliver the promised results. The dominant theme within the shifting ideological framework was the emergence of a New Right philosophy emphasising the advantages of market processes, the role of the private sector in generating wealth and the moral and economic dangers of both a large public sector and other forms of collective action such as trades unionism. The stand of the government against the long and painful miners' strike of 1984–5 was emblematic of this anti-unionism.

However, other ideologies also emerged and would, from time to time, challenge Thatcherism. The third parties of the Liberals and Social Democratic Party (SDP), which became the Alliance and finally the Liberal Democrats, saw a rise in their attractiveness to voters. The Green Party increased its support in recognition of the environmental damage caused by the postwar period of growth. And the Labour Party undertook a painful re-examination of its approach with different elements within the Party promoting a quasi-Thatcherite line, the professional managerialism of the SDP or the radical socialist democracy of Ken Livingstone's rule at the Greater London Council (GLC) and the socialist–feminist wing. While disparate in their approaches a common theme can be discerned among these anti-Thatcherite ideologies. They combine a commitment to a managerialist state retaining some element of overall direction, with an element of the 'small is beautiful' approach, a recognition of the value of autonomy, privacy, self-help and community based action (see Summary Box 3.1).

Summary Box 3.1 *1980s*

Economic and social change:	Recession (and recovery)
	New technology
	Collapse of mixed economy consensus
Salient political issues:	Unemployment
	Track record of public sector
Key planning activities:	Urban regeneration
	Countryside policy
Planning profession:	Retrenchment
	Privatisation
Conceptualisation of planning:	A – Economic development
	B – Community participation
	C – Arena for mediation
Theoretical framework:	A – New Right
	B – New Left
	C – Institutional approach

□ *Problems and policies*

Certain aspects of the planning system, which had in any case been in decline during the 1970s, were finally killed off by the Thatcher administration. Regional economic planning councils were disbanded in 1979, ODPs abolished soon after and regionally-based grants significantly cut back. The areas in which they applied were redefined reducing their applicability. This had knock-on effects in that only development areas as defined by a national government were eligible for grants from the EC. Industrial development certificates followed ODPs in 1984 and the automatic entitlement to grants in development areas ended in 1988. Regional planning was effectively replaced by the application of inner city policy in depressed regions and an a-spatial training policy administered through numerous special employment schemes. The apparatus of the new towns programme was finally dismantled with the accelerated winding up of the New Towns Commission. The ailing Community Land Act was repealed in 1980 with the exception of the LAW, which remained on a self-financing basis as a means of directing land to private sector developers in pursuit of urban regeneration. The LAW's function was 'to make development land available as quickly as possible where the private sector finds it difficult to complete transactions'. Development Land Tax was abolished in 1985.

Within land use planning, the twin elements of development planning and development control were restructured in line with a more market oriented approach. Government advice on development control made it clear that a more 'positive' approach to planning was to be adopted. This was particularly the case where small businesses were involved. The 1985 Department of Trade and Industry report *Business in the Community* led to a White Paper in the same year *Lifting the Burden*, which set out the need to reduce planning constraints on business. A 1986 White Paper *Building Business – Not Barriers* again echoed this theme. DoE Circular 14/85 established clearly that there was a presumption in favour of planning permission being granted unless planning objections could be sustained. And a series of circulars (DoE Circulars 2/86, 22/80 and 9/80) stressed the need to take account of market forces. Three DoE Circulars focused on the needs of industrial development and business enterprises particularly: 16/84 on *Industrial Development*, 14/85 on *Development and Employment* and 2/86 on *Development by Small Businesses*.

Several procedural changes were made to ensure that this advice was heeded. Joint housing studies were introduced as a factor in deciding residential development planning applications by DoE Circular 9/80. Changes to the Use Classes Order in 1987 and the General Development Order in 1981 and 1988 removed some important and many minor developments from local authority control. Central government advice, such as Circular 31/85, emphasised that aesthetic control in particular should be removed from routine development control. Following the idea of zoning contained in enterprise zones (see below), special planning zones under the 1986 Housing and Planning Act created areas where development in compliance with an approved plan did not need specific permission.

The negotiation by planners of community benefits during development control, known as planning gain, was also regarded less favourably. Following a 1981 report on planning gain by the Property Advisory Group, a DoE Circular 22/83 was issued which restricted the use of planning gain by local authorities. In 1989 draft guidance and proposed legislative amendments were put forward for altering the nature of the planning agreements by which most planning gain was achieved. This was eventually instituted in the 1991 Planning and Compensation Act. The use of planning conditions was also restricted by DoE Circular 1/85. Throughout planning procedure, the emphasis was on speeding up the process and league tables of the speed of development control in different districts were published. There was a price to pay for such 'improvements' to development control – planning fees were introduced in the 1980 Local Government, Planning and Land Act. Similar fees for planning appeals were dropped from the Bill after opposition.

Development planning was also considerably affected, indeed diminished in importance. Early on in the decade the Secretary of State for the Environment made it clear that structure plans should be rapidly prepared and approved, and considerable departmental effort was put into processing the large number of structure plans still in the system awaiting final submission and approval. As part of the effort to speed up development planing, the DoE placed considerable emphasis on restricting the scope of structure plans to land use matters. In modifications to development plans, the Secretary of State removed policies considered to stray outside such planning concerns. The requirements for survey work and public participation were also reduced. These procedural changes were summarised in DoE Circulars 23/81 and 22/84, the latter providing a memorandum on structure plans and local plans.

The net result of these changes was that structure plans became shorter compared to the bulky documents of the 1970s. The relevant parts were even shorter as the 'reasoned justification' for policies became a non-statutory part of the plan after 1979 changes to regulations. These were readily identified as capitals were used for policies and lower case print for all other parts of the plan. But it is not just that structure plans were shorter and more up to date. They were downgraded compared to local plans. The Inner Areas Act of 1978 allowed local plans to be prepared and adopted in advance of structure plans in specified inner city areas. The 1980 Local Government Planning and Land Act extended this to all areas.

This downgrading of the county council's role mirrored the removal of certain areas of development control from the county to the district council. This took effect from January 1981 following the 1980 Local Government, Planning and Land Act. County matters now covered only minerals, waste disposal, cement workings and development across national park boundaries.

The government's attitude to local plans varied over this period. The changes in regulations meant that survey work for local plans was discouraged and, in the early 1980s, it was strongly suggested that local plans would not be needed for all areas. However, statutory local plans were clearly preferred compared to the non-statutory plans which had previously been commonly used by district councils. By the end of the decade, full local plan coverage was seen as a potential way of replacing structure plans altogether. The ideas for restructuring development planning were contained in the 1986 Green Paper *The Future of Development Plans* and a 1989 White Paper.

A further bout of local government reorganisation also had implications for development planning. In 1985 the Local Government Act abolished the metropolitan counties, sweeping away six sites of increasingly troublesome opposition to Thatcherite policies. This also removed the structure plans that the metropolitan county councils used to prepare. Therefore, the Act and DoE Circular 30/85 provided for unitary development plans in metropolitan areas. These were to be prepared by the district council, comprising strategic and detailed policies and conforming to statutory central government policy guidelines. Passenger transport authorities were resurrected as separate organisations to replace the transport planning functions of metropolitan county councils. In London, London Regional Transport had already been established in 1984 to take public transport out of the GLC's hands.

Taken together, structure and local plans were given less importance within the overall planning system during the 1980s. Two quotes from circulars illustrate this. From DoE Circular 14/85: 'the development plans are one, but only one, of the material considerations that must be taken into account in dealing with planning applications', and from DoE Circular 16/84: 'where a developer applies for planning permission which is contrary to the policies of the approved development plans, this does not in itself justify reason for refusal'.

Urban conservation was represented in the 1983 National Heritage Act which established the Historic Buildings and Monuments Commission for England, known as English Heritage. This body also took over the role of the GLC's historic buildings division, including its listed building control. The Commission has an Ancient Monuments and Historic Buildings Advisory Committee to support its work and an Ancient Monuments Board and Historic Buildings Council exists in each county. In Wales the relevant body is CADW or Welsh Historic Monuments, and in Scotland, the historic buildings and monuments directorate of the SDA, now known as Historic Scotland.

Following on from the 1979 Ancient Monuments Act, five areas of archaeological importance were designated in 1984: Canterbury, Chester, Exeter, Hereford and York. Within these areas an operations notice was now needed before development, even permitted development, could proceed. The criteria for listing buildings of historic and architectural importance were also extended in 1988. Previously only pre-1939 buildings could be listed in England and Wales, although in Scotland buildings over 30 years of age were eligible. Under the new rules buildings of only 10 years' life have been listed. The policies and procedures for listed buildings and conservation were set out in DoE Circular 8/87.

Thornley (1991, p. 161) describes the net effect of Thatcherism on land use planning as:

> to retain a strong planning system operating in certain areas where conservation and environmental factors are considered important. Elsewhere the system has been much modified and weakened and market criteria are expected to dominate with the removal of many previously adopted criteria.

Countryside protection formed the basis of an unexpectedly popular piece of legislation, the 1981 Wildlife and Countryside Act, followed by the 1985 Wildlife and Countryside (Amendment) Act. This legislation covered a number of issues. Protection of specific species, such as bats and badgers, was enhanced and earlier Acts concerning birds (1954 and 1967), wild creatures and wild plants (1975) were replaced. A system of reciprocal notification, between the landowner and Nature Conservancy Council, was set up with regard to sites of special scientific interest (SSSIs) and special protection given to moorlands. A system for monitoring applications for agricultural capital grants from an environmental point of view was also introduced. Generally, the Acts encouraged a voluntary approach on the part of the agricultural industry towards nature conservation. The 1985 Wildlife and Countryside (Amendment) Act extended this to the Forestry Commission also and conservation oriented planting grants were introduced in the 1985 Broadleaved Woodland Grant Scheme.

The legislation also covered the role of the Countryside Commission and access to the countryside. Under the 1981 Wildlife and Countryside Act a duty was placed on all county councils to inform the public about their access rights and, in 1985, a Countryside Access Charter was published. In Scotland the policy deliberations of the 1970s bore fruit in the 1981 Countryside (Scotland) Act which established regional parks, and provision for management and access agreements between rural landowners and local planning authorities.

While reforms in the Common Agricultural Policy (CAP) were for the first time reducing financial support to farmers, countryside policy tried to ensure that the reduced subsidy to agriculture did not lead to a shift of land out of predominantly rural use. The set-aside policies of the 1986 Agriculture Act exemplified this. In this Act it was set out that the Minister of Agriculture had a statutory duty to balance agricultural interests with the economic and social interests of rural areas, conservation and the enhancement of the beauty and amenity of the countryside, together with any archaeological features, plus public enjoyment of the countryside. The Act also provided for the designation of environmentally sensitive areas (ESAs), where grants for farming practice in line with conservation objectives were made available.

These pressures towards balancing the different interests in the countryside in the face of changing circumstances also led to the Farm and Countryside Initiative. This was jointly sponsored by the Ministry of Agriculture, Fisheries and Food (MAFF), DoE, Manpower Services Commission, Development Commission, Countryside Commission, Nature Conservancy Council (now known as English Nature) and Agriculture Training Board. It investigated the appropriate ways of changing the rural economy and training labour for a new economic structure. Relevant inputs into this debate included the 1984 Countryside Commission report *A Better Future for the Uplands* and the 1986 Country Planning Officers' Report *Agriculture and the Countryside*. In 1987 MAFF further investigated alternative land uses, diversification and the environment in the countryside. This led to policies for encouraging farm woodlands, extending the ESA scheme and promoting diversification on farms with grants.

Concern for the rural environment guided several statements of minerals policy during this decade: 1981 saw a Town and Country Planning (Minerals) Act. The 1981 Act covered Scotland, England and Wales and created several possibilities for enhanced planning control of minerals workings. The case of coal, and in particular of opencast mining, was addressed by the Flowers Report on *Coal and the Environment* in 1981, a 1983 White Paper on *Coal* and subsequent 1984 guidelines. Opencast coalmining had been considered merely a wartime emergency measure and had been controlled by the Minister of Power and, from 1958, the Secretary of State for Energy. Only in 1984 did such workings come within the general framework of development control. The separate need for Secretary of State authorisation was repealed in the 1986 Housing and Planning Act so that such workings now require planning permission in the same way as any other mineral working.

There was significant activity in the environmental policy area, heralding the changes that were to come in the 1990s. At the beginning of the decade the policy changes were marginal. In the case of noise pollution, the Noise Advisory Council was disbanded, but the 1980 Local Government Planning and Land Act allowed local authorities to designate their own noise abatement zones. Environmental concerns were introduced into derelict land policy. The 1982 Derelict Land Act, largely a consolidating measure, clarified the availability of grants under a range of existing legislation spanning two decades but it also extended the power to declare derelict land clearance areas on environmental as well as economic grounds. Higher rates of grant assistance operated in these derelict land clearance areas and also in national parks and AONBs.

But by the end of the decade more significant change was occurring. Moves were finally made towards implementing the integrated pollution control proposed by the Royal Commission on Environmental Pollution in the 1970s. In 1987 Her Majesty's Inspectorate of Pollution (HMIP) was created from existing pollution control agencies to control emissions to all environmental media: land, water and air. This was in pursuit of the 'best practicable environmental option' (BPEO) for controlling pollution.

Particular attention had to be paid to water quality because, on the one hand, the EC were introducing new standards and, on the other, privatisation of the English and Welsh water industry in the 1989 Water Act created new structures of water management. Under EC law a new system of regulatory control was also required. The 1989 Water Act, therefore, allowed the Secretary of State to set water quality objectives, which the new watchdog body for the water industry, the NRA, should strive to achieve. By the late 1980s the DoE had also set up a Drinking Water Inspectorate and implemented part of the Control of Pollution Act 1974 on public registers of consented discharges and effluent samples.

A significant addition to environmental protection came in 1988 with the introduction of regulations requiring environmental assessments as a standard element of planning procedure. The Conservative government had opposed the 1985 European Commission directive on such assessments but eventually had to comply. This presaged a key theme of the 1990s with European integration and the 'greening' of planning going hand-in-hand to reshape many of the changes of Thatcherism.

By contrast, urban policy of the 1980s exemplified the approach of Thatcherism. In housing policy there was a marked shift away from public sector provision. Local authority housebuilding fell from 130 000 completions in 1975 to proposed levels of only 6000 in England for 1991/2. Public spending on council housing fell by 80 per cent in real terms over 1979–89 (Spencer, 1989). This shift confirmed the importance of public–private sector partnership in rehabilitation as the main way of improving the existing housing stock. There was a growing emphasis on private sector finance and complementing local authority grants with households' own resources. This was evident in the 1985 Green Paper on *Housing Improvement* and the improvement sections of the preceding 1980 Housing Act. DoE Circular 29/82 encouraged the use of enveloping schemes where the local authority undertook the basic external works on a group of dwellings providing the physical and financial framework for other work. Meanwhile, DoE Circular 22/80 established the local authority improvement for sale scheme and homesteading, where local authority housing was sold for improvement by the purchaser.

The 1985 Urban Housing Renewal Unit of the DoE and its Action Estate Programme was the logical extension of this shift where provision was made for whole local authority estates, to be transferred to trusts, tenants' cooperatives or developers on the basis that this would facilitate their upgrading. Funds were provided under the Housing, Manpower Services Commission and DoE Urban Programmes. Housing action trusts (HATs), introduced in the 1988 Housing Act, were an extension of this idea.

In Scotland, less change in housing policy occurred. The 1985 Housing Improvement Green Paper proposed three types of housing action area for demolition, improvement and a combined strategy. This confirmed the greater role that the public sector continued to play, often in cooperation with local community groups. Ad hoc housing associations have often been the instrument for this cooperative policy under the Housing (Scotland) Act 1974.

In urban areas more generally, urban regeneration was based less on public sector development and direction and more on private sector development levered in by subsidy and land transfers. A review of inner city policy in 1981 soon established the important role that the private sector was to play. The Financial Institutions Group and Business in the Community were early examples of this. The Financial Institutions Group consisted of 25 managers seconded for a year during 1981–2. This produced some 35 unpublished reports but only one idea that took root. This was the proposal for urban development grants (UDGs) along the line of American leverage grants, a proposal which reinforced existing thinking within the DoE (Jacobs, 1985). These flexible grants were introduced in 1982 in 80 local authorities in England and Wales: designated districts or those with enterprise zones (see below). Scotland had its own equivalent – local enterprise grants for urban projects (LEGUPs). They were intended to encourage the marginal private development, with public sector funds levering in multiple quantities of private money. The legislative basis for the grants scheme was the 1969 Local Government (Social Need) Act. This was supplemented by urban regeneration grants for large scale projects introduced in the 1986 Housing and Planning Act. The traditional Urban Programme was further revamped by a management initiative, which produced the City Action Teams of 1985.

However, the enterprise zones (EZs) and urban development corporations (UDCs) of the 1980 Local Government, Planning and Land Act were the mainstay of inner city policy during this decade. EZs are relatively small areas, proposed for Secretary of State designation primarily by local authorities. They last for 10 years, during which financial assistance in the form of 100 per cent capital allowances against tax and exemption from business rates apply. A zoning scheme is prepared by the local authority which, when approved, overrides any local plan and structure plan in case of conflict. Development in accordance with the scheme does not require specific planning permission. The assumed problem that EZs were designed to tackle was a shortage of good quality property and an excess of bureaucratic red tape. They were a unique planning experiment. 25 zones were designated throughout the UK during 1981–5, covering some 3800 hectares in total with only exceptional cases of designation thereafter.

UDCs cover areas, usually larger in scale than EZs, where a specially created body – the corporation – undertakes a policy of levering in private sector development through cheap land and infrastructure investment. The inner city problem was seen in terms of local government inefficiency, a lack of business confidence and problems in the supply side of the development process, principally the availability of land. The UDC also has extensive planning powers within its area which effectively replace the mainstream land use planning system creating, as Thornley (1991) argues, 'a dual planning system'. The first two UDCs announced were the London and Merseyside docklands, followed by five more in 1987: Cardiff, Trafford Park, Tyne and Wear, Teesside and the Black Country. A further three, in Leeds, Central Manchester and the Lower Don Valley in Sheffield, together with an extension of the Black Country Corporation area were introduced by the end of the next year, with Bristol following, after local authority objections, in 1989.

Transport policy continued to place emphasis on road provision and private sector transport. The 1980 statement on *Policies for Roads in England* set out that the first priority must be national economic recovery in which road provision would play a part. Environmental benefits would flow from this, it was argued. Freight transport focused on heavier lorries, in line with EC axle-weight regulations, the 1981 Armitage Committee Report and the 1981 White Paper on *Lorries, People and the Environment*. In the case of public transport, conflict between local authorities and central government over the provision of a subsidised service eventually led to the 1987 Transport Act which increased central government control over such financial matters. In the 1986 Transport Act, following the 1984 White Paper *Buses*, bus services outside London were deregulated to allow private sector operators to compete with the public sector on services over 30 miles.

There was a general aim to introduce private sector funding where possible, for example through toll roads. The 1987 *Policy for Roads in*

England established the principle of developer involvement in financing road improvements. Similarly great emphasis was given to city, rail and tube systems where private sector funding could be demonstrated: for example, the Docklands Light Railway and the Jubilee Line extension in London. Meanwhile British Rail restructured its services with an eye to breaking even and eventual privatisation and the Channel Tunnel struggled towards completion totally on the basis of private funding. In line with a more general policy move (see below), leaseholds on motorway service stations were sold in 1983, realising £48 million.

In contrast to previous land nationalisation attempts, the Thatcher government sought to privatise much of the public estate. The sale of individual council housing was a major plank in the Conservative Party's manifestos. Some 1 million council houses were sold at a considerable discount over 1979–89, contributing to the increase in owner occupation among the population. As mentioned earlier, under the 1988 Housing Act, whole council estates could be privatised as HATs. Nationalised industries such as British Rail were encouraged to sell any 'surplus' land and the 1980 Local Government Planning and Land Act set up Part X derelict land registers which collated data on and publicised the extent of surplus public sector land, available for voluntary or forced sale. These registers operated in designated areas: all districts in England, six areas in Wales, with no such provision in Scotland. Such privatisation moves were considered to be an important element in Thatcherite urban policy.

□ *Theory*

The planning profession came under severe attack during the Thatcher years. Planning departments were cut back in size and some even disbanded altogether. As with so many other areas of public sector activity, privatisation occurred. Planning consultancies grew apace, drawing professionals from the public sector, as private sector developers sought their expertise to challenge revised planning constraints in conditions of property boom and, also, as local government made use of private sector planners to develop planning strategies. In this climate, planning theory took three routes. Along one, the New Right political perspective was applied to the case of planning. Along another, the New Left were developing a radical answer to the New Right. Meanwhile in more purely academic circles, the criticisms of the 1970s were being synthesised into a new theoretical framework which can now be termed the institutional approach.

The New Right approach, while lacking analytic depth, launched a thorough assault on the very notion of planning itself (Thornley, 1991). Arising out of this, a much reduced role for planning could be established. The central notion was that free markets generate wealth in society and that most public sector activity hindered the generation of this wealth. Planning, along with many other state activities, was characterised as potentially so much 'red tape' and an extravagant use of public funds. Planners were essentially state bureaucrats who, following the iron law of bureaucracies, sought to create and expand their empires. It was, therefore, essential for the economic well-being of society to cut back on such areas of state activity and minimise the effect on the public sector. Planning could be justified only to the extent that it reconstituted itself as economic development, a role which many planners actively took on. In this role, the planning system was directed towards facilitating development. The extent to which it achieved this goal, depended on its responsiveness to market signals and the ability to cut back on unnecessary bureaucratic procedures (see Summary Box 3.2).

Summary Box 3.2 *New Right*

Definition of planning:	Economic development
View of planners:	State bureaucrats
Process involved:	Potentially facilitating development
Relation to economy:	Intervention in free markets
Relation to politics:	Potentially an example of the authoritarian state
Outcomes:	Dependent on relation between planning goals and market signals
Research focus:	Markets
Theoretical antecedents:	Critique of **Procedural Planning Theory** and **Liberal Political Economy**

To counter this view, left wing movements began to develop, albeit incoherently, a vision of planning as community participation. Drawing on the experiences of the GLC Popular Planning Unit and the occasional success story, such as the Coin Street redevelopment in Central London, a radically deprofessionalised planning was proposed (Brindley *et al.*, 1989; Wainwright, 1987; Montgomery and Thornley, 1990). In this model the planner would merely act as an advocate, ensuring that a form of local pluralism operated. Any other role for the planner would constitute the suppression of local wishes by professional interests or other vested interests operating through the medium of local planning. The rise of planning aid and the growth of community activism could be related to this theoretical development. The allocation of resources was seen as a process of struggle between political groups formed around common economic interests. Community groups thus struggled for power in the context of constraining economic processes. Through struggle, an element of control over both private sector actors, central and local government could be exerted, resulting in environmental change for local needs.

The state, therefore, had a dual role to play. It should focus its energies on opening up the political arena to community involvement, decentralising state structures and actively empowering community groups. But the state's power resources could also be used by those on the New Left to challenge other interests in society (Stoker, 1991). This view of local politics implies a debate about the concept of citizenship (Gyford, 1991). For some on the New Left (as on the New Right) there is a moral duty to engage in politics and contribute fully to debate and struggle. For others, such action can come only after economic and social change, otherwise all citizen action is token and empowerment is an empty shell.

In academic circles, there was an attempt to marry the lessons learned from New Left local authorities and other political actors on the ground, with the criticisms of the radical political economy of the 1970s. In particular, the aim was to reconstruct a radical, left wing analysis which was not driven by the inevitable dynamics of capital accumulation. This debate (within planning) originally centred around the work of Manuel Castells. Castells was one of the key figures in the development of an urban marxism. The 1977 translation of his book *The Urban Question* was widely cited for its discussion of state planning, particularly urban planning, in relation to capital accumulation processes and its Althusserian methodology, derived from the philosophy of Louis Althusser. This methodology proposed three structures which jointly determined social outcomes: economics, political and ideological. However, in accordance with the precepts of marxism, the economic structure was considered to be 'determinant in the last instance', that is, in the end, it was the economics of capital accumulation which drove the system. This results in a functionalist analysis (which Castells was later to reject in favour of an emphasis on urban social movements – see Chapter 10 below).

A profound disagreement grew up between those marxist analysts who wished to maintain the primacy of the economic structure and those (of varying political persuasions) who wished both to elevate political and ideological factors to greater importance *and* to question the notion of structures driving social change. Some argued that a greater role should be accorded to human agency, to the actions of groups (classes, institutions, gender and ethnic groupings) and individuals within those groups in generating outcomes, outcomes which could both reproduce the existing social system and achieve change (Dunleavy, 1980, p. 44). For many, the philosophical framework of realism has provided a method which can draw on marxist insights without determinist conclusions (see Summary Box 3.3).

Summary Box 3.3   *New Left*

Definition of planning:	Community participation
View of planners:	Advocates
Process involved:	Struggle for local power
Relation to economy:	Economics as constraint on achieving community goals
Relation to politics:	Local pluralism
Outcomes:	Dependent on ability to control public and private sectors
Research focus:	Communities
Theoretical antecedents:	Integrating development of **Political Sociology** and **Radical Political Economy**

The other strand of planning theory reflected the, by now, substantially separate professionalisation of academics and practitioners in planning fields (Breheny and Congden, 1989, p. 230). It sought to take on board the insights of both liberal and radical political economy as well as organisation theory and political sociology. Indeed one of the potential difficulties of this institutional approach is its attempt to reconcile the insights of essentially critical approaches to planning (radical political economy and political sociology) with the approaches of liberal political economy and organisation theory, which take a more positive view of planning practice and are more sanguine where potential reform is concerned. This strand also sought to incorporate other new developments in social theory such as structuration theory (Giddens, 1984). Institutionalist writings in the 1980s were just developing the approach and at the time of writing this approach is still in its infancy and lacks a definitive statement of the total framework (but see Healey, 1990; Healey and Barrett, 1990; Healey, 1992a). It currently appears very eclectic, taking on board many different points from different disciplines and theoretical persuasions. Its importance in the 1990s, however, warrants discussion in some depth.

The central concern of the institutional approach was to incorporate analysis of the constraints placed on planning activity by economic processes, while at the same time recognising that actors, individually and collectively, can influence policy and its impacts. The institutionalist approach rested on the argument that social outcomes, including environmental change and planning policy, are the result of both broad structural processes and the active involvement of agents, such as planners, politicians, community groups and specific business interests. Healey and Barrett, in an important article, explained the approach as follows (1990, p. 90):

> The approach adopted in this paper draws in particular on the work of Anthony Giddens, who argues for a relational approach between structure and agency in which 'structure' is established by the way agents operate: deploying, acknowledging, challenging and potentially transforming resources, rules and ideas as they frame and pursue their own strategies. Structure, in terms of the framework within which individual agents make their choices, may be seen to inhere in the various *resources* to which agents may have access, the *rules* which they consider govern their behaviour, and the *ideas* which they draw upon in developing their strategies.

These key concepts were defined as follows (1990, p. 94):

(a) the *resources* for development, as channelled via the financial systems and the inter-relation of supply and demand;
(b) the politico–juridical *rules* which limit the construction of development opportunities; and
(c) the *ideas and values* people hold about what they should build, what they would like to occupy and what kind of environment they seek.

In this way it was intended that institutional analysts could use the underlying idea of economic, political and ideological structures current in much marxist thought in the 1970s and early 1980s, but in a non-functionalist and more flexible manner.

In the institutional approach, the state undertook a mediating role, mediating between the different interests involved in urban and environmental change. However, the state also had a structuring effect, influencing the way in which actors may pursue their interests and strategies. Planners were seen as a sectional interest group interacting with other interests in a structured society. The planning system provided one arena where structured mediation between these interests could occur, and planners played an active role in handling that mediation. The outcomes of the planning system were in part dependent on this mediation but also on the dynamics of other economic and social processes. Planning further had significant impacts in that resources were reallocated through the planning system, thereby maintaining or changing structures in society.

The problem in analysis is 'keeping all the balls in the air' and allowing for: the dynamics of economic processes and the interrelation of actors; planners as mediators and a sectional interest group; planning as promoting change and being constrained in so doing; planning as structured by and involved in structuring social processes. To some extent the problems of this approach lie not in its analysis of political processes but in its model of economic processes. While attracted by many of the insights of radical political economy, few of the adherents of institutional approach fully espouse a marxist model. But the market model of much conventional economics seems closely linked to the New Right case or liberal political economy. The contribution that institutional economic analyses can make in underpinning institutionalist planning theory are only just being recognised (see Part 4 below) (see Summary Box 3.4).

Summary Box 3.4   *Institutional approach*

Definition of planning	Arena for mediation
View of planners	
	One sectional interest among many
Process involved	
	Mediation
Relation to economy	Economics as one source of structuration
Relation to politics	Planning involves conflict between sectional interests
Outcomes:	Dependent on contingent relation of factors
Research focus:	Locality case studies
Theoretical antecedents:	Integrating development of **Organisation Theory, Radical and Liberal Political Economy** and **Political Sociology**

■ The 1990s: taking stock and looking ahead

Writing at the beginning of the decade it is clearly not possible to set out the key characteristics of the planning system in the 1990s, in the way that hindsight has allowed for the past. In this section, I will therefore draw together the key changes that are occurring now and speculate about policy developments. The detail of planning policies in the 1990s is presented in Part 2. I will also consider which of the theoretical frameworks discussed so far are likely to prove relevant in the 1990s and be developed further. Such policy speculation is of course a dangerous activity and apparent policy trends can be bucked, but the first few years of the decade do seem to indicate such a clear trend. The theoretical discussion will form the basis of the analysis in Parts 3 and 4 of the actors and institutions of planning and the relation with market processes.

□ *Economic and social change*

The early 1990s saw the economic ups and downs of the 1980s culminate in a major world recession which hit all regions and both manufacturing and service industries. Given the policy legacy of Thatcherism, there seemed little the government could do to raise economic output. The replacement of Margaret Thatcher with John Major as leader of the Conservative Party did not change economic policy in this respect, and the election result of 1992 which returned the Conservative Party for a fourth consecutive term confirmed the continuation of anti-Keynesian economic policy.

The new issue of the decade was undoubtedly the environment. This issue took on a new significance because of the global scale at which problems were perceived and solutions being discussed. The scientific predictions of depletion of the ozone layer, enhancement of the greenhouse effect and loss of biodiversity meant that the environment became an issue of planet survival rather than of local amenity. Global arenas became the key forums for developing environmental policy such as the Montreal Protocol on limiting ozone depleting substances and the 1992 Earth Summit's tentative agreements on greenhouse gases and biodiversity.

As far as Britain is concerned, the EC firmly established itself as a major policy actor for both economic and environmental problems. 1992 saw steps being taken towards greater European integration with the removal of trade barriers. While this move has promised economic growth its effects are likely to be highly regionally differentiated. Debate continues to rage over the desired extent of such integration, not only in economic but also in political terms. Together with economic recession and the environment, Europe completes the trio of issues dominating the early 1990s.

☐ *Problems and policies*

Since the replacement of Margaret Thatcher by John Major did not really herald the end of Thatcherism, many of the planning policies of the early 1990s were continuations of those of the 1980s. However, there was a small, quiet but highly significant shift in land use planning. The 1991 Planning and Compensation Act seemed to mark an end to the anti-plan attitude of the 1980s. Whereas during the 1980s development control was urged to have regard to market factors often in preference to the development plan, the 1990 Act made it clear that development control decisions were to be based on the development plan unless there was a good reason to the contrary. This is not the return to strategy-led planning that it might seem. The reassertion of the development plan occurs in the context of the probable abolition of the structure plan and the development plan is therefore equated with the district-based local plan. This trend is likely to be reinforced by the local government restructuring that will follow the recommendations of the Local Government Commission in the 1990s (see Part 3 below).

In countryside policy, the debate within the EC over the CAP continued with reforms put in place which cut the subsidies to agricultural production. In the context of heightened concern with the environment, the opportunity was taken to link these reforms with further measures for environmental protection. This continued a slow but significant trend of the late 1980s.

Environmental planning achieved new importance in the policy climate of the 1990s. The most significant environmental policy document to date has been the 1990 White Paper on the environment, the first such White Paper ever produced. *This Common Inheritance* (which derived its name from the 1987 Brundtland report of the United Nations' World Commission on Environment and Development *Our Common Future*) was a glossy compilation of environmental statistics, description of current policy and outlines of future policy commitments. On the one hand, it in no way addressed the global environmental concerns in a manner to satisfy environmentalists but, on the other hand, it did represent a new innovation in the DoE's policy thinking. A commitment was made to producing an annual update on the White

Paper and further policy developments have followed. A 'green' minister in each government department was appointed to represent the environment's interests and the DoE's own research has been skewed towards examining the implications of global environmental change on its traditional concerns such as land use planning. The recommendations of such research, if translated into policy, could significantly alter traditional practice. The DoE has also issued advice to other government departments on how to incorporate environmental assessment into their own policy appraisal (1991a). This draws heavily on the advice that the DoE has received from environmental economists, such as Professor David Pearce. Professor Pearce led a team on a DoE research project into the implications of the Brundtland report's concept of sustainable development for the UK. In this research report (published as *Blueprint for a Green Economy*: Pearce *et al.*, 1989) the use of environmental economics techniques to value the environment was advocated, and many of these techniques are mentioned in the DoE's policy appraisal advice.

One of the implications of basing environmental policy at least in part on environmental economists' ideas has been the claim that it is possible to have sustainable development, in which economic growth is married with environmental protection. In this way it has been politically possible to advance a degree of environmental policy innovation at a time of economic recession. This is certainly the view of the European Commission which has vigorously argued for high environmental standards as a corollary of economic growth, and the European Commission is one of the main actors pushing for a higher profile for the environment in British planning. It is clear that the European Commission is leading Britain into whole new policy areas and new modes of policy practice. The British government would claim that it is developing its own particular environmental approach but, while more environmental policy documents are emanating from the DoE, there is substantial criticism by the Commission of the quality of their content and conflict with Europe over the detail of their content continues.

In urban and transport policy the 1990s have seen the trends of the 1980s continued. Urban regeneration was still dependent on local economic development. Continued reliance was placed on UDCs; continued emphasis was given to business services, now through training and enterprise councils (TECs); and there was a continuing shift away from the traditional Urban Programme as local authorities were required to bid for inner city money in partnership with business and voluntary organisations through City Challenge. Meanwhile local authorities had to cope with the imposition of another regime for local government finance, the council tax. Since this occurred in the context of recession and tight central government budget restrictions, there was considerable concern over the contribution that urban local authorities would be able to make to regenerating their areas, or even preventing further local economic and social decline.

Perhaps mention should also be made of John Major's 'big idea', the Citizen's Charter. While many doubt the relevance of this mix of public relations and policy targets, the approach has impacted on planning with a greater emphasis on customer care within planning, greater scrutiny of public sector agencies and, in some selected cases, more power for the client-based organisations scrutinising recently privatised activities.

■ Theoretical approaches for the 1990s

A large number of theoretical approaches have been introduced, each of which has had an influence on planning thought over a period of time. It is perhaps a reflection on the intellectual insecurity of the planning profession and its academic colleagues that so many influences have held sway but it is also apparent that, after a period of fragmentation and conflict in the 1970s and 1980s, a degree of synthesis has occurred and the lines of theoretical debate are likely to be more clearly drawn over the next decade.

Figure 3.1 illustrates the interconnections between the various theoretical approaches, some critical (−ve) and some reinforcing (+ve). Of these, I would argue that four will continue to influence intellectual and political debate in the 1990s: the political thought of the New Right and New Left; and the academic analyses of liberal political economy and the institutionalist approach. The politically-oriented approaches are becoming more distinct from the growing literature on the two academic approaches, indicating the end of the period of radicalisation of academics, whether by the Left in the 1970s or the Right in the 1980s. It also reflects the decline in the ferocity of political debate, in that right wing and left wing political ideologies are not strongly leading theoretical developments. Thus the relatively profession centred approaches of liberal political economy, pushed by those with an economic training, and the institutional approach, firmly based in the professional planning schools, are currently in the ascendancy. However, it is in the nature of professional activity that it cannot meet its own promises, and conflict with professionals and challenge to their ways of thinking are bound to arise. The political poles of Left and Right remain the source for such challenges, even if at the moment they seem weak.

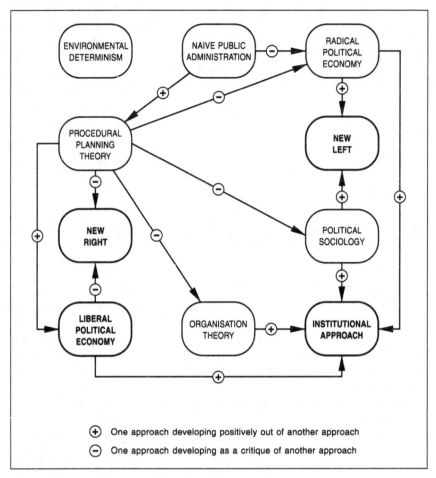

Figure 3.1   *Relationships between theoretical approaches*

These four approaches will be used to organise the discussion in Parts 3 and 4 of the socio–political and economic dimensions of planning activity respectively. To enable the reader to find a ready reference point for that discussion, the four approaches will be briefly outlined in relation to these dimensions (see Figure 3.2).

The **New Right** model is not as strong as in the 1980s and the dismissal of Margaret Thatcher, with whom it was so strongly associated in Britain, has robbed it of a key spokesperson. However, it still informs Conservative government actions and remains a potent ideology for focusing discontent with current state activity and proposing restructuring of that activity, removing and weakening some areas of government control while strengthening others. It provides a continuing

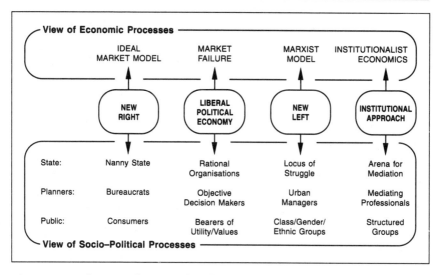

Figure 3.2   *Theoretical approaches for the 1990s*

rationale for reducing the scope of local authority activity and centralising power at the nation state level. Adaptations to the growing influence of the EC in the 1990s can be seen in the anti-Maastricht treaty movement within the Right and it is also possible to conceive of a right wing form of environmentalism which might bring a green tinge to New Right thought.

New Right theory brings a certain viewpoint to the study of the socio–political processes of planning practice. The question it asks of planners is whether they are not acting as bureaucrats within a 'nanny' state of red tape and regulation. The central concern remains as to whether state interference in market processes delivers any real benefits which might compensate for the constraints on economic activity, job and wealth creation, that it represents. There is little justification for the objective professional in this view, and hence the role is demoted to that of bureaucrat. In this market-dominated view, the public are essentially consumers. They express the majority of their wishes and desires through purchases in the marketplace, and the New Right propose that public services should be no different. It suggests that public participation in planning, whether as applicants, objectors or pressure group members, should be seen as a form of consumer involvement, the public as clients and shoppers of planning services. This contrasts with the viewpoint offered by other approaches (see Figure 3.2).

The New Right's understanding of these central market processes is based on an idealised market model. Here, the forces of competition constrain consumers and suppliers in the pursuit of their own self-interest, so that the public interest is served best by an unrestricted free market. The ideal of perfect competition is seen to approximate sufficiently to the economic reality to justify remodelling the state and its activities, in order to achieve this ideal of the unfettered market.

New Left theory is currently struggling with the challenge of the final dismantling of communism in Eastern Europe. While New Left thinking has moved on from the strictures of radical political economy of the 1970s, it is rooted in an alternative economic analysis to the dominant paradigm. The marxist analysis of the economy still has much to offer according to the New Left. As such, it has to reinterpret its analysis of the linkage between an economy based in capital accumulation processes and the nature of social and political activity in a liberal representative democracy. That reinterpretation continues, and consideration of relations between civil society and the state remain an integral element. A largely philosophical debate about the value of realism in preventing a determinist analysis is now informing more empirically-based work which is exploring the actual relationships between economy, state and political action.

In terms of analysing planning practice, New Left thought continues to raise relevant questions. In particular it offers a critical perspective on the role of state professionals in allocating resources as urban managers, and questions both the distributive impact of their decisions and their relation to major economic interests. The New Left focus attention on the nature of the struggles that occur in and around the state at local and central levels, examining the resources that are available in such struggles and the ways in which disadvantaged groups can best achieve a greater share of policy benefits. The conception of the groups that participate in such struggles has altered so that the public is not conceived purely in terms of class but also in terms of divisions based on ethnicity, gender and sexuality. The processes by which groups define themselves in these terms are themselves a significant form of political struggle.

Liberal political economy has enjoyed a renaissance in the 1990s based on the arguments of the environmental economists and the favour they have found in policy circles. This is firmly based on a mainstream welfare economics and, in particular, the concept of market failure. While some of this analysis is rooted in the heavily-jargonised techniques of neo-classical economics, proponents in the environmental and urban planning areas have sought hard to use more accessible language to put over arguments in support of planning activity.

Liberal political economy also suggests a particular perspective on the processes of planning activity. In many ways it harks back to procedural planning theory for it suggests a view of the planner as a rational decision maker, balancing all the costs and benefits of a policy or project. The planner can recoup a role as an objective, expert professional. This also emphasises the rationality of state organisations and the need for them to operate smoothly and efficiently. Liberal political economy recognises that problems of urban administration can arise and that state planning activities are not costless, but the aim is to minimise these costs and then feed them into the analysis. The assumption often is that when such costs are taken account of, the benefits of planning activity will be valued well in excess of administration costs.

In this approach the public are seen, rather technically, as bearers of utility functions, expressions of preferences. This means that the public's preferences are considered important but that they are best accessed by professionals using a variety of valuation techniques. This goes beyond the idea of the public as consumers as it encapsulates the difference between marketed and non-marketed products, and emphasises the relevance of people's preferences even where a quasi-market cannot be created. Preferences are, however, a matter of markets or quasi-markets rather than democratic processes. Politics may set the policy agenda and prioritise goals, but the detail of policy formulation and implementation is the proper concern of planners.

Finally, the **institutional approach** promises to come to fruition in the 1990s, building on the difficult work of theoretical synthesis and interactive model-building using empirical research that occurred in the 1980s. In many ways, given that this task is not yet complete, the discussion in Part 3 of planners as mediating professionals, the state as a series of mediating organisations and the public as structured groups will be part of the evolution of institutional theory rather than simply its application. In particular, the economic model underpinning the approach has been relatively undeveloped and the discussion Part 4 represents an attempt to extend the theory in this direction.

The questions that the approach so far offers concerns the way in which planners, as state professionals, engage with individuals who represent social groups and economic interests in society. Knowing the social and economic stakes that these individuals represent is important for understanding the extent to which planners can influence their actions. The ways in which planners perceive these stakes and negotiate with individuals is also relevant. While key cleavages in society will produce major groupings of community and business interests, the institutional approach is highly flexible in its identification of the structured groups which the planning system faces. It is also agnostic in terms of the likely outcomes of planning activity: major social reform may be possible or it may be highly constrained. The circumstances of each case provide the parameters for the mediating state and its professional planners.

Further reading

A historical overview of the 1980s can be found in: Brindley *et al*. (1989) which focuses on land use planning and urban policy; Lowe *et al*. (1986) which looks at countryside policy; and Weale *et al*. (1991) which provides an account of environmental planning. Healey and Nabarro (1990) gives a flavour of the concerns facing planners and planning academics in this period. For accounts of the key theoretical aproaches, the reader is referred to: Thornley (1991) for an analysis of New Right ideas; Montgomery and Thornley (1990) for some suggestions of a New Left position, Mishan (1982) for an accessible yet rigorous account of welfare economics, which includes a highly critical conclusion; and Healey and Barratt's article (1990) which sets out the institutionalist position.

■ PART 2 ■

PLANNING TODAY

Part 2 surveys the current planning system with a view to providing a description of its main elements. The emphasis is on clarifying the procedures of the planning system. This survey of the planning system should enable the reader to progress to Parts 3, 4 and 5 where the processes at work within the system are more fully explored. The planning system is taken to comprise: land use planning and conservation (development planning, development control, conservation); countryside policy (countryside access, nature conservation, agriculture and minerals); environmental policy (pollution control, waste management); and urban and transport policy (urban grant and subsidy systems, transfers of landownership, and transport policy). Each area of the planning system is covered in terms of: the organisations involved; the focus of this specific planning activity; the aim of that activity; the timing and geographical scope involved; and the main methods used to achieve the desired end result. The emphasis is on the situation in England. This situation in Wales is usually broader similar. Reference to the main differences in Scotland is made at the end of each section. Generally, the situation in Northern Ireland is not covered, although particularly interesting points of comparision are made where appropriate.

Reference will be made to many different political actors, in particular agencies of the state at national, regional and local levels. These are discussed in more detail in Part 3 but a summary is provided in Figure 4.1. In addition, exhibits in Part 3 amplify some of the policies outlined here. Chapter 8 looks at the conflict over green belts, UDCs, and the EC in relation to environmental assessment. Chapter 9 provides case studies of professionals in the water industry, joint housing studies, and planners negotiating planning obligations. In Chapter 10, the environmental big public inquiry, gentrification and conservation, and the Royal Society for Nature Conservation are considered. Chapters in Part 4 also provides analyses of the economic dimension of problems in major policy areas: housing land policy; minerals exploitation; pollution control; and the inner city problem.

For any practical application, the reader will have to make reference to up-to-date policy documents, indicators of current practice and data. This text does not attempt to replace such reference material. To guide the reader to more detailed material, references are given to sources of data and policy statements at the end of each chapter. A Glossary to the numerous acronyms used is provided on p. xiv.

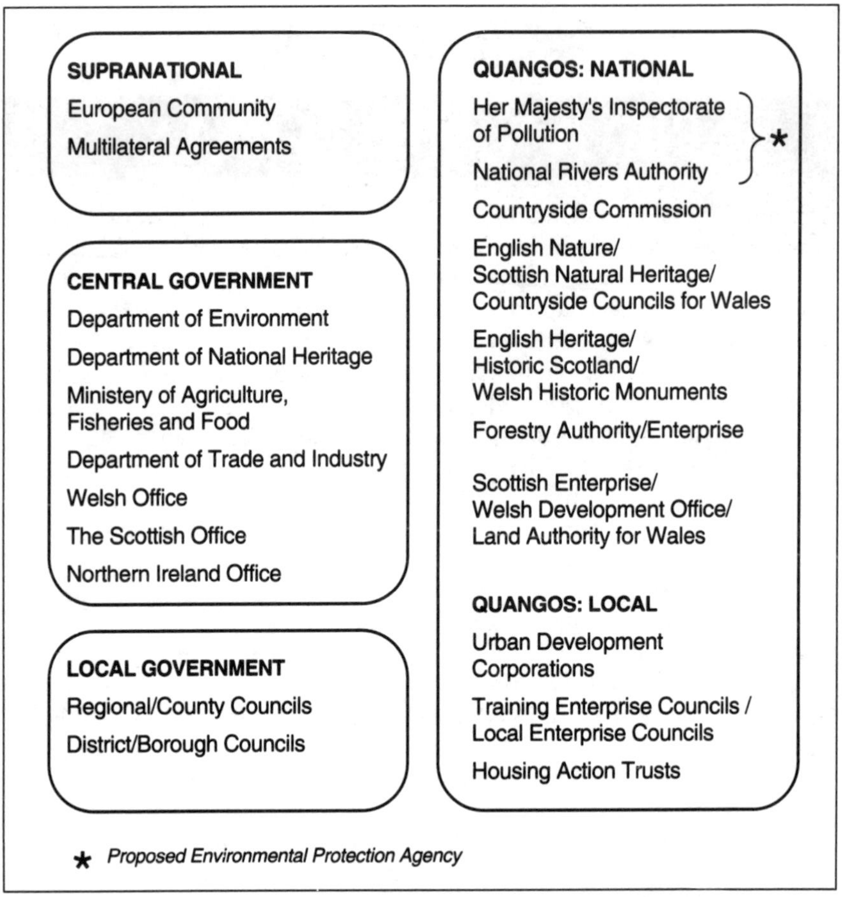

SUPRANATIONAL

European Community

Multilateral Agreements

CENTRAL GOVERNMENT

Department of Environment

Department of National Heritage

Ministry of Agriculture,
Fisheries and Food

Department of Trade and Industry

Welsh Office

The Scottish Office

Northern Ireland Office

LOCAL GOVERNMENT

Regional/County Councils

District/Borough Councils

QUANGOS: NATIONAL

Her Majesty's Inspectorate
of Pollution

National Rivers Authority

}*

Countryside Commission

English Nature/
Scottish Natural Heritage/
Countryside Councils for Wales

English Heritage/
Historic Scotland/
Welsh Historic Monuments

Forestry Authority/Enterprise

Scottish Enterprise/
Welsh Development Office/
Land Authority for Wales

QUANGOS: LOCAL

Urban Development
Corporations

Training Enterprise Councils /
Local Enterprise Councils

Housing Action Trusts

* *Proposed Environmental Protection Agency*

Figure 4.1   *State organisations involved in the planning system*

■ *Chapter 4* ■

Land Use Planning and Conservation

This chapter sets out the procedures and policies of the comprehensive system of land use planning which is at the core of the planning system. Many aspects of countryside, environmental, urban and transport policy are dependent on the powers contained within the land use planning system. The two central elements are the provision of indicative guidance through development plans and the control of development proposals on a case-by-case basis through development control. Conservation planning is a special case of land use planning in areas of heritage value, supplemented by a limited range of subsidies.

■ Development planning and simplified planning zones

Summary Box 4.1 *Development planning*

Organisation:	County councils, district councils, metropolitan district councils, regional councils, island councils
Focus:	Scale of development, patterns of land use
Aim:	Comprehensive planning
Timing:	As change in strategy necessary
Scope:	Local authority areas or sub-areas
Planning tool:	Indicative guidance

Development planning (see Summary Box 4.1) is one of the two key elements of the comprehensive land use planning system in the UK: the other is development control (see below). Under development planning, plans are prepared by local authorities to guide development and environmental change for all parts of the country. These plans operate at two levels: a strategic level and a detailed local level. Above these levels, there is the control afforded central government by certain statutory provisions and the guidance offered by certain policy statements. The exact form of this tiered structure varies across the country, from England and Wales to Scotland, from metropolitan to non-metropolitan areas.

In non-metropolitan areas of England and Wales, strategic planning is currently provided by *structure plans* prepared by county councils. These are documents which set out general policies, in respect of the development and use of land, and must include specific policies relating to the conservation of natural beauty and amenity, and proposals for improving the physical environment and traffic management schemes. They have a timescale of 10–15 years and, under the 1991 Planning and Compensation Act, it is the intention that full coverage of a local authority area will be provided by one structure plan.

Under recent government advice (set out in Planning Policy Guidance Note 15 – see below), structure plans should be made concise by concentrating on key land use issues and excluding detail more properly left to local plans (see below). Key structure plan topics are listed as: new housing; green belts and conservation; the rural economy; major employment-generating development; strategic transport and highway facilities; minerals; waste disposal, land reclamation and reuses; and tourism, leisure and recreation. Economic issues must be considered and social issues may be considered only in so far as they relate to land use and development. Structure plan policies should also make reference to any regional or strategic planning guidance, current national policies, the availability of resources and other matters that the Secretary of State identifies.

The structure plan document comprises a written statement of policies, supported by a key diagram (including inserts as necessary), which is explicitly not a map. Individual properties and the precise boundaries of areas where policies apply are not identifiable. The structure plan is accompanied by an explanatory memorandum which sets out the reasoning for the policies or any alterations to previous policies. This is not strictly part of the structure plan and carries less force than the policies themselves, because it is non-statutory in nature.

The policies may be further supported by descriptive material such as a report of survey, in which statistics and other data are used to analyse the situation in the county. Local authorities have to keep under review the need for a fresh survey examining the local area particularly with regard to physical factors, economic structure, population trends and communication networks. Where the review of strategy in the light of this survey work indicates that a change of structure plan policies is needed, then fresh policies can be devised resulting in an alteration to or complete replacement of the plan. A structure plan may be revised or replaced without any fresh survey work at all but, in all cases, an

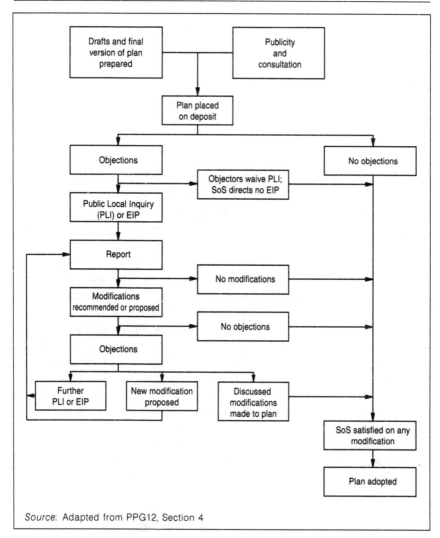

Source: Adapted from PPG12, Section 4

Figure 4.2 *The development plan process*

explanatory memorandum is needed. Government advice is that plans should be revised every five years. While local authorities have discretion in reviewing structure plans, they can be directed so to do by the Secretary of State.

Until the 1991 Planning and Compensation Act, the structure plan was submitted to the Secretary of State who approved or rejected it, following any appropriate modifications. However, county councils are now able to approve their own structure plans, subject to certain reserve powers held by the Secretary of State. This change is intended to speed up the overall plan process. Plans are subject to specified consultation and publicity before the final version is placed 'on deposit' for public inspection. Prior to the council's final approval and adoption of the plan, an examination in public will usually be held. Here a chairman, appointed by the Secretary of State, invites selected participants to debate selected policy issues. There is no right of appearance at an examination in public, and not every policy will necessarily be examined in detail.

In all non-metropolitan areas of the country, detailed land use policies are set out in *local plans* (see Figure 4.2). These are written documents accompanied by one or more annotated maps, specifying the location of new development and areas of protected land. There are two kinds of local plans. District or general plans cover whole or part of districts. They are also known simply as local plans and provide the main basis for development control. Subject or topic plans cover a specific policy issue. There used to be a category of action area plan, but such action areas, selected for comprehensive treatment by development, redevelopment or improvement, can now be designated in district plans. In general local plans are prepared by districts with certain topics of county-wide interest being dealt with by county council subject plans: e.g. derelict land or recreation. County councils and national park authorities must prepare separate subject plans for minerals and (in England only) waste management covering the whole of their areas. National park authorities also have to prepare a general local plan for their area. Under recent legislation and policy advice it is the clear intention that every local authority should prepare one local plan for their area. This is in line with proposals to reduce the relative importance of structure plans. Full coverage in England is expected by 1996.

Local plans fill in the details left unspecified by the strategic policies of structure plans, and generally should conform to them. The county council, in response to being sent a copy of a local plan in compliance with publicity requirements, sends the district a statement of conformity or non-conformity. A similar statement is issued if the structure plan is revised and modified. If there is conflict between a structure plan and local plan prepared by the same local authority, the local plan will prevail. But a statement of non-conformity acts as an objection to a newly prepared local plan and, where it arises from a modified structure plan, may suggest the need for alterations to the local plan. It is intended that, after allowing for the timescale of the plan making process, local and structure plans should agree with each other. However, conflict between local authorities over development planning can occur and has done so in the past. An exhibit of green belt designation in development plans is provided in Exhibit 8.1.

Local authorities are entitled to prepare alterations to or replacements for their local plans at any time. In doing so, they are encouraged to rely on the survey supporting the structure plan rather than preparing their own. Once a local plan or proposals for alteration to or replacement of a plan are prepared by the local planning authority, they undergo public consultation and are placed on deposit for a time to allow for objections to come forward. If there are any objections, then a public local inquiry is held before an Inspector. Any modification arising from the local inquiry process must be advertised but the final local plan is adopted by the council without reference to a higher-tier authority. Nevertheless the Secretary of State does retain the reserve power of calling in a local plan or proposals for alteration to and replacement of such a plan for final decision and approval. The Secretary of State can also make a direction modifying a local plan.

In the metropolitan areas of England and Wales, structure and local plans have been replaced with a *unitary development plan* (UDP) prepared by the district councils. Such a plan has two parts. Part 1 consists of general policies (along similar lines to a structure plan) and Part 2 sets out detailed proposals. The detailed (Part 2) policies have to be in general conformity with the strategic (Part 1) policies. Adoption of UDPs closely follows the procedure for local plans including the provisions for a public local inquiry. A Secretary of State may call in any part of a UDP, including individual policies or one of the two parts. Public participation already undertaken for an existing local plan may be taken into account when preparing a UDP.

In any area where a structure plan, local plan or UDP has not been prepared and a development plan under the 1947 Town and Country Planning Act exists, then the 'old-style' development plan has statutory force as 'the development plan'. Some local authorities also prepare supplementary planning guidance and other 'bottom drawer' plans. Central government advice (in the form of Planning Policy Guidance Note 12 – see below) makes it clear that informal plans which have not been subject to public consultation and formal procedure are discouraged. Supplementary planning guidance, which has been through such processes, may form a material consideration in development control decisions (see below) but will not be accorded equal weight with the statutory development plan.

While *simplified planning zones* (SPZs) were presented as a way of removing areas from planning control, in practice they have become areas where a distinctive form of development planning operates. Under the Housing and Planning Act 1986, the plan for the SPZ itself conveys permission to develop. In effect, in a SPZ a system of zoning operates rather than the plan being a precursor and guide to case-by-case development control. The plan for a SPZ is known as a scheme and new schemes or proposals for alterations to existing schemes are prepared under procedures akin to those for any development plan: the 1991 Planning and Compensation Act has effectively created one streamlined set of plan making procedures (see Figure 4.2). SPZ schemes can take two forms: a specific scheme which itemises the desired development in detail, leaving all other development proposals to fall within normal development control; and a general scheme which gives a very broadly-defined planning permission and lists specific exceptions to that permission. The scheme may grant planning permission for almost any development or specify permitted development very closely. It can specify whether the planning permission granted under the scheme is unconditional or subject to certain conditions. All development which is not specifically permitted requires permission under normal development control procedures (see below). This contrasts with zoning schemes in certain other countries where a change to the zoning scheme itself would be required in such circumstances. SPZs last for 10 years and on their demise only permitted development which has already begun continues to carry planning permission.

SPZs cannot be set up in national parks, conservation areas, the Broads, AONBs, green belts or SSSIs (see Chapter 5). Certain types of development are also not considered suitable for SPZs: minerals workings; waste disposal facilities; special industrial areas as listed in Use Classes B3-B7 (see section on Use Classes Order below); and some other development such as slaughterhouses and funfairs. SPZs are considered particularly appropriate for large sites which are either proposed for new development (such as an industrial park or residential estate) or consist largely of derelict land (an old industrial estate or railway siding, for example). They can be used to implement a development brief prepared by a local authority, but the legislation does permit the initiative for a SPZ to come from outside the local authority, say a private developer. Anyone can request a local authority to make or alter a SPZ scheme and the Secretary of State has default powers to direct the preparation or alteration of a scheme and to call the scheme in for approval. Relatively few SPZs have been designated: Corby, Nottingham and Derby in England, Dingwall in Scotland, with a few more in the pipeline.

While much of this development planning activity occurs at the local level, central government retains control through the various reserve powers identified. In addition to these control mechanisms, central government also issues guidance. In England and Wales, the DoE has prepared a series of *planning policy guidance* notes, setting out its

Summary Box 4.2   *Planning policy guidance notes (as at May 1992)*

PPG1	Green Policy and Principles	March 1992
PPG2	Green Belts	January 1988
PPG3	Housing	March 1992
PPG4	Industrial and Commercial Development and Small Firms	January 1988
PPG5	Simplified Planning Zones	January 1988
PPG6	Major Retail Development (Town Centres and Retail Development)	January 1988 (Draft October 1992)
PPG7	The Countryside and the Rural Economy	January 1992
PPG8	Telecommunications	January 1988
PPG9	Regional Guidance for the South East	February 1989
PPG10	Strategic Guidance for the W. Midlands	September 1988
PPG11	Strategic guidance for Merseyside	October 1988
PPG12	Development Plans and Regional Planning Guidance	February 1992
PPG13	Highway Considerations in Development Control	November 1988
PPG14	Development on Unstable Land	1990
PPG15	Regional Planning Guidance, Structure Plans, and the Content of Development Plans	May 1990
PPG16	Archaeology and Planning	November 1990
PPG17	Sport and Recreation	September 1991
PPG18	Enforcing Planning Control	December 1991
PPG19	Outdoor Advertisement Control	March 1992

interpretation of policy on a number of issues to guide local authorities in their local planning activity (see Summary Box 4.2).

In England there is also *regional planning guidance* which takes account of advice given to the Secretary of State by regional conferences of local authorities. The purpose of regional guidance (see Summary Box 4.3) is to provide a broad development framework for the next 20 years or more (15 years in the case of housing).

These guidance notes, both planning policy guidance and regional policy guidance, are advisory not statutory documents. They gain their authority from: the ability of central government to use its reserve powers to influence local planning; the widespread consultation under

Summary Box 4.3   *Regional planning guidance (as at May 1990)*

RGP10	Greater Manchester	1988
PPG9	The South East	1989
PPG10	The West Midlands	1988
PPG11	Merseyside	1988
RPG1	Tyne & Wear	1989
RPG2	West Yorkshire	1989
RPG3	London	1989
RPG4	Greater Manchester	1989
RPG5	South Yorkshire	1989
RPG6	East Anglia	1991

taken before final versions are issued, particularly among local government itself; and the general relationship of local to central government in which greater authority is claimed by the latter (see Chapter 8). Other forms of central government guidance include White Papers, minerals planning guidance notes, development control policy notes (DCPNs) and Department circulars, although DCPNs are being progressively withdrawn and the use of circulars restricted.

An important addition to the statutory development plan is the *joint housing study*. This is prepared jointly by local authorities and housebuilders and compares the housing land requirement for each district over the next five years, as derived from structure and local plans, with an assessment of the land which is agreed to be available for housebuilding. Each study usually covers the area of a county and identifies all potential housing sites of 0.4 ha or more, with an allowance being made for the contribution of smaller sites, known as intensification. Joint housing studies are normally reviewed every two years.

There is some debate over the methodology to be used for determining housing land requirements over the joint housing study period. Where the year period coincides with the development plan period, including any of its phasing programmes, there is little difficulty. Assessments for identified land can be compared with structure plan proposals. Where the periods do not coincide, then central government advice, contained in PPG3, is that the 'residual method' should normally be used. This subtracts dwelling completions to date from plan targets and transforms the resulting figure into an annual requirement. This is then grossed up to cover the five year period. The main exceptions are when local housebuilding rates in the recent past have diverged substantially from the level provided for in the development plan. Further discussion on joint housing studies is provided in Exhibit 9.3.

☐ *Scotland*

While the broad structure of development planning is the same in Scotland, there are some important differences.

First, structure plans are prepared by the regional councils with local plans falling to the district councils. However, the three island councils are unitary authorities and the regional councils of Dumfries and Galloway, Borders and the Highlands are also unitary authorities for the purpose of planning, combining regional and district functions. Second, there is the scope for regional planning authorities to prepare regional reports, quite separate from structure plans. The Scottish Office is the central government department with overall responsibility for planning in Scotland and it issues guidance in the form of *national planning policy guidelines* (NPPGs). These are the equivalent of the NPGs and RPGs in England and Wales. They are replacing National Planning Guidelines and the Land Use Summary sheets which supported them. The Scottish Office also issues *planning advice notes* (PANs), which set out good practice in relation to local planning and cover some of the material set out in NPGs.

There are also differences in the legislative basis for development planning. The key planning statutes are the 1972 Town and Country Planning (Scotland) Act, 1973 Local Government (Scotland) Act (both as amended) and certain provisions of the 1991 Planning and Corporation Act. Schedule 4 of the 1991 Act for streamlining the development plan system does not apply to Scotland and the relevant provision for SPZ schemes is Schedule 11. The requirement to prepare joint housing studies is not operative in Scotland.

■ Development control

Summary Box 4.4 *Development control*

Organisation:	Usually district councils, the Planning Inspectorate
Focus:	Individual development proposals
Aim:	Implementing development plan, other material considerations including environmental impact
Timing:	Ad hoc, responsive
Scope:	Development site and surroundings
Planning tool:	Regulation and bargaining

Development control (see Summary Box 4.4) is the cutting edge of the land use planning system. It is the mechanism by which planning affects most people and, arguably, could be said to have its most direct effects. The essence of development control is that prior permission is required for most categories of development (Figure 4.3). This is a comprehensive requirement, covering all locations and it means that a vast number of development proposals are discussed and decided on within local planning authorities, that is the district council for most purposes. In 1990/1 English and Welsh local authorities dealt with 548 000 planning applications.

The *definition of development* for which planning permission must be sought is given in Section 55 of the 1990 Town and Country Planning Act. Broadly speaking this covers all building, engineering, mining or other operations and any material change of use of land and buildings. Exceptions include operations which affect only the interior of a building and which do not materially affect its external appearance (but do not include underground excavation). Partial demolition has always required planning permission but under the 1991 Planning and Compensation Act all demolition has been formally brought within the definition of development. In most cases it will be considered permitted development under the General Development Order (see below). The intention is that most residential demolition should be controlled. Two other important exceptions from the definition of operations subject to development control are works for road improvements or maintenance within the boundaries of a road and work on sewers, mains, pipes, cables, etc. by local authorities or statutory undertakers.

There are also three exceptions from the definition of material changes of use: use incidental to the enjoyment of a dwellinghouse; use for agriculture or forestry; and change of use within the same use class (see the Use Classes Order below). Changes of use that are specifically included within development control are the use of a dwelling as two or more units and the deposit of refuse and waste material. Case law has clarified that in certain cases intensification of a use may also constitute a material change of use. This is where there is a change in the character of the use such that the use before and after the change can be identified by separate names. Resuming a temporarily discontinued use is not development but resuming a permanently discontinued use does require a further planning application. Where there is doubt as to whether a planning permission is required, the developer can apply to the local authority for a *certificate of lawful use or development*. Such a notice can be applied for before or after any development is carried out, that is to decide whether a planning application is necessary or as a defence against enforcement action

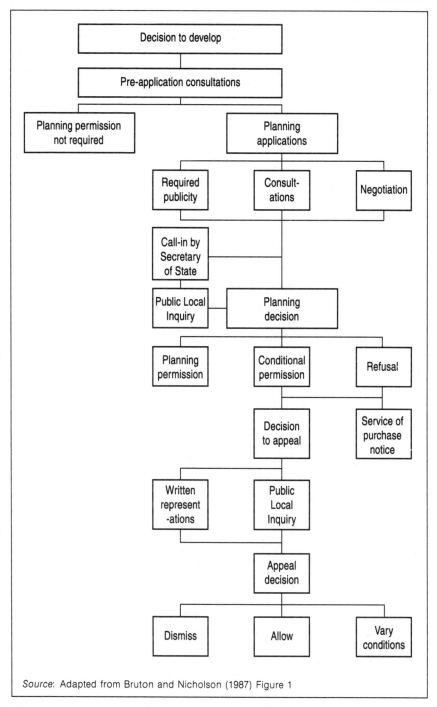

Source: Adapted from Bruton and Nicholson (1987) Figure 1

Figure 4.3 *The development control process*

(see below). Appeal against such a notice can be made to the Secretary of State. The issue of such a certificate effectively grants planning permission so that, thereafter, uses may lapse and be legally resumed.

While the use of a site for agricultural or forestry does not require specific planning permission, a system of prior notification now exists for all farm and forestry building proposals (see Chapter 5). Where development is proposed, notification must be given to the local authority to allow intervention on matters of siting, design and external appearances, nature conservation and heritage. New buildings, significant extensions and alterations, farm and forestry roads and certain excavations and engineering operations are covered. Fish farming has been brought fully into the development control system under an amendment to the definition of development by the 1991 Planning and Compensation Act.

Exemptions and exceptions from development control are further provided by two central government policy instruments: the Use Classes Order (UCO) and the General Development Order (GDO).

The *Use Classes Order* defines 16 classes of use to which a building may be put; change of use within a class does not constitute development and does not, therefore, require planning permission. It does not necessarily mean that a change of use from one class to another is always development. It will still be necessary to decide if a material change of use has occurred. The Order divides uses into classes under the headings shown in Summary Box 4.5.

Summary Box 4.5   *The Use Classes Order (England and Wales)*

Part A A1	Shops	
	A2	Financial and Professional Services
	A3	Food and Drink
Part B B1	Business	
	B2	General Industrial
	B3–7	Special Industrial Groups A to E
	B8	Storage and Distribution
Part C C1	Hotels and Hostels	
	C2	Residential Institutions
	C3	Dwellinghouses
Part D D1	Non-residential Institutions	
	D2	Assembly and Leisure

The *General Development Order*, which requires parliamentary approval, defines minor forms of development, such as extensions, which may be undertaken without explicit planning permission. Legally such actions still constitute development. The list of such permitted development is categorised under the parts shown in Summary Box 4.6.

Summary Box 4.6 *The General Development Order (England and Wales)*

1	Development within the curtilage of a dwellinghouse
2	Minor operations
3	Changes of use
4	Temporary buildings and uses
5	Caravan sites
6–7	Agricultural and forestry buildings and operations
8	Industrial and warehouse development
9–10	Repairs to unadopted streets, private ways and services
11	Development by local or private acts or orders
12–15, 17	Development by local authorities, local highway authorities, drainage bodies, water authorities and statutory undertakers
16	Development for sewerage and sewage disposal
18	Aviation development
19–23	Mining-related development
24–25	Telecommunications development
26	Development of Historic Buildings and Monuments Commission for England (English Heritage)
27	Use by members of certain recreational organisations
28	Development at amusement parks.

Many of the provisions have size restrictions which limit the general applicability of the GDO. The Order also provides that certain changes of use between different classes as identified in the UCO shall not require planning permission. This covers certain changes between Part A uses (shops, financial and professional services, and food and drink) and between B1, B2 and B8 uses (business, general industrial, and storage and distribution). The GDO may not apply in all instances. The Secretary of State or a local authority may issue an Article 4 direction removing GDO rights in respect of an area, such as a conservation area. Planning conditions may also remove GDO rights in respect of a site or building.

Strictly speaking applications for planning permission are not required in the case of development on Crown land or development by government departments or the local authority themselves, though the removal of the Crown exemption is being considered. In these cases, deemed planning permission is currently granted for which there is a simplified non-statutory procedure. Some types of development by local authorities and statutory undertakers is covered by the provision in the GDO and local authorities have deemed permission for development which has been authorised by a government department.

For developments and changes of use which do require planning permission, a *planning application* is made to the relevant district council on specified forms, providing all the necessary detailed inform-ation and, in 82 per cent of cases, paying a fee (Audit Commission, 1992, p. 5). Pre-application negotiations with the planning authority are encouraged: under a recent House of Lords ruling, local authorities may not charge for this. Planning applications may be made for outline planning permission, where certain 'reserved matters' are held over for further approval by the local authority at a latter date (usually within three years), or full planning permission. Reserved matters may include siting, design, external appearance, means of access and landscaping. Submission of a planning application involves a certain amount of publicity, which is the responsibility of the local authority not the applicant. All applications, other than those for reserved matters or amendments to applications, require a site notice or letters to neigh-bours. Applications for major development trigger newspaper adver-tisements while any development requiring environmental impact assessment (see Chapter 6), involving a departure from a development plan or affecting a right of way implies mandatory site notices as well as press advertisements. Construction of oil refineries and private hospitals require additional authorisation to accompany the planning applica-tions.

Once submitted, the application is investigated by a planning officer who consults with affected parties, for example the Health and Safety Executive in the case of hazardous development or development within a hazard consultation zone (see below), or MAFF for development on more than 20 ha of Grade 1, 2 or 3a agricultural land. In most non-minor cases, the highways authority and water authority are important consultees and parish and community councils have specific rights of notification.

In the case of *hazardous installations* the role of planning has been extended by the 1990 Planning (Hazardous Substances) Act, itself a response to a strengthened EC directive. Already, in 1990, local authorities consulted with the Health and Safety Executive on 5046 applications, with 620 applications considered by its major hazards assessment unit. The 1990 Act now requires local authority consent for the storage of prescribed quantities of defined dangerous materials, as set down in regulations (see Chapter 6). The removal of the distinction between processing and storage of hazardous substances increases the number of sites covered by the regulations from 300 to 450. In addition there is a proposal to make public all safety reports (as prepared by operators or owners and vetted by the Health and Safety Executive) for such hazardous sites.

Environmental policy and development control have also been brought closer together by the introduction of environmental assessments, again in response to an EC directive (see Chapter 6). The 1991 Planning and Compensation Act now includes the requirement for environmental impact assessment of certain development proposals in key planning legislation. Exhibit 8.3 discusses environmental assessment further.

The *decision* on the application is formally taken by a planning committee of the council, to whom the planning officer presents advice, although the decision may be delegated to sub-committees or the chief planning officer. In some exceptional cases, the application may be 'called in' for decision by the Secretary of State, following a public inquiry held before an inspector, in a manner similar to an appeal (see below). This power is used in only about 140 cases each year in England and Wales. In recent years central government has placed great importance on the efficiency of the development control and tried to minimise delays. The goal set for local authorities is that they should decide 80 per cent of applications within eight weeks.

The councillors on the committee or the planning officer (or the Secretary of State) cannot take any view they wish on the proposal. The planning legislation requires the decision to be made as follows: 'Where, in making any determination under the planning officer, regard is to be had to the development plan, the determination shall be made in accordance with the plan unless material considerations indicate otherwise.'

This is a significant change introduced by Section 26 of the 1991 Planning and Compensation Act and creates a presumption in favour of the development plan. Included within material considerations is central government advice on development control as provided in DoE circulars and planning policy guidance notes. In general material considerations must relate closely to the purpose of planning legislation and must also fairly and reasonably relate to the application itself. In addition acceptable decisions may be based on: the fear of creating a precedent, the availability of alternative sites, the risk of piecemeal development, preservation of existing uses and, exceptionally, the personal circumstances of the applicant. Planning permission can be refused on the grounds of prematurity, that is because the relevant development plan is in process of being revised. However, in such a case, it must be clearly shown how the development will prejudice the outcome of the development plan process. Refusal on the basis of prematurity is allowed, for example where the development contravenes a phasing programme in a development plan setting out how much development should occur each year or over a specified number of years. Local authorities may also refuse to determine repetitive applications where an appeal has been dismissed by the Secretary of State within the last two years.

The planning decision taken by the local authority need not be a simple reject or accept. *Conditions* may be attached to the planning permission provided that they: fulfil a planning purpose; are necessary, precise and enforceable; are related to the permitted development; and are not unreasonable. This can include limitations on changes otherwise permitted under the UCO. Advice on planning conditions is contained in DoE Circular 1/25 or WO Circular 1/85.

Under Section 106 of 1990 Town and Country Planning Act or Section 52 of 1971 Town and Country Planning Act, a planning agreement may be made between the applicant and the local authority to obtain *planning gain*. Such an agreement is an enforceable local land change which can restrict the use or development of land, require specified operations or activities to be carried out, require land to be used in a particular way, or require money to be paid to the local authority. Whereas previously, such matters had to be agreed between the local authority and the landowner, a planning obligation can now be offered unilaterally by the landowner under Section 12 of the 1991 Planning and Compensation Act, in which case it may be become a material consideration, particularly in an appeal situation. After a specified period of time, there are provisions for discharging a planning obligation on application to the local authority or, on appeal, to the Secretary of State.

Further advice on planning agreements is given in DoE Circular 16/91 or WO Circular 53/91 which sets out two tests for their acceptable use. First, the planning agreement must fall into one of five categories: required for the development to proceed; directly related to the development; used to finance facilities in near future; necessary to secure an acceptable balance of use or the implementation of local plan policies; or intended to offset loss of amenity arising from the development. Second, the agreement must be fairly and reasonably related in scale and kind to the proposed development. Agreements which fail these two tests are seeking 'extraneous benefits' and cannot be used by local authorities. Exhibit 9.3 is on the role of planners in negotiating planning gain.

If a planning permission is refused or unacceptable conditions attached to a planning permission, then the applicant has the right to *appeal* to the Secretary of State for the case to be reconsidered. In 1990/1 26 000 appeals were decided in England and Wales. Currently no charge is made for lodging an appeal but this is likely to change soon, with the transformation of the Planning Inspectorate into an executive agency. In completing the appeal forms, the appellant must choose the procedure by which the appeal will be considered: written representations, that is by correspondence; or public local inquiry, that is in a fairly formal local tribunal. 80 per cent of cases are dealt with by written representations. For certain minor categories of development, local informal hearings can be used which attempt to overcome some of the offputting procedural aspects of local inquiries. Exhibit 10.1 discusses these aspects of public local inquiries in relation to projects with major environmental impacts. The procedures for appeal cases are set out in detail in regulations, which include a timetable for the exchange of statements of case by the parties and for the holding of the inquiry and the decision itself.

Once both sides have put their cases in public or in writing, then the inspector allocated to the case will write a report. In 95 per cent of cases, the inspector will also make the binding decision, but the Secretary of State has the right to recover a case for final decision. For major developments the inspector's report will be passed on the Secretary of State for this decision. The appeal decision can be challenged in the courts only on fairly restricted legal ground, referred to as proceedings for statutory review.

Costs may be awarded against either party to an appeal under the Local Government Act 1972 and Town and Country Planning Act 1990. The principles on which costs are awarded are set out in DoE Circular 2/87: unreasonable, vexatious or frivolous action which has resulted in unnecessary and unreasonable expense, including unreasonable cancellation of a public local inquiry. Under the 1991 Planning and Compensation Act, the Secretary of State has the right, with due notice, to dismiss an appeal if there has been an undue delay on the part of the appellant.

There is provision for the Secretary of State to constitute a Planning Inquiry Commission to deal with applications that have been called in, appeals or other public sector projects. This provides for a broader ranging debate over the development than may occur at a public local inquiry. Although this provision has been on the statute book for over 20 years, a planning inquiry commission has never been convened.

Central government can, in occasional cases, take over the role of the local authority in development control and grant planning permission through a *special development order*. As such the development order is debated in the Houses of Parliament and signed by the Secretary of State. They are generally used for particular areas, such as new towns, urban development corporations (see Chapter 7), national parks or AONBs (see Chapter 5) or particular developments which raise issues of national significance such as Stansted Airport or the Windscale nuclear reprocessing plant (see Exhibit 10.1). Planning consent can also be granted by *private bill procedure*, again debated within the Houses of Parliament rather than at a public local inquiry. Under the 1992 Transport and Works Act many of the types of development involved with orders and private bills will be dealt with in future by a ministerial order making procedure, operating outside Parliament and using a public local inquiry. This is of particular relevance to transport schemes.

If a development occurs without the benefit of planning permission then the district council has certain *enforcement powers* (see PPG18 and DoE Circular 21/91 or WO Circular 76/91). These include the power to issue a variety of notices. A recent innovation under the 1991 Planning and Compensation Act is the planning contravention notice which a local authority issues to give warning of a breach of planning control without instituting full enforcement proceedings. Such a notice can be used to ascertain information about the development, owners of interests in the site and the extent of compliance with planning consent and, further, to encourage contact with the local authority with a view to rectifying the apparent breach of planning control. There is an equivalent breach of conditions notice. An enforcement notice requires the developer to comply with a particular planning permission, including its conditions or to discontinue an existing use. An enforcement notice must be issued within four years of any building, engineering, mining or other operations occurring to be effective. In the case of unauthorised uses, enforcement action must be taken within 10 years. There is a right of appeal against the issue of an enforcement notice to the Secretary of State and it is possible to apply for a certificate of lawful use or development retrospectively to obtain planning permission for the unauthorised activity. Under the 1991 Planning and Compensation Act the local authority can serve a breach of condition notice requiring that any conditions attached to a planning permission are complied with within a prescribed period. There is no appeal against this notice. Non-compliance with any of these notices is an offence. The maximum fine is currently £20 000.

The use of these notices is further strengthened by the right of the local authority to enter a site with a warrant to ascertain if a breach of planning control is occurring. Local authorities also have the power to enter the site, take steps to ensure compliance with any planning consent and recover the costs if an enforcement notice has not been taken notice of, and can also apply for an injunction to prevent breaches occurring. Where the breach involves demolition, then a replacement building may be required.

A stop notice is issued after an enforcement notice and requires the developer to stop all activities on site in breach of planning legislation. If the developer successfully appeals against a stop notice, then the local authority may be liable to compensation for the financial loss incurred. The scale of such financial loss, particularly to a commercial developer, can be many times the scale of fines for non-compliance with an enforcement notice. Registers of both enforcement and stop notices are held by local authorities for public inspection. Finally, a completion notice seeks to encourage completion by stating that the planning permission will lapse after a certain period of time, of one or more years, unless development is begun. Otherwise planning permission lapses if development has not begun within specified time limits, usually five years or two years from the approval of reserved matters.

In addition to these enforcement powers, local planning authorities have certain powers for *altering planning permissions*. A revocation or modification order is issued prior to development beginning and negates or changes an approved planning permission. Such an order requires ministerial confirmation. A discontinuance order requires the developer to halt development even if permission has been granted. A strong case must be made before the necessary ministerial confirmation is given. Current central government advice in DoE Circular 22/80 states that enforcement or discontinuance powers are not normally to be used in the case of small businesses unless alternative premises can be found. Issuing a revocation or modification order will render the local authority liable for compensation for expenses incurred by the developer since the grant of planning permission and any loss of development value. The developer is also entitled to compensation for the costs of complying with a discontinuance order.

Finally, the allocation of land for certain uses by public authorities or its designation as a new town, urban development area, clearance or renewal area, general improvement area or for roadbuilding may 'blight' that land in the interim period before the development or designation takes effect. In these cases the landowner may find the value of the land has fallen substantially and a *blight notice* may be served on the local authority requiring the authority to purchase the land. Ministerial confirmation is necessary.

Local authority development control powers are extended in the case of specific categories of development, notably advertisements, caravans and minerals (the latter are dealt with in Chapter 5). *Advertisement control* is covered by Section 220 of the Town and Country Planning Act 1990, relevant regulations, PPG19 and DoE Circular 5/92. The display of advertisements also constitutes development under Section 55(5) of the 1990 Act so that local authorities may use either development control or advertising regulation powers to control unauthorised advertisements. With limited exceptions advertisements require consent, although some, such as bus stops, have deemed consent. The Secretary of State can make directions removing the benefit of deemed consent from specific classes of adverts in defined areas. This power is rarely used. Rural businesses are entitled to advertise their whereabouts in line with the government principle that outdoor advertising is essential for commerce.

Consent for advertisements is given on the basis of two criteria only: amenity and public safety. A discontinuance notice can be issued which requires the display of an advert with consent to cease: there is a right of appeal. The local authority can designate areas of special control in which stricter advertisement controls apply, including prohibitions on certain types of advert. Such areas have to be reviewed every five years and local consultation is expected before designation. Currently, 45 per cent of the land area of England and Wales is so designated. However, government advice continues to argue that advertisements have a place even in sensitive locations such as conservation areas.

Caravans are covered by the 1960 Caravan Sites and Control of Development Act and the 1968 Caravan Sites Act. Sites require prior permission in the form of a licence from the local authority as well as the usual planning permission. For travellers in particular, local authorities now have a duty to provide sites within their area, but compliance has been very patchy. Guidance is provided in DoE Circulars 28/77, 57/78 and 23/83.

□ Scotland

While, again, the broad principles of development control are similar in Scotland to the situation in the rest of Britain, there are procedural differences. Of course, where reference is made to the DoE, in Scotland the relevant reference is the Environment Department of The Scottish Office. Again, whereas PPGs are material considerations in England and Wales, NPPGs and PANs are relevant in Scotland. Other differences are more specific.

First, the reference point for the definition of development for which planning permission is required is provided by 1972 Town and Country Planning (Scotland) Act, not the 1990 Town and Country Planning Act, which did not apply to Scotland. Second, there are separate policy instruments setting out the provisions of the UCO and GDO for Scotland. These are: the Town and Country Planning (Use Classes) (Scotland) Order 1989; and the Town and Country Planning (General Permitted Development) (Scotland) Order 1992. The terminology to describe the classifications in these instruments varies slightly from the English and Welsh equivalent.

Third, the 1991 Planning and Compensation Act does apply to Scotland but the section which establishes the presumption in favour of the development plan in development control decisions is Section 58. Fourth, the provisions on Section 12 of the 1991 Planning and Compensation Act relating to planning obligations do not apply to Scotland and the reference point for planning agreements is S.50 of the 1992 Act. Fifth, the power to call in planning applications for decision rests with the regions. Sixth, planning appeals are dealt with by a recorder, not an inspector.

■ Conservation

Summary Box 4.7 *Conservation*

Organisation:	Department of the Environment, The Scotish Office, English Heritage, Welsh Historic Monuments, Historic Scotland, district councils
Focus:	Heritage areas and buildings
Aim:	Amenity protection
Timing:	Ad hoc, both positive and responsive
Scope:	Conservation areas, buildings, trees
Planning tool:	Regulation, subsidy

Conservation policy (see Summary Box 4.7) is concerned with protecting amenities. However, as Cullingworth states (1988, p. 196) '"Amenity" is one of the key concepts in British town and country planning, yet nowhere in the legislation is it defined'. In many cases, protection of amenity is seen as equivalent to maintaining existing buildings, trees and patterns of land use. The historic nature of urban landscapes is thus seen as an indicator of high levels of amenity.

The *public estate*, in the form of English Heritage (CADW in Wales and Historic Scotland north of the border), own and maintain large numbers of historic buildings and sites. In addition, major historic buildings are managed by the Historic Royal Palaces Agency. The Secretary of State also has powers to purchase or accept a listed building or ancient monument (see below) for the public estate, local authorities may purchase a listed building by agreement and properties can be accepted into the public estate in lieu of tax liability. However, the main method of conservation planning takes the form of designating areas, sites and buildings for special protection rather than transferring property ownership.

Conservation areas are a measure whereby a district council (or English Heritage in Greater London) designates a geographic area for enhanced protection under development control. There are 7500 conservation areas in the UK covering 1.3 million buildings. Local authorities have a duty under the Planning (Listed Buildings and Conservation Areas) Act 1990 periodically to review their area for designating conservation areas, and the Secretary of State can also decide to designate such an area. The designation document for a conservation area undergoes consultation procedures and notification to Secretary of State and English Heritage (or equivalent agency) before being adopted by the council. This document will include policies to be adopted in respect of the area for preservation and enhancement of amenities. Such policies must be submitted to a public meeting within the conservation area, and note taken of views expressed. However, the most significant elements of protection arise from the legislative effects of the designation. These ensure that all demolition within a conservation area constitutes development and thus requires conservation area consent unless it involves a church in use, a listed building or ancient monument, when separate provisions apply (see below). DoE Circular 8/87 and WO Circular 61/81 set out other limited exceptions.

The regime for dealing with conservation area consents is identical to that described below for listed buildings in relation to authorising works, taking enforcement action, undertaking urgent works to preserve unoccupied buildings and providing for purchase notices. As far as the operation of normal development control is concerned, the definition of material changes of use and physical alterations is interpreted more tightly within such an area. Development control within conservation areas also involves extended publicity arrangements. Furthermore, Article 4 directions under the GDO are often made to extend the definition of development for which planning permission is required. There are about 200 Article 4 directions relating to English conservation areas (EHTF,1992). These provisions allow greater opportunity for the operation of development control as well as the inclusion of broader amenity-based material considerations in development control decision making. Following a 1988 legal case concerning the London Borough of Camden, it was held that in all planning decisions concerning conservation areas 'special attention should be paid to the desirability of preserving or enhancing the character and appearance of that area'. This was interpreted as meaning that any permitted development should perform a positive role in meeting the conservation area's aims. However, another case in 1992, concerning the South Lakeland District Council, has reaffirmed the prior principle that development which has a neutral effect on the local area should also be permitted: only development detrimental to the amenities of a conservation area can be refused consent.

As with listed buildings, the costs of preservation and enhancement in conservation areas largely remain with owners and occupiers. However, there are two possibilities for grant aid. First, the Secretary of State and English Heritage, or equivalent organisations, can make grants or loans on a discretionary basis. In 1989/90, English Heritage allocated £33 million for such grants. Second, local authorities, singly or jointly, may enter into a town scheme agreement with the Secretary of State or English Heritage (or equivalents) which provides for a specified sum of money to be set aside for grant-aiding the repair of selected buildings over a fixed period of years. About 400 of the 7000 English conservation areas are eligible for such grants. In some cases, the interaction of the local property market with conservation area designation may actually increase property values. This is explored in Exhibit 10.3.

The other area-based policy concerns the designation of *areas of archaeological importance* (AAIs) where enhanced provision is to be made for 'rescue archaeology' during development. There are five such AAIs designated under Part 2 of the 1979 Ancient Monuments and Archaeological Areas Act: York, Canterbury, Chester, Exeter and Hereford. Within designated areas of archaeological importance it is a criminal offence to carry out operations resulting in disturbance to archaeological remains without having served an operations notice on the local authority at least 6 weeks before operations including tipping, disturbance or flooding, are due to commence. Then an 'investigating authority' has the power to enter, inspect and excavate the site within the next 4½ months. Thereafter they have the power to enter for inspection and recording only. Development can be delayed for up to a maximum of 6 months. Grants are available from the DoE and local authorities to aid such rescue archaeology, but there is no statutory funding under the legislation.

Recent government advice in PPG16 on 'Archaeology and Planning' emphasises the importance of preserving nationally important archaeological remains, stating that in cases where development is proposed, there should be a presumption in favour of their physical preservation. Such nationally important remains are usually scheduled ancient monuments (see below). In other cases the relative importance of archaeology will have to be weighted against other factors. Whether scheduled or not, the desirability of preserving an ancient monument is a material consideration in development control and policies for archaeological conservation should be included in development plans. The resources of the county archaeological officer (or equivalent) who maintains the sites and monuments records can be important.

In many cases of proposed development, rescue archaeology will be the preferred option. Such rescue archaeology recognises that the excavation occurring during development often creates opportunities for archaeological exploration, through clearance of surface buildings and landscape. However, such development can of course threaten archaeological remains with disruption, damage and eventual burial. Rescue archaeology aims to influence the physical process and timing of development to allow time and opportunity for recording archaeological remains and to ensure their preservation in a form of reburial which would allow re-excavation. This is generally achieved through planning agreements and conditions attached to planning permissions. A code of practice exists for voluntary agreements between archaeologists and developers, issued jointly by the British Property Federation and the Standing Conference of Archaeological Unit Managers, through the British Archaeologists' and Developers' Liaison Group.

Marine archaeology has no equivalent system of protection as yet but an enhanced system of control for historic wrecks is being developed. The Advisory Committee on Historic Wreck Sites and the Archaeological Diving Unit have advised on new procedures of designating historic underwater sites and issuing licences for diving and other activities in their vicinity.

Inside and outside such designated areas, additional protection of important features of the built and natural environment is afforded by a variety of means. The Royal Commission on Historical Monuments, English Heritage (or equivalents) and several local authorities provide a record of historic buildings and monuments. This is currently being organised into a systematic database. Individual buildings of special architectural or historic significance throughout Britain can be 'listed' by central government. Indeed, the DoE under the Planning (Listed

Buildings and Conservation Areas) Act 1990, and The Scottish Office have a duty to compile such a list or approve such lists prepared by the Commission or other relevant bodies. The DoE's responsibility for listing will now pass to the new Department of National Heritage. There are three grades of *listed building*: I (the highest quality), II* and II. Currently there are some 500 000 listed buildings in England, about 2 per cent of the building stock. 58 per cent of listed buildings are in rural areas; 42 per cent in urban areas. Just over half of all listed buildings are also in conservation areas: 77 per cent of urban listed buildings, 40 per cent of rural listed buildings.

The criteria for listing are set out in DoE Circular 8/87, and the 1990 Act. The older the building is, the more likely it is to be listed but it is not just the quality of the individual building that is important. Its location as part of a group may render it worthy of listing. If it appears that an important unlisted building is in danger of demolition or alteration which would alter its character, then local authorities can serve a building preservation notice on any unlisted building (but not a church or ancient monument) which will lead to a six month stay of action pending the departmental listing procedure. Objection to listing may be made informally to the Department resulting in a second opinion from an Inspector being sought. If the Department formally decides not to list the building, then the building preservation notice ceases to have effect and no further such notice can be issued for 12 months. Any owner, who has received planning permission for work to an unlisted building, may also apply to the Secretary of State for a certificate stating that the building will not be listed. This certificate prevents any listing, including temporary listing, for a period of five years. This can be useful where time elapses between the grant of outline planning permission and approval of reserved matters. In cases of alteration, destruction, misjudgement or mistake, buildings may be removed from the list.

The demolition of any listed building is subject to control, as are any works for alteration or extension in a manner likely to affect its character as a building of special architectural or historic interest. In each case, listed building consent is required. These powers are exercised by the relevant development control planning authority, usually the district council. But in London these functions are performed by the borough councils, subject to directions from English Heritage.

Application for consent results in an extended consultation and notification procedure. Under directions from the Secretary of State these include English Heritage, CADW or Historic Scotland and in the case of any proposed demolition, and amenity groups such as the Georgian Society or Civic Trust. In addition the local authority must inform the Secretary of State of any listed building consent they propose to give, subject to notified exceptions. This creates the opportunity for the Secretary of State to call in an application. The final consent may be conditional and there is provision for appeals to the Secretary of State. Any consent for demolition must make allowance for recording the building by the relevant Royal Commission on Historical Monuments or Ancient & Historical Monuments in Wales.

Subject to Secretary of State confirmation, local authorities may revoke or modify listed building consent, and there is an expedited procedure for so doing where the owner-occupier and all others affected do not object. The Secretary of State may also revoke or modify consents. Where development under the Town and Country Planning Act is also intended, then planning permission will be needed in addition to listed building consent. As with planning consents, listed building consents expire after five years.

Carrying out works without listed building consent is an offence punishable by a fine and/or imprisonment. Fines are exacted in proportion to the financial benefit the developer has gained, or is likely to gain. This differs from the situation with other planning consents where standard fines can be levied only for non-compliance with an enforcement notice. It is no defence to argue ignorance of the listing but it is possible to argue a defence on the basis that: there was a need for urgent works to ensure preservation of the building or for reasons of health and safety; that no temporary alteration was possible; that the extent of the works was minimised; and that the local authority was given written notice as soon as possible. The local authority or the Secretary of State can issue a listed building enforcement notice stating the breach of control, specifying remedial action, and giving the owner and occupier at least 28 days to object and lodge an appeal. If the remedial action is not taken within the stated compliance period, then the local authority may enter and undertake the works, recovering the costs from the owner. Injunctions preventing damage can also be sought.

There are a number of financial consequences arising from listed building control. Compensation may be payable by the local authority for loss arising from: refusal of listed building consent for works which would not themselves require planning permission; modification or renovation of the consent; and serving of a building preservation notice.

There is an onus placed on the building owner to ensure adequate repair and maintenance for such building. Grants are available to assist in this but mainly for Grade I and some Grade II* buildings. English Heritage makes grants available for the repair of historic buildings and monuments and the National Heritage Memorial Fund is a further source for major sites. For the 13 world heritage sites designated under the UNESCO World Heritage Committee, funds are available from the World Heritage Fund. Relief from capital taxes exists for owners of heritage properties which are opened to the public.

But the responsibility for ensuring the continued contribution of such important buildings to the urban and rural environment rests with the owner and thus knowledge of any listing is important information for a prospective purchaser during the legal and planning searches. Where the owner neglects to maintain a listed building the local authority has the option of compulsory purchase. If the building has been deliberately left derelict then compulsory purchase can be at 'minimum compensation' if the Secretary of State so directs, which excludes all development value. Prior to such compulsory purchase the local authority must serve a repairs notice setting out the necessary repairs in detail. The local authority also has the power to execute any urgent works necessary for building preservation, provided that the building or parts of it are unoccupied and they give the owner notice. They can then recoup the cost.

While parks and gardens cannot be formally listed, English Heritage maintain a register of parks and gardens of special historic interest. This carries no statutory force but highway and local planning authorities are advised to take note of the register in their decisions by DoE Circular 8/87.

Ancient monuments are protected under the 1979 Ancient Monuments Act. The degree of protection afforded depends on whether a site is classified as a 'scheduled monument' or an 'ancient monument'. Scheduled monuments are of national importance in the view of the Secretary of State. An ancient monument is any monument of public interest in the view of the Secretary of State by virtue of historic, architectural, traditional, artistic or archaeological importance. Some 20 100 monuments have been scheduled in Britain. PPG16 sets out the criteria for scheduling as: period or age; rarity; extent of documentation; group value, condition and surviving features; fragility or vulnerability; diversity; and potential. Development affecting a scheduled monument requires an additional consent in the form of scheduled monument consent from DoE, English Heritage or equivalents; this covers proposal for demolition, destruction, damage, removal, repair, alteration, extension, flooding or covering up. The scope of control is more detailed and extensive than for listed buildings but there are six class consents in force which allow owners to undertake certain specified works without explicit consent. Crown land is subject to scheduled monument clearance which broadly follows the consent procedure, and refusal in certain limited cases gives rise to liability for compensation. It is a criminal offence to undertake prescribed operations without such a consent and injunctions preventing operations may be sought. Central government, local government and heritage agencies can all take action.

There are proposals contained in a 1991 DoE Consultation Paper to tighten up the control of ancient monuments. The definition of 'damage' would be extended to any disturbance of the land. Removal of any finds, not just those using a metal detector, would be an offence and ignorance of the status of the site would not be an adequate defence, placing ancient monuments on an equivalent footing to listed buildings. Finally, works to an ancient monument to ensure public health and safety would be constrained to the minimum necessary.

Where works are urgently needed for the preservation of a scheduled monument, the Secretary of State may enter the site and undertake the works. There is no provision for recouping the costs incurred. Grants are available from heritage agencies mainly for repair, archaeological recording and consolidation of monuments. Occasionally they are available for purchase. Where the owner enters into a management agreement with central or local government or heritage agency, funds may also be made available. Any ancient monument, not just scheduled monuments, may be compulsorily purchased by the Secretary of State in order to preserve it or may be accepted into the public estate. Alternatively the Secretary of State may be appointed 'guardian' of the monument, providing for its preservation without a transfer of ownership. Public access is a condition of such guardianship.

Ecclesiastical buildings are exempt from certain listed building protection measures. They may be listed but building preservation notices, listed building, consent, provisions for urgent works to unoccupied building and compulsory purchase provisions do not apply. This means that listed building consent is not necessary for churches in use or for demolition of redundant churches. This exemption applies only where denominations can demonstrate internal arrangements which meet with standards of a proposal code of practice. For Church of England churches an additional statutory system of protection already exists under the 1983 Pastoral Measure, operated by the Church. By agreement with the Secretary of State a non-statutory local inquiry may be held for the demolition of a listed church or one in a conservation area. The Redundant Churches Fund preserves Church of England churches of historic or architectural interest.

Trees are also covered by their equivalent of listing, in this case the placing of a *tree preservation order* (TPO) on an individual tree, a group of trees or a woodland. Such an order prevents cutting, topping, uprooting, wilful damage, destruction or coppicing without express permission from the district council and encourages preventative tree surgery and woodland maintenance. Permission for felling may require replanting. Dead, unsafe and dying trees are exempt. Non-compliance with a TPO may result in fines of up to £20 000 being imposed and the enforcement powers of local authorities in relation to areas have been strengthened by Section 23 of the 1991 Planning and Compensation Act allowing applications for injunctions and warrants for right of entry. Replacement planting may also be required up to four years after non-compliance. Appeals on matters of TPOs can be made to the Secretary of State. Tree planting may also form an acceptable planning condition and, indeed, a local authority has a duty to consider the preservation and planting of trees in granting any planning permission.

☐ Scotland and Wales

As the above text has made clear, the equivalent body to the DoE is the Environment Department of The Scottish Office and the equivalent heritage agencies to English Heritage are CADW, or Welsh Historic Monuments, in Wales and Historic Scotland north of the border. There are some 3000 listed buildings in Wales and 36 000 in Scotland, but resurvey is likely to increase these figures substantially. In Scotland listed buildings are graded A, B and C not I, II and II*.

The legislative basis for listed buildings and conservation area control is the 1972 Town and Country Planning (Scotland) Act and the reference point for TPOs in Scotland is Section 54 of the 1991 Planning and Compensation Act.

Further reading

In this area there is little substitute for consulting the actual policy documents themselves: legislation, circulars, PPGs, etc. They are often more accessible than the student fears! Documents for England and Wales are gathered together in the *Encyclopedia of Planning Law*. A parallel text for Scotland is the *Scottish Planning Sourcebook*. Useful journals are *Planning*, the weekly magazine for the profession, and the monthly *Journal of Planning and Environmental Law*. The annual reports of relevant organisations – the Planning Inspectorate, English Heritage (and equivalents) – can also be consulted. A guide to conservation policy and procedure is provided by Suddards (1988).

■ *Chapter 5* ■

Countryside Policy

Planning policies for the countryside attempt to balance the goals of preserving the natural features of the landscape, providing for public access and enjoyment and supporting the economic activities that occur in rural areas. The former two goals, in the view of the Sandford Committee, are not in fundamental conflict, as they both seek the conservation of the countryside although short-term and specific trade-offs may be necessary. More recent government planning policy guidance has recognised that situations of conflict may be more common than previously assumed. Certainly in the case of certain economic activities, principally agriculture and minerals extraction, the threat to nature and landscape conservation and public access can be severe. This chapter considers countryside planning under four headings: general policies and specific designations for countryside protection together with the provision for public access; measures aimed at nature conservation; planning for rural economies, particularly agricultural activities, forestry and rural housing; and minerals planning.

■ Countryside protection and access

Summary Box 5.1 *Countryside protection*

Organisation:	National park authorities, local authorities, Countryside Commission, Countryside Council for Wales, Scottish Natural Heritage
Focus:	Areas of natural beauty
Aim:	Leisure and visual amenity
Timing:	Continuous
Scope:	Large and small areas
Planning tool:	Regulation and estate management

The general principle of countryside planning (see Summary Box 5.1), that development should benefit the rural economy *and* maintain or enhance the environment, assumes that 'the countryside can accommodate many forms of development without detriment' (PPG7, para 1.10). Development planning and development control in the countryside should take a positive attitude in particular to rural business, tourism, sport and recreation and sensitively manage the location and detail of any new development. Outside special designations (see below) PPG7 advices that proposals for new development should take account of: the need to encourage rural enterprise; the need to protect landscape, wildlife habitats and historic features; the quality and versatility of land for use in agriculture, forestry and other rural enterprises; and the need to protect other non-renewable resources. Re-use and adaptation of rural buildings is encouraged to prevent dereliction and avoid new build. Development control has also always sought to protect agricultural land of the best quality by resisting development on Grade 1, 2 and 3a land in England and Wales: about one-third of agricultural land in England and Wales falls into these grades. Proposals which conflict with the development plan and involve the loss of more than 20 ha of such land require consultation with the MAFF.

However, *agricultural development* itself used to be exempt from development control. The use of land and existing buildings for agricultural purposes, as defined in the 1990 Town and Country Planning Act, does not require planning permission since it does not constitute development. New construction, alterations or extensions to farm buildings or excavations and engineering operations do constitute development but, if reasonably necessary for the purposes of agriculture much is permitted development under the GDO. More extensive rights are available to agricultural units of at least 5 ha; more limited rights to units of 0.4–5 ha. Details are given in PPG7.

Since 1992, however, a system of prior notification for such development operates which allows local authorities to regulate certain aspects. This is a significant innovation, affecting over 12 million of agriculture and forestry land in England and Wales. Under this system the farmer or developer must give the local authority 28 days to decide whether prior approval will be necessary for the details of development: that is, siting, design and appearance. The principle of development is not open to debate. The purpose of prior approval is to safeguard the visual amenity of the landscape and promote natural and heritage conservation. Approval may be conditional and there is no right of appeal.

Such sensitive management of all development in the countryside runs alongside a range of more restrictive rural policies. The policy tools discussed here focus on special designations for small and large areas.

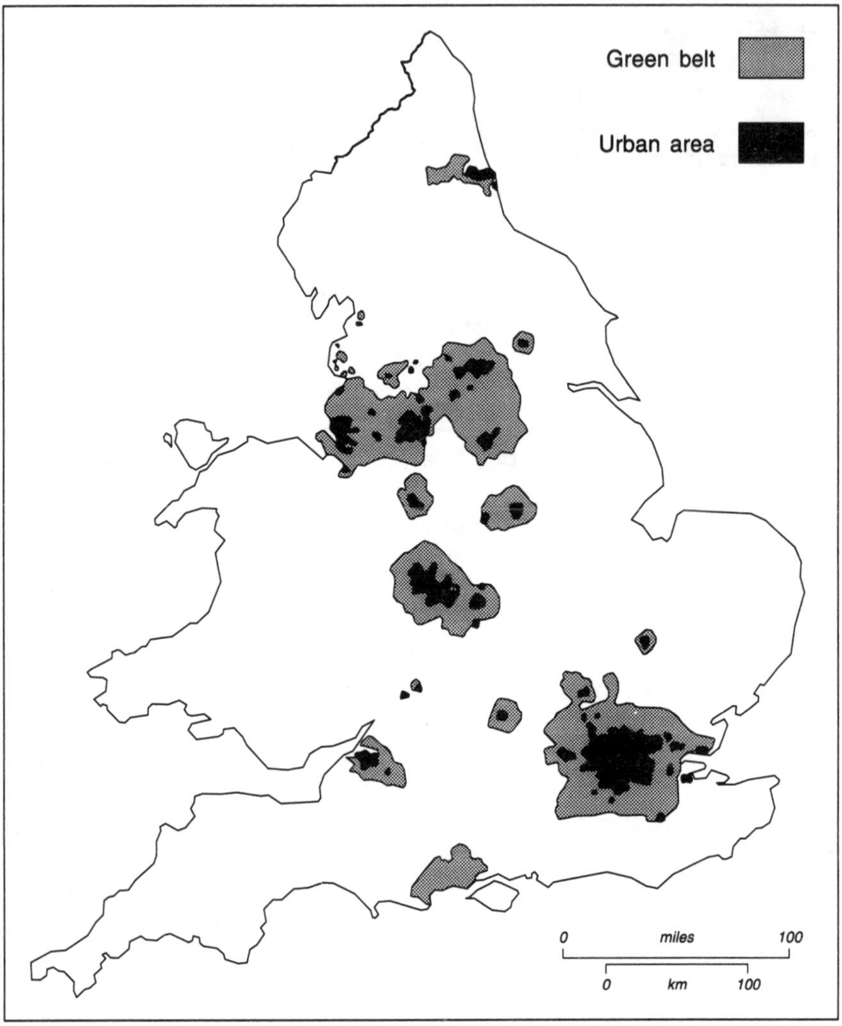

Map 5.1   *Green belts*

The designations covered below are: green belts, national parks, AONBs, heritage coasts and public rights of way.

Green belts are probably the planning tool of greatest longevity and popular support. They apply to 15 separate areas covering 1.6 million or 14 per cent of England (see Map 5.1). Designation is undertaken by local authorities through the development plan process with detailed boundaries established in local plans and old-style (pre-1968) development plans. The purpose of green belts is fivefold (PPG2):

- to check the unrestricted sprawl of large built-up areas
- to safeguard the surrounding countryside from further encroach-ment
- to prevent neighbouring towns from merging into one another
- to preserve the special character of historic towns
- to assist in urban regeneration

They are essentially tools for resisting and diverting urban development and largely negative in nature. While mention is made in PPG2 on green belts of their positive role in providing public access to countryside and space for sports and leisure, green belts in themselves imply no special land management practices to this end. Neither is the quality of the landscape relevant to designation or a part of green belt policy implementation (PPG2, para 7): 'The essential characteristic of green belts is their permanence and their protection must be maintained as far as can be seen ahead.'

This means that alteration of green belt area and boundaries is rarely sanctioned and green belt policies in development plans will follow a longer timescale than for other aspects. Green belts are not intended as a reservoir of development land for beyond the current plan period; other land between the urban area and green belt should be safeguarded for this purpose. Within green belts there is a general presumption against inappropriate development, with 'appropriate development' defined as agriculture and forestry, outdoor sport, cemeteries, institutions standing in extensive grounds or 'other uses appropriate to a rural area'. Mineral extractions may be permitted due to their locationally fixed nature. No other development is to be allowed even 'in exceptional circumstances'.

Pressure for the re-use and conversion of buildings already within the green belt has led to additional policy advice. Re-use of redundant farm buildings may be permitted for business, tourist or residential use with suitable conditions controlling the conversion works and final use. The shift away from institutional health care towards a 'care in the community' policy has left many former hospitals in green belts redundant. Government policy is that these should be converted for appropriate green belt uses but, if there is little or no prospect of such re-use being viable, then other uses are preferable to the buildings remaining empty or being grossly underused. Conversion is preferred to redevelopment and no extension of the mass of the buildings is allowed on redevelopment.

Green belts are thus the exemplar of a restrictive planning policy designed to prevent change in rural areas bordering onto urban concentrations. Many local authorities operate other restrictive policies for stretches of non-green belt countryside but none carry the statutory force of green belts. An exhibit on the conflicts involved in designating green belts in development plans is provided in Exhibit 8.1.

Turning to more positive planning tools for the countryside, the principle major designation is the creation of 10 *national parks*, 7 in England and 3 in Wales, under the 1949 National Parks and Access to the Countryside Act (see Map 5.2). These are designated by the Countryside Commission in England and Countryside Council in Wales, subject to confirmation by the relevant Secretary of State. They cover 13 600 km^2 or 9 per cent of the area of England and Wales. Planning for the parks is currently the responsibility of a planning board in the Lake District and Peak District, while elsewhere national park committees within county councils take on this role supported by joint advisory committees where more than one county council is affected by a national park.

In January 1992, in its response to the report prepared by the ad hoc National Parks Review Panel, the government announced that it would be moving towards an independent planning authority for all national parks, thus placing them all on the same footing as the Lake District and Peak District. In 1989 the Norfolk and Suffolk Broads were given status comparable to a national park and a planning board was created to take responsibility for the area. It is intended to make the same arrangements for the New Forest area.

The current statutory purposes of national parks are conservation of the natural beauty of the countryside and promotion of its public enjoyment. Proposed legislation will restate this purpose as relating to 'quiet enjoyment' and the understanding and conservation of wildlife and cultural heritage, thus clarifying that in cases of conflict conservation overrides public access and enjoyment. However, parks also have a duty to take full account of local communities' economic and social needs, under the Countryside Act 1968. There is a proposal to impose a statutory duty on all ministers and public agencies to take these aims of national parks into account in any development they are concerned with.

Planning responsibilities for a national park authority include, under the 1991 Planning and Compensation Act, the preparation of a single park-wide local plan and separate minerals and (in England) waste local plans. Authorities are also responsible for development control within their areas including minerals and waste applications, although in the Broads applications are first submitted to the relevant district council before being passed to the Broads Authority. Enhanced development criteria operate within the parks, ensuring a more critical approach to planning applications. Agricultural development in national parks has

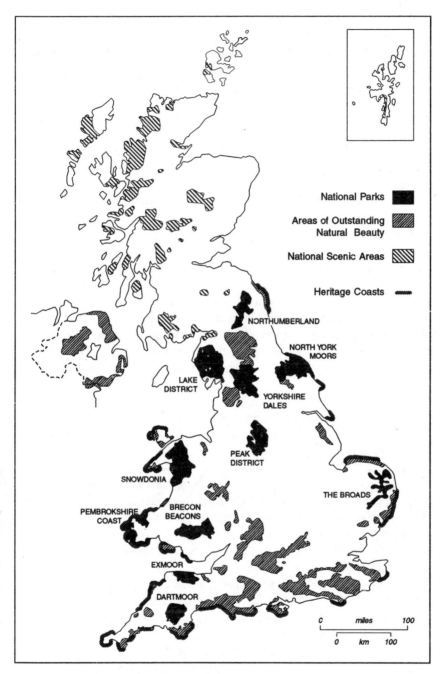

Map 5.2   *Countryside protection policies*

long been subject to a partial form of development control – the notification system that, since 1992, has been extended to all agricultural development. Certain development that carries permitted development rights outside the national park requires consent within the boundaries: some larger extensions to dwellings, industrial buildings and warehouses; roof extensions; stone cladding; satellite dishes in certain locations; microwave antennae; excavations and engineering operations. Government advice in PPG7 on 'The Countryside and the Rural Economy' proposes a single test for considering applications for major development in parks: that such development should be demonstrated to be in the public interest before being allowed to proceed.

But national park planning implies positive management also. Each park authority prepares a national park plan which is a management plan for the area, and Exchequer funds are made available to implement this. 75 per cent of national parks funds are provided by central government. In 1990/1 the average net expenditure for a national park was £1.89 million with average staffing of 99 full-time staff (Crabtree, 1991). Some management functions are carried out jointly by the park committee or board and a district council: principally trees, derelict land and country parks, and district councils can act on an agency basis for the county or board. Park authorities also have powers to enter into agreements with landowners to achieve management of the land in line with park objectives. £500 000 was paid during 1989/90 under such agreements.

The 1949 National Parks and Access to the Countryside Act also provides for the designation of *areas of outstanding natural beauty*. There are 39 such AONBs, covering 19 900 km^2 or 13 per cent of England and Wales. AONBs may also be designated by the DoE in Northern Ireland, where there are 9 such areas covering 20 per cent of the land area. The purpose of AONBs is to conserve the natural beauty of the landscape, rather than to provide means for public access and enjoyment. Permitted development rights are withdrawn on the same basis as in national parks, and development plans and development control are required to have regard to such conservation aims. There are no special organisational provisions for AONBs and local planning authorities remain responsible for them. There are Exchequer grants available for the maintenance and enhancement of AONBs, activities which are also undertaken by the local planning authority under specific powers. Grant decisions reflect the fundamental landscape conservation purpose of the designation.

Certain other areas are also designated for landscape and leisure purposes. In coastal areas the Countryside Commission (or Countryside Council in Wales) designates *heritage coasts* to protect the landscape and also provide for managed recreation. 44 such heritage coasts cover one-third of the coastline in England and Wales. This is not a statutory designation and there is no withdrawal of permitted development rights but 37 of the 44 heritage coasts are in national parks or AONBs where there is enhanced protection. In addition recent government advice on coastal planning (issued in draft in March 1992) proposes a presumption against building on all undeveloped stretches of the English coastline. Even in built up areas, permission should be restricted to those developments which require a coastal location such as tourism, recreation, mineral extraction and marinas/harbours, etc. Currently some 75 per cent of the English coastline is undeveloped.

Coastal planning advice also covers the need to restrict development in areas prone to flooding and at risk of such flooding in the foreseeable future. In a situation of global warming and sea-level rise, this could be a significant new consideration for local planning in many areas. Managed retreat for low-level coastal areas is also put forward as a possibility in undeveloped stretches.

In cases of conflict between public access for recreation and nature conservation, the government advice in PPG17 on 'Sport and Recreation' makes it clear that priority should be given to conservation and the enhancement of natural beauty in national parks and heritage coasts, and conservation of natural beauty and the needs of agriculture and diversity in AONBs. *Public access* for leisure purposes is more specifically provided for in country parks and the provision of local authority picnic sites. Here local authorities have powers to provide special facilities for leisure activities in the countryside. The aim is not just to provide for public enjoyment but also, by doing so in selected spots, to take the pressure off other more vulnerable parts of the countryside.

The provision of public rights of way ensures continued access to large parts of the countryside. There are currently 140 000 miles of public rights of way. Under the 1949 legislation, they are set out in definitive maps, to which there have been rights of appeal and representation both to county councils, who prepared them, and the law courts of the Quarter Sessions. These definitive maps were largely completed by 1960. The 1981 Wildlife and Countryside Act provides for the continuous review of these definitive maps to give up-to-date information on public rights of access. This 1981 act is now the reference point for such definitive maps. Local authority finance is available for footpath maintenance and signposting and the 1981 Act sets out a variety of other powers and duties concerning the enhancement of footpaths and bridleways: for example, appointment of wardens and reinstatement after ploughing. Obstructing a footpath is an offence and landowners must maintain stiles, claiming the expense from the county council. A public path can be closed or diverted only after a formal procedure, including publicity, a hearing or objections and confirmation by the Secretary of State.

Long distance footpaths provide further sources of public enjoyment. These are initiated by county councils, in discussion with other local planning authorities, and presented to the Secretary of State for the Environment. They are eligible for Exchequer grants for maintenance, this being the responsibility of district councils. A recent footpath initiative is the Countryside Commission's parish paths partnership, a £1 million package announced as part of its 1992 'Action for the Countryside' programme. The aim is to involve local people in managing local rights of way. This is part of the Countryside Commission's general approach that bringing together voluntary and statutory groups with farming interests in the countryside is the best way of achieving the protection of rural areas, environmentally, socially and economically.

□ Scotland

The general policy for development planning and development control in rural areas follows similar principles in Scotland although there is separate legislation and guidance reference points. The equivalent planning bodies in Scotland are: the Environment Department of The Scottish Office rather than the DoE; the Department of Agriculture, Fisheries and Foods in The Scottish Office rather than MAFF; and Scottish Natural Heritage, formed from the Countryside Commission for Scotland and the Nature Conservancy Council in Scotland, instead of the Countryside Commission. In addition to these administrative differences, there are a number of substantive policy differences.

A major difference in countryside policy is that there are no national parks, although the 1945 Sandford Committee clearly intended that 5 Scottish parks should be created alongside the English ones. National park direction orders were issued by the Secretary of State under the 1947 Town and Country Planning Act, so that all planning applications in specified areas are submitted up to The Scottish Office for consideration, but no further steps were taken. A recent 1991 report by the Countryside Commission for Scotland (now part of Scottish Natural Heritage) entitled *Mountain Areas of Scotland* proposed four National Parks in the Cairngorms, Loch Lomond and Trossachs, Glen Loch, Ben Nevis and Black Mount, and over parts of Wester Ross. However, this did not succeed in achieving such designations either. Neither are there any AONBs as a result since national parks and AONBs are based on the same enabling legislation.

Instead 40 national scenic areas, covering 13 per cent of Scotland's ground area, have been identified to date. In these areas all planning applications are considered by Scottish Natural Heritage but there are no funds attached to the designation. The 1991 Natural Heritage (Scotland) Act also introduced the designation of national heritage areas. These areas are proposed by the Scottish Natural Heritage and formally designated by the Secretary of State. In these areas integrated management is to form the basis of countryside planning, focusing on positive rather than restrictive planning. In particular the negotiation of management agreements between Scottish Natural Heritage and landowners is encouraged to promote public access into the large areas of private rural land in Scotland. Existing national scenic areas may continue or, over time, be converted to national heritage areas.

There is a partly implemented Park System in Scotland. Country parks are established and maintained by local authorities, who may also designate areas of scenic heritage for protection under their normal planning policies. Under the 1981 Countryside (Scotland) Act provision is now made for regional parks in which the local planning authority and landowners can enter into management agreements. They are designated by the regional councils and confirmed by the Secretary of State for Scotland. There are 4 regional parks covering 718 km^2.

Coastal areas have additional protection through the means of coastal conservation zones. These are intended as areas where applications for development permission should be subject to wider consultation and stricter control. Policies for such zones are contained in local plans. 74 per cent of the mainland and island coastlines are so designated, some 7546 km.

The status of footpaths is also different in Scotland. There is no duty to map paths and the paths themselves are not rights of way but carry permissive powers of access. Formal rights of access are only granted following a procedure which involves the local courts. Continuous use by the public and a formal assertion by the local authority is required. Long distance footpaths are initiated by regional councils and confirmed by The Scottish Office.

☐ *Northern Ireland*

As with most planning powers in Northern Ireland, control is largely vested in the DoE for Northern Ireland under a heavily centralised system. In addition to the occasional points made in the text, it is worth noting that the Environment Service of the DoE(NI) runs 6 country parks, 1 peatland park and 2 additional countryside centres, as well as coordinating a regional park.

■ Nature conservation

Summary Box 5.2 *Nature conservation*

Organisation:	English Nature, Countryside Council for Wales, Scottish Natural Heritage, local authorities, voluntary organisations
Focus:	Habitats
Aim:	Wildlife conservation
Timing:	Continuous
Scope:	Sites of Special Scientific Interest, nature reserves
Planning tool:	Management

So far the emphasis has been mainly on public access and landscape conservation. However, nature conservation is an integral element of these countryside policies (see Summary Box 5.2). The main bodies responsible for ensuring that the needs of nature conservation are taken into account are the three national successors to the Nature Conservancy Council (NCC), whose duties include the provision of scientific advice, establishing and maintaining national nature reserves and developing relevant research. The NCC was reorganised into three national agencies under general powers contained in the 1981 Wildlife and Countryside Act, the 1990 Environmental Protection Act and the 1991 Natural Heritage (Scotland) Act. There is a NCC for England known as English Nature which works with the Countryside Commission for England; the NCC in Scotland combined with the existing Countryside Commission for Scotland to form Scottish Natural Heritage; and in Wales a new body called the Countryside Council took on the work of the NCC and Countryside Commission in Wales. There is a joint committee for international liaison and representation between the organisations, called the Joint Nature Conservation Committee.

However, the 1968 Countryside Act places a duty on every local authority, government department and public body to have regard to nature conservation alongside the enhancement and maintenance of natural beauty of the countryside. Advice on nature conservation for local planning authorities is contained in DoE Circulars 27/82 and 1/92;

WO Circulars 52/87 and 1/92. A PPG is due shortly. The wildlife of inland water-based areas is further protected by the specific duty imposed on the National Rivers Authority (NRA) (see Chapter 6), water and sewerage undertakers and internal drainage boards to conserve and enhance natural beauty, conserve flora and fauna. Advice in DoE Circular 17/91 requires water companies to take special care in putting forward water and sewerage treatment plant proposals in areas designated for landscape and wildlife importance.

Specific provision is made for nature conservation in the form of *nature reserves* and SSSIs. There are 242 national nature reserves in Great Britain covering 1681 km^2 designated by the relevant nature conservation agency with another 44 in Northern Ireland covering 44 km^2. Nature reserves are protected under management agreements between English Nature (or equivalent) and landowners. These are the responsibility of English Nature (or equivalent) though, by agreement, they may be managed by district councils. Local authorities can enter into similar agreements and create local nature reserves. There are some 241 local reserves in the UK, 171 km^2 in all. There are also marine nature reserves, managed by English Nature (or equivalent). 7 potential sites have been identified and two designated, Lundy in 1986 and Skomer in 1990.

Special additional reserves were created under the Ramsar Convention 1971 for protecting wetlands, i.e. marshes, estuaries, etc. Some 44 areas in Britain have been designated by the Secretary of State under the Convention. 40 Special Protection Areas for Birds have also been designated by the Secretary of State under the EC Wild Birds Directive 79/409. Within Ramsar Sites and special protection areas for birds, nature conservation considerations should normally outweigh the need for development projects by the water industry. The EC is further expanding their wildlife protection work with a habitats directive which will set up a European network of special conservation areas, known as the Nature 2000 sites. In the UK sites likely to be included are bogs, heathland, dunes and key forests.

There are nearly 5700 *sites of special scientific interest* (SSSIs) in Great Britain covering 17 800 km^2 or 7 per cent of the land. They are designated by the relevant nature conservation body under Section 28 of the 1981 Wildlife and Countryside Act, which replaces the 1949 National Parks and Access to the Countryside in this respect. The 1981 Act requires the designation of all SSSIs to be reviewed with a view to removing the designation from damaged areas and extending boundaries where appropriate. Designation is based on scientific criteria and the sole purpose is nature conservation. Planning decisions concerning any SSSI automatically involve consultation with English Nature (or equivalent). However, the government view is that there is no presumption against development in or near SSSIs.

Further protection is given under the 1981 Wildlife and Countryside Act, as amended in 1985. Under a system of reciprocal notification English Nature (or equivalent) has to inform landowners and other relevant bodies of the intent to designate a SSSI and landowners have to inform English Nature (or equivalent) of any intended operations within such a site, giving four months notice. This does not apply to development with planning permission. The fines for not complying with these requirements are, however, relatively light at up to £500. If English Nature (or equivalent) objects to proposed operations they have a limited period of time (currently four months) within which to negotiate a management agreement for the land, with compensation being payable for operations foregone by the landowner. This contrasts with other areas of planning control where there is no compensation for loss of development rights. Currently 6 per cent of the area of SSSIs is subject to management agreements. At the end of the negotiation period English Nature (or equivalent) can apply to the Secretary of State for an Section 29 extension order. However, at the end of this extended period (of up to 12 months) the only remedy available to English Nature (or equivalent) is compulsory purchase.

Added protection is available for sites of national importance, which are designated by the Secretary of State and require written approval from English Nature (or equivalent) for operations. The designation of such sites invokes compensation if the value of the land is reduced. There is a proposal for establishing consultation areas around SSSIs of major importance identified by English Nature or the Countryside Council for Wales. 16 areas have been proposed, ensuring wider consultation for any schemes of development or operations in or near the SSSIs.

The 1981 Wildlife and Countryside Act also provides for the protection of a SSSI to be taken into account by the Minister of Agriculture in giving farm capital grants. These essentially negative measures are being supplemented by English Nature's Wildlife Enhancement Scheme which aims to promote positive management of SSSIs. Under this scheme, launched in 1991, payments will be available for wildlife protection works. These will cover the one-off costs of preparing management plans and agreements, and also annual payments for works.

In addition to these area-based policies there is a list of *protected species* which encourages protection of their habitats and constrains development in the vicinity, as well as preventing capture, killing and/or export in specified cases. For example the 1991 Badgers Act protects badgers' setts, requiring any disturbance to be authorised by a licence from English Nature (or equivalent). The schedules of the 1981 Wildlife and Countryside Act also detail the protection afforded various plants, animals and birds. Some 400 species are so listed. The DoE has a Wildlife Inspectorate which seeks the implementation of the register on protected species.

Local environmental pressure groups play a major role in nature conservation policy. They can act as watchdogs for instances of local habitat destruction and lobby for enhanced protection. Their expertise is often called upon by local authorities and others, seeking knowledge of local nature resources. And policy implementation can be delegated to local groups, who may manage nature reserves and take an active role in local conservation. An Exhibit 10.3 concerning the Royal Society for Nature Conservation in Chapter 10 discusses one such group.

□ *Scotland*

As the main text has indicated, many of the provisions for nature conservation listed above are relevant in a Scottish context. There are two points of variation which are worth mentioning.

First, in relation to SSSIs, an Advisory Scientific Committee has been set up to review objections to current SSSI designations and to any new designations or amendments under the current redesignation procedures. This has provoked considerable controversy as it allows landowners to appeal over the head of Scottish Natural Heritage.

Second, there is a Marine Consultation Area Scheme in Scotland, under which areas identified by Scottish Natural Heritage have the protection of extended consultation arrangements over any works affecting them. This scheme was the model for proposals to establish consultation areas around SSSIs of national importance.

□ *Northern Ireland*

In Northern Ireland many of the functions of English Nature are performed by the Countryside and Wildlife Branch of the DoE(NI). There is an advisory body, the Council for Nature Conservation and the Countryside, set up in 1989.

The equivalent designation to the SSSIs is the area of special scientific interest. There are 26 such areas of special scientific interest, covering 69 km^2. These areas replaced the designation of areas of scientific interest previously used.

■ Planning for rural economies

Summary Box 5.3   *Rural economic development*

Organisation:	Ministry of Agriculture, Fisheries and Food, The Scottish Office, local authorities, Countryside Commission, Scottish Natural Heritage, Countryside Council for Wales, Rural Development Commission
Focus:	Mainly agricultural production
Aim:	Balance economic and environmental concerns
Timing:	Continuous support
Scope:	Agricultural areas
Planning tool:	Regulation and subsidy

The effect of agricultural practice on landscape and nature conservation has long been a source of dispute between farming and environmental lobbies. On the one land, protecting countryside areas requires active, economically sustained rural communities, in practice this has meant supporting agricultural production. On the other hand, the economic activities that sustain such communities may threaten established natural habitats and landscape features (see Summary Box 5.3).

For a long time it was held that supporting agricultural activity was sufficient safeguard of the countryside in itself but, more recently, the fundamental nature of the underlying conflict has been recognised. The 1986 Agriculture Act now states that a reasonable balance must be maintained between the agricultural industry, the economic and social structure of rural communities, conservation and public access. This section looks at the subsidy and grant schemes for agriculture and forestry and how they have been altered to give a better balance between increased production and environmental protection. It then goes on to consider the other means of supporting rural communities, including planning for residential development in the countryside.

The main form of support to agriculture has been through the subsidies of the EC CAP. However, reform of the CAP, in response to rising costs and overproduction, have forced a change in policy for agricultural areas. Thus many *subsidy schemes* have been changed to reduce production, take land out of agricultural use and achieve more acceptable patterns of farming. For example, there is a pilot Extensification Scheme for Beef and Sheep whereby farmers receive payments in return for reducing output by at least 20 per cent and doing so in an environmentally acceptable way: for example, maintaining hedges, ponds, meadows, moorland and heaths. Hill livestock compensatory allowances give payments to farmers in designated less favoured areas: some 80 per cent of Wales falls in this category and 90 per cent of Scotland. In the past these allowances have led to overgrazing and revisions to the scheme are now being introduced. There is also a proposal for an Organic Conservation Scheme supported by grants.

Under the 1981 Wildlife and Countryside Act, applications for capital grants now trigger a series of representations and notifications, creating the potential for such applications to be refused on 'countryside' grounds. Farmers may, however, be compensated in cases of refusal. For example, the 1981 Act makes provision for maps of areas of moor or heath within national parks to try and protect them from ploughing and these maps can provide information for grant decision makers. And in 1989 farm and conservation grants were introduced to replace grants aimed at increasing capital investment. These are targeted instead at environmental improvements such as the handling of farm waste, regeneration of woodlands and moorland and repairs to traditional buildings, hedges and walls.

The most significant policy initiative is probably the *Set-Aside Scheme*, an EC initiative which provides for payments to the farmer where at least 20 per cent of arable land is taken out of production for five years and put to fallow, woodland or non-agricultural use. Conditions attached to these payments structure the management of the land. The reforms to the CAP in May 1992 generalise the proposal for set-aside to all farms so that reductions in guaranteed prices goes with a required set-aside of 15 per cent acreage and compensation payments. The Countryside Premium Scheme further provides for additional payments to farmers in selected areas for managing set-aside land to the benefit of wildlife, landscape and countryside communities: for example, as feeding areas for winter geese.

In the case of *forestry*, schemes were introduced in 1985 (the Broadleaved Woodland Grant Scheme) and in 1988 (the Woodland Grant Scheme) to encourage high environmental standards in woodland management and provide higher rates of grant for planting native pinewoods and broadleaves. Since then grants have also been intro-duced for the environmental management of all woodlands, with higher rates operating for woods of special environmental value. The Pilot Farm Woodland Scheme provided supplementary grants for planting on agriculturally improved land but this has been replaced by a revision to the main Woodland Grant Scheme which now generally encourages farmers to convert farmland into woodland. This is seen as an environmentally acceptable way of taking land out of agricultural production. The grants are front loaded to cover the costs of planting, and subject to environmental and silvicultural checks by the Forestry

Authority (see below) and its consultees. Higher ratios of broadleaves within the tree mix attract more grant. Farm woodland grants are not available for ESAs and there are limits on planting in less favoured areas.

Some measures are more purely environmental in focus, not trying to marry reduced agricultural production with environmental aims. Another initiative promoted by an EC directive (No. 797/85) concerns *environmentally sensitive areas* (ESAs) designated by the appropriate agricultural department under the 1986 Agriculture Act (see Map 5.3). ESAs are areas of special landscape, wildlife or historic interest, considered vulnerable to agricultural intensification. Incentive payments are made to encourage farmers to maintain traditional, more ecologically sensitive, farming practices. There are currently 23 such areas covering 7900 km^2 or 4 per cent of agricultural land. Each ESA has quite distinct management agreements reflecting the special ecology of the area. They have no significance in relation to planning policies.

Concern with the water pollution arising from farming activities has led to the designation of *nitrate sensitive areas* to control nitrate leaching from soil due to fertiliser use. Monitored by the NRA they encourage agreements to restrict the use of nitrate-based fertilizers in designated areas (see Chapter 6).

Generally, though, the emphasis has been on a voluntary approach in encouraging the farming community to take a more responsible attitude towards nature and landscape conservation issues. The 1981 Wildlife and Countryside Act allow for agreements for managing agricultural land. Local planning authorities can use Section 39 of the Act to enter into such agreements with farmers. The North Yorkshire Moors National Park Authority have used this means to negotiate five year agreements with farmers by which payments are made for specified farm practices, both in the form of annual income and improvement-related grants.

This voluntary approach has been supplemented by a wave of incentives from the DoE, mainly via the Countryside Commission (or equivalent in Scotland and Wales) and, more reluctantly, from MAFF (and its equivalents). The Countryside Commission's 1992 'Action for the Countryside' programme includes a number of measures aimed at agriculture, including an extended Countryside Stewardship Scheme for England. This scheme, run by Countryside Commission with consultation from English Heritage and English Nature, identifies specific categories of landscape, which are seen to be under threat; currently these are: chalk and limestone grassland; lowland heath; coastal land; waterside landscapes; uplands; historic landscapes; and pasture and meadow land. In these areas £13 million is available over three years for

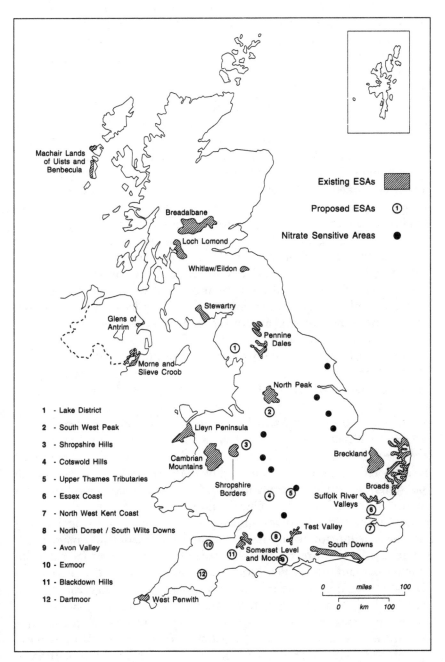

Existing ESAs
Proposed ESAs ①
Nitrate Sensitive Areas ●

Machair Lands
of Uists and
Benbecula

Breadalbane
Loch Lomond
Whitlaw/Eildon
Stewartry
Pennine
Dales

Glens of
Antrim
Morne and
Slieve Croob

North Peak

Lleyn Peninsula

Cambrian
Mountains

Shropshire
Borders

Breckland

Broads

Suffolk River
Valleys

Test Valley

South Downs

Exmoor
Somerset Level
and Moors

West Penwith

1 - Lake District
2 - South West Peak
3 - Shropshire Hills
4 - Cotswold Hills
5 - Upper Thames Tributaries
6 - Essex Coast
7 - North West Kent Coast
8 - North Dorset / South Wilts Downs
9 - Avon Valley
10 - Exmoor
11 - Blackdown Hills
12 - Dartmoor

0   miles   100
0   km   100

Map 5.3   *Environmental policies for farmland*

annual per hectare payments to farmers and landowners in the private or public sector, who enter into 10 year agreements to recreate landscapes, restore wildlife habitats and allow public access. Specified sums are set down for different types of land and works carried out, including some one-off capital payments. In its first year, 900 agreements were made. The scheme may shortly be extended to Wales. Another Countryside Commission initiative is the hedgerow protection scheme under which £3 million is available to complement MAFF's own hedgerow grants.

Economic development within rural communities remains of continuing importance within countryside policy, as emphasised in the advice contained in PPG7 on 'The Countryside and the Rural Economy'. Given the somewhat reduced emphasis on agricultural production, this has involved attempts to promote forestry and other economic activities in rural areas. The Rural Development Commission (RDC) is charged with specific responsibility for rural economic development. It grant-aids development in 27 rural development areas covering a third of England and 5 per cent of its population and encourages cooperation between local organisations to enable community-led development. The organisations include local authorities, RDC Business Services (formerly COSIRA), rural community councils and English Estates. Together they are to prepare rural development programmes for the next 5–10 years.

The Farm Diversification Grants Scheme provides funds to enable farmers to develop farm trails, holidays, livery and similar activities to maintain their livelihood in an appropriate rural way. Local authorities are required to support such changes in their planning policies.

Forestry has also been pursued as an employment-generating activity and the organisation of forestry planning has reflected this. To date all forestry activities have been covered by the Forestry Commission which has sought to expand treeplanting and currently owns 2 million acres worth over £2.2 billion. This is now being reorganised prior to privatisation. This involves splitting it into two parts: the Forestry Authority will regulate all forestry, administer research and manage the grant schemes; Forestry Enterprise will be the commercial arm, managing plantations. The latter is to be a self-sufficient enterprise. There is a regional structure with seven regional advisory committees. Recent changes mean that the number of environmental interests on these committees now balances the commercial forestry interests. This recognises the effect of the 1985 amendment to the Wildlife and Countryside Act which placed a duty on the Forestry Commission to balance its economic interests with conservation, countryside and wildlife concerns. In 1991 the Countryside Commission launched a new forest programme with a new National Forest in the Midlands and up to nine community forests. Under a community woodlands supplement to the Woodland Grant Scheme, funds for planting will be provided with the aim of both increasing treeplanting and providing an appropriate location near urban areas for recreation and appropriate development.

In addition to supporting agriculture and forestry and ailing small rural business, it is now recognised that some residential development in the countryside is necessary to support rural communities and their economies. To this end rural housing has become a focus of planning policy in the countryside. Isolated dwellings have always been restricted to those needed by agricultural and forestry workers. PPG7 recommends functional and financial tests of whether such need is genuine and sufficient to warrant residential development and the Agricultural Development Advisory Service (ADAS) can provide an appraisal if required. Any such development is usually subject to an occupancy condition.

More substantial residential development in the countryside is generally resisted. Proposals for complete new settlements were frequently put forward during the 1980s but advice in PPG3 suggests that they are appropriate only in limited circumstances. Any such development is likely to attract households from urban areas and is not intended primarily to meet rural housing needs. However, it is accepted that 'a community's need for affordable housing is a material planning consideration which may properly be taken into account in formulating development plan policies' (PPG3, para 38). In urban locations the provision of affordable housing is encouraged using negotiation, planning obligations and conditions and controls over density. But such mechanisms work best in areas of high demand and on larger sites and may not be appropriate in rural areas. Therefore, special arrangements can be made under the rural exceptions scheme.

This operates in two ways. First, local plans may include policies stating that small sites will be released for housebuilding, even in areas where housing would not normally be permitted, if they provide low-cost housing for local people. Second, in order to ensure that this housing is available for local needs, both initially and on subsequent change of occupant, housing associations are involved to prevent house price rises in open market exchanges.

□ *Scotland*

The geography of Scotland has meant that some of the reforms of the CAP, with their focus on arable farming, have been less important than in lowland England. However, the merging of environmental and agricultural policy has had an impact here too. One issue of particular concern has been fish farming and the pollution generated in coastal locations which can severely affect local ecosystems. Fish farms are now subject to development control throughout Britain and discharges have been brought within pollution control and, therefore, subject to control by river purification boards (see Chapter 6). The Scottish Office have issued draft supplementary guidelines in 1991 to the Crown Estate who are responsible for managing coastal resources as the legal owner of the seabed. This proposes identifying 44 very sensitive areas where there should be severe constraint on fish farming, with location policies identifying preferred sites for such activities elsewhere. Even outside very sensitive areas there is a presumption against very large farms. Thresholds are given for triggering environmental assessment (see Chapter 6) and separation distances specified to prevent a proliferation of such farms.

Economic development in rural Scotland remains a matter of great concern. The Agriculture Development Programme for Scottish Islands provides grants with an environmental emphasis to maintain the local economy of the islands and the Rural Enterprise Programme for the Highlands and Islands has now been launched. This fits within the general work of Highlands Enterprise, formerly the Highlands and Islands Development Board.

■ Minerals planning

Summary Box 5.4   *Minerals planning*

Organisation:	Department of the Environment, national park authorities, local authorities
Focus:	Mineral production
Aim:	Balance national and local interests
Timing:	Ad hoc response, continuous monitoring
Scope:	Mineral deposits
Planning tool:	Regulation and indicative planning

Minerals extraction is often regarded as an immediate and substantial threat to the countryside (see Summary Box 5.4). It disrupts surface landscapes, destroys habitats and generates considerable noise, dust and transport movements. With effective restoration, the land may in due course be returned to agricultural or alternative leisure use but no-one would deny that the interim effects are not environmentally degrading. However, it has been held that the national interest (as opposed to that of local rural communities) is served by mineral extraction. The DoE produces forecasts of the demand for aggregates, using external consultants, and this provides the basis for local minerals planning and development control decisions on minerals applications. It is assumed that sites should be made available to meet forecast demand; the main approach adopted by local authorities has therefore been to use development control policies to manage the release of mineral land and to influence the extraction process. For example, for cement quarries a plan must be drawn up by the operator for each site, discussed with the minerals planning authority to agree current operating and restoration practice. Landbanks of permitted reserves are also established at each site to safeguard future cement supplies. Recent planning legislation has extended the application of these policies. Under the 1991 Planning and Compensation Act, all county councils and national park authorities must prepare one area-wide mineral local plan. These indicate where mineral working may occur, where minerals wastes should be disposed of and where minerals resources should be safeguarded for the future. The plans also include policies for development control, restoration and aftercare. National policy guidance is provided by a series of minerals planning guidance notes. Other relevant policy advice includes the PPG16 on 'Archaeology and Planning', which recommends the CBI's Code of Practice for Minerals Operators for dealing with archaeological remains on sites of excavations.

The 1981 Town and Country Planning (Minerals) Act, incorporated in Town and Country Planning Act 1990, covers England and Wales, and tightens up aspects of mineral development control, and the new agreement powers of the Planning and Compensation Act 1991 also apply. Mineral planning authorities, generally county councils, national park authorities or metropolitan district councils are given extensive control powers, including enforcement and stop notices. For minerals workings, a stop notice may be served at the same time as an enforcement notice and, if necessary, a stop notice can take effect within three days or even, exceptionally, immediately. Planning injunctions can also be served. Restoration and aftercare conditions have been improved to ensure proper replacement of soils and management of the site to a required standard for agricultural, forestry or recreational after-use. Approval of aftercare schemes by the mineral planning authority may be required. Furthermore conditional planning permissions can be changed with reduced or no compensation to reflect improvements in restoration and aftercare techniques. All planning permissions since February 1982 are subject to an implied 60 year time limit.

On sites where work has ceased but there is an outstanding planning permission, special orders can be made. Suspension orders can be applied, to hold minerals not worked for at least 12 months for future working. This provides for temporary restoration and environmental protection. Prohibition orders can be introduced to prevent resumption of works, where no operations have been carried out for at least two years and no further working is desirable. Generally a duty is placed on all mineral planning authorities to review every mining operation in their area with a view to using the full range of development control powers.

Special provisions apply for permissions granted in the 1940s and proposals are also being put forward for updating permissions from the 1950s, 1960s and 1970s. Some minerals operations have permissions granted as interim development orders in the mid-1940s. Prior to the 1991 Planning and Compensation Act these were valid planning consents. Under this legislation a register of interim development orders granted during 1943–8 is set up. Registered consents may be made subject to conditions meeting current day standards for after-use and restoration. Notice is also given for the cessation of the use within 50 years' time. Where there is an interim development order on a site which has not been worked between July 1948 and April 1989, then permission is deemed to have lapsed since 1979. This means that the site comes under the Town and Country Planning Act 1990 and the mineral planning authority can decide on a new form of consent. Where there is no substantial working between April 1989 and May 1991, no working can begin until a scheme of operation and restoration conditions are determined by the planning authority.

Planning permissions from the 1950s to the 1970s may also be subjected to new procedures for updating. In particular, current procedures may be simplified and speeded up. Proposals to this end were contained in a March 1992 consultation paper. This paper also proposed incorporating British Coal's special permitted development rights for opencast mining within the general scheme for minerals.

Minerals extraction may also have implications for other areas of planning. For example, PPG14 on 'Development on Unstable Land' points out that various forms of underground mining cause subsidence and ground instability. This then becomes a factor to be taken into account in preparing development plans and determining planning applications in affected areas.

□ *Scotland*

A broadly similar pattern of planning and control operates in Scotland since the Town and Country Planning (Minerals) Act 1981 and certain minerals-related provisions of the 1991 Planning and Compensation Act are applicable.

Further reading

As recommended in Chapter 4, the legislation, other policy documents and annual reports of relevant organisations should be consulted. Gilg (1992) is an up-to-date edited collection about the changes occurring in countryside policy after the CAP reforms. Selman (1988) is a useful text for countryside planning in Scotland, and Gillet (1983) also contains relevant sections.

■ *Chapter 6*

Environmental Planning

Environmental policy is a rapidly growing area of planning activity. Public concern, the results of scientific research, and the role of the EC are all increasing the scope and stringency of environmental policy tools. In this chapter four aspects of environmental planning are covered: the management of water resources; pollution control including integrated pollution control; waste disposal; and the recent 'greening' of the land use planning system, already outlined in Chapter 5. Environmental impact assessments are included under this last section. Issues relating to derelict and contaminated land are left to Chapter 7.

■ Water supply management

Summary Box 6.1 *Water management*

Organisation:	Water utility companies, National Rivers Authority, Offwat, Scottish local authorities
Focus:	Supply of water
Aim:	Matching demand
Timing:	Continuous
Scope:	Lithosphere
Planning tool:	Investment, regulation and charging

Water management used to be a wholly public sector activity under-taken in England and Wales by river water authorities, until water privatisation split responsibility between the private water companies and the regulatory body, the National Rivers Authority (NRA) (see Summary Box 6.1). Investment in water supply infrastructure, whether reservoirs or pipe networks, is planned and implemented by the water companies using a mixture of public and private finance. For example, under the 1989 Water Act the companies may levy an infrastructure charge on developers of new residential estates. Since many of the water companies are based on the old regional water authorities and, there-fore, cover river basins and their catchment area, in theory this enables integrated management of the basic water unit to continue. In practice, a mixture of commercial considerations and regulatory constraints drive investment decisions. Whereas in the past most investment went into new reservoir capacity, attention is increasingly being focused on the loss of supplied water through leaky pipes. Demand management is also receiving more attention, with the use of pricing and metering to restrict the demand for water. The water consumers' watchdog, the Office of Water Services or Offwat, is playing an important role here in monitoring the water companies' use of the price structure as a tool of water management in a commercial, profit making context. Meanwhile regulatory pressures are pushing more investment into meeting pollution control conditions.

The NRA remains responsible for overall water resource management alongside functions with respect for water pollution (see below), flood defence and land drainage, fisheries, navigation and harbours. Under the 1991 Water Resources Act, these functions are carried out having regard to the conservation and enhancement of natural beauty and amenity, conservation of flora and fauna and recreational use. A number of regional and local advisory committees aid the NRA to perform its functions having regard to these goals.

The water management function charges the NRA with conserving, redistributing and augmenting water resources in England and Wales and securing the overall proper use of such resources. This is achieved by agreeing water resources management schemes with water companies, determining minimum acceptable flows and minimum acceptable levels or volumes for inland waters and issuing certain licences. Such licences are required for abstracting water and for impounding water by means of some obstruction. Conservancy notices may also restrict the use of wells or boreholes which otherwise might not need a licence. Applications for licences may be called in by the Secretary of State and provision is made for appeals against refusal or failure to issue a decision. Existing licences may be modified or revoked, although compensation may then be payable. The NRA is required to keep details of licences available in a public register.

In situations when a serious deficiency of water exists or is threatened, then the Secretary of State may make drought orders, either ordinary or emergency orders. These allow extra restrictions on the taking of water from any source, the discharge of water, its supply and any treatment. The use of water by consumers may also be regulated under such an order. This is the source of the numerous hosepipe bans in south east England and elsewhere.

Privatisation has made a considerable difference to water management in England and Wales, effectively removing a major area from the remit of the planning system. However, in many ways the explicit regulatory framework has been improved. Decision making discretion within the public sector has been replaced by external scrutiny of the private sector. The implications of these changes for the role of professionals in the water industry is explored in Exhibit 9.1.

□ *Scotland*

The Water Act 1989 did not apply in Scotland so that water management and supply remains within the public sector and is largely administered by the local authorities. The regional and island councils, as local water authorities, directly manage the use of water resources, sometimes cooperating in joint boards. They are subject to regulation by the river purification authorities with regard to abstractions and treatment. There are proposals for altering this longstanding system of public sector planning of water.

■ Pollution control

Summary Box 6.2   *Pollution control*

Organisation:	Her Majesty's Inspectorate of Pollution, National Rivers Authority, River Purification Authorities, local authorities
Focus:	Discharges, hazardous substances
Aim:	Integrated Pollution Control, Best practicable environmental option, Best available technology not entailing excessive cost, Polluter Pays Principle
Timing:	Prior authorisation, nuisance control
Scope:	Sources of pollution
Planning tool:	Regulation and inspection

Pollution control covers a great variety of incidents from smoky bonfires to major accidents at hazardous installations and can affect all media: land, air and water. The range of pollution control measures reflect this variety (see Summary Box 6.2).

Smoke control and local nuisances are dealt with by local environmental health authorities, that is district and island councils. In general this is ex post control, coming into effect after the nuisance is created. Pollution from domestic chimneys is controlled under the successive

Clean Air Acts by local authorities creating smoke control zones. Within these zones only smokeless fuels may be used and, in newly declared areas, grants for installing new boilers and fires are available. In 1990 there were 6342 smoke control orders covering 962 000 ha and over 9500 premises in the UK. Local authorities also have powers to control a variety of other specific sources of air pollution, such as bonfires, under the 1974 Control of Pollution and various Public Health Acts.

The Environmental Protection Act 1990 extends the powers of local authorities to deal with the air pollution aspects of a number of industrial processes as well. These are referred to as *local authority air pollution control processes*, or Part B processes. The control of these process dovetails into Integrated Pollution Control (see below) by ensuring prior authorisation for some 11 000 manufacturing processes and 10–15 000 waste oil burning plants. Both new and existing processes require such authorisation. The system for such processes is run by local government through air pollution officers or chief environmental health officers within district or metropolitan borough councils.

More complex industrial operations, or Part A processes, are covered by *integrated pollution control* (IPC) under the 1990 Environmental Protection Act. IPC considers emissions to all media – air, water and lands – and recognises their interrelation. In 1976 the 5th report of the Royal Commission on Environmental Pollution suggested that each industrial process should be looked at as a whole so that the best overall pattern of discharges from the environmental point of view might be authorised. This means that a higher level of air emissions, say, may be acceptable if it can be traded off against a lower level of water discharges, providing a net environmental benefit.

The first move towards integrated pollution control was made with the creation of Her Majesty's Inspectorate of Pollution (HMIP) for England and Wales in 1987 from three other organisations: the Industrial Air Pollution Inspectorate; the Radiochemical Inspectorate; and the Hazardous Waste Inspectorate. HMIP liaises with the NRA on authorisations concerning emissions to water (see below). The government proposes to amalgamate HMIP with the NRA and waste regulation functions of local authorities to create an Environmental Protection Agency, probably by 1994.

The pollution inspectorates have a statutory responsibility to control emissions from scheduled industrial processes to all environmental media in a system of prior authorisation. Controlled processes for IPC are classified into some 35 process areas with a distinction drawn in most cases between Part A processes (which are subject to IPC) and Part B processes (which can be left to local authorities to consider air pollution alone) (see Figure 6.1).

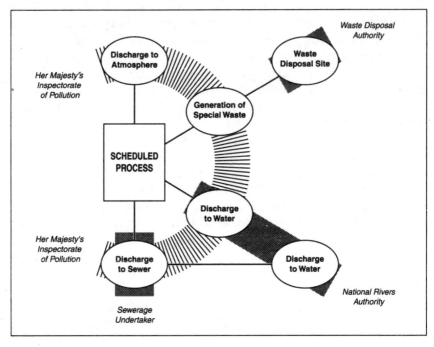

Figure 6.1   *Integrated pollution control*

Summary Box 6.3   *Classification of integrated pollution control processes*

Acid processes; animal and plan treatment; asbestos

Carbonisation; cement and lime; ceramic production; chemical fertiliser production; chemical wastes treatment; chemical bulk storage; coating processes; combustion for energy

Di-isocynates; dyestuffs inks and coatings

Gasification; glass manufacture and production Halogens

Inorganic chemical processes; iron and steel

Non-ferrous

Organic chemicals; other mineral fibres; other mineral processes

Paper and pulp; pesticide production; petrochemical processes; petroleum processes; pharmaceutical production

Rubber processes

Smelting processes

Tar and bitumen; timber processes

Uranium

Waste incineration; waste recovery; waste derived fuel

Currently there are 3500 scheduled processes operating on 2300 sites. IPC will cover 5500 complex industrial processes (see Summary Box 6.3). In issuing a licence for these processes the Inspectorate traditionally required the operator to use the 'best practicable means' to prevent pollution and render any residue harmless and inoffensive. This has been amplified by the concept of BATNEEC, best available technology not entailing excessive cost, under Section 7 of the 1990 Environmental Protection Act. Licences require operators to use BATNEEC to: prevent or minimise the most polluting emissions; render harmless all substances released; and control releases to achieve the best practicable environmental option. The onus of proof with regard to BATNEEC lies with the operator of the process.

Guidance papers covering some 200 processes are being published which detail the operation of IPC. Each guidance note is issued in draft form for a four month consultation period. Prescribed processes, whether existing or proposed, have six months to apply for authorisation from the issue of the final guidance note. The government's timetable is that all new and substantially altered processes should have been brought under control as from 1 April 1991, with existing processes covered under a rolling programme by the end of 1996. Fees are charged for the issue of the licences, the aim being that 75 per cent of the Inspectorate's costs would be recouped. Three types of fee apply: for the application; for inspection, monitoring and enforcements; and for variation of a licence. The fee depends on the complexity and size of the process involved. Applications are made to the regional office of the Inspectorate, and a response is required within four months.

The authorisations and any conditions attached are legally binding so that breach carries financial penalties. In addition to granting the initial authorisation, the pollution inspectorate has the power to issue notices; vary the conditions attached to a licence; revoke an authorisation; enforce compliance with a licence; or prohibit the continuation of an authorised process. Appeals in each case may be made to the Secretary of State. In cases of a breach the courts may order the harm to be remedied or the pollution inspectorates and river purification authorities have the power to undertake remedial actions themselves, subject to the Secretary of State's approval and that of any other land users affected (other than the prescribed operator).

The public have an opportunity to comment before any authorisation is granted and information on authorised processes, including breaches of authorisation, are held on a public register. The registers are held nationally and locally by the pollution inspectorate, NRA, and local authorities. However, commercially confidential material and information affecting national security is excluded. The idea is that the public will have greater opportunity than before to assess the effectiveness of IPC.

In addition to this control over emissions, there is a separate set of controls over particularly *hazardous materials*. For the manufacture of dangerous chemicals an Advisory Committee on Major Hazards has been appointed by the Health and Safety Executive. This has produced reports which have increased the safeguards for such installations including the production of a written safety report, on-site and off-site emergency plans and the provision of public information on the hazard. EC directives also control hazardous chemical production. The 1990 Planning (Hazardous Substances) Act establishes a new system for authorisation of the storage of hazardous materials. Hazardous substances consent must be obtained from the relevant authority for holding more than certain controlled quantities of specified substances. These are obtained from district or London borough councils, except in the case of statutory undertakers' land, when the appropriate minister issues the consent. The Secretary of State can also call in applications. Prior to the issue of consent, the Health and Safety Executive must be consulted (or the Health and Safety Commission in the case of a Minister) and there is provision for appeals against refusal or the imposition of conditions. Holders of consents can also apply for consents to be varied or revoked, and hazardous substances authorities can revoke or modify given consents, subject to confirmation by the Secretary of State. In the latter case, compensation may be payable. Although the consent runs with the land, application must be made for continuation of the consent if control of that land changes hands. Compensation is payable if continuation is not granted under such circumstances. Enforcement is dealt with by issuing hazardous substances contravention notices and details of all consents are held in a public register.

Discharges to water are the prime responsibility of the NRA. The NRA was created to act as a regulating body in England and Wales following privatisation of the water industry and the creation of private water companies. It has the responsibility imposed on it by the 1989 Water Act now consolidated in the 1991 Water Resources Act to monitor water quality and achieve water quality objectives. The NRA has general responsibility for controlling pollution in inland, coastal and esturial waters. To this end a licence for discharges to water is required, either from the NRA under the 1991 Water Resources Act or under some other specified legislation such as the 1974 Control of Pollution Act. Where discharges of 'special wastes' or 'Red List' substances are involved, NRA must gain authorisation from HMIP under the 1990

Environmental Protection Act. Disposal into sewers is under the control of the water companies who own the sewerage network but discharge from the sewers requires consent from NRA. Compliance with authorisations is monitored by the NRA and public registers on the consents and effluent samples are kept. The NRA has powers to prosecute offenders in Magistrates Courts or Crown Courts with penalties of fines up to £20 000 or up to two years in jail. It can also undertake remedial works and reclaim the costs if a site operator knowingly caused or permitted water pollution.

The NRA have been given powers to charge for processing consents and monitoring them. These charges seek to recover the costs of administration; they are not primarily targeted at generating incentives for pollution abatement. However, the banding for determining annual monitoring charges does relate to the quantity and type of discharge and some crude estimate of the carrying capacity of the affected water course.

Where the NRA consider that a particular area requires special protection from pollution then a *water protection zone* may be designated by the Secretary of State. This extends the potential scope of regulation. Nitrate sensitive areas (NSAs), which affect agricultural activities, are a particular form of such protection zones. Pollution from agricultural sources is a particular problem for water resources. Run-off and seepage from slurry, silage, yard water and herbicide or pesticide application all pollute rivers or aquifers. A 1989 joint survey by MAFF and NRA highlighted this issue. The Farm and Conservation Grants Scheme provides 50 per cent grants for capital works to prevent such pollution. MAFF and ADAS provide free advice including codes of good agricultural practice, and standards will be set to enable NRA to monitor such pollution. The designation of NSAs is, however, a more effective way of tackling the problem as it allows for management agreements to control farming activities with payments to encourage farmers to enter into such agreements. 10 pilot NSAs were originally designated in England and, at the end of 1991, 24 were designated or proposed for designation.

Due to the continuing evidence of pollution of groundwater sources, NRA proposes to establish *source protection zones* or vulnerability zones (so called to avoid confusion with the SPZ acronym). Within these, certain development would be restricted to protect water supplies. This is likely to affect waste facilities, chemical stores, mineral excavations, intensive livestock units and chemical spraying. Three types of zone are suggested: inner source protection, outer source protection and source catchment areas. This would be an extension of the water protection zone concept.

The effectiveness of pollution control is judged in relation to *quality standards* set for water and air. Air quality standards are set for smoke and sulphur dioxide, lead in air and nitrogen oxide under EC directives. Ozone standards are also likely to be introduced. A network of monitoring sites record levels of pollution for these emissions. A variety of EC directives cover other aspects of air quality. The 1989 Water Act provided for statutory water quality objectives and these are currently being established. Under the proposed scheme, put forward by NRA, all water (inland, coastal and groundwater) will be covered by a three-part classification. This will consider the application of EC directives, set standards for key chemical parameters and biological measurements, and consider appropriate uses for the water. The objectives will be formally set by the Secretary of State serving notices on the NRA (or the successor EPA) in relation to specific stretches of water. Prior consultation and a period for objections is allowed for. Regulations are expected by the end of 1992. The objectives will then become relevant in granting and receiving discharge consents. Overall compliance with the objections will be monitored by five yearly river quality surveys.

This system operates within an EC framework. A 1980 EC drinking water directive set numeric quality standards according to 44 parameters and offered guidance on another 22. The Drinking Water Inspectorate within the DoE, established in 1990, covers compliance with this directive. It also monitors the concentration of pesticides in drinking water, currently controlled by the Food and Environmental Protection Act 1985. Other EC directives cover other aspects of water quality, including bathing waters, shellfish waters, fishlife and dangerous substances. EC directives are increasingly going to govern pollution control: for example, directing investment in sewage treatment to control discharges from coastal towns.

In relation to noise pollution the local authorities have the power to set up *noise abatement zones* of mixed residential/industrial or commercial areas in which they can control noise levels. Local authorities also have powers to control noise from construction sites. They have a general duty, under the 1974 Control of Pollution Act, to inspect their areas from time to time to detect noise nuisance against which action can be taken. This would take the form of noise abatement notices. The maximum fine for non-compliance with such a notice of £20 000 for commercial and industrial sources. However, only 3180 such notices were issued in England and Wales during 1989/90, 90 in Scotland in 1990. Less then 300 proceed to prosecution. Between a quarter and a half of all complaints are dealt with informally.

Advice on planning decisions in relation to noise is contained in DoE Circular 10/73 and WO Circular 16/73, with a PPG also expected shortly. However, noise pollution control is a fairly technical matter depending heavily on methods of measuring noise levels. Central government provides a Code of Practice regarding noise measurement procedures. The introduction of a new British Standard BS4142/1990 is likely to introduce more stringent noise control, as it adopts a tighter standard for situations of varying noise.

☐ Scotland

As in England and Wales, local authorities have responsibility for smoke and local nuisances, together with minor air pollution control. The district and island councils administer this system. But, for IPC, Scotland has its own administrative structure. The relevant agencies are HM Industrial Pollution Inspectorate (HMIPI) and the Hazardous Waste Inspectorate, with river purification authorities taking the role of NRA. IPC here is achieved through HMIPI and the river purification authorities working closely together before authorisation is given. The river purification authorities carry the powers of authorising emissions of Red List substances. This structure is due to be replaced by a separate Scottish EPA which will assume the pollution control and waste regulation responsibilities of river purification authorities, district and island councils.

☐ Northern Ireland

In Northern Ireland the role of pollution inspectorate is taken by the Alkali and Radiochemical Inspectorate and consultation over emissions to water is with the Environmental Protection Division of the DoE NI. The timetable for implementing IPC new processes in Northern Ireland runs one year behind that in mainland Britain. The proposals for EPAs is unlikely to have any effect in Northern Ireland as pollution control will probably remain within the control of the DoE(NI).

■ Waste management

Disposing of waste is a major public and private sector activity (see Summary Box 6.4). Industry generates some 100 million tonnes p.a. and households another 20 million tonnes p.a. The 1990 Environmental Protection Act instituted a new regime for waste disposal. Currently

Summary Box 6.4   *Waste management*

Organisation:	Waste Regulating Authority, Waste Disposal Authority
Focus:	Waste
Aim:	Environmentally acceptable disposal
Timing:	Prior licensing, continuous monitoring
Scope:	Disposal sites
Planning tool:	Regulation and inspection

some 90 per cent of waste is disposed of in some 4000 controlled landfill sites. As previously, sites for disposal of waste must by licensed and controlled waste can be disposed of only at a licensed site. This is known as a *waste management licence* and it is an additional requirement to a valid planning consent. The relevant licensing bodies or waste regulating authorities (WRAs) are: county councils in non-metropolitan England; London Waste Regulating Authority; Greater Manchester WRA; Merseyside WRA; district councils in metropolitan areas outside the WRAs; district councils in Wales and Northern Ireland. Further WRAs may be set up as appropriate.

Licences for site may be refused on grounds of environmental pollution, harm to human health or serious detriment to local amenities. In addition, the authorities must be satisfied that the applicant is a 'fit and proper person'. WRAs must consult with the NRA, and Health and Safety Executive before issuing a licence and details of licences are held on a public register (subject to commercial confidentiality and national security). As with pollution control, conditions may be attached and there are powers to vary, revoke and suspend licences with appeals to the Secretary of State. WRAs will be able to charge site operators for licences and subsequent monitoring and they hold enforcement powers. They also have a duty to inspect old sites, undertake any necessary remedial work and charge owners for costs incurred. If the site poses an environmental hazard, remedial action is a mandatory requirement on local authorities. Some £33 million is available in 1990/1 for such work. Central government provides technical guidance to WRAs in the form of waste management papers and will, in due course set standards for disposal techniques. HMIP is currently the organisation responsible for monitoring the performance of WRAs. Upon creation of the new EPA, waste regulation functions will be removed from the local authority level.

The remaining 10 per cent of waste is disposed of by dumping at sea (to be phased out) and incineration. There are 35 municipal incinerators and four specialised high temperature incinerators. These are controlled under IPC by HMIP.

Waste regulation authorities also have to draw up *waste disposal plans* which forecast future waste generation and consider the adequacy of existing disposal facilities. Plans for future development of new facilities are then made. The legislation requiring waste disposal plans is the 1974 Control of Pollution Act. Under the 1991 Planning and Compensation Act county councils and national park authorities must also prepare a *waste local plan.* In metropolitan areas, waste policies will be contained in the unitary development plan, and in Wales within the general local plan. These waste local plans or policies address the land use implications of authorities' waste policies. They set out the considerations to apply in identifying sites for new treatment and disposal facilities and deciding planning applications. The two plans should be complementary and not conflict with each other. There will be a PPG on waste disposal facilities to advise local authorities on the preparation of such plans. Among other matters, these are likely to propose restrictions on development in the vicinity of landfill sites due to dangers from methane gas explosions.

Under the new rules in the Environmental Protection Act 1990, waste regulation is to be kept separate from waste disposal. Waste disposal authorities (WDAs) are: county councils, metropolitan WDAs, metropolitan district councils where there is no metropolitan WDA, and elsewhere district councils. Any authority that is both a WRA and a WDA must administratively separate these functions and notify these arrangements to the Secretary of State, who has the power to direct revised arrangements. The aim in many cases is to encourage the formation of arm's length waste disposal companies. These would work alongside private sector disposal contractors and compete with them for contracts.

All parties – producer, regulators, and disposers – have a *duty of care* imposed on them under Section 34 of the legislation which has also created greater opportunities for enforcement action. Applicants for waste management licences have to demonstrate financial and technical resources to manage sites competently. Nor can incompetent managers walk away from sites which breach their licence. They remain responsible for pollution already caused. There is also a duty of aftercare for sites where tipping has ceased to ensure no continuing risk of pollution. The penalty for an offence can be two years in prison and/or up to a £20 000 fine. For special wastes the prison term rises to five years. Carriers of waste have to register with a WRA under 1991 Regulations implementing the 1989 Control of Pollution (Amendment) Act.

Attempts are being made to increase *recycling* by a system of 'recycling credits'. Under the 1991 Environmental Protection Act WDAs have a duty to pass the savings in landfill costs due to recycling onto waste collection organisations and voluntary organisations promoting recycling. This should make recycling more profitable. Local authorities are also required to draw up and publicise recycling plans and to take the provision of recycling facilities into account when granting planning permission for large shopping developments. The WDA may make agreements with waste disposal contractors to encourage recycling.

Two types of waste have special additional systems of control: *marine disposal* and radioactive waste. Any discharge from land to sea requires the consent of the NRA. Dumping or incinerating waste at sea in the past further required a licence from central government agricultural departments, that is MAFF in England and Wales. However, such disposal methods are being phased out (see below). Operational discharges from ships are the responsibility of the DoTr while discharges from off-shore installations, such as oil rigs, are under the DoEn's remit.

The use of the seas for waste disposal has been the subject of much international concern and bi-lateral or multi lateral agreements. Of particular concern to Britain have been the agreements reached at the North Sea conferences.

The 2nd North Sea Conference was convened in November 1987 and agreed a ban on dumping all harmful industrial waste by 1990, a ban on incineration at sea by 1995 and a 50 per cent reduction in outputs of dangerous substances (the Red List) by 1996. An international task force was to be established to research and monitor the environmental quality of the North Sea.

The 3rd North Sea conference was held in the Spring of 1990. This further agreed that all use of polychlorinated biphenyls (PCBs) would be phased out by the end of 1999 and other pollutants discharged to sea further reduced. Dumping liquid industrial waste and flyash from power stations would end by 1993 and dumping sewage sludge by 1998. The timetable for ending incineration at sea was brought forward to the end of 1990. While the end of waste incineration at sea is to be welcomed it accounted for only 2000 tonnes in 1985. However, 30 per cent of UK sewage sludge was disposed of by marine dumping, amounting to 5 million tonnes in 1985. The government published an implementation guidance note in 1990. The implication is that more incineration facilities will have to be built.

Radioactive waste remains a special category. All users of such materials have to be registered, currently amounting to 7000 users.

Commercial nuclear installations are inspected by the Nuclear Installations Inspectorate, part of the Health and Safety Inspectorate, who are responsible for monitoring normal working operations. Such operators have to work to a level of nuclear safety known as ALARP – as low as reasonably practicable. Transport of radioactive material is subject to DoTr regulations based on standards set by the International Atomic Energy Agency. Specific authorisation for discharge of radioactive materials is needed from HMIP in England, the Welsh Office in Wales, HMIPI in Scotland and the Alkali and Radioactive Inspectorate in Northern Ireland. 1000 premises currently discharge wastes, all of which are inspected. Continuous environmental monitoring is carried out at the larger sites. Discharges from the major nuclear sites in England in addition require authorisation from MAFF, who monitors the levels of radioactivity in foodstuffs and other materials.

Advice on waste disposal is provided by the Radioactive Waste Management Advisory Committee but there is a commercial body, UK NIREX Ltd. whose role is to undertake such disposal. This public company is owned by BNF plc (the fuel reprocessing company), CEGB, UKAEA, South of Scotland Electricity Board with the Secretary of State for Energy holding a golden share. Jointly all these organisations devise the strategy for radioactive waste disposal. Currently the location of long-term disposal sites is the key planning issue. Low-level waste (gloves, overalls, laboratory equipment) is mainly disposed of at a controlled landfill site at Drigg in Cumbria. Intermediate and high-level waste (totalling about 6 per cent) is currently stored at nuclear establishments.

☐ *Scotland*

In Scotland the district and island councils are the waste regulating authorities, with the river purification authorities taken on the consultative role of NRA. Districts and island councils are also the WDAs but here the requirement to form arm's length waste disposal companies does not apply. The WDAs also directly undertake recycling of waste.

■ Environmental policy and land use planning

The concept of environmental assessment of projects is now well established in land use planning (see Summary Box 6.5 and Figure 6.2). The origins lie in the 1985 European Directive No.85/337, implemented in 1988 through amendments to a variety of regulations

Summary Box 6.5   *Environmental policy and land use planning*

Organisation:	Local planning authorities
Focus:	Environmental impacts
Aim:	Sustainable development
Timing:	Continuous
Scope:	Projects, extending to plans, programmes and policies
Planning tool:	Research, indicative guidance, regulation, negotiation

which deal with different types of development: for example, ports, harbours, roads. Exhibit 8.3 discusses the role of the EC in promoting environmental assessment. The main form of implementation in England and Wales was through the Town and Country Planning (Assessment of Environmental Effects) Regulations 1988. This effectively required environmental considerations to be specially considered during the development control process for certain projects. The 1991 Planning and Compensation Act gave this process statutory recognition.

Developments which fall within the remit of the schedules attached to the 1988 Regulations may require an environmental statement to be submitted with the planning application. The 'environmental statement' presents 'environmental information' which allows an 'environmental assessment' to be made. An environmental assessment is defined in DoE Circular 15/88 as:

> a technique for the systematic compilation of expert quantitative analysis and qualitative assessment of a project's environmental effects, and the presentation of results in a way which enables the importance of the predicted results, and the scope for modifying or mitigating them, to be property evaluated by the relevant decision-making body before a planning application decision is rendered.

Schedule 1 lists all those developments for which an assessment is compulsory, subject to specified size limits (see Summary Box 6.6).

Schedule 2 lists all those developments for which an assessment may be necessary if it is of a type, scale or form to have significant environmental consequences by virtue of factors such as the nature, size or location of the process or land use (see Summary Box 6.7).

DoE Circular 15/88 gives guidance as to when an environmental assessment should be undertaken with regard to Schedule 2 uses and activities, including various 'indicative thresholds'. The general rule is that an environmental assessment will be needed for projects which are of more than local importance, or where they are in particularly sensitive or vulnerable locations or for unusually complex projects

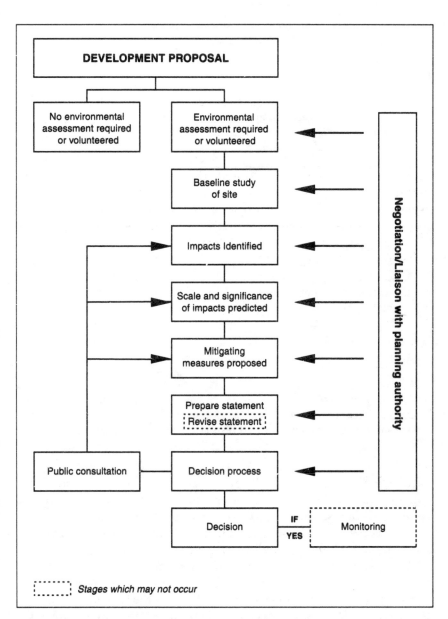

Figure 6.2 *Environmental impact assessment*

Summary Box 6.6   *Environmental assessment: Schedule 1 projects*

1. oil refinery or liquefaction/gasification plant
2. power station (other than nuclear power station)
3. radioactive waste storage or disposal
4. cast-iron and steel melting
5. asbestos processing
6. integrated chemical installation
7. special road; long-distance railway; aerodrome
8. trading port; inland waterway; inland port
9. waste disposal, including treatment of special waste

Summary Box 6.7   *Environmental assessment: Schedule 2 projects*

1. agriculture
2. extractive industry
3. energy industry
4. processing of metals
5. glass making
6. chemical industry
7. food industry
8. textile, leather, wood and paper industries
9. rubber industry
10. infrastructure projects
11. other projects
12. modification of Schedule 1 developments
13. short-term development and testing for Schedule I activities

with potentially adverse environmental effects. There are proposals for extending the application of environmental assessment to golf courses, coast protection schemes and wind power projects.

A developer may choose to submit an environmental assessment with the planning application without waiting to discover if the local authority requires it. Alternatively a developer may make an application to the local planning authority for a determination on the need for an assessment. Otherwise the local authority, or the Secretary of State in the case of called-in applications, will decide whether an assessment is necessary. Any appeals against any determination or decision are made to the Secretary of State.

The environmental statement is prepared by the developer with the local planning authority undertaking the assessment but, in practice, the process of preparation and assessment involves considerable consultation with various bodies and communication between developer and planner. The environmental statement may become a focus of debate in appeal or call-in situations and resulting public local inquiries (see Exhibit 10.1).

It is intended to extend this process of environmental assessment beyond specific projects to plans, programmes and policies as well. DoE (1991a) have published general advice on incorporating environmental concerns within policy formulation and guidance on development planning now also includes a section on the environment. PPG1 on 'General Policy and Principles' states the government's commitment to a 'sustainable' planning system and PPG12 has a whole chapter on development plans and the environment. Currently advice is against full environmental assessment of a plan or its policies, arguing that an environmental appraisal will underpin plan drafting. While central government continues to argue that development and conservation need not necessarily be in conflict, PPG12 does recognise that (para. 6.7): 'Environmental concerns weigh increasingly in the balance of planning consideration.'

Of particular significance are the attempts to give land use planning, through development plans, a role in combating global warming. Energy conservation and altering assessment patterns to reduce CO_2 emissions could have a substantial effect on policies governing built form, development location and transport infrastructure planning. The DoE is currently sponsoring research on these topics and new planning policy guidance is expected which could greatly alter the content of current planning policies.

□ *Scotland*

In Scotland environmental assessment was introduced through a separate range of regulations: the main one being the Environmental Assessment (Scotland) Regulations 1988.

Further reading

Again the reader is referred to the primary sources: legislation and other policy documents. HMIP (and equivalent) produce annual reports and much useful data, including policy details, is included in the annual Digest of Environmental Protection and Water Statistics. The annual White Paper on the Environment is another source of up-to-date policy information. The DoE is also producing a range of publications on environmental issues from guidance on policy and prodcedures (1991a, 1991b) to research reports (Owens, 1992). There is a broad literature on environmental assessment procedures and practice: Wathern (1988), Clark and Herington (1988), Mertz (1989) and Fortlage (1990). Guides to the growing amount of EC environmental policy are provided by the European Commission itself (1992), Haigh (1989) and the law firm Clifford Chance (1992).

■ Chapter 7 ■

Urban Policy and Transport

This chapter completes the overview of the institutions and instruments of the planning system by considering urban policy and, briefly, transport planning. Urban policy and regional policy too has traditionally been conceived in terms of public investment and subsidy. The period of Thatcher government in the 1980s confirmed a shift towards a more market oriented approach which persists today. The key concepts are leveraging in private finance and transferring land to the private sector, which are covered in the first two sections. In the final section it is shown that transport planning too has been based on these concepts in preference to a public sector directed programme of investment. However, considerable amounts of public money continue to underpin the operation of these policies, as Chapter 16 will show.

■ Urban grants and subsidies

Summary Box 7.1   *Urban grants and subsidies*

Organisation:	Department of the Environment, local authorities, Welsh Development Agency, Scottish Enterprise
Focus:	Private development
Aim:	Urban regeneration
Timing:	Ad hoc, responsive
Scope:	Areas of marginal development interest
Planning tool:	Leverage

The concept of attracting private investment into an area by grants and subsidies (see Summary Box 7.1) is not new. Regional planning was based, from the earliest days, on a combination of carrot and stick, with grants, subsidies, tax allowances offsetting the costs of investments in depressed regions while planning restrictions sought to inhibit development in the more congested, prosperous regions. Such regional policy effectively died in the 1980s. All regional development grants have now been scrapped, leaving only regional selective assistance. Project-specific, these funds are available for proposals which can be demonstrated to be viable but requiring government assistance to go ahead. Plans for revising the boundaries for the assisted areas – development and intermediate areas – where these grants may apply, were announced in June 1992 (see Map 7.1). This limited the areas, focused them more clearly on urban areas, and included areas in all regions of mainland Britain. The overall budget of regional aid was cut in Autumn 1992 also. Plans are proposed for an Aid Challenge programme to parallel City Challenge (see below). The EC may broaden the applicability of its regional grants as it intends to delink eligibility for EC funds from national designation of eligible areas. But this will be EC not British regional policy.

There is now little distinction between British regional and urban policy, both being concerned to lever private funds into areas of depressed demand. 'Leverage' embodies the idea that a small initial sum of public investment can attract a larger sum of private investment, with a multiplier effect ensuring the continued attraction of private funds in ever larger amounts. Even subsidies that were originally conceived in terms of the direct social effect of the public monies are now frequently justified in terms of their cumulative effect on the local economy.

Subsidies to encourage *home improvement* have long been available as part of the shift from a slum clearance policy to one of rehabilitation. Such subsidies have, on occasion, underpinned social change as well as physical improvement (Exhibit 10.2). Local authorities still have a duty under the Local Government and Housing Act 1989 to inspect housing in their area and take steps to repair, close or demolish unfit housing. Clearance areas in which extensive compulsory purchase and demolition is proposed can still be declared, but the emphasis is on improvement through grants.

The 1989 Local Government and Housing Act sets out a new system of improvement grants replacing that formerly available under the 1985 Housing Act. The provisions of the Act have been implemented by 1989 and 1990 Regulations with advice given in DoE Circulars 4/90, 10/90 and 12/90 and WO Circulars 13/90, 15/90 and 16/90. Four types of grant are available: renovation grants for improvement, repair or conversion; common parts grants for improving or repairing the common parts of buildings; disabled facilities grants for the provision of facilities for disabled persons in dwellings or the common parts of buildings; and houses in multiple occupation grants to improve or repair houses in multiple occupation or create such houses by conversion.

Grants are available to private owner-occupiers, current or intended, of dwellings and to tenants in the case of renovation or disabled facilities grants. Tenants must be responsible for carrying out the relevant works

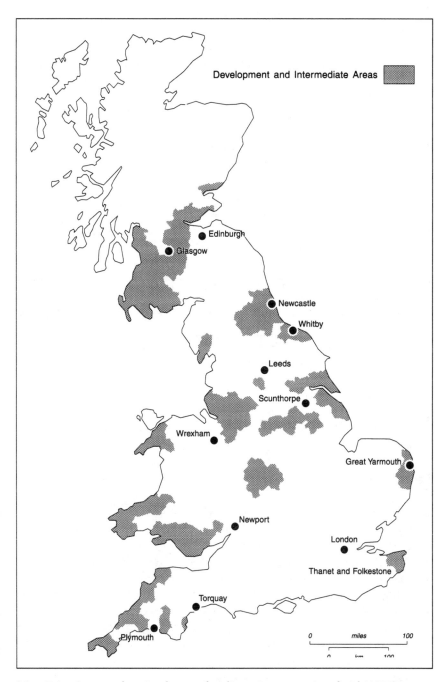

Map 7.1 *Proposed assisted areas for discretionary regional aid (1992)*

under the terms of their lease. In each case a certificate of ownership must accompany the application. Dwellings must be at least 10 years old and there are no exclusions based on rateable value. Instead the amount of the grant payable is subject to means-testing based on the housing benefit system. Renovation grants must bring the dwelling up to a specified 'fitness standard'. Grants beyond this standard are discretionary, not mandatory. Grants may be subject to conditions regarding the nature of the works and the availability of the dwelling for letting. Grants may have to repaid, at least in part, in the case of sale, within five years if it was intended to let the dwelling or within three years if it is owner-occupied.

Minor works may also be assisted by local authority grants, for example for thermal insulation. 75 per cent of eligible local authority expenditure under these provisions is met by central government grant. Higher rates of subsidy are available in renewal areas (see below).

Under the 1989 Local Government and Housing Act local housing authorities may designate *renewal areas*, consisting primarily of living accommodation, where living conditions are unsatisfactory. They are not intended for areas of publicly owned housing or HATs (see below). Such renewal areas replace general improvement areas and housing action areas. A report accompanies the designation detailing the existing conditions, the powers and proposals for improvement, their costs and the resources available for implementation. Draft proposals must be publicised and account taken of representations and Secretary of State guidance. Detailed guidance is provided in DoE Circulars 6/90 and WO Circular 14/90. These currently indicate that a renewal area should be at least 75 per cent privately owned, consist of at least 300 dwellings, have at least 75 per cent of dwellings in poor physical condition and that at least 30 per cent of households should be significantly dependent on specified state benefits.

Renewal areas are temporary measures intended normally to last for 10 years. Within a renewal area the local authority can compulsorily purchase properties, provide housing accommodation, carry out works and assist others to carry out works. 50 per cent of eligible expenditure will be provided by central government up to a total average expenditure of £1000 per dwelling. Local authorities are under a duty to inform residents of actions they are undertaking concerning such areas.

A further improvement subsidy provided under the 1989 Local Government and Housing Act concerns *group repair schemes*, otherwise known as enveloping. This refers to a programme of public sector repairs to the external fabric of a group of houses, say a row of terraced housing, which will then encourage further individual actions. Under the Act, local authorities can enter into agreements to undertake enveloping of privately owned homes and recover costs as agreed between the parties. Sale of enveloped dwellings allows the local authority to recover further costs from the sale proceeds.

As part of the current drive towards energy efficiency £60 million of funds are available under the DoE's Greenhouse Programme to improve the energy efficiency of selected *council estates*. 140 or so schemes are to act as demonstration projects, encouraging other local authorities to follow their example using local funds. Another estate-based programme is the Estate Action Programme, formerly the Priority Estate Project under which funds are available for physical works and establishing new management structures. Within these schemes, the participation of tenants is seen as essential to estate renovation. Local management trusts and community refurbishment schemes are encouraged.

In addition to these housing policies, there are a range of subsidy schemes aimed at urban regeneration. A traditional urban grant system that continues to the present day is the *Urban Programme*. The background to this programme has been covered in Chapter 2. Basically grants are still available under the urban programme for specific projects in the 57 programme authorities which meet social needs in the inner city (Map 7.2). This is now interpreted in terms of improving employment prospects or the ability of inner city residents to compete for jobs or reducing number of derelict site and vacant buildings. Applications are made to and decided by the local authority who pays grants out of its Urban Programme budget. Following the 1988 White Paper *Action for Cities* there has been a shift away from local authorities as the 'natural' agency for urban regeneration. Urban Programme statements prepared by local authorities are now vetted by local chambers of commerce. The whole Urban Programme has been the subject of a private sector-style performance review under the 1985 Urban Programme Management Initiative.

The urban programme framework has been used over the past decade to fund private sector development and redevelopment projects, the public sector monies explicitly attracting a larger amount of private sector money. Previously known as urban development grants or urban regeneration grants, these forms of subsidy have now been replaced by *city grants* available for projects of over £200 000 in City Challenge areas (see below), £500 000 elsewhere. While priority in the city grant applications is given to the City Challenge authorities and then other urban programme authorities, local authorities are not involved in vetting and preparing grant applications or handling grant monies, as is the case with all Urban Programme schemes. Applications are made to and decided by central government, who continue to seek leverage. The

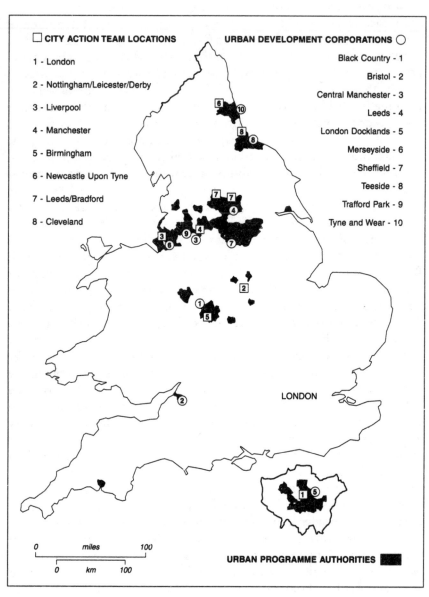

Map 7.2　*Urban policy initiatives*

initial sum of grant must be at least matched by subsequent private investment. In the first year of city grant, 11 local authorities received funding; in 1992/3 20 more authorities were granted £37.5 million p. a. each for five years. Most of this money is a transfer from other programmes, particularly the traditional Urban Programme.

Urban Programme local authorities can also compete for central government monies in an annual round of bids called *City Challenge*. City Challenge bids are required to show evidence of partnership between local government, the business sector and voluntary organisations. Other initiatives which depend on the involvement of the private sector in strategy planning, management and detailed implementation include the activities undertaken by training action points, local employer networks, *training and enterprise councils* (TECs). A particularly important initiative, TECs were announced in the 1988 White Paper on *Employment Policy for the 1990s* and launched in March 1989. They are private sector-led and took over the Youth Training Scheme and Employment Training. The aim was to develop a structure with local flexibility, which would build long-term business–education links. TECs are companies limited by guarantee and may issue shares. Each TEC board has 9–15 directors, two-thirds of whom must be from the private sector with the remaining one-third selected by the private sector directors. The aim is for 80 TECs in England and Wales (Bennett, 1991; Bennett *et al.*, 1992).

The bypassing of local authorities can also be seen clearly in the Merseyside Task Force, set up after the 1981 riots, the other inner city task forces and city action teams (see Map 7.2). In the 16 *task forces*, a small team of civil servants work with local business secondees to stimulate inner city private enterprise. They operate with a small budget available for grants as task force development funds. Over 1986–91, £58 million has been spent on 2600 projects with another £25 million committed. They have no standard approach, responding to local circumstances. As a central government initiative, they report directly to ministers. In the eight *city action teams*, the regional directors of DoE, DTI and DoEm develop strategy approaches to coordinate their separate areas of work. They also work with local government, local business and voluntary organisations. Again their budget is small.

Powers are still available under the 1980 Local Government, Planning and Land Act for designating *enterprise zones* (EZs)(see Summary Box 7.2). These are areas identified by central government, with or without local authority support, in which a range of incentives to development and business activity apply. These incentives include: exemptions from business rates; tax allowances for capital expenditure; exemption from industrial training levies; reduced requirements to provide statistical information; a simplified planning regime using an EZ scheme and rapid development control; priority handling in all regulatory regimes. In the past exemptions from IDCs and development land tax were also relevant. Such zones are designated for a period of 10 years only. As a result, the first of the EZs identified in the first round in 1981 have already been wound up. A second round of 12 EZs was put forward in 1983 but central government has announced that there will be no further designation rounds, although occasional individual designations may be appropriate, for example at Motherwell. The legislation is still in force and it is possible that the scheme may be implemented again on a more substantial scale in the future, for example in response to the coal pit closures.

Summary Box 7.2   *Enterprise zones (1992)*

Dudley	N.E. Lancashire	Sunderland
Glanford	N.W. Kent	Wakefield
Isle of Dogs	Rotherham	Wellingborough
Middlesborough	Scunthorpe	Workington

Despite the removal of many powers and resources from local authorities, they are still given a general responsibility for *economic development* within their areas under Section 33 of the 1986 Local Government and Housing Act and required to produce an annual statement on their policy and activities. This general role is circumscribed by guidance from central government as to the form of this activity and restrictions placed on local government by way of orders. Traditionally local government has had the power raise the result of a 2p rate to fund such economic development. This has now been updated, following the changes in local government finance, to the product of the local authority's population and £2.50 for country councils or non-metropolitan districts, £5.00 for metropolitan districts. While the 1980s saw a range of economic development activities occurring within urban local authorities, there is now a greater emphasis on involving the private sector and voluntary organisations following the 1988 White Paper *Action for Cities*.

Another major urban policy concern has been dealing with *derelict land*. Some such land requires additional aid beyond simply encouraging development proposals. Derelict land grant is available for actions necessary to overcome dereliction and contamination of abandoned sites. Any non-local authority owner of derelict land is eligible and grant is paid for a proportion of the net loss incurred during reclamation work: 80 per cent in assisted areas and derelict land clearance areas (see below), 50 per cent elsewhere. Derelict land is defined for the purposes of giving grants as 'land so damaged by industrial or other development that it is incapable of beneficial use without treatment'. In England the powers to make grants and treat derelict land fall to the local authorities and UDCs. These are only permissive powers but are relatively unrestricted in their scope, drawing as they do on a variety of planning and other legislation. In 1985/6 the budget for approved grants was £75 million, a nine-fold increase from 1974/5. Demand outstrips this allocation, with applications in 1984/5 totalling £165 million. About two-thirds of all reclamation is for hard land uses, stressing the economic rather than environmental role that much derelict land policy plays (Kivell, 1987). There are specific powers for the acquisition and restoration of derelict land within national parks under the National Parks and Access to the Countryside Act 1949. Derelict land clearance areas where enhanced rates of grant apply can be declared by the relevant bodies. Such grants are available for use by voluntary organisations, private companies and nationalised industries as well as local authorities.

Proposals are being put forward to give local authorities more powers in relation to derelict land with the greater use of restoration conditions and, as a last resort measure, the provision for local authorities to reclaim sites and recover the costs from owners. Other possibilities include bonding, bank guarantee and sinking fund schemes to protect against dereliction. Garden festivals have been another approach to derelict land. Five festivals have been funded since 1984: Liverpool, Stoke on Trent, Glasgow, Gateshead and South Wales. Each cost about £50 million to turn an area of dereliction into a landscaped tourist attraction with the aim of securing longer-term investment and environmental improvement when the festival is over. About 23 per cent of the total monies goes on land reclamation, with the remainder used to stage the temporary tourist event.

It is proposed that a new Urban Regeneration Agency will be created in 1993 to oversee policy for reclaiming and developing some 150,000 acres of derelict land in Britain. It will be a policy making executive agency with responsibility for a large slice of the DoE's budget, namely £250 million p. a. for city grant and derelict land grants, together with the work of the public sector industrial developer, English Estates. It is expected to work closely with but not incorporate the UDCs (see below). Legislation will give the Agency compulsory purchase powers and, in designated areas, it will take over development control functions.

Over half of all derelict sites may also be contaminated land and district councils have a duty under Section 143 of the 1990 Environmental Protection Act to compile a register of land that is also potentially contaminated, where additional aid is needed and developers will wish to be aware of the risks. The use of the term 'potentially' contaminated means that large numbers of sites are eligible for registration. The registers will identify sites, prioritise them and classify them in terms of use and need for long-term monitoring. These are due to be made public by April 1993, but concern over the effects of the register on land markets has sent proposals for implementation back to the drawing board.

☐ *Wales*

In Wales a number of agencies are involved in urban and economic regeneration activities: the Welsh Development Agency (WDA); Development Board for Rural Wales; Land Authority for Wales, a survivor from the Community Land Scheme of the 1970s; Cardiff Bay Development Corporation, a UDC (see below); Welsh Tourist Board; and Housing for Wales, a housing association. The WDA administers the grant schemes, including derelict land funds, and certain specific programmes: Landscape Wales and Urban Development Wales. There is also a Programme for the Valleys to run from January 1988 to March 1993 which coordinates agencies involved in regeneration of industrialised valley areas.

☐ *Scotland*

In Scotland the Scottish Development Agency (SDA) has pioneered a number of programmes in the past with emphasis on a sectoral approach using local self-help to achieve economic development. The Glasgow Eastern Area Renewal (GEAR) project is one such project which operated through the 1970s and 1980s. Under a 1988 White Paper *New Life for Urban Scotland* four further partnership initiatives were set up for Glasgow, Paisley, Edinburgh and Dundee. Many of these initiatives were instigated by the SDA. This role is now taken by Scottish Enterprise. The sister organisation, Highlands and Islands Enterprise, was created out of the Highlands and Islands Development Board.

The emphasis on enterprise is now a key theme in recent urban regeneration policy. This follows the 1988 White Paper on *Scottish*

Enterprise: a new approach to training and enterprise creation and The Scottish Office document *New Life for Urban Scotland* of the same year. Another example of this approach is given by the 22 local enterprise councils (LECs). These will be coordinated by Scottish Enterprise and Highland and Island Enterprise. These bodies take on the responsibility for economic development and for central government training programmes (Fairley, 1992). It should be noted that the requirement for local authorities to prepare economic development plans does not apply in Scotland.

☐ Northern Ireland

In Northern Ireland, the Department of Economic Development is in charge of local economic regeneration. Because of the political and economic situation here, economic development has always had a high priority and economic development policy has been highly centralised. Historically there has been a high level of reliance on government grants, and also EC grants, and on a restricted range of major employment opportunities. The latest strategy was set out in the 1987 *Pathfinder* document which aimed to develop the area's independence from grants, subsidies, public sector employment and multinational investment.

■ Transferring land to the private sector

Summary Box 7.3   *Land privatisation*

Organisation:	Public corporations
Focus:	Transfer of landownership
Aim:	Urban regeneration
Timing:	Ad hoc disposal
Scope:	Public land
Planning tool:	Leverage

A key theme throughout the 1980s was privatisation: of nationalised industries, of public utilities, and of public land (see Summary Box 7.3). The transfer of land from public to private ownership was presented as a key factor, in itself, in generating development, wealth and economic activity. A number of examples of this approach can be found.

Urban development corporations (UDCs) were set up by the 1980 Local Government Planning and Land Act (see Figure 7.2). They involved the transfer of large areas of land, usually from other public bodies such as statutory undertakers, to independent corporations, often by way of a vesting instrument which shortcuts complicated and lengthy procedures for the sale of statutory undertakers' land. UDCs are designated by statutory instrument and require Parliamentary approval. Public objections to designation are possible only via a petition to the Select Committee considering the designation.

The UDCs have wide ranging powers including that of purchasing land in the designated area. A UDC can apply to the Secretary of State for a vesting order to transfer public land to the corporation's ownership. They also have powers of land assembly, reclamation, servicing land and development or of disposal to developers. Substantial Treasury funds are available to package the land for sale onto the private sector as development sites.

UDCs usually hold all development control powers for their areas including conservation powers over conservation areas, listed buildings and preserved trees. In some cases local authorities carry out development control functions on an agency basis for the UDC and, in the case of Cardiff UDC, a partnership arrangement was made between the UDC and the city council. Although UDCs do not have formal development planning powers, their development schemes are effectively de facto local plans. Such schemes are, however, corporate planning documents and not open to public consultation and scrutiny in the same way as a development plan. The UDC submits proposals directly to the Secretary of State for development of land in its area. After consultation with the local authorities the Secretary of State can then approve the proposals with or without modifications. Planning permission for all development is granted via a special development order for any conforming development.

The essence of UDCs is the discretion they have to promote the development of their areas. Altogether 11 UDCs have been designated: Merseyside and London Docklands in 1981; Trafford Park, Cardiff Bay, the Black Country, Teeside and Tyne and Wear in 1987; Central Manchester, Leeds and Sheffield in 1988; with Bristol in 1989. Later UDCs have been much reduced in scale compared to earlier ones. The last four received only £15 million each over five years compared to £443 million over 1981–8 for the London Docklands Development Corporation and approximately £150 million each over 6 years for the rest. The overall budget is £470 million in 1991/2 for a programme covering over 16,000 hectares. There is further discussion of UDCs in Exhibit 8.2.

It was hoped that a similar approach could be made to work for *housing estates*. The most well-known example of privatisation is probably the sale of individual council houses to tenants. Although the numbers sold under this initiative are now well down on the peak years, the provisions for sale still exist and a new rent-to-mortgage scheme has been introduced. Tenants can purchase their home at a discount to market value and with the aid of a public sector mortgage. The 1988 Housing Act made provision for the privatisation of whole estates of council houses under the 'pick-a-landlord' scheme. The new owner could be either a developer, housing association or tenants' cooperative.

But the housing privatisation initiative most closely akin to the UDC is the creation of housing action trusts (HATs) under the 1988 Housing Act. These are designated by the Secretary of State and are eligible for public funds to aid estate improvement. The designation process involves consultation with affected local authorities, a ballot of all tenants (a majority of whom must vote in favour) and debate in the Parliament. However, the Secretary of State has wide discretion in making the designation. The resulting HAT is run by a small board of five to eleven people with all the housing powers of the local authority, as well as planning powers and certain public health powers. These HATs are intended to be temporary institutions with an expected life of five years. The original aim was that the housing would be disposed of before the end of the five years. On such disposal tenants become assured tenants, unless they are transferred back to a local authority. Any disposal must be to an 'approved landlord' and local authorities do have first refusal.

It was intended that the bulk of the monies would come from the private sector. The return on this private investment would be in terms of profits on sales forward or increased rents, improvement by a HAT resulting in a shift from fair rents to 'reasonable' rents, that is an increase in rents. However, designation was dependent on local consultation and such arrangements proved unattractive to tenants and, indeed, to developers. Recent revisions to HATs maintain fair rents and allow for later transfer back to the public sector and the most common conclusion will be for the housing to be transferred back to the local authority with no change in tenants' standing.

Elsewhere attempts have been made to transfer land from public bodies to the private sector by two means. First, the 1980 Local Government, Planning and Land Act created *Part X Registers* on which all land held by public bodies surplus to their requirements was to be identified. This register was a public document and the idea was that publicising this land would lead to offers for its purchase by a developer who would bring it into economically beneficial use. The Secretary of State also has the power to direct the sale of land held on the register. From 1991, there are stricter regulations requiring local authorities to publicise information about unused and underused land, in sites of 0.1 hectare or more. This information must be updated each March and made readily available to the public.

Second, central government has frequently encouraged public bodies to sell their land in order to improve their financial position. (This did not apply to council housing, however, where local authorities were constrained in terms of their use of 'right-to-buy' receipts.) In order to raise funds a variety of bodies have been selling their land portfolios: local education authorities selling playing fields, health authorities selling institutions no longer required under the 'Care in the Community' policy, even local authorities selling their graveyards in one celebrated case in the London Borough of Westminster. This has created substantial pressures for the grant of planning permission and subsequent development, often in greenfield or green belt areas. Such release of land has not necessarily been in line with the goal of urban regeneration either.

Under the 1991 consultation document *Encouraging the Use of Vacant Public Sector Land* there are further proposals to transfer public sector land to private landowners. Franchising has been proposed whereby options to purchase all the vacant land held by public bodies in a defined area would be offered to a single purchaser, who would then act as a 'pure' developer, reparcelling land for sale and construction.

□ *Wales*

Of the agencies listed above as involved in urban regeneration, two are specifically focused on transferring land to the private sector. The Cardiff UDC is charged with transforming the Cardiff Bay area. And the Land Authority for Wales retains a role from the 1970s Community Land Scheme in buying land for resale to developers.

□ *Scotland*

UDCs, one of the main initiatives discussed above, do not apply in Scotland. Similarly the privatisation of council houses has had much less effect, with 5 per cent of the public stock sold in Scotland compared to 15 per cent in England and Wales (Midwinter *et al.*, 1991, p. 174). Direct land privatisation measures have, perhaps, been less emphasised in Scotland. But there has been considerable scope for the transfer of assets to the private sector arising from institutional change. The replacement of the SDA by Scottish Enterprise, with its change in policy emphasis, creates the potential for selling the former SDA's assets. And the formation of Scottish Homes from an amalgamation of the Scottish Special Housing Association and the Housing Corporation in Scotland gives rise to similar possibilities, given that Scottish Homes was given a remit to act in a strategic planning capacity, rather than as a direct housing agency.

■ Transport planning

Summary Box 7.4   *Transport planning*

Organisation:	Department of Transport, county councils, Passenger Transport Authorities, Passenger Transport Executives
Focus:	Transport networks
Aim:	Mobility
Timing:	Rolling programmes
Scope:	Network boundaries
Planning tool:	Public investment and subsidy

While transport planners frequently emphasise the need for coordination in the planning of transport networks to create an efficient integrated system, the reality is closer to fragmentation of policy making both between and within transport sectors at central and local government level (see Summary Box 7.4).

Central government, in the form of the DoTr and counterparts within the Welsh and Scottish Offices, have responsibility for motorway and trunk roads while local authorities cover other roads. Central government has more extensive road responsibility in London following the abolition of the GLC and are proposing the creation of a Director of London Transport. All rail services, except local services in metropolitan areas, are also the responsibility of central government.

In most metropolitan areas, passenger transport executives (PTEs) have been created to administer public transport, both local rail and road, on behalf of passenger transport authorities (PTAs), themselves a joint board of district representatives from the relevant metropolitan district councils. These PTEs used to operate their own bus services but these services have now been formed into independent companies, supported by public subsidy. Following the abolition of the GLC, the London PTA and PTE were not resurrected as in other metropolitan areas. Here all public transport remains under central government control through London Regional Transport and British Rail. Outside these metropolitan areas, county councils have the duty to coordinate an efficient system of public transport. The principal means of achieving this is via specific local subsidies.

Bus deregulation abolished fares control, network subsidy and coordinated planning of bus services. Under the 1985 Transport Act, operative from 1986, a streamlined system of registration for private bus service was introduced and all PTEs and district councils had to create companies for their bus services. Some of these are being privatised. All such arms' length services had to operate according to market criteria of viability, and local transport authorities were given a general duty to promote value for money and not inhibit competition. Subsidy is now restricted to social desirable routes (Stoker, 1991, pp. 216–8). As a result of this system the level of public subsidy to the bus system has fallen by 30 per cent.

In terms of policy documents, separate and ad hoc policy statements for the different transport sectors are issued by the DoTr. Only in the case of motorways and trunk roads is there a requirement to issue an annual policy statement, in this case in the form of a White Paper on roads. This lists the programmed roads for construction by region, following advice from the Standing Advisory Committee on Trunk Roads which considers national road needs. Currently this roadbuilding programme is supported by substantial funds on the basis of its contribution to economic prosperity.

Local policy documents comprise development plans, transport policies and programmes (TPPs) and passenger transport plans (PTPs). Structure and local plans are required to include traffic management proposals. And PPG12 amplifies this in terms of policies and proposals for the development of the transport network and related services, including indications of timescales and priorities. Traffic management is defined as including the coordination of public transport services, the movement of freight, the control of parking and the improvement of cyclist and pedestrian safety. Particular emphasis is given though to proposals for improvements to the road network and safeguarding land for new routes which will be developed within 10 years. Roads which already have permission may not be the subject of an objection to a local plan but it is also intended that new road permissions should conform with the relevant local plan. Transport policies and programmes were originally intended to be broad ranging documents integrating transport and structure plan policies, but they have been narrowed in scope to the point where they comprise an annual single purpose bid to central government for highways capital funding. These funds are provided in the form of a Transport Supplementary Grant, a form of block grant. Local authority attempts to use the general rate fund to supplement this grant were curtailed by the House of Lords ruling over the GLC's 'Fares Fair' policy. PTPs focus on public transport but bus deregulation has limited their relevance.

Specific proposals for *major transport schemes*, usually roadbuilding, are subject to DoTr procedures. Under these procedures public inquiries are held for all major schemes where there are objections and local authorities usually follow similar procedures for other road proposals. The Inspector is chosen by the Lord Chancellor, rather than by the Minister of Transport as has been the case in the past. Information on the reasons for the road proposal must be published in advance along with practicable alternative routes. Consultants' reports must be made available to protestors and library facilities provided. This includes the advice on landscaping of trunk roads and advice on alternative routes provided by the Expert Advisory Committee on Landscape Treatment of Trunk Roads. All trunk roads are subject to an environmental assessment following the 1992 DoTr manual *Assessing the Environmental Impact of Road Schemes* proposed by the Standing Advisory Committee on Trunk Road Assessment. There has, however, been a tendency to use Private Bills for new railways and tramways. This includes both major development associated the Channel Tunnel and various innovative urban light rail schemes. Under the Private Bill procedure, the proposal is heard and considered within the Houses of Parliament. There is no public local inquiry and the method of making representations is both archaic and expensive. Under the 1992 Transport and Works Act, the private bill procedure has been reformed, so that proposals for new railways, tramways, etc. are covered by an order making procedure which is subject to Ministerial rather than Parliamentary approval. This provides for public consultation, environmental assessment and a public local inquiry if there are objections.

The general emphasis is currently towards reduced subsidy to public transport and greater private sector involvement in all transport schemes. Subsidy to British Rail on an operating basis is being cut back and Network South East in particular is being asked to increase its coverage of current costs by fares from around 80 per cent to 100 per cent in the foreseeable future. Separate business sectors have been created within British Rail to which quasi-commercial remits have been applied, in anticipation of privatisation beginning in 1992/3. The government has been forced by a spate of rail accidents and subsequent inquiry reports to increase capital spending on the railways to improve safety. However, new rail projects are expected to be virtually self-financing. This applies to the various light rail schemes which are being implemented across the country. It also applies to the massive Channel Rail Tunnel project, which has struggled to raise sufficient private finance for all its stages, and to the Channel Rail link, effectively halting its implementation once the full cost of all the environmental features became clear.

The government has recently announced proposals to increase the contributions property developers make to road improvements. The intention is that the DoTr would examine draft development plans and provide costings for the road improvements that would be necessary as a result of new development. Not surprisingly, this has met opposition from the development industry.

However, transport policy more than any other area of planning activity is affected by the environmental challenge arising from increased knowledge of global climate change. This could well result in a shift from private to public transport in the wake of a carbon tax and the introduction of policies such as road pricing and road calming. The 1991 Road Traffic Act is a small step in this direction. It provides for a full network of red routes by 1996, routes on which all stopping and parking is restricted. The Act also introduces a new system of decriminalised on-street parking control operated by local authorities. Local authorities can also prepare parking policies, subject to DoTr guidance, which match the needs and character of their areas. Residential areas may be designated as 20 mph zones as part of local traffic calming measures. These measures have proved popular with many urban local authorities and are going some way to altering local traffic management and driving patterns. However, a shift towards a more sustainable transport policy is likely to be much more far reaching. The European Commission are already considering moves in this direction with a 1992 Green Paper on *The Impact of Transport on the Environment: a Community Strategy for 'sustainable mobility'*, to be followed shortly by a White Paper. The Royal Commission on Environmental Pollution are also due to report on this topic in 1994.

□ *Scotland*

The emphasis in transport policy has been similar in Scotland to the rest of Britain. Deregulation of urban public transport was a UK-wide initiative and the initial decision not to privatise the Scottish Bus Group was later reversed.

Further reading

Lawless (1991), Parkinson (1989) and Bovaird (1992) provide a guide to the intricacies of urban policy. The reliance on discretionary measures and initiatives by central and local government means that legislation and comparable sources are less helpful here. Similarly the shift in urban policy towards marketing reduces the value to students of many annual reports from central and local government and quangos. Useful guides to the Scottish experience are found in Gillet (1983), which also covers housing and transport in some detail, and Donnison and Middleton (1987), which focuses on the GEAR initiative (see also Brindley *et al.*, 1989). The TEC/LEC policy initiative has not been dealt with at length here and can be followed up in Fairley (1992), Bennett (1991), Bennett *et al.* (1992), and Stoker (1991, p. 69).

Transport policy has been dealt with here fairly briefly and there is, indeed, a lack of texts which deal with the contemporary transport planning system. Richards (1990) provides a brief overview of transport issues, with more substantial coverage in Hoyle and Knowles (1992). Both texts are well illustrated. For details of procedure and policy, the reader is refered to the Department of Transport's own publications. The recent trends towards a proposed greening of transport policy is indicated by the European Commission's 1992 Green Paper on transport, with very readable, grass-roots accounts provide by Sherlock (1990) and Engwicht (1992). An excellent analysis, in the North American context, of alternative measures for reducing congestion is found in Downs (1992).

■ *PART 3* ■

THE POLITICS OF PLANNING

Part 3 outlines the main institutions and agencies which together formulate and implement the policies of the planning system outlined in Part 2. It begins by considering the various state organisations at central and local government level and in the various 'quangos' and international arenas. It goes on to examine the current conception of professional planners' role within the policy process. Finally it looks at the various interfaces between the public and the planning system, through pressure groups, party political pressure and the climate of public opinion.

Throughout use is made of inset 'Exhibits' of particular policies, procedures and issues. This serves to both amplify the operation of the planning system and to raise questions about the politics of planning. The four theoretical perspectives identified at the end of Part 1 as the most relevant for understanding planning in 1990s – the New Right, the New Left, liberal political economy and institutional approach – are used to identify key issues in these Exhibits. Each Exhibit is kept short and deliberately provocative in style. It is hoped that they will be used to stimulate debate in classes and seminars. To this end, a limited number of further reading references is given at the end of each Exhibit.

■ *Chapter 8* ■

The State

This chapter looks at the different organisations which together constitute the public sector where planning is concerned, outlining the main features of the different types of organisation. Four types are distinguished: central government, local government, quangos and international organisations, particularly the European Commission. Much of the detail of how these different organisations are involved in different areas of planning practice has been covered in the separate sections on particular policies. It is not intended to rehearse those details here; rather, the emphasis will be on the characteristics of the different types of organisation and the broad patterns of interrelation. The chapter begins with a brief discussion of this interrelation in the policy process.

■ The policy process

The term 'the state' can suggest a unified set of public sector organisations, responsible for formulating and implementing public policy. This is a view of the state fostered by the liberal political economy approach with its emphasis on rational decision making within the public sector. However, in practice the state is neither unified, nor is it the sole arena for the policy process. In this chapter a number of different organisations within the state are reviewed, ranging from parish councils to the Commission of the European Community. These organisations interact in a series of complex dynamics in debates and actions over policy. Within each organisation, there is a different balance between the influence of politicians, administrators, and professionals, each with their own approach to policy issues and their own claims to legitimate influence. State organisations are also subject to influence, pressure and claims from the public, exerted through pressures groups, political parties and general public opinion.

The policy process involves this wide range of actors and institutions. It is possible to provide a diagrammatic representation of the interrelation between these actors and institutions (for example, see Midwinter *et al.*, 1991, Figure 4.1) but a full coverage of the complexity of relations can render such a diagram unintelligible while a simplified version can, of necessity, highlight only certain aspects. In the following it is preferred to draw attention to specific linkages in the context of particular institutions. In any case, the precise pattern of the linkage with vary depending on the focus adopted. Stoker, discussing central–local relations, defines a number of policy networks (1991, p. 148): territorial communities, based in regions such as Scotland or Wales; policy communities, based on specific policy areas such as housing renewal; the national community of local government (the national pressure groups representing local government), an example of an interorganisational network; producer networks based round a specific industry; and issues networks, the inner city problem being an example. Each policy network comprises a particular set of linkages between state organisations, and between the state and outside groups.

Linkages between specific organisations only tell one part of the story. The strength of that linkage vis-à-vis others and the direction of power or dependency it represents is essential knowledge for understanding the interaction of organisations in practice. Rhodes (1981) has analysed this power-dependency relation between state organisations, particularly central and local government, as bound up with the resources available to the various organisations. Such resources may take five forms: financial, including the power to levy taxes or to give grants; constitutional and legal, set down in legislation, including the various reserve powers granted central government under planning acts; hierarchical, based on the supervisory role of one organisation over another and including the various forms of planning guidance that central government provides; political, founded on the electoral base of the organisation, either directly elected as with central and local government, or with political representation, say, on the board of a quango; and informational, using the expertise of professionals within an organisation, particularly important, say, in some pollution control quangos. These resources are used by actors in state institutions in a complex process of exchange, where resources are employed to achieve each organisation's goals according to the understood 'rules of the game'.

The institutional approach is particularly adept in understanding these rules of the game and the interaction of actors within a policy framework. It looks for the variety of resources used by actors in achieving policy outcomes. But the issue of resources is also relevant to the other three approaches outlined towards the end of Chapter 3. For the New Right there is an emphasis on the extent of resources that the state in general commands, particularly financial but also in other terms, in relation to the public and private sector organisations, and on the difference between the role of the individual in relation to the state compared to the freedom and power of the individual in the market-place. The 'Citizen's Charter' idea is supposed to reduce this difference.

The New Left also see an imbalance between the resources available to some sectors of the public and the state but, seeing scope for public sector action to restructure the distribution of resources in society, they pay more attention to the resources available to different state institutions. By using the institutions of the state, redistribution may occur. Knowledge of the resources held by those institutions which the working class and other disadvantaged groups may capture and use in their struggles is therefore a necessary element of political action. The development of political resources is an active dimension of altering power-dependency relations with the state. Meanwhile for the liberal political economist, resources are both an input into rational policy formulation and a constraint on policy implementation. Knowledge of the distribution of resources across state organisations gives an indication of the institutions which need to be brought into the policy process and where certain policy functions should best reside. In these decisions, financial and informational resources will be given particular importance, the others considered more amenable to change through policy reform (hierarchical and constitutional) or less relevant (political).

■ Central government

The British government structure involves three main institutions at the national level: the Cabinet, which formulates Government policy; Parliament, which is the legislature and passes binding policy in the form of Acts; and the executive in the form of the civil service which provides non-partisan advice to Ministers and organises the implementation of policy, according to the standard constitutional account. In practice, the formal division of labour is overlaid with a complex pattern of interaction between the different roles. In the day-to-day running of the planning system, it is the executive that is most involved. The Cabinet may propose and the Houses of Parliament decide or legitimate new policy, but it is the civil service who administers. All three institutions will be the focus of lobbying for policy change since all three have a degree of influence on new and emerging policies. The influence of the executive in shaping new policy initiatives has been extensive in the past, although the 1980s has seen a shift towards greater ministerial control over policy formulation (Laffin and Young, 1990). The implementation of such new policy ideas remains the concern of the executive and it is the executive that has the ongoing responsibility for the operation of the system. The only exception to this is the system of Parliamentary committees which provide ongoing supervision of the activities of the executive. The House of Commons Select Committee on the Environment is particularly important as a watchdog over the planning system. Royal Commissions, established by Parliament, can also play such a role and the Royal Commission on Environmental Pollution (RCEP) has proved influential over the years.

Summary Box 8.1   *Links with other institutions: central government*

Cabinet:	Parliament	
	Executive	
	European Community	
	Political Parties	
Parliament:	Cabinet	
	Political Parties	
	Executive:	Select Committees
		Royal Commissions
Executive:	Cabinet	
	Parliament	
	Local Government	
	Quangos	
	Pressure Groups	

The executive, or civil service, are distinguished by a particular administrative culture. Civil servants are career administrators and generalists. They are not trained experts in the areas they administer nor is much use made of political appointees. They are sensitive to changes of political bias and hence tend to avoid controversial issues if at all possible (Chapman, 1984, p. 175). There is a strong sense of departmental loyalty and ethos, so that civil servants in one department tend to see themselves as much in (a sometimes conflicting) relation to other departments as to outside groups whether pressure groups, quangos or local government (see Summary Box 8.1). These outside groups are often perceived as 'clients' of the department so that the world outside the executive is seen by civil servants to be divided up into the responsibilities of the various departments. Overall the civil service culture is a 'bounded culture' (Chapman, 1984, p. 178) which politicians, professions, policy advisors and the public can find difficult to penetrate.

Much of the actual implementation of planning policy for which the executive is responsible will in fact be delegated to regional- or local-level institutions. These may be local offices of central government departments or ministries, or delegation may involve more autonomous institutions: local government or quasi-governmental organisations (quangos) discussed below. Certain aspects of central government activities may also be hived off to quangos operating at the national level. At times it may be difficult to distinguish between the work of a central government department and that of a quango; it is a matter of degree. For example, the system for appeals against development control decisions by local authorities is administered by the Planning Inspectorate. This used to be a branch of the DoE exercising central government control over local authority decisions. But during the 1980s the DoE emphasised a view of the Inspectorate as an independent body operating as a neutral, sometimes professionally informed, referee in planning disputes. The proposals to charge fees for planning appeals and make the Planning Inspectorate a self-financing executive agency are an extension of this approach. Indeed it has been a feature of central government policy in the urban and environmental field to favour the creation of agencies at arm's length from the Government and the executive. The implications of this trend will be discussed further in the section on quangos below.

At central government level, the main institution responsible for the planning system in England is the DoE (see Summary Box 8.2). This 'super-department' was created in 1970 under the Heath administration, modelled on the Scottish Development Department set up in 1962 (Selman, 1988). It currently has 3000 staff based in London alone. It combined the former ministries of housing and local government, public building and works, and transport and was charged with the responsibility for 'the whole range of functions which affect people's living environment'. In fact it focused and continues to focus heavily on housing (particularly local authority housing), local government (especially local government taxation) and overseeing the operation of the land use planning system. As of February 1989 the staff within the DoE dealing with purely environmental issues (narrowly defined to exclude land use planning and the built environment) amounted to only 10 per cent (McCormick, 1991, p. 17). The DoE also acts as the 'sponsoring' department for the construction industry, a function performed by the DTI for most other industries. It also has a regional structure (as does the DoTr), which can act as 'the eyes and ears' of central government (Stoker, 1991, p. 145).

Recently the DoE has lost certain responsibilities due to the creation of a new Ministry of National Heritage in 1992. This covers historic buildings, royal parks and ancient monuments as well as sports, the performing arts and the media. It has taken over the listing of historic

Summary Box 8.2   *Central government departments relevant to planning*

Base	Department	Directorates and Groups
Whitehall	*Environment*	Environmental Policy and Analysis
		Housing and Urban Group
		Finance and Local Government
		Planning, Rural Affairs and Water
		Planning and Development Control
		Construction Policy
		Environmental Protection (incl. Her Majesty's Inspectorate of Pollution)
	Ministry of Agriculture, Fisheries and Food	
	Transport	
	Energy	
	Trade and Industry	
	Treasury	
	Ministry of National Heritage (from 1992)	
Wales	*Welsh Office*	
Scotland	*The Scottish Office*	
	Environment:	Environment and Planning
		Housing and Local Government
		Statistics
		Inquiry Reporters
		Building
		Engineering, Water and Waste
		Her Majesty's Industrial Pollution Inspectorate
	Industry:	Urban Policy and New Towns
	Agriculture and Fisheries	
Northern Ireland	*Northern Ireland Office*	
	Agriculture (NI)	
	Economic Development (NI)	
	Environment (NI)	

Source: Civil Service Yearbook (1992).

buildings but the DoE retains its development control function in respect of such buildings.

Certain key policy areas remain outside the DoE's remit. Energy planning has always comes under the DoEn. Industry policy, including selective grant aiding of industry in particular regions and locations is the responsibility of the DTI. The proposal to set up an Urban Regeneration Agency, under the remit of the DTI will further shift urban policy out of the DoE. The Ministry of Agriculture, Fisheries and Food (MAFF) has the overall remit for agricultural land in the countryside. In addition, transport functions were removed from the DoE in 1976 to a separate DoTr, which interprets its role largely in terms of road construction. Herington has noted the conflicts that exist between these central government departments over the direction of planning policy. For example, the separation between the DoTr and DoE, and hence between land use and transport planning, means that the 'DoTr has been uninterested in the spatial impact of its programme' (1984, p. 75), both in the past in relation to green belt protection and urban regeneration and now with regard to constraining energy consumption and pollution. Ironically both the nature conservation concerns of the DoE and any policy of planned urban growth, potentially brings the Department into conflict with MAFF.

Even within the DoE, separate directorates or groups will sometimes clash. While the housing and construction sections may seek to promote speculative housebuilding, the planning directorate may be seeking to constrain it. While the inner city directorate may promote concepts such as EZs where planning regulations are relaxed, the environmental protection group will be concerned over the possible consequences for local air and water quality. In particular, 'the present division of responsibility within the DoE clearly makes it difficult for it to coordinate the twin policies of countryside protection and urban growth' (Herington, 1984, p. 63). Separating central government functions off and handing them to quangos, such as the Countryside Commission which took over many rural concerns in 1982, or even private sector bodies such as the privatised water companies which replaced the regional water authorities in England and Wales in 1990, will only make this lack of policy coordination worse, in the absence of strong mechanisms for integration.

Over all the work of the different departments stands the financial control exercised by the Treasury. As Chapman (1984, p. 176) says: 'The Treasury has, in effect, a controlling role over all other departments through its financial responsibilities.' In addition Chapman notes that this functional control has been reinforced by the Treasury's elite status within the civil service and by the flow of staff in and out of the Treasury to elsewhere in the executive. Similarly the financial work of the DoE, in regard to local government finance, has been a major influence on DoE's other policy work. The policy on the uniform business rate may have had at least as much influence in determining the location of industry as urban policy or land use planning.

The problem of developing a unified policy stance within the DoE and within central government more generally is shown in the recent Environment White Paper (1990) *This Common Inheritance*. This was a document designed to respond to growing environmental concern, both at a local level and in relation to global issues such as the enhanced greenhouse effect and the depletion of the ozone layer. It aimed to be broad in focus. 'Environment' was loosely defined to include the built heritage, the countryside, nuclear waste, genetically modified organisms and energy use. The problem of interdepartmental coordination was met by a standing committee of Cabinet Ministers who considered the draft document and advised on their particular ministry's concerns. Despite these arrangements, the White Paper was widely criticised for the extent to which it sacrificed demonstrable commitment to achieving environmental goals by way of institutional change and innovative policy tools, to the gloss of presentation. Little in the way of substantial new initiatives was announced. Instead the emphasis was on listing the existing policies and practices of the various, largely divorced, government departments and quangos.

The standing committee of Cabinet Ministers has been retained and a minister nominated in each department responsible for the environmental implications of that department's policies and spending programmes. But this has not really met the criticisms concerning inter-departmental and intra-departmental conflicts over policies and objectives, nor the environmentalists' concerns that the current institutional arrangements create a degree of inertia which prevents changed policies to enhance environmental protection.

Outside England, the Welsh, Scottish and Northern Ireland Offices are the key central government departments. The Welsh Office is the least powerful of the three. It largely takes the lead from the DoE, setting out parallel policies for the Principality where necessary. Most planning policy is common for England and Wales. In contrast, The Scottish Office is a much more powerful institution. There is a quite distinctive administrative and legal structure in Scotland with the promise or threat of devolution and a Scottish Assembly standing behind the institutional arrangements for Scotland. There are many policy areas, such as planning, where The Scottish Office has widespread autonomy, and other areas where the responsibility between Whitehall and The Scottish Office is at least ambiguous (Midwinter *et al.*, 1991, p. 79).

The situation in Northern Ireland is quite distinct. The centralisation of most planning powers within the Northern Ireland Office and the curtailed powers of local government since 1973 both creates departments with more diverse responsibilities and absolves the DoE of many supervisory and coordinating functions.

The extent, scope and continuing growth of the bureaucracy of the executive at central level has given much ammunition to the theorists of the New Right. They have pointed to the empire-building tendencies of faceless bureaucrats, extending their control over an increasingly restricted and frustrated private sector, and also citizenry. The liberal political economists have been of little support to the bureaucracy against this critique for there is limited evidence of rational decision-making, and examples of administrative failure abound. Neither has the institutionalist approach proved useful to the executive. Primarily developed to account for local level planning, its normative statements on the mediating role that the state can play is undercut by first, the lack of consultation and negotiation over many areas of policy and second, by the inequitable structuring of any mediation that does occur, which the approach also draws attention to. The discussion of the relationship between pressure groups and central government in Chapter 10 highlights this aspect. Based on similar empirical material, the New Left continues the longstanding critique of marxism that capitalist interests have captured large elements of the central state and, instead, has placed its faith in local-level mobilisation against the centre.

Thus central government bureaucracy finds little support and much criticism among the various theoretical frameworks. Yet even the vigorous critique of Thatcherism did not, in practice, reduce the power of the executive. Many functions have been transferred to 'executive agencies' or quangos but this is largely a transfer within the state. And, many commentators from the New Left (for example, Hall, 1988) have argued that the process of conflict with local government that the centre engaged in during the 1980s actually involved a great centralisation of power and the strengthening of central government control. The power of the central state is, in the end, highly attractive to those who seek to govern whether from the Left or Right or in the name of professional expertise and thus a strong executive remains an attractive instrument of government. This is the counterpart of attitudes held concerning local government.

■ Local government

Byrne (1986, p. 6) describes local government as a form of self-government providing for local initiative and freedom. As such it goes beyond both the decentralisation of central government functions to local offices and their delegation to non-elected but quasi-autonomous organisations (see Summary Box 8.3). Local government and central government exist in an uneasy partnership, both claiming authority by virtue of their elected nature but with central government clearly in a position of greater power through various financial and administrative controls. Central government can also claim greater legitimacy through the higher turnout at general than local elections (Stoker, 1991, p. 51). Local authorities are, after all, the creation of statutes enacted at the central level. They are bound quite tightly by the doctrine of 'ultra vires' which means that local authorities can undertake only activities for which they have specific statutory authority; this contrasts with private sector bodies, who can undertake any activity unless prohibited by law. It is also distinct from the situation in many other European local government systems.

Summary Box 8.3   *Links with other institutions: beyond the centre*

Local Government:	Executive
	Quangos
	Political parties
	Pressure groups
	European Community
Quangos:	Executive
	Local government
	(Pressure groups)

However, the existence of a variety of resources at both central and local government level ensures that local government does not degenerate into a mere agency of the centre (see the discussion of Rhodes, 1981, above). As a result, 'difference and the possibility of conflict is structured in to the relationship' between central and local government (Ranson *et al.*, 1985, p. 24). The conflictual aspect has been particularly apparent since the mid-1970s, with the issue of local government finance being a flashpoint. Conflict is based in the fact that local government comprises political institutions capable of choice but it is exacerbated by organisational differences (see Summary Box 8.4), a lack of learning at both levels, a fragmented approach within central government (see above) and the random nature of the set of policy instruments used in the relationship between the tiers.

There are a number of specific control mechanisms included within the various policies of the planning system by which central government can limit the actions of local government. Many of these have been indicated in Part 2. For example, development control decisions are subject to appeal to the Secretary of State. There are numerous reserve powers held by the Secretary of State. Central government can influence

Summary Box 8.4   *Differences between central and local government organisations*

Central Government	Local Government
National, international	Local
Large scale	Smaller scale
Administrative culture	Professional culture
Ministerial control	Control by committee
Sets framework for action	Engaged in service delivery plus quasi-entrepreneurial activity

Source: Adapted from Ranson *et al.* (1985) pp. 27–8.

local areas by a variety of designations, even removing areas from local government control by UDCs. There are also the supervisory aspects of the planning system and the mass of advice and information flowing between the tiers.

Most important though, local authorities are dependent on central government for finance; 85 per cent of local authority income now comes direct from central government as grant. This level of grant, the revenue support grant, is based on centrally assessed notions of needs known as standard spending assessments. Central government also closely circumscribes the amount that local authorities can raise from local taxation and loans. Local business rates are now levied according to their assessed property values and a nationally set, uniform rate poundage: rates paid are equal to the rateable values of the property multiplied by the rate poundage. The receipts from the uniform business rate are then redistributed according to local authorities' share of population. Local taxation of residents (first domestic rates, then the community charge or poll tax, and now the council tax) is levied according to central government regulation. The amount that can be raised annually through loans and credit is also limited so that councils cannot exceed an annual capital expenditure allocation. Within housing, controls are even tighter. There can be no transfer from or into the housing accounts, say from the general rate fund. A fixed percentage of housing capital receipts (largely from council house and land sales) must go to repaying debt with only the remainder available for new capital spending. The budget of a local authority may be 'capped' if central government consider it too high, and this may 'cap' local domestic taxation.

Changes in local government finance and the use of central government powers have meant that the relation of 'control' has increasingly replaced that of 'partnership' in recent years. A number of strategies have been used in engineering this shift: legislation, minimal consultation, targeted funding, bypassing local government procedures, and reorganisation and reform of local government (Stoker, 1991, pp. 153–7). The goal of this control has been fundamentally to alter the nature of local government. As Stewart and Stoker argue (1989, p. 2):

> From the mid-1980s the Government's concern about local government became wider in its focus and more far-reaching in its implications. The Government's programme has gone beyond the search for public expenditure restraint to a more broad-ranging attempt to restructure local government.

Stewart and Stoker identify a number of key themes in this restructuring process: the fragmentation of responsibilities, with service delivery, regulation and strategic planning shared with other institutions and agencies; a commitment to local authorities competing with private sector bodies and in the process separating service delivery from the responsibility for that service; a closer relationship between receiving the service and paying for it and a greater emphasis on consumer choice; all involving a challenge to current producer interests within local government and the development of a commitment to a more 'business-like' management.

Examples of this can be seen in: the opening up of building regulations inspections to approved private sector consultants; the payment of fees for planning applications; the competitive tendering for refuse collection and the creation of arm's length bodies for waste disposal; the need for direct labour organisations (local authorities' internal construction, repair and maintenance organisations) to achieve a 5 per cent return, keep trading accounts and compete with private contractors; the requirement for bus undertakings to operate on a commercial basis. This list is potentially a very long one.

The result has been a new style of management. Discussing land use planning, Maitland and Newman (1989) argue that there is a shift away from hierarchical and functional organisational structures, towards new working practices which are customised to specific tasks. There is a new emphasis on 'customer care', on mimicking private sector planning organisations and developing new organisational cultures, often directly opposed to previously-held values. Stoker argues (1989a, p. 159) that the 'aim is to create a local government compatible with the flexible economic structures, two-tier welfare system and enterprise culture which in the Thatcher vision constitute the key to a successful future.'

This has also involved a challenge to the existing political nature of local government, not just its role as service provider. Two more of Stewart and Stoker's 'key themes of restructuring' involved: initiating new forms of accountability to the centre and the local community; and challenging existing mechanisms of local representative democracy (1989, p. 3). The creation of local decision making bodies which bypass directly elected local authorities (such as urban development corporations or TECs/LECs) has been complemented by tightening the constraints on local councillors. The Widdecombe Report of 1986, followed by a 1988 White Paper and the 1989 Local Government and Housing Act made substantial changes in the ways in which committees (the key decision making arena) are convened in local authorities, the use of political advisors and cooptees on committees and the scope for local government officers to undertake political activity. The tasks of maintaining financial probity (avoiding unlawful expenditure), legal propriety (avoiding illegality or maladministration) and management coordination were also given a higher profile by the appointment of three separate senior officers to these posts.

These reforms were initiated largely to deal with urban local authorities who were seeking to implement and work out on the ground the ideas of the New Left (Gyford, 1985; Blunkett and Jackson, 1987; Livingstone, 1987; Boddy and Fudge, 1984). Drawing on spatially distinct social practices and cultures, these councils sought to mobilise local communities against the central state, in order to influence the local pattern of resource allocation, occurring through capital accumulation and (dis)investment and public sector policies. In doing so they often created innovative new political and organisational structures at the local level and sought to develop policy which both produced new benefits for the local community, particularly women, ethnic minorities, the disabled and other disadvantaged groups and also politicised these groups. Empowering people, enabling them to govern themselves, was a watchword of such councils.

Seen as a reaction to this activity within radical left local authorities, the reforms of Thatcherism have, in their own terms, been largely successful, refocusing local authorities on service provision rather than broader political activity: 'What is clear is that the "tidal force" of the politicisation of local government will receive a severe and possibly terminal setback from the legislative proposals' (Leach, 1989, p. 121). Examples remain though of local councils and areas within local government activity where the reforms continue to be resisted. Of course, in many conservative local authorities the reforms will just mean business as usual, with the political actions of local business interests and even amenity groups subsumed within the acceptable, apparently apolitical activities of local government.

The structure of local government has also been the subject of central government attention during this period, adding to the several, confusing reorganisations that have occurred since the Second World War. At the time of writing (1992), local government structure is based on the reorganisation of 1972 in England and Wales and 1975 in Scotland, which created a two-tier system throughout most of the country, as amended by the 1985 Local Government Act which abolished the metropolitan county councils and the GLC.

Therefore, in England there are 39 county councils and, beneath them, 296 district councils (some of them still called boroughs) covering all non-metropolitan areas. In the metropolitan areas of West Midlands, South Yorkshire, West Yorkshire, Greater Manchester, Merseyside and Tyne & Wear, there are now only district councils, some 36 in all. The Greater London area is covered by 32 London boroughs. In Wales there are 8 county councils and 37 district councils. These local authorities are represented at national level by three special pressure groups: the Association of County Councils (ACC), Association of District Councils (ADC) and Association of Metropolitan Authorities (AMA). Meanwhile in Scotland there are 9 regional councils and 53 district councils plus 3 island areas with a single, unitary local authority or island council. The Scottish regions differ from other local authorities in that they often take on the functions of The Scottish Office, for example some development control functions, and are generally regarded as much more successful in relating both to central government and the districts in a spirit of partnership rather than conflict. The Scottish local authorities are represented in negotiations with central government by the single organisation, the Convention of Scottish Local Authorities (COSLA).

Below this main structure of local government there is a patchy coverage of very localised organisations: over 900 active parish and town councils in England, about 800 community or town councils in Wales and over 1200 community councils in Scotland. These bodies have a largely consultative role vis-à-vis the rest of local government (Gyford, 1991, p. 89; Stoker, 1991, p. 57; Midwinter *et al.*, 1991, p. 141) although they can undertake some local environmental management.

Although it would seem that a knowledge of this structure is essential for discovering which authority does what at the local level, it is not so simple. Responsibilities are allocated between district and county councils, district and regional councils (see Stoker, 1991, Table 2.1) with, broadly speaking, strategic planning, transport, policy, fire services, education and social services (plus water in Scotland) going to the higher-tier authority. But there is considerable scope for sharing these responsibilities in a variety of ways: jointly providing a service;

providing a service concurrently; dividing up the responsibility (as with development control); higher-tier authorities having reserve or default powers; lower-tier authorities claiming a responsibility back from a higher-tier authority (as with the maintenance of certain unclassified roads); or agency powers where one authority agrees to perform a function for another authority, usually for payment (Byrne, 1986, p. 59). Broadly speaking there are pressures for a higher-tier authority to perform a function where: there is a strategic dimension to the responsibility, involving some negotiation with central government and/or neighbouring authorities; the service is most economically or efficiently provided over a larger geographical area; or the function carries 'kudos' and the larger authority uses its political power to capture the function.

The abolition of metropolitan county councils and the GLC has necessitated alternative arrangements for many local government functions with a strategic dimension in these areas. For example, London has a London Planning Advisory Committee and a London Waste Regulatory Authority among many other joint boards and committees to coordinate the work of the boroughs.

Local government functions, therefore, are spread across the organisational structure of local government like a net, and the mesh of the net represents a complicated pattern of intraorganisational and interorganisational communication. This communication is vital for resolving actual and potential conflicts between tiers of government or departments within local government. Such conflict arises not only from the existence of two tiers with organisational boundaries but also due to different professional and political judgements about policy and priorities (Midwinter *et al.*, 1991, p. 126). Godschalk (1991) distinguishes three types of conflict, each with its own resolution technique: issues resolved by informal negotiation or facilitation; disputes resolved by formal negotiation or mediation; and impasses resolved by arbitration, often to an external hearing or court. The institutionalist approach is particularly useful at identifying and analysing these forms of local government activity. It can also help pinpoint where there is insufficient liaison between departments, as with the conceptual and practical gaps between expenditure-based plans, such as HIPs and TPPs, and development plans which prevent local government taking an enabling role in relation to local development (Carter *et al.*, 1991). An example of this is given in Exhibit 8.1.

The structure of local government over which this net of communication spreads is, however, under discussion again. The Government recently announced a thorough review of local government to consider the possibility of unitary authorities in non-metropolitan areas, that is

Exhibit 8.1   *Conflict over green belts*

While green belt policy has enjoyed a high degree of consensus and support, specific green belt designations have been a focus of conflict. Central government and both tiers of local government have sought to express their own views about development allocations through representations on the appropriate boundaries of belts. This was particularly the case during the late 1970s and 1980s when green belt boundaries were being changed. The designations of postwar development plans were proving out of date. In some places, development had occurred rendering green belt notation irrelevant, but in most cases attempts were being made at the local level to extend the width of green belts to protect land from heightened development pressures. The first round of structure plans were used as the vehicle for redefining green belt areas. While this suggests that county councils were the prime movers in green belt designation, conflicts with both upper and lower tiers were equally important. The DoE sought to contain the spread of green belts, pruning back extensions, removing 'interim' status from large areas and refusing to approve some new belts. The power of the Secretary of State to approve structure plans was a strong control over county councils' actions.

The motives for this stance by central government is open to interpretation. The New Left would see this as evidence of the capture of the DoE by speculative housebuilders keen to obtain development land generally and planning permission on their landbanks in particular. On the other hand, the New Right would see this as a move against overly restrictive, anti-development policies of NIMBYist (Not In My Back Yard) local councils. The liberal political economist would also argue that overruling local councils' policy could, however, be justified, on the grounds of the need to mesh together county council policies on a regional scale and meet regional demographic forecasts: that is, the strategic planning needs at higher level.

But county councils also had to deal with pressure from below, from district and parish councils. The nature of this pressure varied from locality to locality: some districts pressed for green belts; other wished to provide for more development land. In general, though, the district councils wished to retain control over detailed land allocations to meet their specific circumstances: local housing needs; the balance of inmigration the council wished to plan for; the demands of local development interests. This meant that district councils often opposed the detailed designation of green belt boundaries in county council subject plans, preferring to implement broad brush structure plans policies in their own district plans. In many cases central government, seeing an anti-restraint alliance between the DoE and the districts, would step in and override such subject plans.

This brief account of green belt conflicts lends itself to the institutionalist approach. It tells of a policy being used to handle the conflicts between tiers of government, conflicts which themselves represent the balance of interests pressing their demands on the DoE or local council. The policy is shaped in detail by the adjustments that the mediation process requires and, indeed, the longevity of green belt policy can be analysed in terms of its usefulness as a mediating tool. For analysts of a different perspective, this account may obscure more important points: the support of development interests by sections of central and local government (New Left); the struggle to contain the tendency for sections of the state to extend their control over the private sector (New Right); and the need to find a rational solution to the problem of allocating land for residential development to meet demographic change in the face of resistance by local vested interests (liberal political economy).

Further reading: Elson (1986); PPG2, *Green Belts*; Herington (1989).

one authority above parish/community/town council level for each spatial area. The possibility of resurrecting a two-tier structure in Greater London has also been mooted. National parks will not be affected by this reform as they are to have their own authorities. Wide discretionary powers to establish a new form of local government have been given to the Secretary of State by the 1992 Local Government Act. This Act also set up a Local Government Commission for England to consider and make recommendations (but not decide) on the appropriate form of local government restructuring. In Wales and Scotland, the Welsh Office and The Scottish Office have put forward alternative scenarios for change already, without the deliberations of the Commission process. The new system is expected to begin operation in April 1994 with completion of the reorganisation by 1998 (1996 in Scotland).

While central government have indicated a preference for unitary authorities and for basing them on existing districts, the Commission has been given a fairly free hand. The aim is that the new authorities should be based on communities, as defined by people's preferences, geography, patterns of economic and social activity and any 'natural institutional focus'. However, cost effectiveness is also a factor behind the reorganisation. Where this dictates, collaborative arrangements between the new authorities and buying in services from the private sector may be appropriate. This means that fairly small councils can be charged with a range of responsibilities. This is attractive to the New Right. In their view, larger authorities can more readily be characterised as bureaucracies engaged in unnecessary strategic planning while smaller, lower-tier authorities are more heavily involved in day-to-day service provision than grandiose planning, have a closer relationship to their clientele/electorate and are more parochial and less ambitious in their attitudes and aspirations.

This restructuring will significantly affect the planning system. New arrangements will have to be made for development plans, particularly structure plans, waste and minerals plans. In some cases there is bound to be duplication of planning effort across the new authorities, under-mining the government's argument that reform will result in cost savings. Joint boards or other consultative arrangements will probably be needed to make strategic planning possible. Many county-led activities such as countryside management, conservation, archaeology, economic development and tourism may not easily be broken up and delegated to a lower tier. From a liberal political economy perspective, this raises administrative problems of great importance for decision making. Rational decision making may be undermined as reorganisa-tion cuts across integrated planning. Political considerations, at national and local levels, may prevent the most efficient spatial unit being adopted for each local government service. From an institutionalist viewpoint, the reorganisation means that there will be a loss in terms of current ways in which conflicts of interest are handled and resolved; it will take time to develop arrangements which can mediate conflicts effectively. From the New Left, this is yet another assault on the ability of local communities to govern themselves and effectively to challenge the central state.

In addition to this central government-led restructuring, it should be noted that many local authorities are adopting decentralised structures within their districts or boroughs. In some cases this is purely administrative, in others is involves mini-town halls. This is discussed further in Chapter 9 in the context of the role of professionals.

■ Quangos

Quangos (quasi-autonomous non-governmental organisations) are non-elected bodies, appointed by cental government to undertake specified functions often with a substantial degree of discretion. They stand between central and local government in the sense that either they have a regional geographical area to cover (for example, national park authorities) or report directly to central government for a local spatial area or policy issue removed from local authority control (for example, UDCs or TECs). But they also stand outside the central–local government relationship in the sense that they are not institutions with claims to representative democracy.

Such agencies may be charged merely with implementing or enforcing a tightly defined policy but they can also be given policy or plan making powers or even a general delegated responsibility. In Britain, delegation is the norm (Rees, 1990, p. 367): 'Agencies not only have considerable flexibility to interpret what their responsibilities mean, but can develop their own strategies to meet them, set their own implementation timescales and decide their own enforcement practices.' In some cases delegation may even extend to discretion over whether to use their powers or not. In theory, notably liberal political economy, these elements of delegation and discretion should enhance rational decision making by allowing for spatial variation in needs and in the preferences of local communities. In practice, as will be explored below, they can insulate the organisation from popular pressure, a point stressed by other theoretical approaches.

The importance and variety of these quangos has grown considerably in recent years as more and more functions have been allocated to them (Stoker, 1991, p. 61). Collective consumption functions, such as waste management and public transport, have been moved from local authorities to quangos. Resource development, as with forestry and water, has been placed in quangos and is now often proposed for privatisation or at least public–private partnership. Many regulatory environmental protection functions are located in quangos where, arguably, expertise and control powers can be strengthened by centralisation. Rees claims (1990, p. 373) 'there has been a tendency for *all* substantive aspects of environmental resource management to migrate away from local control'. In large part this arises from the ideology of the Conservative Government of the 1980s; but also from the requirements of increased regulations under EC rules; and from the heavy constraints that local government finds itself under (Shaw, 1990). Shaw identifies a number of different organisations which can now be considered as quangos: central government arm's length agencies such as UDCs (see Exhibit 8.2); local government arm's length agencies such as enterprise boards; corporatist development agencies such as English Estates, Scottish Enterprise or the WDA; joint boards such as police authorities; and hybrid agencies including TECs or LECs. Stoker (1991, p. 65) replaces corporatist development agencies with public–private partnerships and adds user organisations (such as housing management cooperatives) and intergovernmental forums (such as the South East Regional Planning Conference, SERPLAN).

In many circumstances, the Government has favoured the central government arm's length agency, terming it the 'executive agency'. Since 1988, 70 such agencies have been created. These agencies are directly modelled on a somewhat idealised private sector. For example, the new agency model Planning Inspectorate will aim to cover all costs with fees and produce a corporate plan indicating other targets such as speed, costs and efficiency savings, against which to measure their performance. Restrictions on the Inspectorate's activities will be lifted allowing them to diversify, say into training and other profit making areas.

The main complaint concerning the proliferation of such quangos whatever their function is their insulation from public pressure (Weale *et al.*, 1991). It is not just that they are unelected bodies and the chains of control from the public are weak. As Rees has outlined with great clarity (1990, p. 373): 'Conflicts of interest are not, therefore, mediated by locating the different functions and decision-making modes of the state at different levels of government, but become buried by the mysticism which surrounds the technical expert.' This has implications for the role of professionals within quangos which is discussed further in Chapter 9. Given this divorce from democratic and popular control, Rees (p. 381) argues that 'Dissatisfaction with [quangos] has rarely resulted in their total abolition, rather new, higher-tier authorities are created as controls, or advisory and coordinating committees are provided to improve performance'.

Isolated from democratic control these agencies can be subject to pressure from sectional interests through corporatist relations between the interest and the quango in which policy practice is effectively jointly decided through extensive consultation. In particular they can develop close relationships with the very interests they may have been established to manage, regulate and control. The Industrial Air Pollution Inspectorate, that preceded HMIP, was criticised by the Royal Commission on Environmental Pollution as having too close a relation with the industry it is meant to control. Rees points out (p. 373) that once 'established central- and regional-level agencies are undoubtedly subject to corporatist pressures.' But she goes on to argue:

> But this should not obscure the fact that the agencies develop an internal, professionally dominated, logic which critically affects the way they interpret their functions and by no means all professional groups support the expansion of private sector production and its profitability.

The nature of the professional and management culture will be decisive as the UDC Exhibit 8.2 illustrates.

Exhibit 8.2 *Urban Development Corporations*

UDCs were the flagship of the Thatcher administration's urban policy. They arose from a classic New Right analysis of urban district councils as obstructive of the wealth creating processes within the city. Land was being left derelict, the argument ran, because local authorities spent too much time discussing rather than facilitating, and were hostile to the very development processes that could regenerate urban areas. The UDCs thus took areas out of local authority control and placed them in the hands of well-resourced quangos with substantial discretionary powers. The quango could operate in a largely autonomous manner and, in London at least, used its powers to underpin a speculative property boom.

The LDDC also provides the ammunition for a New Left critique of UDCs. The quango, having arisen from a dissatisfaction with elected local authorities, was explicitly divorced from local communities. It responded neither to pressure from the London boroughs nor the local groups which arose from within the Docklands communities. The New Left could readily present this as central government intervening to benefit private profit making at the expense of local working class peoples. The heavy involvement of individual property developers within the LDDC, the close relations they formed with developers working in the Dockland area and the high-handed attitude to local people all confirmed this view.

The role of the LDDC in acting as the property developers' organisation meant that the degree of planning, understood as purposive, rational decision making, was limited. The form of facilitative planning that the LDDC espoused does not fit easily with the liberal political economist's view of a planning organisation. Neither did the rather one-sided consultation that the LDDC engaged in lend itself to any analysis of mediation as in the institutionalist approach.

However the LDDC of the early 1980s proved to be the exception rather than the rule. Towards the end of the decade, the LDDC was developing relations both with local councils, who decided to enter planning gain agreements with the Corporation and try thereby to salvage some benefits from the UDC designation, and with local communities through the LDDC's social programme. The New Left continued to see these adjustments in the Corporation's attitude as marginal and as representing a climb down by the local community and boroughs in their struggle over the land resources of Docklands. But the experience of other UDCs suggests that a shift towards an accommodation between the local community and the corporation is the general model. In Merseyside, the lack of private sector involvement meant that, from early on, the corporation and local authorities worked together in consultation. Later UDCs were based on negotiation between quango and local government from the start. In some cases the district council operated development control and other functions for the UDC on an agency basis. In such situations the UDCs operate neither as an aloof, autonomous, professional-dominated quango nor as a representative of private capital in conflict with the local community. Rather the institutionalist approach highlights the extent of negotiation, liaison and consultation that occurs between quango and local government, as well as infrastructure agencies and community groups, over the planning of development in an urban area.

This does not mean that a cosy consensus emerges. Conflicts and tensions over jurisdiction remains. Furthermore this more cooperative approach is heavily dependent on the attitudes of both local authorities and UDCs. The second round UDCs were in areas where the local authority had already adopted a leverage style of planning due to the nature of the local property market and the other constraints they faced on their own investment activities. The UDCs also were generally more conciliatory in tone, unwilling to emulate the conflict-ridden history of the LDDC.

Further reading: Stoker (1989); Brownill (1990); Brindley *et al.* (1989).

Whether this isolation from public pressure and tendency to corporatist pressures matters depends on the viewpoint adopted. For the New Right links with the commercial sector at the expense of local democracy are justified since the private sector is seen as dependent on and hence able to represent the public as consumers. Again for the liberal political economist the isolation is a problem only if it results in valuable information for decision making being lost or the political goals of policy being misinterpreted. However, the institutionalist approach would argue that such quangos lose out in the opportunity to mediate between the full range of interests affected by the quango. Both the institutionalist approach and the New Left also draw attention to the way in which the manner of a quango's decision making can mask the inequalities arising from its actions. As Rees argues (1985, p. 346), many of these institutions become heavily influenced by the technocratic approach commonly adopted by the managers that run them. These 'tend not to see the political and allocative nature of their activities' and see their role rather in terms of technological fix, maintaining output or achieving economic efficiency.

Thus Rees concludes on the Industrial Air Pollution Inspectorate and its US counterpart (p. 397):

> the élitist and technocratic stance of the Inspectorates and their continued reluctance to involve the public in the bargaining process has produced much hostility and suspicion. The political nature of control decisions is ignored. Rather the whole process is viewed as a neutral technical matter. Calls for greater freedom of information have been dismissed as a 'waste of expert professional time' a 'distraction' from the 'highly technical job' which inspectors 'are employed to do' . . . However, no technical exercise can be neutral – all decisions on pollution control standards inevitably affect the distribution of real income and welfare between different groups within society.

This distributive issue is repeatedly ignored in the way many quangos tackle their tasks.

In some cases quangos may actively try to suppress concerns about this distributive impact. McCormick argues that agencies such as the NCC have in the past actively tried to moderate the demands of pressure groups with whom they are in contact in order to present a professional, apolitical face to central government (1991, p. 25). One of the advantages of maintaining a technocratic approach, which largely disregards outside political claims, is that central government will look on the agency with more favour and, after all, such agencies are dependent on central government for their very existence. For example, the NCC and the Countryside Commission were widely regarded as ineffective, powerless and secretive in the early 1980s (Lowe *et al.*, 1986, p. 133). They remained divorced from public concerns over the countryside and sought to remain aloof from the conflicts between farming and forestry interests on the one hand and rural conservation on the other. They were seen to be having a corporatist relation to these farming and forestry interests. But, as McCormick details (1991, pp. 17–18), by the late 1980s they were taking a more critical line with regard to government policy and the activities of key rural business interests. Many environmentalists saw a link between this shift in attitude and the proposals for merging the councils that central government announced in July 1989: 'There was a suspicion among environmental groups that the two agencies became too effective at slowing down the conversion of natural habitat to farmland.' This is a cautionary tale for quangos indeed.

Does this account of the critique of quangos and their operation suggest that quangos have no legitimate role? Certainly there has been widespread support for the new EPAs for England and Wales and for Scotland (Wilder and Plant, 1992). Such quangos can raise the profile of environmental protection and create career opportunities for specialists and thus foster education and training in these areas. It is also argued that the requirements of economies of scale in technical and research facilities and of integration in decision making in pollution control support the need for such an agency. These are all points the liberal political economy approach would emphasise. However the above criticisms emphasise that safeguards are also needed to ensure the openness of the agencies' operation and the scope for democratic control of their activities in any particular locality. All other theoretical approaches imply such safeguards, though they differ in terms of which outside groups should be given most access and control.

■ The European and international dimension

There is no doubt that urban and environmental planning policy within Britain is increasingly having to conform with policy decisions made at the European and the international level (see Summary Box 8.5). This section briefly reviews the nature of that influence.

Summary Box 8.5   *The policy making institutions of the European Community*

Institution	Function	Composition
European Commission	Policy formulation and implementation	Commissioners appointed, substantial executive
Council of Ministers	Decisions on Commission's proposals	Representatives of national governments
European Council	International summit	Heads of government
European Parliament	Debates, limited power	Directly elected Members of the European Parliament

The EC was originally formed as the European Economic Community (EEC) with an emphasis on establishing a free trade area. Within this two areas of policy activity had considerable significance. First, the strength of the farming lobby within original member states led to the CAP whereby an expensive system of financial support was provided for agricultural production. As Chapter 16 will explore, the CAP has had profound consequences for the British countryside. Eventually the high cost of the policy and the continued evidence of administrative failure in terms of butter mountains and wine lakes led to its reform, beginning with milk quotas introduced in 1984. This reform has continued to reduce the amount of money directly pumped into encouraging agricultural production, although the total sum remains extremely high (Fennell, 1990).

Second, the EC has always sought to mitigate the effects of its competitive trade policy through programmes of grants to depressed areas, such as the Social Fund and Regional Development Fund. For a time these European monies reinforced British regional policy but as domestic regional policy has declined in importance so have the European supplements. For it has always been required that European Funds can go only to areas and projects where some British government monies are already available: European support has been regarded as a supplement not a replacement for national programmes. There are now proposals for delinking EC and national subsidy programmes, in part as a response to the economic effects on regions of the integrated European market.

In the 1990s it is clear that the most significant area of EC activity for the planning system concerns the environment (see Summary Box 8.6). The original Treaty of Rome establishing the community made no reference to the environment. However, following the 1972 United Nations Conference on the Human Environment, the first of five environmental actions programmes at the EC level was announced. The first two contained largely remedial measures but more recent programmes have been increasingly proactive. Since these environmental programmes had no specific basis in the Treaty, policy measures were authorised under Article 110 concerning the removal of trade barriers or the 'catch all' Article 235. Specific responsibility for environmental protection was given to the EC by Article 25 of the 1986 Single European Act, provided that the objective of the policy could be better obtained at the community rather than at nation state level. The 1986 Act also requires environmental protection to be written into all EC policy and states a commitment to the 'polluter pays principle', the latter underpinning moves towards full corporate liability for environmental damage. The 1986 Act and announcements at European Council meetings in 1988 and 1990 continued to argue that the single market and high standards of environmental protection were integrally related, the one supporting the other.

Under these various provisions, some 280 measures of environmental protection have been passed at community level since 1973. The Fifth

Environmental Action Plan, beginning in 1992 and to be supported by a community environment fund, is set to expand EC involvement even further. McCormick (1991, p. 20) concludes that:

> Against a background of variable government interest in environmental regulation, the role and influence of the EC in environment policy-making has grown. In fact, it is now arguably the single most important and effective influence on British environmental policy and politics.

Summary Box 8.6   *Key Community environmental policies*

Water:	Drinking Water Directive
	Surface Water Directive
	Bathing Water Directive
	Ground Water Directive
	Urban Waste Water Directive
Air:	Air Pollution from Motor Vehicles Directives
	Pollutant specific measures, for example on lead and NO_2
	Industrial Plants Directive
	Large Combustion Plants Directive
	Ozone depletion (the Community is a party to the 1975 Vienna Convention and the 1987 Montreal Protocol)
Waste:	Framework Waste Directive (1975 and 1991)
	Hazardous Waste Directive
	Incineration of Hazardous Waste Directive (proposed 1992)
	Civil Liability for Damage caused by Waste (proposed 1991)
	Landfill Directive (proposed 1991)
	Package and Package Waste Directive
General:	Integrated Pollution Prevention and Control (Framework Directive proposal in preparation 1992)

Source: Clifford Chance, *European Environmental Law Guide* (1992)

Part of this shift has involved a move away from the use of advisory policy documents and selective subsidies and grants to steer domestic policy, towards a greater use of formal legislative tools. The European Commission (the powerful executive of the community) has five such tools available to it: regulations which apply equally in all member state and are directly binding; decisions which bind only the parties involved in the specific issue on which the Commission has been asked to adjudicate; directives which bind member states to the objectives of the policy but allow each state to find its own way of implementing these objectives; and recommendations and opinions which have no binding force but carry some weight given the other powers at the Commission's disposal. The significance of these tools is that the European Commission is the only international organisation in the world with the power to agree environmental policies which bind member states.

The EC has particularly relied on directives to prompt national-level legislation. The directive on wild birds required the government to enact new legislation leading to the Wildlife and Countryside Act 1981. Despite opposition from the Government and major lobby groups such as the CBI, EIAs were introduced using the 1985 directive. In 1988 the EC directive on large combustion plants required the introduction of new technology to reduce the emissions causing acid rain. In 1989 the EC took the British Government to the European Court of Justice over failure to meet EC water quality standards set down in a directive.

The directive has proved a very effective policy tool from the EC's viewpoint and new directives are in the pipeline. But it seems likely that the EC in the future will take a more directly involved role in environmental matters. This will take four forms. First, there is likely to be greater use of fiscal or market-based instruments, such as carbon taxes. These receive specific mention in the Fifth Environmental Action Programme. Second, there will probably be a shift from directives to regulations in proposing policy for member states. Third, there is the imminent operation of the European Environmental Agency (EEA) and the possibility of other European environment agencies. The EEA itself is intended to be an information clearing house, with an EC-wide environment database, supporting enforcement activity and policy making. Proposals have also been put forward for a European Inspectorate with direct regulatory powers and, less radical, an auditing body which will examine the environmental protection enforcement agencies in the various countries (Westbrook, 1991). Fourth, the EC is developing a sophisticated form of strategic policy advice to guide local policy making. In 1990 they issued a Green Paper on the Urban Environment which sought to air some guidelines for urban planning practice and promote a vision for European towns and cities. In 1991 the *Europe 2000* document was published setting out spatial trends within the community. This established a form of regionalism as the likely key unit for EC indicative strategic planning. And in 1992 a Green Paper on *The Impact of Transport on the Environment* was produced which tackled the problematic issue of the relationship between transport and environmental policy, and suggests EC-led constraints on traffic growth.

Certain EC actions also greatly strengthen the ability of third parties within Britain to challenge environmental policy practice. The 1990 EC directive on Freedom of Access to Information on the Environment will open up public bodies to watchdog activity by pressure groups. And the proposed directive on Civil Liability for Damage caused by Waste opens up the prospects of new categories of environmental liability which can be enforced in British courts. This form of liability already operates in the USA and imposes considerable costs on polluters in accordance with the 'polluter pays principle'. As Faulks (1991, p. 20) says: 'It would not be unrealistic to suggest that the introduction of the concept of impairment of the environment as an actionable tort heralds a new era in the European Community environmental legislation programme.'

This increase in EC activity is likely to be resisted by the British government as it has been resisted in the past. For example, Rees (1990, p. 366) tells of how the British Government repeatedly used exemptions to ensure that the newly privatised water companies at least complied with the letter if not the spirit of EC water quality directives:

> All the discharges which have not been granted exemption will be eligible for an 'authorisation' or 'deemed consent'! In this way, the EEC requirement that they must come under control has been formally fulfilled without doing anything to actually reduce the pollutant loads of potentially dangerous substances.

Currently the British government is using the uncertainty over the 1991 Maastricht Treaty to try and 'repatriate' environmental policy to the national level, using the principle of subsidiarity – by which policies should be dealt with at the lowest possible level for effective implementation – as a negotiating tool. The Conservative government (and in particular New Right elements within it) have seen this growth of EC activity as creeping, or galloping, bureaucratisation (see Exhibit 8.3). To date debate about subsidiarity in relation to environmental policy has resulted in the Commission's power to enforce some directives being devolved to nation states, including water quality directives where the Commission was in conflict with Britain. The proposed legal action over failure to comply with the EIA directive in the case of the M3 extension has also been dropped.

The whole attitude of the EC has been considerably influenced by the concept of 'sustainable development' promoted by the Brundtland Report (WCED, 1987), itself a product of the United Nations. The 1972 UN conference on the Human Environment in Stockholm played a significant role is raising awareness and produced a declaration comprising 26 statements which forms the basis for current international environmental law. Following on from this conference, the UN created UNEP, its environmental programme which has been operating since 1974. This largely plays a coordinating and catalysing role. It sees its role as complementing the many non-government organisations which operate at the international level, undertaking

Exhibit 8.3 *The EC and environmental assessment*

The relationship between the EC and Britain over environmental assessment (EA) has not been a happy one. Britain held out against the imposition of the EC directive, contributing to the lengthy delay between first draft and final version. When the adoption of the directive required that Britain introduce EA within two years, the DoE sought to simply graft EA onto land use planning by means of amended regulations. The view that Britain was complying with the words rather than the spirit of the directive was reinforced by the apparent reluctance to apply EA to infrastructure proposals approved by Private Bills and to projects which were in the pipeline at the time the EC directive came into force on 3 July 1988.

The latter led to an acrid exchange of letters between Britain and the EC Commissioner for the Environment, including a request from the Commission not to proceed with four major transport projects: the Hackney Wick-M11 link; the East London River Crossing; the Compton Down M3 extension; and the Channel Tunnel rail link. Only in the 1990s has EA been integrated into the Private Bill procedure and new orders under the Transport and Works Act, and given statutory recognition in the Planning and Compensation Act. Even so the EC remains unhappy that British regulations require only that the environment statement, and not the assessment of information it contains, is recorded in writing. The statement is provided by the developer while it is the public body who undertakes the actual assessment.

The British Government's point of view has been that the Commission were imposing unnecessary regulations, that the British land use planning system took environmental factors into account in development control anyway, and that the EA directive was an example of exactly the creeping bureaucratisation that the Thatcher government has been trying to dismantle since 1979. Further it represented not only more red tape within Britain but also the empire-building tendencies of the Commission. In this context the bureaucratic nature of the Commission, as opposed to the relatively less powerful but elected European Parliament, is significant.

Against this New Right argument are ranged the liberal political economists. They see the EC as acting rationally to impose a decision in the public interest. The environment is seen as a public good on a European, if not a global, scale. The EC is acting in the best interests of all members by insisting on a common and rigorous standard of environmental protection. Certainly EA has added another layer of procedures to the planning system. Documents have to be produced, information obtained, and organisations consulted. The relevance of EA to the role of local government in taking planning decisions depends on the use made of such documents. If the information and judgements therein do not influence planning decisions, then there has been unnecessary procedural red tape, but the lack of effective constraint on the development process means that the term 'nanny state' is hardly justified. Rather, it would seem as if the state is engaged in a legitimation exercise, appearing to promote environmental protection when really the development process has continued as before. Such a view would be consistent with the New Left position.

However, if it appears that EA is influencing planning decisions – and the early experience supports at least some marginal impact – then the role of government must be construed differently. Enhanced environmental protection will restrict development, preventing projects from going ahead or requiring extra expenditure along the way. Whether this restriction is seen as unnecessary interference or a rational policy tool depends on the value placed on the environment compared to the economic activity of the development process and also on the assumed interrelation between environment and economy.

Meanwhile the institutional approach remains largely agnostic as to the benefits of EA. It notes the extent of interorganisational contact involved in the apparently technical EA process. It also notes the constraints that these organisations face within the process, seeing the outcomes as dependent both on those constraints and on how organisations and actors work within them and seek to push them outwards. Over the longer term, it may be possible to detect an impact on the development process, not just in terms of marginal environmental protection, but also in restructuring the development process itself. The evidence is not yet available for tracing this line of causality from the EC to British development activity.

Further reading: Wathern (1988); Clark and Herington (1988); Jones *et al.* (1991).

research, spreading information and encouraging debate and it also creates channels of communication between nations which can be used for policy progress.

One major success story for UNEP has been the creation of the World Commission under the chairmanship of Gro Brundtland to examine issues of Environment and Development. The open participatory way in which the Commission, operated and the resulting report *Our Common Future* (1987), have had a significant impact. The DoE White Paper on the Environment was a response to the arguments of the Brundtland report for 'sustainable development'. Following on from this initiative, a Centre for Our Common Future was set up in Geneva and a major conference, The Earth Summit, convened in 1992 in Brazil. The working papers for this high-level conference covered a wide range of urban and environmental planning policies, with an enormous potential impact.

The practical outcomes of the Earth Summit were two conventions, on global warming and biodiversity, and three statements with lesser legal standing: a statement on forest principles; the Rio Declaration (the downgraded Earth Charter); and Agenda 21 (the agenda for implementing sustainable development). This last item may prove to be more significant over time, as the UN will set up a Commission on Sustainable Development to monitor the implementation of Agenda 21. This will call for statements from all countries on its proposals for achieving sustainable development, a call which will have moral if not legal force.

For the full impact of the Earth Summit to be felt, discussion must be transformed into agreements and action. However, as Rowlands emphasises (1992, p. 315)), achieving international agreements involves a degree of mutual trust between participants. This element is missing, particularly in negotiations between the South and the North, the developed and less developed countries.

> Thus, many governments, especially the weak and the suspicious, may think that environmental data will be used for other ends – goals which do not bring worldwide collective benefits, but instead entrench a renewed imperialist, dependent relationship.

Looking at the reasons why economically powerful countries, such as the USA, refuse to accept international agreements, Johnston (1989, p. 141) has argued: 'the powerful states in the world have been unprepared to sign a treaty which recognises certain resources as a "common heritage" because to do so would mean renouncing some of their power.' He is therefore pessimistic about the prospects for much further effective international agreement on environmental problems.

However, there is not doubt that there is a new international level of awareness about environmental issues which is being translated into a number of agreements and having a significant impact on local level policy. Rowlands (1992) cites three factors as underpinning the growth in international environmental awareness: increasing domestic environmental concern which has then been reflected onto the international arena; increases in the quantity of pollution generation and the level of environmental degradation at a global level; and the greater scientific knowledge, often couched in probabilities and ranges rather than certainties, about environmental impacts. Liberal political economists have been particularly forceful in arguing that it has become increasingly clear that activities in one nation state impinge on others and, further, that there can be genuine mutual benefits of cooperation. Environmental policy need not be a 'zero sum game' in which one nation can benefit only at the expense of another, but a national response to a pressing problem.

However, while the Brundtland Report and various EC and DoE documents seek to argue that sustainable development means that economic development and enhanced environmental protection can go hand-in-hand, the economic barriers remain substantial; Part 4 will further explore this important issue.

Further reading

For an overview of the issues raised in this chapter the reader is referred to Stoker (1991), which covers much more than just local government, and McCormick (1991), which discusses state organisations and the policy process in relation to the environment. For more detail on local government, Stoker (1991) is excellent while, for the analysis of central–local relations, Rhodes (1981) is still useful. The particular situation of Scotland is well introduced in Midwinter *et al.* (1991). Quangos are discussed in Stoker (1991) , in the context of non-elected local government, and Rees (1990), in the context of natural resource management. For a brief introduction to the role of the EC, Franklin with Wilke (1990) is also helpful.

■ *Chapter 9* ■

The Planners

It is possible to consider professions as just another pressure group seeking to influence public policy (see below). It is true that national-level representatives of professionals do lobby government for policy change. For example, the Royal Town Planning Institute (RTPI) and Royal Institute of British Architects (RIBA) were both consultees on the annex to PPG1 on 'Aesthetic Control and Design Guidance'. And the RTPI is currently lobbying to keep waste disposal a local authority function rather than transfer it to the new EPA. But professions play a much more significant role in the policy process, for they are the recipients of much delegated power to implement and even formulate policy. The importance of the professional culture within quangos has already been noted in Chapter 8 and is explored further in Exhibit 9.1 on water management. This chapter considers the range of professions concerned with urban and environmental planning, their claims to authority and knowledge, and the values they profess.

The majority of the professions that today deal with the built and natural environment were founded before the Second World War, particularly in the late 19th century and the 1930s (see Table 9.1).

Table 9.1 *Dates of founding of the main planning professions*

1834	Royal Institute of British Architects
1868	Royal Institution of Chartered Surveyors
1883	Institution of Environmental Health Officers
1886	Royal Institute of Public Health
1895	Institution of Public Health Engineers
1896	Institution of Water Engineers and Scientists
1901	Institute of Water Pollution Control
1903	Institute of Hygiene
1914	Town Planning Institute
1919	Chartered Institute of Transport
1927	Institute of Energy
1930	Institution of Highways and Transportation
1931	Society of Housing Managers (now Institute of Housing)
1937	Royal Institute of Public Health and Hygiene
1944	Institute of Road Transport Engineers

The activities of these professions vary considerably from the more technically-minded public health engineers to 'the' planners within the Royal Town Planning Institute (originally just the Town Planning Institute) who undertake more of a coordinating role. Some draw on knowledge from the natural sciences, others from the social sciences. Some of these professions are found almost entirely within the public sector, such as environmental health officers; others are oriented firmly towards the private sector, especially chartered surveyors and architects; some professions which were based within the public sector are facing privatisation (see Exhibit 9.1). Some professions are high status, others lower status. Some professional organisations are large and powerful, others weak. The lines of division are many. It is the nature of these activities as 'professions' which is the common unifying thread.

■ Occupational control

Johnson (1972) argues that professionalism is a specific form of occupational control, of organising and restraining the working practices of specific groups of workers. It is a form of control which distinguishes these workers, termed 'members' of a profession, as being in middle class, higher status, service occupations. Entry is restricted and usually based on achieving formal educational qualifications. Higher salary levels are then retrospectively justified in terms of the income and leisure foregone during this period of education. The education, usually conducted at under-graduate or postgraduate level, also justifies higher salaries in terms of the command over specialist knowledge acquired and greater autonomy in work practices on the basis of the professional's superior knowledge. But as Collins (1990, p. 19) makes clear, technical knowledge by itself is not a sufficient guarantee of a professional occupational structure. It is the status that society confers on certain types of knowledge and the restrictions placed on access to it that is important.

The education process, involving selection at point of entry and at various examination points, is also part of a process of creating a uniform social grouping out of aspiring professionals. Collins argues (1990, p. 19) that: 'the academic organisational structure has a social rather than a technical impact: it affects the way in which an occupation is organised but not the amount of skilled performance.' Such educated, professional workers are distinguished by what they wear, how they conduct themselves, where they congregate for work and leisure and the common language they speak. They can be described as: 'communities with a certain style of life, code of ethics and self-conscious identity and

Exhibit 9.1 *Professionals in the English and Welsh water industry*

Professionals in the private sector sell their services to clients, who therefore exercise a degree of control over professionals, although a degree of autonomy based upon the professional's own expertise and status always remains. Where the employing firm is also owned by external investors, then consumer control is supplemented by owner control, and professionals may find themselves having to respond to quite distinct and potentially conflicting sets of pressures: concerning quality of service from clients; concerning expanding market share and cost cutting from shareholders. Professionals in the public sector have a similar dual system of control. Here the 'client' is the user of the public sector service, traditionally a source of little pressure within the public sector, and the 'owner' must be the local electorate to whom the service is ultimately responsible. In the English and Welsh water industry, professional water managers have had to come to terms with a shift from the public to the private sector and this has highlighted the particular role they play within water management.

Prior to privatisation, water managers were located within quangos, the regional water authorities (RWAs). Here the 'control' exercised by the water authorities' customers, the users of water supplies, was fairly minimal since it was exercised indirectly. The scale of the RWA's organisation gave customers little effective access. Central government could influence RWAs on water customers' behalf and the boards of RWAs had a majority of local government delegates. In this way, democratic control was supposed to guide professionals in their work. Then, under the 1983 Water Act, the elected members were replaced by a small management board appointed by central government. Local authorities were represented via consumer consultative committees, where they held about a third of seats with RWAs themselves appointing the remainder. However, in practice this made little difference since water managers had come to operate with substantial autonomy, subject mainly to fiscal controls from their central government paymasters.

As a result, for much of the 1970s, water managers were promoting major public investment projects such as dams and reservoirs subject to relatively little external scrutiny. This has been severely criticised for being an inappropriate strategy, ignoring more mundane problems such as leaky pipes and inadequate sewage treatment. Even in relation to planning infrastructure for new development, water managers remained distanced from the land use planning authorities, preparing their own strategies first and consulting afterwards rather than liaising during development planning. The RWAs in this period provide a good example of the New Right's bureaucracy running out of control. They were aloof from the community they served, hardly engaged in any negotiative activities inside or outside government and cannot be considered to have made rational planning decisions over water supply.

The transfer of the water supply industry from the public to the private sector has coincided with the greater influence of the European Commission. This meant that water managers have had to respond to a quite different pattern of pressures. The EC has required substantial upgrading of treatment facilities to improve water quality. Prior to privatisation this upgrading was blocked by financial restraints, but continued pressure from the EC and some private sector funding have helped loosen central government purse strings. As a result water managers are dealing with major new investment programmes again but are doing so under conditions of a requirement to produce profits for shareholders and the greatly enhanced consumer and environmental protection that followed privatisation.

The NRA monitors water managers closely and this is comple-mented by the work of the consumer watchdog, the Office of Water Services (Offwat). Offwat operates with a central and regional office structure, monitoring day-to-day management and guiding major policy decisions. It has responsibility for overseeing economic regulation, the standards of service, customer complaints and competition and discrimination. Thus the increases in water bills and the moves towards metering are not left to water professionals' discretion any more but are negotiated with a number of organisa-tions: the same is true of water treatment investment. This suggests a shift towards a situation more readily recognised as structured mediation within the institutionalist approach. The direct control exercised by the community remains weak. Here quangos control each other, the public do not control the professionals directly. For water managers, this still represents a loss of autonomy but their authority as expert, objective professionals had already been eroded by the evidence of planning failures in the 1970s.

Further reading: Rees (1989); Pearce (1982); Saunders (1985).

boundaries to outsiders' (Collins, 1990, p. 15). While not intending to imply there is no scope for individuality within a profession, nevertheless there are similarities between members of a profession which, in the majority of cases, are more marked than individual differences.

This raises the question of how the professionalisation process deals with the major structural differences within society, those of class, gender and ethnicity. In many cases the filtering of entrants to the profession ensures a relatively homogeneous base on which professionalisation can work. But there is evidence that, at least in the case of gender, the barriers to entry are coming down. There are growing number of women entering all the professions associated with the environment. However, this is operating from a low base (see Table 9.2).

Table 9.2 *Women within the built environment professions*

Royal Institute of Chartered Surveyors	60,000 members	3 per cent women (6 per cent including students)
Royal Town Planning Institute	11,750 members	15 per cent women (18 per cent including students)
Royal Institute of British Architects	28,000 members	8.5 per cent women 4 per cent of working members are women
Institute of Housing	9,000 members	39 per cent including students
Chartered Institute of Building	28,400 members	Less than 1 per cent
Institute of Civil Engineers	70,100 members	2 per cent including students

Source: Greed (1991) pp. 202–4.

In all the land use and construction professions, Greed estimates that less than 5 per cent are women. As she says (1991, p. 3):

These factors may be irrelevant to urban policy-making, if women's needs are perceived as being no different from those of men; or if it is believed that the professional man is capable of sufficiently disinterested neutrality to plan equally well for all groups in society . . . But as research and human experience have shown, women suffer considerable disadvantages within a built environment that is developed by men, primarily for other men.

Greed argues that professions need to be restructured to allow more women access to senior posts in order to overcome this discrimination in the outcomes of planning activity, although she recognises (p. 181) that not all women in senior positions, particularly those that have achieved those positions on the basis of an agenda set by men, will automatically operate in a way that is conscious of this discrimination. The professional socialisation process may ensure that a female professional operates primarily as a professional (defined in terms of her male counterparts) than as a woman (defined in terms of exploitative relationships in society).

While these features of uniform socialisation and controlled entry are hallmarks of the traditional profession, what Johnson calls the 'collegiate professions,' he points out that professions can operate under two other forms of occupational control, and that the traditional collegiate form may coexist with one of these. Some professions operate under corporate patronage in which one industry employs the majority of the members and, therefore, exercises a significant influence on their ways of working. For example, architects are predominantly employed by property developers and the values and norms of that industry affect their work. Alternatively, some professionals' work is defined by the actions of the state and they become subject to state mediation in establishing their professional identity. Many planning professions exist to operate a variety of regulations, from development control to pollution abatement to assessing suitability for council housing. The state, in setting the guidelines for this work and indeed creating the opportunity for its existence, is a pre-eminent influence on the profession.

State mediation has been a major factor in the creation of 'the' planning profession, the chartered town planner. This professional remains the central figure in much planning policy for planners are charged with coordinating and synthesising the inputs from many other, more specialist professions. Data and policy inputs on roads from transport engineers, air quality from environmental scientists, housing need from housing managers, land drainage from water engineers all feed into the strategic planning and development control decisions of planners. The new informational requirements of EIAs are also being handled by planners given the incorporation of most EIAs into development control decision making. This description of a planner's work reflects the image presented by the liberal political economy approach, the planner as rational coordinator of data inputs, but a large amount of planning work is more bureaucratic in nature, particularly development control. Yet another area of planners' work is neither rational decision making nor bureaucratic rubber stamping. It involves negotiating with groups, whether from the commercial sector, pressure groups, or the general public and liaising between the public and private sectors (Underwood, 1980 and see Exhibits 9.2 on planning gain and 9.3 on joint housing studies).

Planners, like other local government professionals, also have to operate within the context of responsibility to elected local politicians. This distinguishes them from professionals, say, in quangos. During the 1980s councillors have become more politicised along party lines (Stoker, 1991, p. 39 – but see Midwinter *et al.*, 1991, p. 137, for the Scottish situation), more aware of policy issues and more expert in managing and challenging their professionals. Laffin and Young (1990) point to a 'new breed' of councillor who is taking back much policy initiative from local government professionals, including planners. This applies particularly to New Right and New Left councils. As a result local government professionals have had to redefine professionalism and reconceptualise both their competence and their claims to represent the public interest. A range of roles are available to the professional in this task: to act as a controller of a budget; to enable and facilitate council policy; to be a policy activist supporting radical councillors; and to be the professional advocate speaking out in the name of rational decision making. Planners, too, have experimented with these roles.

■ Town planners under attack

The planning profession (as we shall call the membership of the RTPI) has been particularly vulnerable to the changes of the 1980s as it is not a strong organisation. It is relatively young and small among the broader range of professions concerned with the environment. It is a common focus of criticism and attack over the inadequacies of the environment and its perceived failure to protect the environment from adverse change. When individuals and firms interact with planners, there is a high degree of dissatisfaction. 29 per cent of all cases referred to the local government ombudsman concerned planners, amounting to some 6728 cases in 1989/90. From the Right have come criticisms of the restrictions that planners place upon development activity and the obvious failure of planners to manage environmental change in a rational manner.

This has been part of a broader attack by Thatcherism on the professions generally, which included a report by the Monopolies and Mergers Commission in 1986 on the provision of professional services (Laffin and Young, 1990). The establishment of the National Council for Vocational Qualifications by the DTI and DES have suggested alternative patterns of education and training to those currently controlled by the professions (Morphet, 1992b). Faced with this attack the professions found little support from the Left, who had long

Exhibit 9.2   *Negotiating planning gain*

Few areas of planning practice have been as controversial as planning gain. To the New Right they epitomise the attempt by the local state to exert undue influence over private sector activity, siphoning off profits and deterring wealth generation. Many uses of planning gain are considered outside the legitimate scope of a planning authority's role. Within this view, the planner would be seen as a bureaucrat, tying up development proposals in unnecessary red tape. But other analysts would argue that planning gain presents, at least potentially, a much more positive role for planners. The liberal political economist places most emphasis on the outcomes, on the ways in which planning gain can deliver a compromise which reflects all the costs and benefits of a proposal. The planner is here cast in the role of an expert assessor of these costs and benefits, using the resources of the governmental organisation to pool internal and external information. The outcome is then judged in terms of the extent to which a balance is achieved and policy goals met.

By contrast, the institutional approach looks back to the process by which the gain was arrived at, and stresses the negotiation involved. The planner is seen as an active mediator between vested interests both within local government and outside. Recognition may be given to the possibility of the planners have vested interests of their own, but it is usually assumed that these do not dominate the mediation process. The skill of the planner lies in balancing the demands of these various interests and devising an outcome which, if not a compromise, is seen as legitimate. In such circumstances, central government plays an important role in providing advice and determinations on what constitutes a legitimate use of obligations, although scope for conflict always remains.

The 1980s saw considerable conflict between local authorities, on the one hand, and developers and central government on the other, over the definition of legitimate planning gain. Recent policy pronouncements by central government represent the temporary halt in that conflict. The current situation reflects both a slight softening in the rather hostile attitude of central government to planning gain and the revised expectations of local authorities in achieving social benefits through planning gain. DoE research has shown that planning agreements are now being used fairly cautiously to control and regulate developments and not to achieve wider planning objectives or community benefits.

To the New Left, however, the existing situation is disappointing. They see considerable potential in planning gain for redressing the inequalities that inevitably result from a weak planning system trying to control powerful capital flows. Planners could use planning gain to channel resources to groups disadvantaged by current patterns of resource allocation. Ethnic minorities, the working class, and women could have their special needs met by diverting some of the developer's profit into community facilities. But planners are heavily constrained gatekeepers and the combination of central government control and the underlying dynamics of capital accumulation ensure that community benefits are limited.

In addition, planners cannot be assumed automatically to reflect the wishes of community groups. Their own interests, in terms of status and career advancement, may result in identification with the promotion of the development process rather than the problems of disadvantaged groups. Community groups, therefore, have constantly to fight to maintain their needs at the forefront of planners' agendas.

The local plans of the 1991 Planning and Compensation Act could provide a new possibility for doing so. Under recent government advice, a planning agreement may legitimately seek to implement local plan policy and research suggests that local plans are recognising that planning agreements are an important policy tool. So the more open debate that occurs about development plan policy may open up the opportunities afforded by planning gain to a wider range of community groups, if planners recognise the opportunities.

Further reading: Grimley (1992); Alterman, 1990; Healey *et al.* (1992).

criticised planners and others for their treatment of disadvantaged groups and the inequitable use of their expertise, powers of negotiation and control over the allocation of resources.

Paralleling these political criticisms of planners, there has been a critique developed in academic circles of the intellectual standing of planning as a profession. Broadbent (1977) has argued that planners had a less established body of knowledge and code of practice than many other related professions. As a result they were over sensitive to other professions poaching their areas of work and tended to be swayed by fashion. They readily adopted new theoretical approaches and sought to capture new planning procedures before other occupational groups. It has proved, therefore, very difficult to identify a coherent ideology for the profession (Foley, 1960). In a stringent attack on planners, Reade (1987) argues that planning lacks any credible theoretical basis, that it is a profession which was prematurely legitimised before its function could be fully clarified and that, consequently, it tries to disguise this fact by jargonising and confusing the issues it deals with: Reade terms this 'legitimation by obfuscation'. Again he emphasises the willingness of planners to take on board new ideas and concerns, without due consideration or a thorough grounding in the knowledge of these new areas.

Exhibit 9.3   *Joint housing studies*

The concept of professionalism implies a degree of autonomy in everyday work and some specialist or monopolised expertise that underpins the higher social status of the professional. In more technocratic areas of planning, such as pollution control or nature conservation, the basis of expertise may be clear cut. But in some areas it is more difficult to conceive of planners as experts in the rational decision making mould of liberal political economy. Joint housing studies provide a good example of the nature of 'expertise' that planning can involve.

Joint housing studies have the appearance of a technical document. They consist of a commentary on a series of tables with figures purporting to identify the availability of housing land. Planning policy guidance indicates the methodology for such studies and refers to the 'residual method' using formula and numeric examples:

The residual method
The general formula used is:

$$TLA = [5 \times (SPT - C)]/Y$$

where: TLA is the target land availability figure
SPT is the structure plan target for dwelling completions
C is the number of dwelling completions to date
Y is the number of years remaining for meeting SPT

This formula has to be adjusted where the structure plan has less than five years to run or there are exceptionally high or low completion figures.

The whole concept of the study fits within a model of planning and development drawn from neo-classical economics: demand for housing land arises from the housing market and is represented by housebuilders seeking planning permission on new development land; supply is controlled by the planning system issuing such permissions and making land allocations in development plans.

Planners could thus collect data on the housing market, demographic and otherwise, and on the outputs of the planning system concerning residential development and make decisions on future policy.

However, joint housing studies were introduced in the early 1980s precisely because a New Right government would not accept this view of planners. It argued that planners did not have the expertise to assess housing and development markets. This expertise resided in the housebuilding industry. Therefore joint housing studies involved planners discussing their land allocations with housebuilders, involving the private sector in planning policy. To the New Left this was further evidence of the Thatcher administration's redirection of the state from the needs of local communities to the demands of private capital. The issue of expertise was an irrelevance since the main issue was the use of planners and the planning system to allocate development rights in line with housebuilders' wishes. In particular, the redefinition of housing land allocations in terms of market-based criteria meant that planners were not allocating land resources in line with the needs of low-income, poorly housed or homeless groups.

In fact, the use of joint housing studies cannot be simply represented in terms of local working class needs versus private capital. For, in many of the areas where conflict and debate between planners and housebuilders over the studies was fiercest, the local community, and in particular the most politically active parts of the local community, were middle class. Joint housing studies were caught in the struggle between housebuilders wishing to build and NIMBYist local populations resisting development. In this situation joint housing studies became a mechanism through which the conflict was negotiated with planners playing a mediating role, as in the institutional approach. The pseudo-technical nature of the joint housing study became a resource in this mediating role. Many of the arguments over the relevance of the residual method and the precise formula used represent the form that the mediation between conflicting interests took. So that, when central government states that the residual method is not appropriate in areas of unusually low or high housebuilding rates, this represents an influence on the outcome of mediation, favouring one party at the expense of the other. Technical dispute is the cover for decisions with distributional consequences.

Further reading: Rydin (1988); PPG3, *Housing*; SLABS Research Unit (1985).

Evidence of the changing flavour of planners' self-perception can be seen in the rapid shift that has occurred from a concern with economic development during the Thatcher years to the current attempts to take on board the growth of environmental policy. In 1983–5 an analysis of papers in the professional journal The Planner found that 45 per cent dealt with economic development, 13 per cent with the environment, and 11 per cent each with the development industry and public administration (Leyland, 1986, p. 34). Now planners are arguing for a key role in local environmental auditing, in EIAs and in plan preparation with a 'green' slant. In support of this, they can cite a debate within the RTPI that took place in 1971 which adopted environmental planning as the broad description of the Institute's concerns. But this option was chosen out of no less than five very different definitions of planning, an indication of the lack of a certain professional identity. Furthermore, these shifts of the 1970s, 1980s and now 1990s build on many previous shifts in the theoretical basis of planning, from environmental determinism to comprehensive rationalism to radical political economy as outlined in Part 1.

Given the recent adoption of environmental concerns within planning, how easily does this fit with current patterns of practice? O'Riordan and Turner (1983, p. 136) find three reasons why planning should be more oriented towards environmental concerns. First, there is the impact of environmental scientific knowledge on the general consciousness of planners and planning policy makers at central and local levels. Second, there is the interconnection between the local economic prosperity and environmental degradation, affecting tourist and farming industries within certain areas. Even with a primary commitment to economic development, this encourages planners to take environmental concerns into account. Third, there are the procedural changes surrounding the introduction of EIAs.

However, O'Riordan and Turner question the ability of planners to deal effectively with the new problems they are facing. Most environmental data draws on knowledge of the natural sciences and thus planners are placed in the position of consulting external experts and assessing their material, often couched in highly technical terms. Second, there is a divergence between the timescales on which environmental research is conducted and that for planning decision making. The latter is relatively short term, geared to local authority or other organisational decision making cycles; the former can require a period of over five years to be conclusive. Third, the environmental scientists providing the raw information have a value system which emphasises their objectivity and neutrality vis-à-vis sectoral interests and is opposed to the political nature of much planning activity. This suggests that the ability of British planners to deal with the integration of environmental issues into planning may be limited: they lack the theoretical base or a consistent value scheme to do so; they are pursuing 'green' topics because they are an intellectually weak profession.

Of course, these types of criticism from planning academics makes the profession even more vulnerable. Breheny and Congden (1989) locate the reason for this in the division that exists between planning academics and professionals, so that the academics tend to develop knowledge, theories and research about planners rather than for them. This contrasts with many other professions, such as surveying and environmental engineering, where the academics and practitioners share common values and approaches, and academic work seeks to support everyday practice. It is, however, evident in other areas of work such as housing management, where radical critiques of the role of state professionals have been developed.

As a result of the political assault on the planning profession by Thatcherism, combined with the lack of intellectual support, the RTPI faced a difficult time during the 1980s. Planning departments in many local authorities were cut in staff numbers, with departments merged or even abolished. Unit costs per planning application actually fell during 1985–9. In the case of the Milton Keynes Development Corporation, the planning functions were privatised to be taken over by Chestertons, a firm of chartered surveyors. There was increasing privatisation of planning work through the use of consultants, with many private sector planners members of alternative professional bodies, such as the RICS, or holding less allegiance to the RTPI which is predominantly public sector focused. At the same time the role of the RTPI in controlling access to the profession came under challenge from the National Council for Vocational Qualifications and from the implications of European integration in allowing foreign professionals to practice in Britain and claim membership of British professions (Morphet, 1992a and 1992b). However, by the 1990s the planning profession had recovered somewhat. Recruitment had increased and only in London were planning departments understaffed, according to the Audit Commission (1992), although many departments still find themselves under daily pressure. The New Right has tempered its views somewhat with an emphasis on customer care, quality and efficiency rather than deprofessionalising planning.

■ The empowering professional

The Left have also sought to find a new role for professionals, looking back to ideas current in the 1960s to develop the concept of the 'empowering professional'. This goes beyond the New Right's concept of the 'enabling' professional who lets people 'help themselves' in the context of market processes. In this context, the 1985 Local Government (Access to Information) Act and 1987 Access to Personal Files Act are as much ways of constraining and checking on professionals as putting information in the hands of citizens. The New Left's concept of empowerment involves people using information to take political control in order to reallocate economic resources in the recognition that market processes systematically disadvantage certain groups. This often involves restructuring of planning organisations, alongside changes in attitude and working practices of planners. Organisations can be opened up to allow community groups to become directly involved in the decision making that occurs within them, as the GLC showed. Organisations can also be decentralised to encourage participation. Local area offices and professional teams, even local mini-town halls can give government a new, more approachable and challengeable face (Burns, 1988; Gyford, 1991; Hambleton and Hoggart, 1984).

As Hambleton and Hoggart have shown, there is a wide range of motives in forming the moves towards decentralisation. It is not automatically linked to radical notions of empowerment but it can be used as part of an attack on a professionalised welfare state. It can not only seek to improve public services and the accountability of those providing services, but also to alter the distribution of resources towards the disadvantaged and, most important, to raise political awareness among the local electorate.

There is now also a concerted effort among planning academics to develop work supportive of practitioners. This has shaped the nature of the institutional approach. For example, the work of John Forester (1989) has had a great influence. This recognises the constraints under which planners work but argues that they can play a positive role in achieving benefits for the environment and disadvantaged groups by means of 'communicative action' and 'mediated negotiation'. Drawing on ideas in American institutionalist politics, the analysis argues that 'political democracy depends not only on economic and social conditions but also on the design of political institutions' (March and Olsen, 1989, p. 17) and further (p. 27) that

> Regardless of the way in which institutions are structured, attention is a scarce good in politics; and control over the allocation of attention is important to a political actor. By inhibiting the discovery of and entry into some potential conflicts, a structure of rules organized into relatively discrete responsibilities channels political energies into certain kinds of conflict and away from others.

Central to this process is the role of language, (p. 25) 'the ways in which participants come to be able to talk about one situation as similar or different from another'.

The professional is important within this process of communication. It is not enough for the planner to stand aloof as the expert. For though Healey (1990, p. 100) argues that 'techno-rational processes have at times been important safeguards for interests not otherwise actively represented in the social relations of policy formulation and implementation', they have also suppressed interests. Hence the new mediating professional must be much more aware of the social and economic position of interests involved, of how the communication involved in planning is structured and of the relation between a mediating planning process and policy outcomes (Healey, 1992b):

> A full understanding of the impact of what planners do must address their contribution to the interrelated activities of knowing, acting and valuing . . . in interactive situations. This means analysing communicative acts.

Above all the planner must be reflexive about his or her own actions (Healey and Gilroy, 1990; Myerson and Rydin, 1991). This is difficult. As Newman (1991, p. 30) says, reasserting the rights of the citizen within planning implies a reassessment of professional practices and values and requires 'a radical shift in attitudes and complete reform of the ways in which local and central government officers are trained. The prize for such a change would be strategic planning decisions arrived at through debate rather than conflict'.

Further reading

Rees (1990) provides a good account of the role of professionals within environmental quangos, while Laffin and Young (1990) is an up-to-date review of the situation in local authorities. The issue of women in such professions is dealt with in Greed (1991), and a more specifically planning oriented study may be provided by Little (forthcoming). Forester (1989) is a good introduction to the idea of the 'empowering' professional.

■ *Chapter 10* ■

The Public

The public interact with the planning system in a number of ways: as a 'client' through applying for permission or authorisation or making representations on planning policy and decisions; through the party political system; by campaigning and through the lobbying tactics of pressure groups; and through creating a climate of public opinion. This chapter covers the last three forms of public pressure. The first form, the client relationship, is implicit in much of the preceding discussion of planners as professionals and the nature of organisations such as quangos.

■ Pressure groups

The term 'pressure group' is not an undisputed one. Indeed 'the tendency of different writers to espouse different terms is a source of confusion for many students approaching the subject for the first time' (Kimber and Richardson, 1974, p. 1). Some political analysts prefer to focus on interest groups where group formation is based on a shared location within economic processes. Pressure groups are then distinguished by also having shared values, which may not relate directly to the participants' economic roles. Others see pressure and interest groups, so defined, as two sides of the same coin with little practical distinction possible. Again analysts differ in terms of how the interests, on which group formation is based, are defined. Some are willing to accept the group's own self-definition. Others argue that this is subjective and clouded by the operation of ideological processes within society. The analyst thus may more clearly be able to relate a group's interests to its role in economic and social processes.

These issues of interest versus pressure groups and subjective versus objective assessment of interests are hotly debated in the political science literature but it is not relevant to cover them in more depth here (see Saunders, 1979). Rather than adopting a strict definition of the type of group to be examined, a broad range of groups will be discussed and issues of definition covered as they arise in particular cases. For working purposes, a pressure group may be defined as 'any group . . . which articulates a demand that the authorities in the political system or subsystems should make an authoritative allocation . . . such groups do not themselves seek to occupy positions of authority' (Kimber and Richardson, 1974, pp. 2–3).

Groups relevant to planning policy can be divided into the following: business interests, particularly the development lobby and the farming lobby and, ranged largely in opposition to such groups, anti-development groups and the other elements in the environmental movement, including discussion of local amenity groups. Each category will be discussed in more detail below.

■ Business interest groups

Business interest groups are the classic case of an interest group, where the members have a common role in the economic process. Although in competition with each other in everyday economic activities, such firms recognise the common benefits of grouping together to influence public policy. The aim is to restructure the policy framework to enhance conditions for profit making. The business lobby thus comprises a number of interest groups from the overarching CBI to sector-specific groups such as the Building Materials Producers' Association or oligopolistic firms, such as the electricity supply industry who lobby directly on their own behalf. In 1972 it was estimated that there were 2500 employers' associations, of which at least 1600 were active (Kimber and Richardson, 1974, p. 10).

The potential membership of such groups is limited and fairly easy to identify and the coverage of that membership by a particular group will depend on the group demonstrating activity in lobbying policy makers on behalf of its members. However there is always the possibility for a potential member to 'free-ride' on the successes of the group without actually joining. For joining and being involved in a group necessarily involves costs, both financial and in terms of time. In some cases the tendency for members to abstain or exit from the group is reduced by the application of specific sanctions or selective incentives (Dunleavy and O'Leary, 1987).

The number of such groups is so great and they are so diverse in nature that is it is not possible to survey them here. Suffice it to say that in many areas of urban and environmental planning one or more business interest group will be seeking to exert influence. This may take the form of the CBI's opposition to the introduction of EIAs. It may represent the demands of chambers of commerce for local economic development aid. Within the general business lobby there are bound to be conflicts and inequalities. Thus the electricity supply industry has different concerns from the energy efficiency industry. The former is represented by a small group of organised firms, until recently forming a nationalised industry. In their pursuit of a particular policy goal, the expansion of nuclear power, former Secretary of State for Energy, Tony Benn, has said: 'In my political life, I have never known such a well-organised, scientific, industrial and technical lobby as the nuclear power lobby' (Roberts *et al.*, 1991, p. 44). Yet, by contrast, the energy efficiency industry (that is, the business interests as opposed to the environmentalists) is represented by a fragmented group of over 20 trade associations.

The strength of all business interest groups lies not in the size of their membership but in the control that members hold over economic resources and their use in production and investment processes. This 'corporate discretion' of business interests means that they are sought as consultees by government and do not have to push against a closed door in their political activities (Lindblom, 1977). Furthermore, those groups representing the more economically powerful firms will hold more sway than those comprising the smaller firms. This feature is particularly seen in the case of development interest groups which are considered further below, along with the farming lobby.

At the national level the operation of corporate discretion will mean that nationally powerful economic actors have easy access to Ministers and, particularly, civil servants in the administration (Saunders, 1985). At the local level, the situation is not so clear cut. In Conservative controlled councils, a local business interest will have ready contacts with local politicians and may even be an elected councillor (Saunders, 1979). In Labour authorities, business interests may more readily make contact with local government professionals and administrators. It will also be easier for business interests to dominate the council where the councillors are not drawn from the commuter community, dependent on external income from outside the local area, but represent local business as employers or employees (Rees, 1990, p. 409). In such circumstances, powerful local growth coalitions can form to harness local planning to the promotion of local economic development (Harding, 1990).

It is clear that during the 1980s business influence at the local government level increased. Since 1984, local authorities have had to consult non-domestic ratepayers, a consultative role usually taken by local chambers of commerce. Some have suggested that business groups can now lead council policy. Reviewing the literature, Stoker and Wilson (1991, p. 30) conclude:

The future world of local pressure group activity is likely to see increased influence for business and opportunities for it to take a leading role. But there are a number of limitations on the capacity of the business sector to offer leadership and on its ability to maintain a coherent and co-ordinated policy programme. It may not be as easy as some analysts imagine for business to usurp the local authorities' control and management of the local political agenda.

For the New Right, business interest groups have a vital role to play in the policy process, for not only do they represent their own interests but also those of their consumers. The public, it is argued, are often represented more effectively by such groups than single-issue or local area pressure groups who will represent only a section of the public. The liberal political economy approach also accepts the relevance of market processes in revealing public preference, though it prefers to look to evidence of market decision making rather than the views of business interest groups. However both the New Left and the institutional approach remain highly sceptical of this view, seeing business interests as, in many circumstances, conflicting with the interests of other groups in society. The influence that business groups hold over central and local government can then be detrimental to many other groups, and represent a manipulation of the political process to meet sectional interests' needs.

☐ *The development lobby*

Development interest groups are a business interest group defined by the common role of its members – housebuilders, property developers and construction companies – in creating and transforming the built environment. They have a primary interest in the land use planning system given its central role in permitting development rights, but also in many of the other regulatory aspects of the planning system. Examples of such groups are the Building Employers' Confederation (BEC), and the HouseBuilders Federation within it, and the Federation of Master Builders. There are also the professions which work for or with development interests, notably the RICS, the RIBA and various property researchers' groups, such as the Society of Property Researchers and the Property Investment Group.

As with other business interest groups, development interest groups use incentives and sanctions to maintain membership. For example, the BEC offers journals, advice services and indemnity schemes. Membership of a group, along with associated insurance or quality vetting, may be a substantial advantage in development activity. Dunleavy and

O'Leary (1987) identify interest groups where selective incentives are used and there is a high percentage membership as one example of a stable group with a relatively long-term presence in policy making. They are further characterised by strong leadership control and low participation by member in political activities. This provides a good description of most development interest groups.

There is, however, a small number of small, more exclusive groups which do not seek a large membership base. These are closed groups of major economic actors who operate effectively as an advisory committee within government decision making. The small number of members is essential for the practicalities of government consultation and to enable the group to represent itself as the pinnacle of the development industry. Such groups, which include the Property Advisory Group, and in the past the Volume Builders' Study Group, are so incorporated into government policy making that they look only inwards towards the public sector and have no function with respect to a wider membership.

The importance of such small development interest groups highlights the point that the influence of such groups is not necessarily related to their membership size, but to their control of economic resources. It is not the case that large numbers necessarily speak louder in policy circles. Hence the closed groups, representing only a few major firms are incorporated into policy making while other, more open development interest groups, such as the Federation of Master Builders, have to engage in the routine campaigning and lobbying of other pressure groups. While their position as economic agents responsible for undertaking development may give them advantages in such political campaigning, it does not always ensure that their viewpoint will prevail over other pressure groups' point of view.

□ The farming lobby

The farming industry is a key actor in planning policy, concerned over the transfer of land to urban uses under the planning system, the use of the countryside for recreational purposes and the pressure of nature conservation policy on their production activities. The farming lobby, comprising the National Farmers' Union (NFU) and the Country Landowners' Association (CLA), has been described as the classic case of an incorporated interest group with a relationship between the NFU and MAFF that was unrivalled in closeness (Self and Storing, 1962). McCormick (1991) recounts how this 'client' relation between the government department and the farmers' trades union arose from the 1947 Agriculture Act, which required government to consult representatives of producers in formulating government policy. By the late 1970s this was resulting in daily, even hourly contact between the two organisations (see also Lowe *et al.*, 1986, pp. 87–95).

In addition to this legislative basis for consultation, the NFU, with its 14,000 members in England and Wales and parallel organisation in Scotland, can claim 80 per cent coverage of its potential membership of farmers, thus speaking with authority for the farming industry. Linkages to the legislature (Houses of Parliament) and Government are also good due to the large number of Members of Parliament with farming interests, either directly or as a landlord. The NFU claims to have regular contact with some 100 MPs. McCormick argues that its relations with local government in rural areas were almost as good as those with central government, with a large number of farmers acting as councillors. But 1976 data suggests that only 7 per cent of non-metropolitan district councillors worked in farming, rising to 10 per cent in shire counties (Herington, 1984, p. 152). Such contact is probably heavily concentrated in specific local areas. As Herington points out (1984, p. 151) the local power of the farming lobby varies depending on the local structure of the agriculture industry, and the size and the productivity of local farms. Political power reflects economic power.

However, McCormick also points to a decline in the influence of the NFU since the 1970s. He identifies five factors behind this decline. First, there is a growing concern among the public and government circles over the cost of agricultural support and its consequences in terms of food surpluses. Second, changes in the countryside receive considerable press and media coverage, usually hostile to the farming industry. Third, more people are questioning the morality of modern farming linking the question of the treatment of animals with 'food scares' such as those over salmonella in eggs and BSE in cows. Fourth, there is growing criticism of MAFF and its role in relation to these problems. Fifth, the urban-to-rural shift in population is resulting in more and more people having a direct stake in how the countryside is used.

As a result of these changes, the farming lobby no longer has as strong a foothold in central government and has to compete on slightly more even terms with other pressure groups. The importance of the farming lobby depends on the significance and extent of its economic power, on the importance that agriculture plays within the economy. As that importance is judged to decline, so will its influence. However, this decline in influence has to be judged against a position of unparalleled access to policy making in the past.

■ The environmental movement

The term 'the environmental movement' covers a broad spectrum of groups from specific anti-development movements, through local amenity groups to ecologists/environmentalists. While there are clear and important differences between the individual groups within this movement, they are united in their support of the protection afforded by planning regulations and the opportunities offered by participation in plan making.

The different theoretical positions see the role of the environmental movement very differently. As mentioned above, the New Right argues that such pressure groups are likely to be captured by highly sectional interests who will disadvantage the general consumer by restricting economic activity. For the liberal political economist, the values held by such groups are seen to have real meaning as representing an element of the public interest, but their concern is to elicit information to enable rational decision making by professionals, not delegate that decision making to pressure groups. It is the New Left and institutional approach which place the most positive emphasis on pressure group activity. Within the institutional analysis, pressure groups are a mechanism by which a variety of interests are represented within the policy process, and it is the role of the planning system to respond to these interests and mediate them. Once sufficiently mobilised to make their view known to the state, the groups move back to a more passive role with professional planners taking over the initiative. For the New Left, however, such groupings can form social movements, in which case they become the active motor of political change. Engaged in struggle with the state as well as groups outside it, they seek to achieve sufficient political power to challenge dominant economic interests and achieve a reallocation of resources. This process of conflict and struggle is a continuous one, which politicises groups and transforms them from mere pressure groups. As will be seen, such a transformation into social movements is rare in practice (Lowe, 1986).

□ Anti-development groups

Anti-development groups are locally-based groups focused on opposition to a specific development proposal. They range from the anti-motorway campaigners of the 1970s to the NIMBYists (Not In My Back Yard) of the 1980s and the tenants' organisations seeking to prevent sale of their council estates in the 1990s.

They differ from other types of environmental group in having a very limited purposed, a tightly defined geographical area of activity, being responsive to an outside stimulus (the development proposal) and, often, having only a limited lifespan. Sometimes an anti-development groups may arise out of or turn into a broader-based amenity group (see below) but then it has lost the specific features of this type of group. Short (1984, p. 131) locates the growth of such groups in the 'failure of the formal political channels to either represent or articulate place-specific issues', itself a feature of the split between workplace and home. The finely grained nature of local community experience centred around the home has not been adequately reflected in the organisation of political parties, even at local government level, leading to an organisational vacuum. When development pressures threaten that local experience, community groups arise, focused on opposition to the development.

The chief tactic of such groups involves intense local mobilisation to demonstrate the strength of opposition to development. This will then be demonstrated through existing formal channels, whether a public local inquiry (see Exhibit 10.1), the use of planning procedures or the vote required under HAT procedures. More radical measures may also be adopted, including squatting, occupation of land and demonstrations. Short (1984, pp. 138–9) describes this as a spectrum of activities ranging from collaboration, through campaigning to coercive and confrontational measures. One common feature, though, is that all such activities are focused on local rather than central government, unless some residents have a particular contact within the Government. This contrasts with development interests which will commonly work through central government as well as using any specific local contact.

Much attention has been focused on middle class, rural or NIMBY groups. Shucksmith (1990, p. 69) relates the rise of the NIMBY phenomenon to the migration of higher status groups into rural locations with a vested interest in preventing further development and the resources, expertise and time to run local campaigns. He quotes the adage 'last one into the village runs the preservation society'. Given the overwhelming predominance of owner-occupiers among such migrants, the economic motive is clear. Short (1984, pp. 132–3) describes it as follows: 'Much resident group activity arises from owner-occupiers seeking to band together to protect and enhance their property values. The rise of owner-occupation has given a material basis for much community actions.'

Thus in their study of residents' groups in Berkshire, Short *et al.* (1986, p. 227) identify the voice of the 'stoppers' (anti-development

---

Exhibit 10.1   *The environmental big public inquiry*

In some areas of planning policy, notably transport and energy, the main strategic decisions are taken at central government level in a highly non-participatory manner. The only opportunities for the public and environmental groups to influence decisions is when the policy is implemented through site-specific development. In most cases major development projects, even if they receive approval through avenues other than development control, are considered at a public local inquiry (PLI). At this forum, the views of various interested parties can be put forward, first to the inspector or panel in charge of the inquiry and then, via a report, to the relevant Secretary of State.

This is a participatory process which, depending on your viewpoint, allows all information to be considered before a rational planning decision is reached *or* allows all interests to be heard and involved in debate before a mediated conclusion is reached. But the reality of PLI procedure, particularly where major projects with environmental consequences are involved, is that the constraints of structure are more apparent than the mediation. This was clearly apparent in a series of 'nuclear' public inquiries into: a nuclear reprocessing plant at Windscale (now Sellafield), Cumbria in 1977; a pressurised water reactor at Sizewell B, Suffolk in 1983–5; and a fast breeder reactor/ reprocessing plant at Dounreay, Scotland in 1986. These constraints take a number of forms.

The resources of environmental groups are a major constraint on their ability to participate on an equal footing with the local authority, let alone the major developer. In the case of the Windscale Inquiry, BNFL spent £750,000. By the time of the Sizewell B Inquiry, the CEGB put £20 million into the preparation for and appearance at the inquiry. The high costs and low perceived benefits were such that the Town and Country Planning Association felt it could not afford to take part in the Dounreay Inquiry. It is not just the length of the inquiry – the Sizewell B Inquiry took 340 working days – and the paperwork that is expensive. The complexity of the issues discussed means that research and expert witnesses are needed to make a case and challenge the other side. This has generated calls for third party funding to allow environmental groups to make their case.

The procedures of a PLI are another constraint. They are highly formalistic, based on a quasi-judicial model. This is reinforced by the use of solicitors and barristers to present the cases of the various parties, using techniques of cross-examination and often obscure legal language. This is a barrier to many community groups presenting their views as they feel overawed, patronised and marginalised. The procedures also influence the debate with an emphasis on two-way claim and counterclaim, on the logical unravelling of single points and on legalistic precision in the use of words. This may not always be the best means by which to reach conclusions over environmental issues. There is often no logical order in the discussion of points either, the material presented depending on the availability of witnesses and the issues raised in cross-examination.

One major problem with development projects which implement a national policy is the division between challenging the project and challenging the policy. In the past inspectors have held that government policy could not be questioned in a PLI, the emphasis had to be on the details of the specific project, assuming that the basic need for the project had already been established. At the Windscale Inquiry only nuclear reprocessing itself could be debated, not its relation to the rest of the nuclear industry. Clearly environmental groups were unhappy with this example of 'salami politics'.

Even where, as at the Sizewell B Inquiry, the issue of need for the project could be discussed, environmental groups were unhappy about the extent to which national policy could really be challenged. The inspector sought to open up a full and fair discussion on the reactor proposal but the significance of this was questioned when statements by the Secretary of State, made during the inquiry, argued that the case for nuclear power was unassailable and when the DoEn authorised CEGB contracts placing advance orders for the reactor.

For many on the New Left these inquiries represent a legitimation tool, used to dispel public concern and support the nuclear industry. The actions of environmental groups are a challenge to a state acting on behalf of an industrial sector. However, the nature of the discussion challenges the notion of the public held by the New Right and the New Left. It is clearly skewing the evidence to present the public as purely consumers when they are represented by environmental groups raising issues of national as well as local significance. NIMBYism is consistent with consumerism: deflecting a nuclear power plant to another area protects local property values and the quality of local living conditions. Challenging the nuclear power programme, and hence the location of such a plant anywhere, suggests a public commitment to a broader range of values. Similarly the groupings that arise cannot be classified in terms of class, gender or ethnicity. Rather the nuclear proposal itself generates a new basis around which a community may form and enter into negotiation, however constrained, within the planning system.

Further reading: Outer Circle Policy Unit (1979) (also in O'Riordan and Turner (1983); Armstrong (1985); O'Riordan et al. (1988).

groups) as middle class, middle aged owner-occupiers. Again Rees (1990, p. 407) argues that:

> It is important to note that in the vast majority of disputes over the location of economic interests, *local* environmental interests have not questioned the need for the development; in other words, they have not challenged any dominant societal values or materialist goals (emphasis mine).

These groups are not concerned with conflicts between protection and development but with conflicts between groups of citizens. In this connection, Short cites the use of conservation area, AONB and other such designations in rural and gentrified inner city locations as an effective tool that middle class anti-development groups seek to use to prevent further building and immigration. This is described by Rees (1990, p. 407) as: 'transforming legislation designed to preserve areas of special historic importance into a weapon for defending smart residential areas'. Shucksmith links this to Peter Saunders' argument (1990, p. 70): 'that owner-occupiers must be seen as a distinct domestic property class because of their market interest in the accumulative potential of their homes, quite apart from their interest as consumers.'

These issues are explored further in Exhibit 10.2 on gentrification and conservation.

However, others have emphasised that economic motive is not the only basis for NIMBYism. Such activity also represents a 'territorial defence of lifestyle' (Shucksmith, 1990, p. 69). Migrants to such rural locations are at least as much in search of particular social networks as a particular physical environment. Ironically as the migrants become established and come to dominate local social and political institutions, they replace the existing social order or, rather, replicate it in their own image.

The short-term, specific anti-development may develop into (or arise out of) a local amenity group. Much research has covered amenity societies along with other environmental groups and they will therefore be covered in detail in the next section. But given their links to anti-development groups, they merit a short discussion here.

Amenity groups share many of the characteristics of middle class rural and urban anti-development groups, but they are usually longer-lived, and focus more generally on the local environment rather than the threat posed by specific developments. Some are locally based, others have a national level of organisation and many span the national and local levels. However they differ from many environmentalist groups (used here to denote groups based on an ecological analysis) in that they concentrate on countryside issues, including access, recreation and wildlife, and on the quality of the built environment. They do not

Exhibit 10.2 *Gentrification and conservation*

While conservation areas are primarily conceived of as a tool for preserving the built heritage, in practice they are also a tool of urban regeneration. This has had significant implications for the relationship of planning to local communities in these areas. At issue is the tendency for areas where conservation policies are successful to undergo gentrification, a process by which local working class communities are displaced by a predominantly middle class population. In some areas the process is developer-led. The refurbishment of 'lofts' in central New York and of dockside wharves in London by development companies has provided accommodation for new groups of high-income service workers. The distinctive physical character of these dwellings, explicitly marketed on the basis of their historic associations, has reinforced the distinctive social status of the new residents, both as new evolving occupational groups and as new occupants of previously working class and industrial areas.

In other areas, the gentrification has been more piecemeal and led by the incoming households. In Islington and similar districts of London, old houses were refurbished by middle class households, on a DIY plus subcontracting basis, or by small builders restoring the building and sometimes converting it into flats. Over a period of time the changing character of the area becomes apparent as tenure shifts from private renting to owner-occupation, as local services reflect the change in population and as new demands are made on the planning system.

In situations of gradual gentrification, the designation of an area as a conservation area is a central resource for the local middle class population. Such a designation attracts certain local government funds for environmental improvements at street level. It can justify alterations in local traffic management to reroute through traffic out of the area. It ensures high standards of aesthetic control on all development in the area. All these factors reinforce the social exclusivity of the area: a more pleasant local environment maintains local property prices; stringent design control raises the costs of refurbishment above the means of lower income groups. Often the new residents use the historic nature of the area to form a community group which reflects, at one and the same time, the unique character of the built environment and the social organisation of the community around that historic environment. Such groups can be highly effective in placing pressure on local planners for further protection and enhancement of the locality.

The previous residents of such an area are relatively powerless in the face of creeping gentrification since the slow, piecemeal pace inhibits effective mobilisation of a community which, in any case, has limited time and resources for mobilisation. Where a developer is seeking to purchase a larger area for comprehensive refurbishment then there is more scope for community action to resist the shift in population implied by the development. However, the particular circumstances of each case determine the success of such community action. In New York an unsympathetic local authority meant that the local artists were unable to resist developers' attempts to evict them. In Docklands the use of largely derelict warehousing meant that some community resistance was bypassed. In Covent Garden, the support of the GLC resulted in a compromise which achieved significant economic revitalisation of the area, conservation of the historic market building and some degree of safeguards and even additional facilities for the local community.

These cases can be seen as situations of mediation by the local planning system of pressures arising from development interests and variably organised and resourced local communities. But the emphasis on gentrification, displacement of local working class communities and the dominant motive of refurbishment to increase property values also lends support to a New Left analysis. The choice between approaches depends on how the various community groups, including artists' colonies and yuppies, are viewed, and the extent to which the social position of these groups and the power they can exercise on the local planning system is seen as dependent on their economic situation.

Further reading: Smith and Williams (1986); Zukin (1988); Christensen (1979).

necessarily link these issues into a broader analysis of environmental systems. Amenity is primarily defined as a 'visual' feature from these groups' point of view.

Another feature of these amenity groups which distinguishes them from all the groups discussed so far, is that their activities are less directly linked to their members' material interests or, at least, relate to their consumption of the rural and built environment for leisure rather than to their ownership of parts of the environment as an investment. Many of these groups could be described as 'attitude' groups where people of like mind gather together irrespective of background (Johnston, 1989, p. 171). Membership is open with no obvious limits to the prospective constituency. This lack of direct material interest and the costs of joining in practice keep the membership well below potential numbers. In order to boost membership, amenity groups have to resort to a variety of incentives ranging from magazines, social activities, recreation information or discounts on entrance fees.

It is possible to overemphasise the extent to which commitment to an amenity group is an ideological as opposed to an economic issue. Some local amenity societies may function as long-term watchdogs against development interests. And the links between attitudes, social position and economic role are definite if not always clearly apparent. The difficulty of disentangling the economic and ideological can be seen in the attempt to understand the growth in local amenity societies. Over 1958–75 the number of such societies increased six-fold to reach a membership of 300 000 by 1977 (McCormick, 1991, p. 33); the number of local societies registered with the Civic Trust grew from 200 to over 1000 from 1957–72 (Kimber and Richardson, 1974, p. 11). This increase did coincide with the surge of environmentalism focused on the consequences of economic growth, the threats of unlimited population expansion and the problems of exhausting certain natural resources. Yet the very fact of economic growth brought with it urban growth and pressures for migration to rural areas. A broader commitment to environmental protection could thus coexist with sectional material interests in preventing development.

Middle class 'stoppers' are not the only form of relevant anti-development or amenity group. Many such groups have been in inner city locations and focused on tenant organisations rather than owner-occupiers. Short (1984, p. 133) describes these groups as forming out of 'dissatisfaction over housing provision in association with discontent over rising rents', but specific development proposals have also provided an impetus. Lack of opportunity to exit the local area by buying into owner-occupation or finding a transfer to another estate provides a captive membership which nevertheless can prove hard to mobilise. Lack of organisational skill, limited resources and resignation by residents all frustrate the formation of such anti-development groups.

Often their formation is linked to broader programmes of social change. Short (1984, p. 134) highlights the role of the women's movement in many of these groups:

> There has been a reciprocal relationship. Much of the community action has involved women while some of the consciousness-raising of women has been because of and through community action. Much of the strength of community action has come from women while some of the new-found confidence within the women's movement has come through community action.

Short describes this kind of grass roots' movement as quite distinct from middle class NIMBYism. This raises the prospect identified by the New Left that some anti-development groups may be seen as radical forces for social change rather than conservative protection of vested interests.

Castells (1983, p. 292) refers to: 'a new situation in which the management of the entire urban system by the state has politicised urban problems, and so translated the mobilisation of communities into a new and significant form of social challenge to established values.' Anti-development movements may, therefore, form such an urban social movement where the resistance to the development fundamentally challenges the premises of capitalist development and the role of the state. To qualify in this way, urban social movements must demonstrably pursue three goals: the organisation of the city as a collection of use values rather than exchange values; the search for autonomous local cultural identity; and the search for decentralised urban self-management (Castells, 1983, pp. 319–20). However, Castells warns that while such urban social movements may restructure the city they will ultimately become institutionalised as they achieve elements of their programme and the change achieved will fall short of full social restructuring. But the appeal of such movements is great: 'when people find themselves unable to control the world, they simply shrink the world to the size of their community' (1983, p. 331).

☐ *Environmental groups*

Environmental groups cover a wide variety of interests and values. As discussed above, some are locally based and are more long-lived, broader oriented versions of anti-development movements. Others are nationally-based, although perhaps with local branches (see Exhibit 10.3). Some focus on amenity, on the visual aspects of the urban or rural environment, such as the Civic Trust or the Georgian Society. Some have developed an analysis of the interrelated nature of environmental systems which guides their work, such as Friends of the Earth and Greenpeace. Some focus on specific aspects of the environment, such as the Royal Society for the Protection of Birds. Others have more general concerns, such as the National Trust, Council for the Preservation of Rural England and the Town and Country Planning Association. Groups vary in size and resources as well. Lowe and Goyder's survey in 1981–2 (1983) revealed a median size of 3000 members but a range from a few hundred to well over 100 000. The National Trust now has over 1 million members.

Exhibit 10.3	*The Royal Society for Nature Conservation*

The RSNC was established in 1912 as the Society for the Promotion of Nature Reserves (SPNR), with Lord Rothschild, the banker, as a key patron. Although it originally worked closely with the National Trust, its specific nature conservation interests and the recognition that active management of land was needed to conserve habitats meant that it soon branched out into ownership of nature reserves on its own account. It was active in the interwar period. Although membership was only 300 by 1939, it was instrumental in setting up the Natural Resources Investigation Committee during the Second World War, which led to the creation of the Nature Conservancy Council (NCC) in postwar legislation. Ever since it has maintained close links with the NCC.

After the war, however, the concentration on an elite membership meant that the society was largely moribund until it developed links in the 1960 with the growing number of country wildlife trusts. In 1969 the SPNR offered associated membership to all country trusts and in 1976 it received a new charter. In its modern form, the RSNC became the national representative and coordinator of these local-level nature conservation groups, and the partnership has benefited both. More recently, the RSNC has also incorporated the urban wildlife movement, again representing local urban groups. It has also extended its national campaigning activities, both in terms of lobbying on legislation and in promoting the concept of Environment City.

The RSNC now represents 47 wildlife trusts and 44 urban wildlife groups. These have a membership of some 250 000 and manage over 1400 reserves amounting to 53 000 ha. 716 full- and part-time staff are employed and the total budget is £1.8 million. Members are in demand by local authorities and the NCC for their expertise and fieldwork, and the RSNC both nationally and in local groups actively monitors, advises and educates on nature conservation issues. Yet, despite the huge membership, only 10 per cent of members were recorded in 1991 as actively contributing time to RSNC activities. This suggests that a large number of people join the groups, not to become actively involved in nature conservation, but because of a general commitment to the cause. Members are not acting as direct consumers of the RSNC's services. Neither do they gain social status and contacts from membership, resulting in new bases of social grouping and cohesion, for many members only rarely participate in the work of local groups.

It would appear that people join the RSNC and its constituent groups because they reflect certain values and policy aspirations. These members value nature reserves regardless of their own 'use' of them. Such people hold an option value or existence value for nature conservation. 'Option value' refers to the desire to protect nature so that the person may benefit in the future or so that others – including but not only descendants – may benefit. 'Existence value' refers to the desire for continued biodiversity regardless of its use to anyone.

The argument that people are willing to put a substantial figure on both option and existence value provides a different perspective on the involvement of the public in environmental issues. It explains the pressures placed on planning policy quite beyond economic self-interest or the social dynamics of group formation. It also undercuts the arguments that all policy is driven by class-based conflict since the holding of such environmental values crosses class barriers.

Nevertheless this emphasis on broad-based environmental values is only a supplement to the other dynamics of pressure group activity. It cannot replace other economic and social cleavages as a political explanation. Indeed the limited extent of nature protection measures suggests that, not only is it not the main factor in explaining pressure groups, it is fairly marginal in explaining policy outputs.

Further reading: Pearce *et al.* (1989); Lowe and Goyder, (1983); Dwyer (1991).

The lines of division are numerous yet the striking feature is that all such groups perceive themselves as part of one environmental movement (Lowe and Goyder, 1983, p. 80). This is partly because of common values, partly due to the perception of the movement as a unity by the media, public and policy makers, but also due to extensive contacts between individual groups. Even at the local level of residents' groups, Short *et al.* (1986, p. 231) found a 'dense circuit of local connections to be used in pursuit of common goals'.

Such connections are certainly a feature at the national level, though they tend to be ad hoc and informal rather than under umbrella organisations (McCormick, 1991, p. 35). Spread of information is achieved by these means together with mutual cooperation on specific issues. McCormick (1991p. 159) records an interview with Jonathon Porrit which suggested:

> that while the coordination of group activities may sometimes seem incoherent and unco-ordinated, most groups are working towards more or

less pre-agreed sets of goals. The role of groups is often complementary. Porritt notes how Friends of the Earth, in working with other groups on changes to the Water Privatisation Bill, was often cast as the confrontational group. By taking this role, it attracted enough of the ire of ministers involved to allow other groups to portray themselves as less confrontational, and to succeed in having some of their proposals accepted.

This does not mean that there is no room for greater coordination. In their study of electricity privatisation, Roberts *et al.* (1991, p. 27) note the disadvantages of there being no convenient coordinating forum for the energy efficiency lobby to challenge the electricity supply industry.

Whether considered individually or as a movement, environmental groups have seen substantial growth over the last decade. In 1981–2, membership of environmental groups was estimated as 2.5–3 million or 4.5–5.3 per cent of the population. By 1990 the estimate was 4.5 million members, amounting to 8 per cent of the population. A 1990 directory of environmental organisations in the British Isles listed 1500 organisations including 65 non-government organisations operating at the national level, 62 local groups and 16 regional groups (McCormick, 1991, p. 34). This growth, which was particularly concentrated in the years 1987–9, builds on two previous phases of growth: the period of establishment in the late 1880s and the first wave of environmentalism in the 1960s and 1890s and early 1970s. The current expanded size of the environmental movement has significantly altered the way that environmental groups operate.

It has increased the financial resources available to groups. Writing in the early 1980s, Lowe and Goyder were already commenting that (1983, p. 46): 'Perhaps the most important consequence of the growth in support for environmental groups has been their ability to take on or expand their professional staff. Increased staffing allows more contact with other groups, more expertise and skills to be brought into the group.' The increased membership itself brings greater skills. Groups do not just regard their members as sources of money, important though this is (see below). They can provide practical assistance at national and local levels and form a network of local watchdogs (Lowe and Goyder, 1983 , p. 40). They also provide authority in relations with government departments though membership size alone will not suffice. The quality of the case is at least as important, and hence the ability to undertake research to support the group's case is central. In the case of the debate over nuclear power, although the groups involved were organisationally weak compared to the nuclear power lobby, the information they provided on the costs of nuclear power was critical, in this case in persuading financial investors that a privatised nuclear power industry was not viable (Roberts *et al.*, 1991, p. 118).

Growth has also brought other changes. The links with green consumerism has meant that environmental groups are faced with new demands from the membership and the public at large: demands which prompt new types of campaign. McCormick (1991, p. 117) argues that there has been a new emphasis on working with industry rather than in confrontation with it and on providing practical advice to the public. Within the movement generally a double approach has developed, using research to talk to government and industry while placing more emphasis on what the individual can do. Yet at the same time there appears to be more public support for the more active groups and for more radical campaigning tactics. The ability to use professional media consultants and fund raising advice has given the environmental movement a higher profile, perhaps a more aggressive corporate image.

The increasing importance of EC policy has meant also changed the way in which environmental groups operate. There is a need for liaison with European environmental groups as well as with the European Commission and Parliament. There is an European Environmental Bureau, established in 1974 to liaise with the European Commission on environmental groups' behalf (Lowe and Goyder, 1983; McCormick, 1991). By 1982 it was representing 63 national groups. But internal problems regarding its direction and organisation has reduced its influence and national groups have increasingly bypassed the bureau and opened their own European offices.

This increased level of European representation has not only been in response to the groups' own perceptions of the need to influence European policy, but also because the Commission has actively sought out pressure groups. It has a habit of using such groups to help draft legislation, to provide information and data, to advise on the level of support for different measures, and to comment on draft proposals (McCormick, 1991, pp. 128–47). This method of proceeding is in line with how British groups seek to influence British policy, but while they have to keep knocking on the British Government's door, the European Commission's door is open wide.

In addition, the possibility of pressure groups themselves seeking judicial review before the European Courts of Justice has given British groups a similar status to their counterparts in the USA under the National Environmental Policy Act. They can challenge policy practice directly, much enhancing their role as watchdogs. In all 'because the British Government has made few concessions on domestic environmental issues, British environmental groups have increasingly seen Brussels as a "court of redress" and a means of outmanoeuvring the government' (McCormick, 1991, p. 132).

The growth of environmental legislation has also meant that government sometimes views environmental groups as a resource for implementing poicy. Local wildlife trusts and offices of the RSPB can perform local environmental mangement and enforcement tasks concerning wildlife protection (Yearley and Milton, 1990).

However, one must not paint too rosy a picture of the environmental lobby. While the membership and resources of groups have grown, they remain vulnerable to financial constraints. All such groups have no obvious constituency and membership is optional. There is therefore no guaranteed resource base (Johnston, 1989, p. 171). In their research, Lowe and Goyder (1983, p. 40) found that 72 per cent of groups surveyed considered membership as important first and foremost to provide income. Income from a stable membership allows the groups to plan its campaigning activities and membership services and gives it a degree of autonomy. Those groups reliant on grants, sponsors or donations find themselves dependent on donors in policy as well as financial terms and sometimes constrained by explicit or implicit conditions on the gift.

In the pursuit of effective influence on government policy, groups are not always successful. Government, particularly at central government level, plays an active role in determining consultation with environmental groups and can elevate some groups in importance while ignoring others (Lowe and Goyder, 1983, p. 24, but see Stoker and Wilson, 1991, on the situation in local government). Among the least receptive government departments to any environmental influence are the DoEn, DTI and DoTr. In some cases groups can be pushed from consultation with the centre of government out to marginal quangos or local government (McCormick, 1991; Lowe et al., 1986, pp. 122–4). In any case, consultation implies acceptance of an unwritten code of moderate and responsible behaviour by the groups. Moving beyond this renders the groups and their demands illegitimate. For groups are dependent on government ceding access, they have no equivalent of business interests' corporate discretion, and attempts to mobilise the membership in overt political activity may be curtailed by the charitable status of many groups.

This suggests that constraints placed on environmental groups by their political role, as much as by their members' interests, may inevitably render them conservative supporters of the status quo. Lowe and Goyder, however, (1983, p. 35) found both emphasis groups, whose demands did not conflict with the status quo, and promotional groups, seeking social or political reform, within the movement. The promotional groups were more likely to be democratic in political structure.

They were described as having a representative leadership, a feature shared with certain recreational groups who drew their membership from a broad social background including substantial numbers of working class members. This was in contrast to other groups, described as 'open oligarchies'. In these the elections were a formality and the leadership exercised strong control subject only to pursuing policies which did not openly split the membership. This covered both the older environmental groups, often formed before the First World War and hence dominated by upper middle class organisers, and also building preservation groups where there was a 'tyranny of taste' (Lowe and Goyder, 1983, pp. 51–3).

This issue of whether environmental groups can be a radical political force is a particular concern of the New Left. Castells (1978, pp. 152–66) reinforces the point that environmentalism embraces a number of fundamentally different elements. First, there are middle class movements which adopt environmental issues on which concession can readily be exacted from dominant interests. Second, there are similar middle class movements where there is a challenge to individual capitalists. Third, there are student movements (so active in the 1970s) which adopt a revolutionary programme and create the potential for linking environmental issues to a class-based challenge to capitalism. Fourth, there are the occasional cases of adoption of environmental concerns by black and other minority groups, primarily formed into urban social movements around other urban issues of collective consumption. Castells notes that this last important source of challenge to the capitalist state has, in fact, rarely taken up the banner of environmentalism.

Castells concludes that environmental politics does have the potential to mount a challenge to capitalism through urban social movements (see above), but the linking ideology of environmentalism serves to mystify the true basis of the politics by reducing social conflicts into an overarching conflict between technology and nature. He questions the view often promoted by such groups that there is the possibility for all 'men of goodwill' to jointly and without internal conflict fight for environmental protection. As he says (1978, p. 159): 'The ideology of the environment, "apolitical", humanitarian, universalist and scientific, transforms social inequality into mere physical inconveniences and blends the social classes into an army of Boy Scouts.'

Therefore, while viewing environmental movements as conservative or, at least, diversionary, Castells accepts that the potential remains for environmentally-based urban social movements to transform the fight the environment into 'a powerful level for change' (1978, p. 166). The problem is to activate this potential. This may be particularly difficult in

Britain where pressure groups rarely seem to transform themselves into urban social movements (Lowe, 1986).

■ Political parties

Pressure groups are not the only form of social organisation that seeks to influence public policy. In a representative democracy, political parties will, of course, play a major role. However, the growth in pressure groups outlined above can be explained in terms of the decline of party politics. As McCormick (1991, p. 41) says: 'it is arguable that interest groups are a more accurate (if not always more efficient) way of representing citizens' interests than political parties.'

Nevertheless parties are a route to political power. Johnston (1989, p. 159) lists five ways in which policies may be brought to the forefront of the political agenda. Beyond influencing individual members of the legislature and changing the views of the population, the other three strategies all relate to political parties: influencing one political party, influencing all political parties, and creating a new political party.

First, one of the existing parties may be induced to adopt certain planning policies and implement them, if elected to government. The success in achieving this depends on the relationship of the new policy to existing ones and the impact those new policies will have on the voting intentions of current and potential voters. A commitment to extensive planning regulations may well deter Conservative voters committed to a free market, while any interpretation of, say, pollution control as a threat to jobs may draw working class votes away from Labour. The *British Social Attitudes Survey* (7th Report) found that the priority afforded to jobs 'suggests that the Labour Party may have some difficulty in persuading its supporters to pay the price of environmental protection' (1990, p. 81).

Second, planning policies (in general or specific aspects) may achieve the status of cross-party support adopted by every party in its manifesto. Green belt policy can be seen to be in this position (Rydin and Myerson, 1990). There is the danger that, if all parties adopt a specific or general pro-planning stance, then its relevance as a means of choosing between parties falls and in effect the policy slips back down the political agenda. As Johnston argues, in relation to environmental policies (1989, p. 159): 'if all parties agree on an issue, then it cannot be used to discriminate between them, unless evaluation of their performance on that issue will be salient when they next appear before the electorate for support'. The signal of this happening is interchangeable policy statements, say in manifestos. But a distinction should be drawn between a common commitment to an existing policy (as in green belts) when the common stance strengthens the policy, and a new policy area (as in reducing carbon dioxide emissions) when the common stance may deflect actual policy action, in the way Johnston suggests.

Certainly, all three major British parties have, until recently, paid little explicit attention to any planning policies (Kimber and Richardson, 1974). Planning policies have been subsumed under the general approach of the party. Therefore, in Labour statements urban and environmental planning is seen as just another area where state planning, in the broader sense, can resolve problems. In Conservative statements, the problems are to be solved by encouraging market processes. McCormick (1991, p. 44), focusing on environmental policies, has been able to say that 'British political parties have played only a marginal role in the environmental debate' and 'the environment tends to be a minor issue in election manifestos'. Considering the 1987 general election manifestos, he says they 'outlined piecemeal environmental programmes, making general reference to issues such as nuclear power, pollution control, energy conservation and green belt protection'.

Between 1987 and 1992, a number of factors appeared to have created the potential for a changed situation. The change in policy stance of the Labour Party, away from bolder forms of socialism, accentuated by events in Eastern Europe, and the departure of Margaret Thatcher as Conservative Party leader have resulted in more flexible party lines. It is less easy to fit planning policy into an example of the overarching party line. At the same time environmental issues, broadly defined, have come to have a much greater political saliency. Even before her departure, Mrs Thatcher made a series of speeches in 1988 and 1989 which demonstrated the significance of environmental concerns. Both inside and outside government and in the opposition parties, restructuring has occurred to give all environmental issues a higher profile.

Chris Patten, who was considered more pro-environment than his predecessors, was appointed Secretary of State for the Environment and a Cabinet Committee convened to prepare an Environment White Paper. Outside the Government, the Conservative Party launched the Tory Green Initiative in 1988 to campaign on the basis of environmentally friendly free-market policies and publicise current government policy in this light. The same year the Green Democrats replaced the former Liberal Green group and was charged with developing an environmental policy within the Liberal Democrats. Labour has had a separate environmental organisation, Socialist Environment and Resources Association, since 1973 but this is probably too radical in its thinking for the current reforming Labour Party. In 1989 the party established a new campaign unit to promote an environmental policy.

However, in line with Johnston's argument (see above), this cross-party stance effectively prevented debate on planning issues at the 1992 General Election. Once again other issues dominated the agenda.

Beyond influence on existing parties, Johnston's third strategy for raising the political profile of environmental policy is the creation of a new party. Given the emphasis that the Green Party places on all areas of planning policy, it is relevant to discuss their growth and fate briefly. In Britain the widespread success of the *Blueprint for Survival* published first by *The Ecologist* magazine and then by Penguin, lead to the formation of the People Party in 1973, to be called the Ecology Party as from 1975 and then the Green Party as from 1985. Electoral success has been much slower coming in Britain than in many other countries. Despite contesting a growing number of seats the Green Party has never polled more than 1.4 per cent of the vote in a General Election. They have fared somewhat better in other elections. In the 1987 local government elections, they received 5.9 per cent of the vote. Their peak performance came in 1989 when they polled a totally unexpected 15 per cent in the European elections. Since then they have lost their high profile, losing members and voters and degenerating organisationally into anarchy.

There is no doubt that the electoral system in Britain works against the Greens. For all their relatively good support at local government level, by June 1989 they had only 1 county councillor, 11 district councillors and 90 parish councillors. When they received 15 per cent of the vote in the European elections they won no seats at all for their 2.29 million votes. On proportional representation, it is estimated that there would be 12 British Greens in the European Parliament (McCormick, 1991). This contrasts with the West German situation where each voter has two votes, one for a constituency MP and one for a regional list candidate, a system which encourages voting for fringe parties. However knowledge of the consequences of the British electoral system can influence voting in both directions. A vote for the Greens may be considered a wasted vote and thus depress electoral support. Yet when there is a move for a protest vote, as in 1989, Greens can be a ready recipient of votes, given that there is no chance of their actually being elected.

The main legacy of the Green Party has been to galvanise other parties into action on environmental issues. Nigel Haigh of the Institute for European Environmental Policy is quoted by McCormick (1991, p. 42) as saying: 'The Euro elections had a dramatic effect. Suddenly ordinary MPs were beginning to bone up on the environment . . .' An internal Labour Party report was arguing that environmentalism was a permanent electoral phenomenon. This reflects a broader growth in environmental concern (see below) which is shaping all areas of planning policy.

■ Values, attitudes and ideologies

The previous sections have looked at the ways in which people form into groups, pressure groups and political parties, in order to influence the policy process. This section looks at a moɾe diffuse form of public influence on the policy process: the role that the values and attitudes play and how they form into discrete but interacting ideologies. An emphasis on these dimensions of public opinion involves consideration of opinion poll and survey data, of the forms that pro-planning and environmentally conscious attitudes take and the ways in which values influence the operation of planning.

Consideration of values and opinions is linked to the conceptualisation of the public adopted. For the New Right, the public are consumers but conceived as such within a strict market framework. The holding of values concerning the built and natural environment which are not priced by the market mechanism is more readily explained by the liberal political economy approach. Certainly any policy action based on such values is only sanctioned by the latter approach. For the New Left and the institutionalist approach, the relevance of such values depends on the extent to which they underpin the formation of social groupings, groupings which can mobilise in political action or groupings which can be mediated by the planning system.

Four sets of values can be identified in the wide range of activities that constitute the British planning system.

First, there is the pursuit of economic development, of urban regeneration, of local economic growth. Although strongly associated with the Thatcherite policy reforms of the 1980s, there is broad consensus across the main political spectrum that economic growth is both necessary and desirable, and this has influenced much planning policy not just the promotion of local economic development. For Conservatives, it represents support of the wealth-creating activities that underpin market capitalist societies. For socialists, it represents the opportunity to increase the material conditions of the working class and, for those in between, it represents the possibility of increasing social provision by giving to the poor from an expanding output without reducing the absolute share of the better-off. Only the Greens stand outside this consensus.

Second, there is the commitment to enhancing social welfare provision regardless of the mechanism of funding. Again a range of political persuasions adopt this attitude from the 'welfare net' paternalism of Conservatives, through the 'social rights' approach of Liberals to the 're-appropriation of surplus value' views of socialists. Greens also have a degree of commitment to social equality and responsibility (Spretnak and Capra, 1985) though it is usually subordinate to the requirements of maintaining ecological systems. Within local planning authorities, this attitude underpins much policy activity in deprived areas where planners actively seek to redress the inequalities suffered by the poor, the elderly, women, ethnic minorities and others.

Third, there is the use of planning to preserve existing amenities, largely for residential or recreational use. The mixture of material interests and altruism that underpins such conservation planning has already been discussed in the section on anti-development pressure groups. These values mainly inform the thinking of higher-income groups and those settled in high-amenity locations.

Fourth, and going beyond the preservation of local amenities, there are the various shades of environmentalism. This term is used to describe a number of profoundly distinct value systems. At the one end, often referred to as 'light green', there are values which move very little beyond the preservationist discussed above. Concentrating on such issues as conservation, waste recycling, wildlife habitat protection, light green values do not seek to question in depth existing social, political and economic practices. Using the term environmentalism to describe this persuasion, Dobson (1990, p. 205) says it is 'concerned about intervention only so far as it might affect human beings'. By contrast, deep green (or Green) values, described by Dobson as ecologism, argue that 'the strong anthropocentrism that this "environmentalism" displays is far more a part of our current problems that a solution to them' (1990, p. 205). Dobson argues that ecologism stands outside and in competition to existing ideologies while environmentalism 'can be slotted with relative ease into more well-known ideological paradigms' and 'that the current vogue to green (small "g") politics shows this cooption at work' (p. 206).

While current planning practice is certainly learning to think in a more environmentally aware way in all its activities, there is little evidence that it will be able or willing to take on board the full import of Green thinking. Environmentalism is therefore likely to coexist with economic development, social welfare and amenity protection as the fundamental values systems of planning. Given these broad value systems, how do they relate to public opinion and policy practice?

The sum of individually held opinions is revealed in a variety of opinion polls and surveys. While it is notoriously difficult to interpret poll and survey data unambiguously, the data seems to reveal a degree of support for all four ideological dimensions. For example, the economy is usually cited as the first priority for government action, followed closely by welfare. State intervention, even when described as socialist planning, is favoured by 38 per cent as a solution of economic problems, compared to 33 per cent rejecting such an approach (*Guardian ICM Survey*, 19 September 1991 p. 3). 64 per cent favour more expenditure on public services even at the expense of higher taxes (*Guardian ICM Survey*) and the first priority for extra government spending include health, education and housing, all social welfare items (*British Social Attitudes Survey* for 1989). There is every evidence, admittedly piecemeal and sometime anecdotal, that protection and enhancement of local amenities is popular with the local residents affected but consideration of the trade-offs that such activities might involve are rarely considered: for example, the effect on employment and on access to housing of restrictive planning or environmental standards or the distributive consequences of deciding against a specific location for a waste disposal site or road link.

Attitudes to various aspects of the environment, ranging from amenity protection to environmentalism, are now a common feature of polls and surveys. The *British Social Attitudes Survey* (1989) found that many environmental hazards were regarded as 'very serious' by those surveyed (see Table 10.1). The increase from 1983 is evident. Including those that considered these hazards 'quite serious', at least 80 per cent of the population is concerned about these threats. There is also evidence that this extent of public concern is consistently under-

Table 10.1   *Environment hazards regarded as 'very serious'*

	1989 %	(1983) %
Industrial waste in water	75	(62)
Waste from nuclear power	67	(63)
Cutting down tropical rainforests	68	(–)
Aerosol chemicals in atmosphere	67	(–)
Industrial fumes in the air	60	(40)
Acid rain	57	(–)
Lead from petrol	45	(48)
Noise and dirt from traffic	31	(23)

Note: – No figures available
Source: British Social Attitudes Survey (1989) p. 80

estimated by public officials who give a less urgent priority to environmental issues than the general public, particularly where air and water pollution, waste disposal, townscape and resource depletion are concerned (Rees, 1990, p. 386). Countryside protection is also highly valued and the farming industry is not regarded as the automatic guardian of rural areas. While 72 per cent thought farmers did a good job in looking after the countryside (76 per cent in 1983), 72 per cent thought modern methods of farming did cause damage to the countryside (64 per cent in 1983) and 46 per cent thought that the countryside was too important to be left to farmers alone (34 per cent in 1983).

Even when environmental protection is traded off against the economic costs involved, there is still considerable and growing support. The *British Social Attitude Survey* found that 88 per cent agreed that industry should be prevented from damaging the countryside even if this sometimes leads to higher prices (78 per cent in 1983) and 72 per cent favoured countryside protection even at the expense of unemployment. In a September 1991 ICM poll for the *Guardian* newspaper, 69 per cent agreed slightly or strongly with the proposition that 'The Government should give a higher priority to environmental policy even if this means higher prices for some goods'. This level of support is broadly unchanged from the survey results of 1989 or 1990 and a substantial increase on the figures that Rees (1990, p. 410) quotes, from a 1983 MORI poll.

Certainly all opinion polls show fluctuation in environmental concern over time. As a report on MORI opinion polls says (*Independent*, 10 September 1991, p. 14):

> When times are good and the economy is growing, people worry about . . . the fate of the planet and future generations. When recession looms or an international crisis blows up, green worries are shoved aside by more immediate concerns about personal security.

But this is against a background of evidence for a substantial and permanent increase in environmental concern since the late 1980s. Since 1988 as many as 30 per cent of respondents in monthly surveys have listed the environment among the most important issues facing Britain today. Using a very broad definition of 'green activity' that includes walking in the countryside alongside green consumerism and pressure group activity, 31 per cent of respondents in July 1991 had undertaken at least five such green activities; this compares with 14 per cent three years ago. The effects of this have been seen in changes to political programmes, planners' range of activities and the details of the planning system. The dynamics between environmental concerns and society is one of the key issues for the 1990s.

Further reading

A good basic introduction to the issues raised in this chapter is provided by McCormick (1991), and Johnston (1989) is also a useful review. For specific work on pressure groups, Lowe and Goyder (1983) is still the most authoritative reference on the environmental movement, with Stoker and Wilson (1991) giving an analysis of groups in relation to local authorities. A recent publication on the role of political parties is Robinson (1992). For detail on public opinion, the best source is the mass of material in the annual *British Social Attitudes Survey*. Midwinter *et al.* (1991) contain detail on pressure groups, political parties and public attitudes in the Scottish context (see particularly pp. 41, 73–6, 210).

■ *PART 4* ■

PLANNING AND THE MARKET

The view that planning is an inherently political activity is now widely accepted, in political, professional and academic circles. It is now also commonly recognised that planning policy has an economic dimension. Economic processes underlie many of the problems that urban and environmental planning seeks to tackle; planning policies have their own economic impacts; and the interaction of planning and economy generates many of the political pressures on the planning system. The nature of this relationship with the economic dimension is, perhaps, less well understood than the comparable political dimension. Part 4, therefore, analysis the interrelationship and argues that a knowledge of economic processes is central to an understanding of planning.

Just as there are differing views on the politics of planning, so there are disputes within the economic literature. These may not be as well known to the reader, so Part 4 proceeds by discussing each of four economic approaches in turn and then applies them in planning case studies. There is a close relation between these four approaches and the key planning themes outlined in Part 1 and used in Part 2. These links are made clear in Chapter 11, which explores: the ideal market model of the New Right; the market failure approach of liberal political economists; the marxist model which informs the New Left; and the institutionalist economists whose work parallels that of institutional planning theory. Chapters 12–15 then apply these to the analysis of four issues: land use planning is represented by the housing land issue; countryside planning by minerals exploitation; environmental policy by pollution; and urban policy by inner city problems. The intention is to provide an account of each economic approach which promotes it, as if by an adherent of that approach. It is hoped this will promote understanding of the alternative positions within the debate on planning and of the links between planning theory and economic analysis. It is also intended to stimulate discussion.

■ *Chapter 11* ■

Alternative Approaches

In this chapter, four alternative approaches to the analysis of economics and planning are outlined. Economics, as a discipline, is concerned with the allocation and accumulation of resources, mainly in the context of a capitalist, market economy. The alternative approaches take different views on the process of allocation and accumulation, identifying different foci for analysis and making different judgements on the outcomes of contemporary processes. This means that each approach suggests a rather different role for the planning system in terms of the policy goals that can be achieved, the policy tools that may be appropriate and the central issue of the relationship of planning activity to the pattern of economic inequality.

The chapter begins by outlining the idealised, neo-classical economic account of the market and then proceed by developing variations and critiques of this account. These come from three main sources: the development of neo-classical thought known as welfare economics; the marxist critique of conventional economics; and the variety of non-marxist critiques which are here labelled institutionalist.

■ The ideal market model of the New Right

The emphasis of this approach is on how the market reacts to and deals with urban or environmental problems. Markets are seen as self-regulating mechanisms which will adjust to rectify imbalances. This approach, therefore, differs from the others to be covered for they tend to emphasise how market processes generate problems.

The idea of markets as self-regulating derives from the 18th century political economist, Adam Smith (Heilbronner, 1983, pp. 33–57). He saw markets as places where self-interest drives the participants and competition controls them. The result of this competition between self-interested actors is social harmony, or (in current language) the public interest. A key link in achieving this outcome is the 'invisible hand' of the price mechanism: the setting of prices and movements in prices.

According to Smith, if high prices are charged by a particular producer, trade will be taken away by competitors undercutting this price. Prices will be driven down to the point at which they cover all the

259

costs of production including an allowance for reasonable profit. If a surplus of a good is produced, prices will be driven down as suppliers seek to entice customers into purchasing the good and production of the good will diminish in response to less attractive prices, drying up the surplus. Conversely a shortage drives prices up as suppliers see the potential for profit and the market, thereby rationing the good between eager consumers. Higher prices further encourage production to meet the shortage. In this way price becomes the signal whereby supplies are regulated within the market and trade allocated between suppliers.

These basic ideas have survived intact into the current formulation of the neo-classical market model. However, the 'marginal revolution' of the late 19th century and the subsequent translation of the elements into mathematical terms have given it the character of a more formal logical model (Lipsey, 1989; Begg *et al.*, 1991). The interaction of supply and demand within the market to generate a price level are now specified in more detail, commonly using equations or a diagram for supply and demand schedules (see Figure 11.1).

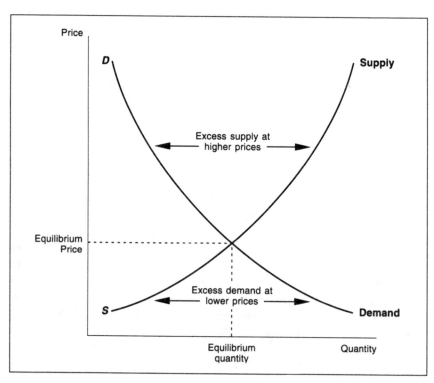

Figure 11.1 *Supply and demand in the ideal market model*

The supply curve in Figure 11.1 indicates the quantity suppliers are willing to make available at any particular price over a given time period and is derived from the marginal cost curves of firms supplying the good or service. Marginal cost refers to the additional cost of producing one extra unit of a good or service beyond the firm's existing production level. The demand curve indicates the quantity consumers or household are willing to purchase at a given price and is, in turn, derived from the aggregate marginal utility curves of consumers, where marginal utility refers to the satisfaction consumers get from consuming one additional unit of a good or service beyond their current level of consumption. By positing certain laws, the general shape of the supply and demand curves indicated in Figure 11.1 can be obtained.

These supply and demand schedules interact to provide an equilibrium price level at which the quantity consumed exactly equals the quantity supplied. Any movement away from this point of equilibrium results in forces which bring the price level back to the point of balance between supply and demand, in much the way that Adam Smith described. New equilibrium points can be established only if the demand or supply schedules alter. In this way, market outcomes are highly responsive to the costs of production and the preferences of consumers.

This analysis does not only apply to markets for final goods and services. The same general supply and demand framework can be applied to factor markets, for land, labour and capital. In these cases the demand schedule is related to the utility derived from employing the factors, that is their contribution to final production termed 'marginal revenue product'. Such a demand is called a derived demand schedule. Derived demand, interacting with the supply of the factors, determines rent, wage and interest levels. Of particular importance to urban and environmental planning is the application of this model to land determining its allocation to uses and price.

The market for land operates to ration space between users so that each site is allocated to its 'highest and best use', that is, to the users who will pay the most for it. Since willingness to pay for the land represents the benefits arising from its use, allocating sites to the highest bidder maximises the total benefits to society from using this resource. In this way the allocation of land to urban and rural uses, to commercial and residential uses, and to high and low income households in free market conditions, can be said to be optimal (Newell, 1977, Ch. 10) (see Figure 11.2).

The model does not only claim to provide an explanation of equilibrium in any particular market. It points out the potential for an efficient equilibrium operating throughout the economy. If all

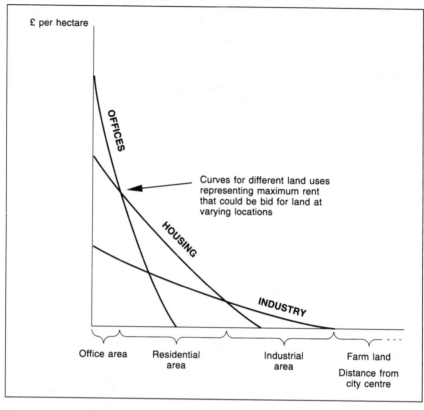

Figure 11.2   *Allocation of land uses in the ideal market model*

markets in the economy are perfectly competitive and are simultaneously in equilibrium (a situation of general equilibrium) then all resources will be efficiently allocated. 'Efficiency' in this context has a very precise meaning: the cost of supplying the last unit will equal the extra revenue gained from its supply or, in neo-classical economic jargon, marginal cost will equal marginal revenue. Furthermore the Pareto condition for optimal resource allocation will be satisfied: this states that a situation is optimal if no-one can be made better off without making someone else worse off.

The central argument of the market model is that such free market processes foster economic growth through their allocation of resources, and thus satisfying a major, if not *the* major social goal. This role of markets in generating wealth and economic growth is an entirely positive one. Poverty and lack of purchasing power are seen as the root cause of urban and environmental problems, creating cycles of degradation whereby aspects of the environment are abused. These include: inadequate maintenance of amenities in an area deprived of inward investment; the use of communal areas in run-down housing estates for refuse disposal and other anti-social activities; the reduction of maintenance procedures in less profitable production activities leading to accidental pollution; the despoliation of the countryside in attempts to combat low and falling farm incomes.

Generating economic growth is, therefore, essential to combat these effects. This is the rationale behind promoting development in economically backward areas. Promoting private sector development, often including an emphasis on physical development or redevelopment of land or other application of capital investment, should be a priority for any urban or environmental planning. This is most readily achieved by giving market forces a free rein. For market actors *will* respond to urban and environmental problems, and do so in the most effective and efficient way.

The underlying argument is that markets respond to such problems because it is in their self-interest to do so. This point has been strongly made in the environmental policy area. As Steve Robinson, Chief Executive of the Environment Council, says (*New Statesman and Society*, 17 August 1990, p. 20): 'Say you make paint and you keep putting in solvents because you don't care, then you run the risk of being legislated out of existence if someone comes up with a water-based alternative.' This point is also made by John Elkington, Director of Sustainability Ltd and co-author of *The Green Capitalists – how industry can make money and protect the environment* (1987, p. 21): 'Environmentally unsound activities are ultimately economically unsound.' The Environment Unit of the DTI, set up in 1990, puts forward a similar message. There are a number of reasons why it is in business's self-interest to respond.

First, such problems are bad marketing. This is particularly the case in the environmental field, where lobby groups have affected consumers' consciousness leading to a direct influence on retailers and an indirect one on manufacturers and growers. It is also the case where property developers are concerned, as the marketability of their product, whether housing, shopping centres or new industrial parks, will depend on local amenities, the absence of problems of congestion, the balance between employment and population and similar factors.

Second, the solution to such problems often creates new economic opportunities. The housing crisis means that potential markets are not being supplied, perhaps because of unnecessary government intervention. Giving rein to free market forces would enable a gap in market provision to be filled. This is a common argument in relation to the rented housing sector (Newell, 1977, Ch. 15). In fact, it is possible to gain a margin over competitors by responding in this way. For example, the shopping centre which provides a dedicated light railway in response to urban congestion will prove more popular with shoppers than other car-based centres. Response to such problems can be an effective way of fending off competition.

Third, responding to such problems now reduces production costs in the long run. Better to tackle polluting emissions now and, perhaps, find a profitable means of recycling or reducing these unwanted byproducts. Short-term profits may even be made by re-using emissions. Better to deal with local unemployment before being forced out of current locations by the filth and crime of a rapidly decaying urban environment.

In addition to individual commercial responses, there are examples of combined action by the private sector. For example, Business in the Community exists to encourage private enterprise to undertake projects which will aid urban regeneration, employing inner city people, retraining the unemployed and improving the local environment. Again the Housebuilders' Federation have developed a recent initiative to enable housebuilders to combine profitable private development with the provision of low-cost housing for local people in rural areas. The activities of building societies in developing rented housing, again at reasonable rents, is another example. The role of numerous organisations, such as the publishers of the *Financial Times*, in sponsoring architectural awards designed to enhance the built environment, is another. In the environmental field, one can point to the work of the Environment Council, which has a Business and Environment Programme to encourage responsible production, and the international organisation, Business Council for Sustainable Development, which participated in the 1992 Earth Summit. And there is the growing number of companies employing consultants such as Sustainability Ltd to undertake environmental audits of their activities and devise programmes of change.

Having outlined how markets respond to such problems, a further use of the model is to argue that the cause of many urban and environmental problems is the absence of market processes in the first place. Proponents of this view readily point to the horrendous pollution and dismal urban environments of the former Eastern Bloc countries compared to the relatively cleaner and more pleasant market-based countries. But they further argue that the absence of active markets anywhere for certain items generates urban and environmental problems. One of the most commonly quoted examples points out that there is no mechanism for pricing and hence rationing the use of the great commons: air, the seas, outer space. Just as the existence of common rights in grazing land or forest leads to their overuse by freely entitled beneficiaries, so absent markets in the great commons leads to their over-exploitation, as a waste sink, as fisheries, as raw materials for production processes (Hardin, 1968).

The same argument can be used to explain the overuse of countryside leisure facilities and urban open spaces, leading to wear and tear and excessive litter. Again, it explains the substantial development in areas of visual amenity in order to gain the free good of pleasant views. The same problem can be seen to arise with the use of urban streets as a waste sink for litter, the overuse of unpriced roads by car-borne traffic, the use of the countryside and coastlines for leisure, and the use of heritage locations for commercial activities and development. It follows that fostering the creation of new markets can be a solution to environmental and urban problems, paralleling the basic policy of ensuring 'freedom' in existing markets. However, proponents of the market model usually limit themselves to calling for the transfer of publicly or commonly owned assets into existing private markets (for example, allowing developers to build toll roads). The level of state intervention involved in creating quasi-markets (for example, road pricing) means that this solution is usually more favoured by welfare economists (see below).

For the proponents of the market model see only a limited role for planning policies: such policies should seek to support and facilitate private sector activity, not replace or interfere with it. Problems are more likely to arise from excessive planning than from too little.

■ The market failure approach of liberal political ■ economy

The first of the critiques of the ideal market model that will be discussed is internal to the neo-classical approach. Firmly based within the discipline of economics alone, it seeks to amend the model at the margins. Using the tools and concepts of neo-classical economics, welfare economics explores the various ways in which market processes do not result in an efficient equilibrium. These are described as situations of market failure. In particular market failure occurs because real life markets fail to live up to the assumptions of the perfect model.

These include: perfectly competitive markets with standardised commodities, numerous buyers and sellers and a ready exchange of market information. Information is available at no cost and the transactions costs of exchange are nil. It is important that no one buyer or seller should be able to have an appreciable effect on the market. The assumption of no monopolies is particularly important for the efficient outcome of general equilibrium to occur. The notion of general equilibrium also assumes that people's perceptions of their utility are representative of their true well-being and that the prevailing distribution of income is ethically acceptable. Examining the ways in which reality diverges from this ideal model identifies four distinct types of market failure (Harrison, 1977).

First, market processes may be 'distorted' by the existence of monopolies or other forms of imperfect competition. Under situations of perfect competition assumed by the ideal market model, each firm will be driven to the point where 'normal' profits are made, a sufficient return just to keep the entrepreneur in business. There will be a balance in which the revenue from the last unit produced just covers the costs of such production. This is efficient in neo-classical economics' terms. However monopolies and oligopolies can exercise a degree of market control, influencing price by altering the amount produced onto the market. In these cases, market equilibrium will occur at a point where the marginal revenue exceeds the marginal cost of supplying it. This is not an efficient allocation of resources since consumption can be expanded while still adding more to consumer benefit than to production costs (Lipsey, 1989). The problems that imperfect competition create are explored further in the context of minerals exploitation in Chapter 13. Identifying these problems raises the question of whether state action is appropriate, either at the industry level to curtail the imperfect competition or at the level of production plants to manage the effects of imperfect competition.

Second, it is not necessarily the case that the marginal revenue and cost schedules facing suppliers and consumers in the market represent the full costs and benefits of production and consumption. Externalities occur wherever the actions of a consumer or producer affect other consumers or producers other than through market prices. In these cases the private cost to the supplier diverges from social costs to all affected actors, and/or the private benefit to the consumer diverges from social benefits. In either case the operation of market processes will result in an equilibrium which is not efficient and at which there is a loss of social welfare (Begg et al., 1991)(see Figure 11.3).

The essence of such externalities is that they are not taken into account by the decision making of firms or households. The route towards dealing with externalities is, therefore, to internalise the externality, to find a way of incorporating them in the relevant actor's decision making processes. There are two main ways to achieve this. First, fiscal measures can be used to force actors to take account of

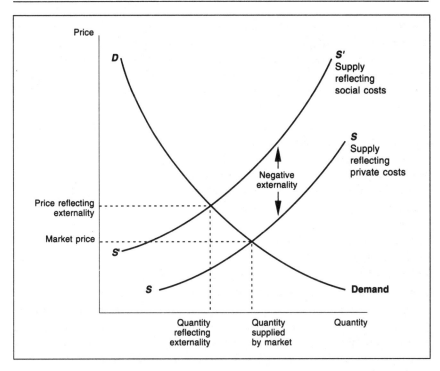

Figure 11.3 *Market failure: the case of negative externalities*

external economies or, more commonly, diseconomies. One of the most frequently cited externalities concerns pollution, and equally common is the advocacy of a pollution tax to deal with the problem. This policy prescription arises from a welfare economic analysis of an environmental problem and is discussed further in Chapter 14 (see also Pearce and Turner, 1990).

A second, less common, way of internalising externalities is to create a market for the externality. This involves compensation passing between parties equal to the social loss arising from a negative externality (or benefit in the case of a positive externality). Where there is a negative externality, the supplier would pay equivalent compensation to those affected by the externality. Where there is a positive externality, the consumer would pay equivalent betterment to the supplier. In each case the payment puts social costs and benefits into balance with each other. Creating and enforcing such a market in compensation and betterment claims can be difficult and costly but, according to welfare economics, the outcome could increase total well-being.

A proxy can be provided by relying on private property rights. This is based on the assumption that externalities are caused by one property owner affecting another. Property rights can then be designed to encompass legal rights: either to demand compensation for infringement of the enjoyment of private property; or to impose a transaction charge in advance for this infringement. If the transaction charge is greater than the loss to the property owner due to the externality then the property owner will accept this transaction charge and the activity will go ahead. If the charge is insufficient to compensate the property owner, the activity and associated externality will not occur. Expanding the scope of property rights can provide an alternative to more direct forms of government involvement, such as land use planning, to minimise the incidence of negative externalities and maximise the number and extent of positive ones.

A third form of market failure is provided by the existence of 'public goods'. A public good is strictly defined by welfare economics as any good where it is impossible to restrict access by consumers. In the case of such goods, the market has little incentive to supply them, for costs cannot be covered by revenue. Consumers have no incentive to pay for the good as they have the opportunity to free-ride on the provision of the good to other consumers. Many of the concerns of British planning have public good characteristics. Enjoyment of a landscape is a public good as is a high level of local amenities: street furniture, planting, maintenance of the built environment, parks and playgrounds. Public rights of way and other access rights are by definition public goods as are also the fundamental functions of the environment in providing clean air and water.

Fourth, market failure can result from other missing markets, in particular those in future goods, risk and information. To ensure that the marginal cost and marginal benefit of future goods are in balance, there should exist futures markets for such goods, trading in goods to be purchased and consumed years hence. But the unknown characteristics of such goods inhibit the creation of such markets. Similarly the limited extent of markets for bearing risk undermine the potential for society undertaking an efficient amount of risky activities. Such a market in risk would equate the marginal cost and marginal benefit of risk-bearing, through a broader range of insurance policies than exist at the moment.

The establishment of futures and risk markets is inhibited by the problems of moral hazard and adverse selection (Begg *et al.*, 1991, Ch. 14). In economics, 'moral hazard' refers to the possibility of the act of insuring increasing the likelihood of the act insured against actually occurring. This makes it difficult accurately to set probabilities, premiums and hence prices in insurance markets. Adverse selection refers to the case where insurance is disproportionately taken up by 'bad-risk' categories, while premiums are based on the 'all-risks' population. This, again, acts as a disincentive to developing insurance markets. The failure of the market to deal adequately with the future and risky events is a central rationale for planning, which is essentially a future oriented activity. If market processes cannot safeguard the future and properly balance risks and benefits then the information gathering and decision making of planning policy formulation may do so.

Imperfect information can more generally create problems of market failure. Gathering information is costly and time-consuming for the private sector but lack of information results in inefficient resource allocation. As with externalities it can result in a social loss. It can also result in cyclical patterns in market allocation, which will be explored further below in the case study of housing land (in Chapter 12).

These various forms of market failure suggest the need for government intervention to rectify such failure or, at least, create a prima facie case for such intervention. However, it is not necessarily appropriate to intervene to remove the particular market failure that has been identified. First, this is because introducing a government policy, such as a tax, in one market may generate distortions in other related markets. Second, the economic theory of the 'second best' argues that the best way to deal with distortions in one market may be actively to create distortion in other markets (Begg *et al.*, 1991, Ch. 14). Third, the costs and benefits of the policy intervention itself must be assessed to ensure that greater inefficiency is not created by intervening than by leaving the market failure alone.

Finally it should be remembered that the goal of welfare economics is efficiency and optimality as narrowly defined in the previous section. It may be thought that the existence of market failures, such as externalities which imply impacts on certain groups due to actions elsewhere, would render the idea of Pareto optimality untenable. If a particular activity will result in a negative externality it would appear that the Pareto criterion has not been met, either in permitting that activity to proceed or, perversely, once it has been established, allowing it to be removed.

But welfare economics has developed a compensation rule (the Hicks–Kaldor formulation) which argues that if the gains from the activity are sufficient to compensate for the externality effect, then the reallocation of resources is acceptable. Hicks assumed that the compensation is actually paid, that a market in property rights is created. Kaldor argued that it didn't matter whether the compensation was actually paid provided that sufficient gains were made to allow such a payment. The assessment and balancing of costs and benefits is thus the central issue in any planning intervention, not necessarily the mechanisms for redistributing these costs and benefits between parties.

It should be remembered that this discussion of an optimal allocation of resources assumes that the resulting distribution of income is ethically acceptable. Each distribution of income implies a different Pareto-optimal outcome. The apparently objective discussion of market failure, efficient resource use and optimal allocations thus implies a highly political debate on income distribution. However, within welfare economics this is rarely recognised and the two discussions are relegated to the separate realms of economics and politics.

■ The marxist inheritance of the New Left

The third economic approach discussed, while tracing its roots back to the classical political economy of Adam Smith, has had a lineage distinct from neo-classical economics since the 19th century (Heilbronner, 1983, pp. 105–30). Marx's development of Ricardian ideas has shaped social science and political practice in direct opposition to the prevailing orthodoxy. Despite the recent collapse of centralised planning under marxist–leninist principles, Marx's analytic framework remains influential. It continues to be the main critique of conventional explanations of market operations and to underpin the thinking of the Left, including the New Left. Marxism, particularly the marxism within geography which supports planning theory, is being redebated (see Sayer, 1991; Peet, 1992 and subsequent replies) but the essence of the framework remains central to any variant of marxism.

Marxists criticise the dominant neo-classical position on the grounds that the focus on supply and demand within a market framework uncritically accepts the appearance of equal exchange between buyers and seller. Neo-classical economics, according to marxism, focuses on epiphenomena rather than the underlying causal processes. The key to unravelling these causal processes is a recognition of the central importance of 'class'. Relations in society are essentially class relations and the actions of individuals and groups can be understood only in terms of their class position. Economic activity, such as the creation of profit, is based upon the class structure of society and political activity too is generated by the self-conscious pursuit of class interests. In this way political and economic analysis is inter-related into a radical political economy approach.

The starting point of any marxist analysis is the production process through which capital accumulation occurs (Ambrose, 1986):

$$M - C \overset{\diagup LP}{\underset{\diagdown MP}{\Big\}}} \quad \ldots P \ldots C' - M'$$

Capital is converted from money form M into commodities C, specifically into the means of production MP (plant, raw materials, buildings) and labour power LP (the ability of workers to work). Through the combination of these two types of commodity, production occurs and a volume of manufactured commodities C' results. The essence of the capitalist system is that the monetary value of this final volume of commodities M' exceeds the value of the initial capital used M. The difference in initial and final value is termed 'surplus value'. In particular surplus value arises because the class system under capitalism allows labour power to be bought at its reproduction cost (the cost of maintaining the labour force) rather than at the value of the final commodities created.

The exploitation of labour through the sale of labour power in the market and the appropriation of surplus value by the owner of capital, the capitalist, is the source of wealth creation under capitalism. The system is driven by the capitalist seeking to use the exploitation of labour to accumulate capital over time, to generate a larger and larger quantity of surplus value and accelerate the rate at which accumulation occurs. That this process of capital accumulation is widely perceived as the operation of market forces, in the manner of the neo-classical framework, is due to the operation of ideology cloaking the underlying processes with a misleading appearance.

Unlike some equilibrium theories of neo-classical economists, the marxist analysis of capitalism does not assume a steady state. On the contrary it presupposes that every situation contains the seeds of its own transcendence, so that the tendency of the system is towards contradiction and crisis. Capitalism continually has to respond to these contradictory tendencies and seek to avoid crisis. The generation of urban and environmental problems is seen in this light. This will be explored by first outlining the main dimensions of capitalist crisis and then examining the ways in which such crisis may be (temporarily) avoided (Harvey, 1985; Burkitt, 1984).

Crises within capitalism can take a number of forms. The most famous, perhaps, is the tendency of the rate of profit to fall. This arises from the contradiction between labour being the ultimate source of all profit and the desire to increase the productivity of any purchased labour power by combining it with fixed capital in the form of plant and machinery. Increasing the amount of fixed capital is one way of increasing the rate of exploitation of labour, through extracting more relative surplus value. However, as the proportion of labour power declines, eventually it becomes more and more difficult to generate more surplus value from the given labour power. Both technically and politically it becomes more and more difficult to continue increasing the rate of exploitation of labour as more plant and machinery is bought. Eventually the rate of profit will start to fall.

The second source of crisis also turns on the central role of labour within the accumulation process. The key factor here is that it is in the interests of capitalists to pay the minimum possible for their labour power, within the limits of reproducing the labour force in terms of quantity and quality (health, training, ideological commitment to capitalism). However, the same labour force constitutes the market for the output of production. Restricting payments to labour also restricts the purchasing power upon which the sale of goods depends. The drive to accumulate capital can result in the overproduction of goods relative to the capacity of the economy to absorb them.

Third, crises can result from the anarchy inherent in a fragmented market system. There is no means by which a balance between supply and demand in the different sectors of the economy is ensured at any given time. Even taking the simplest case of a two-sector economy with wage goods and capital goods sectors, there is no assurance that sufficient wage goods will be produced for the labour employed in both sectors, nor sufficient capital goods for both sectors' needs (Desai, 1979, Part III). The result is a crisis of disproportionality.

A particular form of this problem, which may be termed a fourth crisis tendency, is posed by the existence of a separate sector focused on landownership and investment in landed property assets. The interests of this sector (or fraction of capital) can conflict with the needs of other sectors (or fractions of capital). In pursuit of increasing returns on landed property, landowners may not necessarily provide sufficient and adequate land to other sectors or fractions of capital for their own functional needs. In addition, landed capital can undermine the profitability of other fractions by demanding a share of the surplus value created during the occupation of land and buildings. The payment of rent by industrial and merchant capital to landowners is an expression of the conflict between fractions of capital and can be a barrier to more profitable capital accumulation by industrial and merchant capital (Massey and Catalano, 1978).

We could now add the environmental crisis to this list. Redclift (1987, p. 48) argues:

Marxists see the commitment to commodity production under capitalism as making ecological externalities inevitable. Indeed it is part of the contradictory nature of capitalism that the environmental crisis presents a massive threat to the earning powers of entrepreneurs, as underwritten by the capitalist state.

An environmental crisis is inevitable under capitalism because markets fail to allocate environmental goods efficiently. This is due to the assumption, bound up in market processes, that all resources are divisible and can be owned. But environmental systems are not divisible: each part bears a relation to other parts. Furthermore environmental change is both uncertain and often irreversible, facts not easily assimilated by market processes. Finally, environmental preferences cannot always be modelled by valuations and, therefore, cannot be subject to market exchange.

The outcomes of such a crisis-ridden process of capital accumulation take a number of forms: cyclical activity in all sectors of the economy, aggravated by speculation; the unemployment of certain resources, coexisting with the overexploitation of others; and periodic collapses of capitalist enterprises. Each of these outcomes has urban and environmental consequences. Furthermore, the actions of capitalists to avert such crises can themselves have additional urban and environmental consequences.

One way of coping with overproduction crises is the devaluation of capital. This can have a spatial dimension when local areas suffer the effect of a withdrawal of capital. Industrial and commercial premises are vacated and, without an alternative use by a capitalist, become derelict and devalued. Harvey (1985, pp. 1–31) has further analysed this in terms of switches between circuits of capital. He identifies three circuits: the primary circuit involves the exchange of wages for labour power and the production process as indicated in the above formula; the secondary circuit involves the flow of capital into fixed asset formation to aid production and the accumulation of a consumption fund to aid consumption; the tertiary circuit comprises investment in science and technology to support production and expenditures on social welfare to help reproduce labour power. The built environment is represented as an element of both fixed capital and the consumption fund (see Figure 11.4).

As overproduction occurs in one circuit, capital is switched to another. Enhanced accumulation occurs in this new circuit while withdrawal of capitalists' interest in the former circuit results in devaluation. In this way capital surges in and out of the built environment, creating periods of development activity followed by slumps.

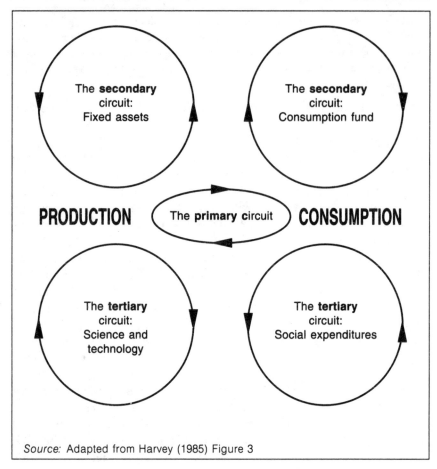

Source: Adapted from Harvey (1985) Figure 3

Figure 11.4 *Harvey's circuits of capital*

Another tactic available to capital is to expand into new markets. Spatially this involves moving into new geographical areas, colonising them politically or economically. Imperialism was the form this tactic took in the 19th century. The capital movements of multinationals charts the 20th century version, although the capitalist developed world's capture of Eastern Europe is also relevant. In this way, capital expands spatially to exploit new markets, new labour forces, new areas and new local environments.

A further possibility is to speed up the turnover of capital, so that the throughput through the system, the rate of surplus value, is increased. This option has urban and environmental implications, in that it requires investment in infrastructure to facilitate the rapid movement of goods, services, information and capital. Mobility over space is an essential element of speeding up the movement of capital through the circuits. Investment in those areas of the built environment associated with the sphere of circulation, such as retailing, will also receive particularly heavy investment under this option. The environment generally has to cope with more rapid exploitation of natural resources, greater use of transportation and the burden of waste and side-products caused by an accelerated rate of production.

Finally, the response for crisis may take the form of increased socialisation of the costs of production: that is, the state may take on an enhanced role in relation to capital accumulation processes (O'Connor, 1973). This can take a variety of forms: infrastructure provision; cheap premises and sites; reproduction costs for labour including housing, training and health care; dealing with waste disposal. In this way, most aspects of the expanding public sector, including regulatory and positive planning functions, can be interpreted as supporting private capital accumulation by taking on part of the costs. Even the various land nationalisation programmes of Labour Governments can be seen as an attempt to deal with the threat that landed capital can pose to industrial capital: the state intervenes in a conflict between fractions of capital to reimpose the overall interests of capital accumulation in the economy (Massey and Catalano, 1978). Overall the role of any planning within a market-based economy will be to tackle the anarchy of capitalism and avert crises.

Whichever tactic is adopted, any beneficial effects can only be temporary since it is in the nature of capitalism that the underlying contradictory nature of wealth creation will generate further crises in the future. For example, the socialisation of costs of production has been shown to generate a resulting fiscal crisis for the state (O'Connor, 1973). The finance for all state activities must be provided by a deduction from the surplus value generated in production: there is no other source. Socialisation of costs is intended to provide an enhanced base for profitable activity by capitalists' but its financing may itself undermine profitable capital accumulation.

Particular attention has been focused on the means by which crisis has to be continually avoided and the expanded social reproduction of capitalism continually secured. The regulationalist school looks to the analysis of social norms, mechanisms and institutions as a way of understanding this process of seeking to achieve continuity and adjust to change (see Cloke and Goodwin, 1992, for a discussion and application of the concepts).

However, the state is not just a switch in the economic machine. It is a political entity and a site for struggle by classes. As capitalist interests are more powerful within a capitalist system and will have captured sections of the state – say, the Treasury – state actions will frequently benefit capital. But there is the scope for the working class using the state to advance their interests against capital (Jessop, 1982). At the local level, the use of the local state as a site for conflict between classes is particularly apparent (Duncan and Goodwin, 1988). The use of the local state to reorientate collective consumption (consumption that is organised for and/or benefited from by a collective group – Dunleavy, 1980) to benefit disadvantaged groups and even attempt local economic restructuring was the seedbed for many New Left ideas. However, at national and international level the dynamics of the underlying economic system are more relevant to marxist analyses, as the case studies in Chapters 12–15 show.

■ Institutionalist economic analysis

The term 'institutionalist' has been applied to or used by a variety of theorists. As seen in Chapter 3, a distinctive branch of planning theory has described itself as institutional. American institutionalist politics contains insights which can reinforce institutional planning theory (see Chapter 9). And there are certain economic theories, which also carry the label and, more importantly, lend relevant economic support to the planning theory.

Neo-institutionalist theory is the variant which is closest to the neo-classical model. It seeks to extend the conventional model to deal with three previously ignored issues (Eggertson, 1990, pp. 4–5). How do alternative sets of social rules and economic organisations affect economic behaviour? Why does the form of economic organisation vary from activity to activity, even within the same legal framework? And what is the economic logic behind the fundamental social and political rules than govern production and exchange, and how do these rules change? To answer these questions, neo-institutionalists relax three of the simplifications of the neo-classical model.

First, explicit consideration is given to the nature of the rules and contracts that govern exchange. Institutions are seen as sets of rules governing interpersonal relations and the institutions of property ownership are considered particularly relevant in understanding economic life. Second, market exchanges are seen to have positive transaction costs, not to be frictionless. Third, the qualitative dimension of goods and services supplied is also examined, not just their price and quantity. However, neo-institutionalist economics remains close to the neo-classical model. Centrally it retains the key assumption of rational choice by actors.

This contrasts with the 'old' and 'new' institutionalists, who accept that there may be alternative bases for decision making, such as satisficing. These theorists have relied more on empirical research and polemical writing than formal model building. Indeed, they have been extremely critical of the pretensions of neo-classical economists to objectivity, scientific method and abstraction from everyday practices. Key figures include Veblen (1976), Myrdal (1957) and Galbraith (1981). While not forming a self-conscious 'school of thought', common themes can be identified.

Social structure is seen as centrally relevant, particularly the issue of social status and the pursuit of goods and economic roles to reflect higher status. The existing inequalities of property ownership are the starting point for much analysis and many trends in economic activity are seen to reinforce, not eliminate, those inequalities. The state is also integrated within the analysis and not a deus ex machina which intervenes from outside the economic system. Institutionalists have a normative analysis of the state which promotes a role for public policy in redressing economic and social inequalities.

J. K. Galbraith's work, with its arguments concerning the manipulation of consumer demand by corporations, the control of corporations by an elite, and the involvement of the state in supporting the profits of these corporations, is characteristic of the approach. Central to Galbraith's approach is the identification of the key economic interests involved and the social groupings they form, together with the power they can wield. Economic processes are seen in terms of the exercise of such power, in terms of conflicts in many arenas and domination through many means. The approach is non-functional but aware of the structural constraints placed on actors. It is sensitive to the possibilities of a situation and sees economics as integrally related to political and ideological processes.

The concern of institutionalists to integrate sociology into economics places them close to the economic sociologists. These writers are trying to overcome the distinction drawn by influential economists such as Samuelson and Pareto that economics is concerned with the rational and sociology with the non-rational (Swedberg, 1990). Economic sociology can be analysed as based on three key propositions (Granovetter and Swedberg, 1992, p. 6).

First, economic action is a form of social action. Therefore, a range of motives for economic action are relevant. Second, economic action is socially situated so that economic action is embedded in ongoing networks of personal relations rather than being carried out by atomised economic agents. This emphasis on networks is reminiscent of the concern with mediation, negotiation and networking of institutionalist planners. Third, economic institutions are social institutions and the analysis of organisational structure and systems of property rights are relevant. In particular, it cannot be assumed that the chosen form of economic institution is necessarily the most efficient.

To this body of broadly defined institutionalist economic analysis may now be added writings in ecological economics (Ekins and Max-Neef, 1992). This is distinguished from environmental economics (Pearce and Turner, 1990) which remains firmly within a neo-classical welfare economics analysis (see above). Ecological economics is highly normative, and recognises the social, ecological and even ethical dimensions of what is commonly regarded as purely economic activity.

From these various writings, four themes can be drawn which together constitute an economic underpinning relevant to institutional planning theory. These are: the centrality of property ownership and the structure of property rights; the range of motives for economic decision making, often associated with particular property ownership and social status patterns; the importance of organisational structure to understanding economic decision making and actions; and the operation of institutions as networks.

In the case studies of minerals exploitation and (to a lesser extent) housing land, emphasis is put on the consequences of organisational structure of firms and industries. In all cases the centrality of property ownership is demonstrated and the varied bases of decision making stressed. Where the planning system interacts with economic actors, or economic actors interact with each other, the requirements of negotiation across networks is seen. This applies particularly to the housing land and inner city case studies. Of all these themes, though, it is the role of property ownership, the ownership of rights in the natural and built environment, and trade in such rights within markets, that is most emphasised. It is worthwhile considering the institutionalist treatment of property ownership and property markets in a bit more detail.

Markets are defined by their trading activities in a particular good or asset and are a mechanism for circulating these goods and assets. But they are constituted by the actions of actors engaged in social relations, including state actors regulating, creating and underpinning the trading activities of the market. Market processes can therefore only be understood in relation to these actors and the existing pattern of social relations. Property is defined, not as capital (as in marxism) nor as a good like any other good (as in neo-classical approaches) but as a right, a claim of one agent against another which is enforceable, which is recognised and enforced by the state (Hart, 1961). Defining property as a right involves identifying an enforceable claim to the use and benefit of things. Such use and benefit can take many forms and property ownership can (and will) involve liabilities as well as positive rights. Reeve (1986, p. 19) lists the following among the bundle of rights and liabilities meant by property: use, management, possession, income, security, capital, transmissibility. Indeed this identification of a variety of different aspects to property beyond the fact of occupation or possession of a thing is the key to the definition of property as a right.

As Macpherson points out (1978, p. 3): 'As soon as any society, by custom or convention or law makes a distinction between property and mere physical possession it has in effect defined property as a right.' Following Macpherson (1978, p. 4):

> We may notice here one logical implication of the definition of property as an enforceable claim: namely, that property is a political relation between persons . . . For any given system of property is a system of rights of each person in relation to other persons.

The discussion of property markets is thus linked with a discussion of relations between agents and the role of the state in structuring and enforcing these relations. As Berge (1990, p. 42) states, reviewing and himself adding to the growing contemporary literature on property rights: 'this view of property rights means that they are a central part of all social institutions and that institutional change means changes in property rights'.

Effecting such changes, or developing planning policy on the basis of such an analysis, involves more detailed discussion of the interests involved in the property market, the way in which owning an enforceable claim to a 'piece' of the natural or built environment relates to agents' economic, political and ideological rationale and the detail of their everyday practice. This involves unpacking the term 'property' into, at first, common and private property and then into further constituent parts.

The definition of property used so far does not imply only private property, the right of a single agent to exclude others. In a society where markets perform the dominant allocative role it is likely that private property will be seen as the exemplar of property, for as Reeve (1986, pp. 95–6) points out: 'a minimum presupposition of exchange is that persons have either the ability or the right to exclude the other partner in the exchange from the "property".' There is therefore a conceptual link between exclusive property and the operation of markets. Reeve relates this to private property, ownership by a single agent, but it applies equally to common property where a right to exclusion exists. To explain this some further discussion of common property is needed.

Following Berge (1990), Bromley (1991) and Berkes (1989), four types of property regime may be distinguished, of which three are frequently referred to as common property: open-access or no ownership (res nullius) in which there is free access at no cost for anyone who wishes to benefit from use of the land or surrounding environment; state property or public ownership (res publica) in which the national state owns the rights – certain use and access rights may be left unspecified but exclusion is possible; communal property (res communes) in which an identifiable group managed the rights to an element of the environment, including the definition of rules concerning exclusion; and private or individual property in which the rights are vested in a specific agent, including rights of exclusion.

Private property was counterposed above to a disaggregated concept of common property. But this term also needs disaggregating for a clearer understanding of market processes affecting the built and natural environments. The purpose for holding landed property and the associated requirements the owner has for performance together distinguish three sub-markets: use, development and investment interests (Healey and Nabarro, 1990; Rydin, 1992).

'Use interests' in land refer to use by occupiers of sites and buildings whether households, producers in industry or agriculture or the service sector, public or private. To have a 'pure' use interest, occupiers should only be tenants on unmarketable legal interests, for example commercial tenants on rack-rented short-term tenancies with no security of tenure, or council housing tenants who cannot legally trade their interest for a price. Where a legal title which commands a price in the market is involved, then the legal right may exhibit features of capital growth and income generation associated with financial assets and hence investment interests in land. Thus the owner-occupier has both use and investment interests in land. Users also undertake development from time to time: those on unmarketable tenancies then combine use and development interests, while the owner-occupying developer combines all three types of interest in land.

Investment interests in land arise from the potential for ownership of the legal title to generate income and/or appreciate in capital value. These are the two desired features of any financial asset. The income return arises from the rental flow from occupants of land and buildings and can provide a yield to a whole series of leaseholders as well as the freeholder. Capital appreciation can be due to rental growth, as well as expectations of rising rents or of capital value themselves. The exemplar of the owner with investment interests in land is the pension fund, with typically 7 per cent of their overall investment portfolio in land, buildings and ground rents (*Financial Statistics*, October 1988).

Development interests in land view land and buildings as sites for the production process of construction, redevelopment and refurbishment. As such, access to land and buildings, and hence the ownership of a legal right granting such access, is an essential means of production. The construction company which owns land temporarily to provide building sites is the main example of this category of ownership. However, much recent research (Ball, 1988; Smyth, 1985) has shown that firms engaged in construction activities often also hold land for its appreciation in capital value, that is as a financial asset. These landowners therefore fall in the overlap category between investment and development interests. The use of this kind of classification will be shown in the housing land and inner city case studies in Chapters 12 and 15.

The analysis implies that planning is best understood in terms of the way in which planning mediates between property interests and the manner in which these property interests are socially structured and themselves influenced by the state. Furthermore understanding the nature of property interests is a necessary precursor to any effective planning activity. As Cox *et al.* (1990, p. 77) argue:

> An appreciation of the traditions and associated practices (of landowner-ship) . . . is crucial in understanding the expectations of landowning interests in response to demands that they manage their land according to the interest which the community in general may be deemed to have in it.

The contribution of institutional economic analysis is to emphasise the interrelation of economic action, social structure and the state. This reinforces the institutionalism of planning theorists and helps underpin their analysis of the planning process.

Further reading

Any one of the numerous conventional economic textbooks will provide an introduction to both the ideal market model and the market failure approach. Suggested texts are Begg *et al.* (1991), Lipsey (1989) or Samuelson and Nordhaus (1989). A simple introduction to marxist ideas in the context of planning is provided by Ambrose (1986) but the best exponent of this approach currently is Harvey (1985). A more formal approach to the marxist model is provided in Desai (1979). The institutionalist writings are very diverse but writers such as Veblen (1976), Myrdal (1957) and Galbraith (1981) are very approachable. A good introduction is provided by the interviews in Swedberg (1990).

■ *Chapter 12* ■

Land for Housing

One of the main tasks the land use planning system faces is allocating land to residential development and then responding to planning applications for such development. This is a major call on the resources of planning departments. It also meshes with local political agendas set by county and district councillors, concerning homelessness and housing needs in the locality and the pressures arising from the flow of households in and out of the area. The interaction of land markets, housing markets and housebuilding activity, together with the land use planning, determine the extent to which housing policy goals can be met by planning activity. The chapter explores the vexed housing land issue from the perspective of the four alternative economic approaches.

■ The ideal market model: the housebuilders' case

The availability of land for housebuilding was a heated political issue during the 1970s and 1980s. The HouseBuilders' Federation and certain academics have been effective in putting forward an essentially neo-classical economic argument concerning the role of the land use planning system in restricting the availability of land and, therefore, pushing up land and house prices. The analysis begins by considering the role of markets in transferring land from one use to another, and in particular from agriculture to residential development.

The demand for housing land, that is land for residential development, is a derived demand, dependent on the demand for housing itself. Both the housing demand and derived housing land demand curves slope downwards when price is plotted against distance from the city centre. This is primarily to offset the increased costs of commuting associated with suburban residence. Land is bid away from agriculture up to the point where the price of housing land is just equal to agricultural land values. As housing demand, and the associated housing land demand increases, the price that land commands at any distance from the city will increase. Thus the point of equilibrium will

282

be at a further distance from the city centre and more suburbanisation will occur.

At the margin, housing land prices should approach agricultural land prices (themselves linked to the price of agricultural produce). If a substantial gap exists between agricultural and housing land prices, then this suggests that market processes are being hindered. Currently such a gap exists. To quote a leading exponent of this view, Alan Evans, in 1987 agricultural land in the south-east was selling for £4300 p.a. while residential sites were fetching £984 000 (1987, p. 132). The planning system is blamed for creating this gap by restricting the supply of housing land. This bids up the price of such land above the free-market equilibrium. As a result the supply of housing is also restricted and house prices are higher than they might otherwise have been. The problem of high house prices, particularly in regions where restrictive planning policies operate, is explained in terms of the free market in land not being allowed to operate.

To quote Evans again (1987, p. 6):

> Firstly . . . [l]and prices can push house prices in that restricting the supply of land can cause both land prices and house prices to be higher than they otherwise would be. Moreover, increasing the supply can cause both land

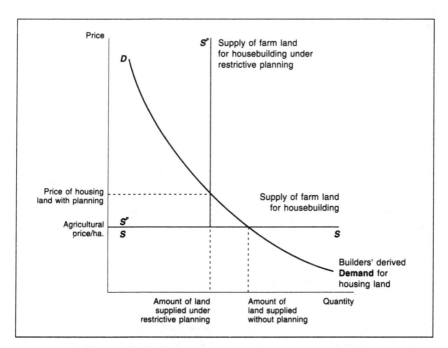

Figure 12.1 *The ideal market model: the effects of restrictive planning*

prices and house prices to be lower than they otherwise would be. Secondly, land prices have risen faster than incomes, house prices, and the price of other goods which suggest that they are a legitimate cause for concern. And thirdly, the price of housing land is far, far higher than the price of agricultural land. Thus if the supply of land on which development were allowed were to be increased the value of development land would fall as agricultural land was developed.

Empirical work to estimate the impact of restrictive planning on house and land prices has been undertaken, using this neo-classical model, by Cheshire and Sheppard (1989). Using data from 1984, they argued that, if the planning system in the south-east had been relaxed so that there was no effective restriction on supply, then housing would have occupied 65 per cent more space and generally been 4–6 per cent cheaper. The proportion of households able to buy their home would have increased from 67 per cent to 71 per cent.

The solution to such problems is clear. Planning restrictions must be eased so that the private housing market can expand to meet demand, driving prices down to more affordable levels. The pattern of sub-urbanisation and rural development that would result represents consumer preferences more accurately than the compact settlements desired by planners and politically active segments of the existing community. The NIMBY ('Not In My Back Yard') attitude of people who already live in pleasant suburban and rural locations is the attempt by the few to exclude others; the market, by contrast, represents all potential residents and is a more democratic, as well as efficient, way of determining where housing should be built.

▌Market failure: planning residential development

There are a number of ways in which the concept of market failure can be applied to the analysis of the housing land market and suggest a rationale for land use planning to rectify the failure (Harrison, 1977, Chs 11 and 13). For example, the concept of externalities can be applied in two ways.

First, there is the total sum of social costs and benefits that will arise from the transfer of land to housing use. Developers, in bidding for a housing site, will take into account only the costs they will directly incur and the income flow they will receive from the eventual housing sale. However, residential development implies an addition to housing stock and, under general conditions of housing need, a growth in local population. This will have a knock-on effect on local facilities. Some of these will be beneficial in terms of availability of labour for local industry and increased demand in local shops. Others will, however, be a cost to the public sector and local community: increased traffic generation may place a burden on the road infrastructure; the sewerage and water supply networks may similarly be stressed; local schools may face rising rolls beyond capacity. In all these ways the social costs and benefits of supplying land to a housebuilder may diverge from the private utility of the land to that builder.

Assuming a net external cost, the result will be a social benefit curve in the housing land market below the builders' demand schedule. Therefore, in terms of efficiency, the uncontrolled market will over-supply land at too high a price. Thus the argument implies a potential role for the planning system in restricting the flow of housing land through the planning system in response to the social costs generated by residential development (see Figure 12.2).

A further application of the concept of externalities is in terms of the spatial coordination of land uses. Each site exists within a network of land uses, and the use of each site impacts on the use of those other sites.

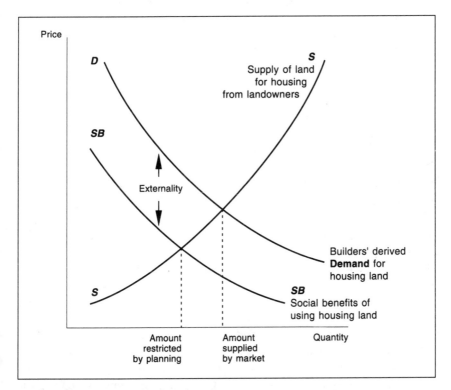

Figure 12.2 *Market failure: the external costs of residential development*

This is particularly relevant for contiguous sites. Thus an area of beautiful countryside will enhance the value of adjoining housing (a positive spatial externality). Conversely a rubbish tip will lower the value of an adjoining golf course (a negative externality). The effect of transferring land into housing use will depend on its current condition and the nature of the adjoining uses. But the transfer is likely to have some form of externality effect. This suggests a further role for the planning system: to allocate sites to land uses so as to minimise negative externalities and maximise positive externalities. Not only should this result in land users deriving the greatest possible enjoyment of their sites, there should be an impact on the pricing of land so that land values in general rise, due to a higher overall level of demand for land commensurate with this greater enjoyment. There should also be an increase in the level of land utilisation, although this will depend on the elasticity of supply of land, that is how responsive the supply of land is to price movements.

One further example of how planning can overcome market failure relates to the problems posed by imperfect information in the new housing market. Such imperfections can generate cycles of development with wide swings in the supply of new housing onto the market. The starting assumption is that a move has occurred away from equilibrium due, say, to a shift in the schedule of demand. The original equilibrium point is no longer applicable but the movement to the new equilibrium does not occur immediately (see Figure 12.3).

The market model would argue that at the prevailing price there will be a shortage which will force the price up to a new equilibrium point. However, it is possible for imperfect information to hinder the process. At the quantity already supplied to the market, the price that the new demand schedule will command is substantially higher. In the absence of information about competitors' actions, each builder will seek to supply a greatly increased quantity of dwellings to match this higher price. When all builders supply these dwellings onto the market, which occurs after a time lag due to the length of the development process, then the price falls as the market is glutted. The price fall then induces a cutback in production and ensuing shortage. This process of underprovision and overprovision will continue with smaller and smaller swings until the new equilibrium is reached. The severity of swings will depend on the number of builders that feel they can beat the competition and supply the market first, and on the length of the development period which introduces time lags into the supply of dwellings.

The assumption in the above discussion, that the swings in price and quantity movements will tend to diminish over time, is based on specified elasticities for the supply and demand schedules, as illustrated

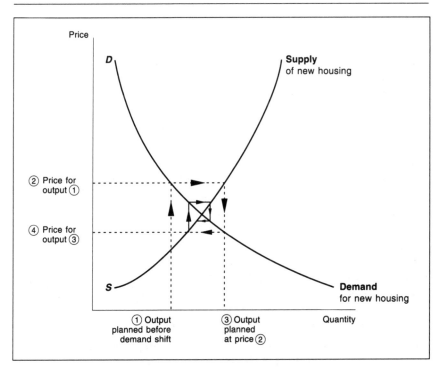

Figure 12.3 *Market failure: instability due to imperfect information*

in Figures 12.3. With different elasticities (slopes of the lines) it is possible for the cycles to become unstable. In practice, the likelihood is of further 'shocks' in the market, shifting the schedules and setting in train a new set of cyclical movements in price and quantity. Again this suggests a role for land use planning, gathering information about future trends and regulating the supply of housing land to prevent such speculative swings in new housing supply.

Planning, therefore, has a role in overcoming market failure and establishing efficient market outcomes. Higher land prices may result from planning activities but such increases should reflect the benefits of better planned housing production and land use patterns.

The marxist model: focusing on housing production

While previous analyses focused on the market for housing land, the marxist approach looks to the production process, in this case the construction process by which houses are built. In his influential study, Ball (1984, and see also 1988) provided an analysis of the housebuilding industry in which he stressed the concentration of capital with a handful of volume housebuilders responsible for the vast majority of output, and the technical backwardness of the industry. Compared to other production processes, there has been remarkably little technical innovation in British construction. Attempts to replace on-site assembly with off-site prefabrication have been unsuccessful since the on-site management of the labour force has not been able to achieve the technical discipline the new methods require. Thus the attempt to introduce timber framed housing in the early 1980s simply resulted in cases of structural failure in the form of damp penetration and fire hazard. Instead of replacing labour with capital, the trend has been towards deskilling labour and (successfully) resisting unionisation to enable greater direct exploitation of labour. As a result construction remains one of the most economically unstable and dangerous industries to work in, with labour relegated to insecure forms of employment.

British housing meanwhile remains poorly built, traditional in design and features, and yet relatively expensive. This is explained in terms of the role that land rent plays in the residential development process. Landowners are able to extract rent from housebuilders in the form of development gains, the increment in the value of development sites over and above their value in existing uses. This can pose a problem for housebuilders as they are faced with high and, in buoyant housing markets, increasing land prices for their development sites. The complaints of housebuilders over land prices must, therefore, be interpreted as a conflict between two fractions of capital, industrial capital producing housing and landed capital holding potential development sites.

One way in which housebuilders have reacted to the problems posed by land rent is to seek to capture development gains for themselves. Housebuilders, particularly the volume builders, have held landbanks, often of substantial size. These may be bought on the open market, acquired in builder-to-builder deals or be the result of asset-stripping when ailing companies are taken over. The spread of land in these banks will vary: some with planning permission, some without, some even in green belts; some for development next year, some for definite future plans, some held with no definite idea of development. These landbanks are essentially a portfolio of investment assets, some highly speculative, some with a fairly certain return. Buying sites cheap and then developing them allows the housebuilder to reap the development gain and cut out the landowner. When market conditions allow, this can be a very profitable route for housebuilders to follow, one which precludes the necessity of increasing the profit rate on the actual construction process by increasing labour productivity. As Duncan (1989, p. 169) argues, the quality of housing (in terms of insulation, materials used, standard of services) and of residential areas (in terms of play areas, cycleways, landscaping) is affected by the focus on extracting development gains from landownership.

The role of the planning system in this process is seen as largely passive. Land use planning is not regarded as constraining the supply of housing land, but rather as permitting landowners and housebuilders to reap development gains through extensive housebuilding. Ball (1984, p. 114) demonstrates this by plotting the construction profitability of housebuilding against land prices for the period 1970–82 and showing how profits lead land prices, without any evidence of land use planning squeezing land supply. The Thatcherite planning programme of the 1980s renewed the laxity of planning practice at a time when the development plans of housebuilders might otherwise have started to come up against the constraints of local authority structure and local plans. The marxist analysis of housing land thus points to the land-banking operations of housebuilders, their use of these landbanks to generate profits and the permissive role that the planning system appears to have played in relation to such speculation in development sites.

By implication and manifesto, the solution to the problem of providing cheap, well-built housing is the nationalisation of either the housebuilding industry or development land to break the deadlock of speculative purchase of housing land interacting with low levels of technical innovation and capital investment.

Institutionalist economic analysis: negotiating about housing sites

Much of the institutionalist research on this topic has drawn on Ball's (1984, 1988) marxist work, but developed it in an essentially institutional framework. The emphasis has been on the degree of imperfect competition in the housebuilding industry and the conflicts of interests over land within the context of local planning policy (Healey *et al.*, 1988, Rydin, 1986). An important starting point has been the analysis of the structure and nature of the residential development industry. In Britain, unlike many other European countries, housing is produced as a speculative good with the developer taking on the whole process from purchase of the site, through construction of the dwelling and estate layout to final marketing of the finished house. This means that the developer has two potential sources of profit: those arising from the construction process itself, the manufacture of the house; and those arising from the development gains that occur when a site is converted into a residential estate. The housebuilder has both development and investment interests in the land, to follow the terminology of the institutional analysis (as opposed to the conflict between fractions of capital identified in the marxist approach).

Recognising these dual interests of landowning housebuilders seriously undermines the neo-classical model. This model argues that the demand for development sites is primarily a function of the prevailing price for the developments, the resulting buildings. This price is determined in a separate market, for final developments both new and existing. The supply of development sites is often viewed as virtually fixed, a view which allows the complexities of interconnected supply and demand to be ignored. However, if, as within institutionalism, supply is viewed as a function of landowners' and others' (such as planning committees') intentions to release sites for development, then the picture becomes more complex. For the landowners' intentions will be affected by expectations of the price level for developments, which may itself be affected by decisions to release development sites, a determinant of the supply of new developments. This points to the interconnection of the markets for developments and development sites, and hence of the supply and demand schedules.

The picture is even more confused when it is recognised that the landowner and the manufacturer of a development can be one and the same agent, as is common in housebuilding. Ownership of a site by a construction company is not equivalent to the holding of factors of production by, say, a clothing manufacturer. For ownership need not mean immediate use for manufacture and holding sites does not incur the same costs as ordinary stockpiling. Indeed holding whole or parts of sites for future development can be rational where site values and development prices increase over time, or where local development prices can be manipulated by the supply of new developments. In such cases, it is meaningless to talk of independent supply and demand schedules for development sites.

The institutional approach links this analysis of the housebuilders' reasons for owning landed property with an analysis of the oligopolistic nature of the housebuilding industry. Like many other industrial sectors, construction and housebuilding within construction are dominated by a few large firms. These firms account for the majority of work done, of employment and, in housing, of units built. There are a very large number of small firms, and fewer medium-sized firms, but they build fewer dwellings and are more important in specialist sub-contracted tasks and in the growing repair and maintenance sector (for example, Pacione, 1990). The decision making of all sizes of firms are important to institutionalists while the marxists tend to focus on the larger capitalists as dominating the production process.

Firms at the smaller end of the size spectrum have fewer resources available for land purchase and usually operate in a more restricted geographical area. They may have a historic landbank of land they have held for many years and are slowly building on. Otherwise they will be seeking to find suitable local sites for their operations, often small–medium sites. In doing so they may find themselves disadvantaged by competition from larger firms, with greater financial resources, an ability to move into local areas at will and a capacity for developing much larger sites. These larger firms also have their landbanks, often substantial ones. They acquire these by a variety of means: some open market transactions, some less visible interhousebuilder transactions, some through takeovers of other firms, particularly in periods of recession.

The significance of landbanking by housebuilders is that the longer land is held in such a 'bank' the greater is the prospect of capital appreciation or development gain or, if market conditions are very uncertain, the landbank can enable upward movements in house prices quickly to be taken advantage of. This does depend, though, on the assumption that planning permission is forthcoming for development on such sites. While marxist accounts assume that the planning system presents no significant barrier to housebuilders' activities, the institutional approach uses a more subtle analysis of the interaction of the planning system and housebuilding.

There are a number of different ways in which urban planning impacts on residential development, affecting the outcome in terms of houses built and providing a structural context for housebuilders' decision making.

First, there is the issue of how much land is 'made available' through the grant of planning permission. The institutional approach argues that the planning system has had considerable effect in restricting land for development in specific areas and at specific times, where and when development would be attractive to housebuilders. Thus, planning restraint can bite, say, in the south east during boom periods. While this is problematic for housebuilders routinely seeking planning permission for development, it considerably increases the development gains for housebuilders who already own land on which planning permission is now forthcoming. Restraint can itself also enhance value through protecting the environmental qualities of an area, an added bonus for those who can get development rights in such a locality. Shucksmith (1990, p. 134) has argued that a planning policy trying to restrict new development in the Lake District to local needs depressed the development land market but increased the price of existing housing, perversely pushing it out of the reach of local people. Thus the planning system influences local patterns of land values and the distribution of development gains between housebuilders. This explains the ferocity, at boom times, of the battle between planners and housebuilders.

Another aspect of planning, influencing which sites are developable and hence more valuable, is the way in which infrastructure networks are extended and improved. Because such infrastructure investment requires a level of strategic planning, if only by the infrastructure agency, it should be less amenable to site-by-site negotiation in the way planning permissions are. However, developers do frequently negotiate extensions and upgradings, if necessary paying in part for the costs via a planning obligation. In this way the speculative residential development process undermines the strategic planning of infrastructure (Healey *et al.*, 1988, p. 109) and negotiation of infrastructure upgrading becomes an element in housebuilders' profit making activities.

Restraint policies and infrastructure investment can also reinforce each other. Healey *et al.*'s (1988, p. 20) found that:

> Public investment can create the conditions which define sites as 'prime' in market terms, and . . . policies of restraint have reinforced this by limiting land release elsewhere and retaining the very environmental quality which enhances an area's attractiveness.

The negotiative processes which allocate serviced housing land also determine the precise locations and nature of those sites. This is significant because size and location impacts forward to the housing market and back to the housebuilding industry. Larger housebuilders will tend to prefer larger sites, where a long programme of work can be sustained, although they are increasingly looking to smaller sites. Smaller builders can cope only with more modest sites, unless they form consortiums, and they may also occupy specialist niches in the market, such as sheltered housing, which have very specific locational requirements. Larger, urban fringe sites may be best suited to the 'mass' housing market, in the low–medium price range. Targeting higher-income groups may require, for example, environmentally attractive rural locations or convenient, waterside urban locations.

It is difficult to generalise on these points as the underlying demographics and economics of the consumer market changes, as does the manner in which marketing actively creates niches for housebuilders to fill. The point here is that planning influences the ability of house-builders to meet identified demand through the nature of the sites released and, in turn, the planning system will face quite specific pressures from housebuilders as they seek planning permission on sites best suited to conform with their marketing strategy.

Finally, there is the issue of phasing. This is the area over which planning has, perhaps, the least control (Brindley *et al.*, 1989, pp. 72–3). While development plans may incorporate timescales over which local development targets are to be reached but not breached, the timing of development remains essentially in commercial hands. In their study of 'growth management on the urban fringe', Healey *et al.* (1988, p. 117) found that 'the phasing programme was largely ignored'.

The planning system thus interacts with the residential development process, a process in search of construction profits and land development gains. The planning system affects the outcomes of residential development, structuring the housebuilding process, and the residential development process in turn structures the activities of planners in pursuit of their goals.

Further reading

An overview of the debate about housing land can be achieved by reading Evans (1988), Harrison (1977), Ball (1984) and Rydin (1986), which cover the four approaches, respectively. Two other useful references, which emphasise policy alongside economic aspects, are Barlow (1988b) and Shucksmith (1988). For the results of recent research which embraced both a behavioural (quasi-institutionalist) and a neo-classical economic approach, the reader is referred to the DoE report by Gerald Eve and the Department of Land Economy at Cambridge University (1992) and various supporting monographs by Monk (1991a, 1991b, 1991c).

■ *Chapter 13* ■

Minerals Exploitation

Minerals deposits only occur in fixed locations with specific geological features. They are a necessary input into construction activity, energy supply and industrial production. And they pose a problem for planning in terms of ensuring a continuous flow of essential resources while protecting local environments from the adverse effects of minerals exploitation. Yet planning often finds itself in a reactive and relatively powerless position when confronted by the economic dynamics of changing minerals production. This chapter explores these dynamics of minerals exploitation from the point of view of the alternative economic approaches.

■ The ideal market model: innovation and trade

While there is a frequent emphasis on the physical reserves of a particular mineral, such as oil, and on the prospect of 'running out of' the mineral within a specified time period, Rees (1990) has argued that scarcity is an economic, not a physical, issue. She has identified the way in which the ideal market model may be applied to various stages of the minerals exploitation process.

The market model assumes that such exploitation occurs so as to just balance marginal costs and benefits to the minerals producer. Thus particular minerals will be mined up to the point where the addition to revenue from the last ton just equals the addition to cost. The three key variables which the model identifies as influencing patterns of production are: the location, size, composition and affluence of market centres; the costs of production, including the provision of essential infrastructure; and the costs of transportation between the production site and the market. The market ensures that profit incentives exist to ensure the exploitation of minerals and their input into broader processes of economic development. When levels of production relative to current demand mean that a mineral is becoming scarce, then extraction costs will go up and, as the supply schedule shifts upwards, price will rise. This will result in a lower quantity being demand by consumers.

Innovations will be spurred. There will be a search for new deposits. By comparing the costs of and returns from different potential minerals sites, the producer will be able to select the most profitable and, providing the level of net return exceeds the costs of finance or returns on alternative investments, funds will be made available to support new exploitation. The three key variables identified by the market model in explaining the search for new mineral deposits are, therefore, the costs, the expected revenue and the net yield from other investments. Other innovations are also encouraged by the potential profitability associated with market scarcity. Time and funds will be invested in finding ways of continuing extraction of deeper or more difficult deposits. Consumers will try to find substitutes for the particular mineral, altering production processes to use an alternative material or using secondhand materials. Both investment in technical knowledge and capital goods may be needed to achieve such substitution. There may also be greater emphasis on recycling the mineral or on conserving it in production processes and final consumption.

The market model can also be used to analyse the rate at which resource exploitation takes place. This involves identifying the efficient depletion path (Rees, 1990, p. 138). This is defined as the path which maximises the sum of the net benefits from mineral use accruing to the present and all future generations, as measured in present value terms by the application of a discount factor to future income streams. Under perfect market conditions, the operation of market signals and the pursuit of maximum profit by producers will automatically ensure that this efficient depletion path is adopted and, therefore, that there is a socially optimal allocation of resources over time. For firms will take their decisions based on future cost and demand patterns, discounting at rates determined by the market and reflecting society's time preferences for receiving goods now rather than in the future. The individual firm's balance between exploitation and conservation will be linked into society's preferred balance through the influence of demand and market discount rates. In effect, the pricing mechanism acts as both an incentive to resource use and a deterrent to overuse.

Where, as often occurs, such minerals are traded across international boundaries, a further dimension to market operations is added. The model argues for free trade across international boundaries on the basis that such trade maximises total consumption and benefits both parties. The relevant theory concerns the principle of comparative advantage of parties to international trade, originally developed by Ricardo (Begg *et al.*, 1991). This states that countries should specialise in goods that they can produce relatively cheaply. Even if Country A produces both goods *x* and *y* more cheaply than Country B there is economic merit in country A specialising in good *x*, which it produces cheapest, leaving Country B to specialise in good *y*. The following, hypothetical example illustrates the point. Assume that the costs of producing coal and manufactured goods in Britain and Bolivia are as follows:

	Cost of coal production	Cost of manufactured goods
Britain	£25/unit	£100/unit
Bolivia	$10/unit	$50/unit

To produce 1 unit of manufactured good, Britain has to give up 4 units of coal. In Bolivia 1 unit of manufactured good costs 5 units of coal. Therefore the Britain has comparative advantage in manufactured goods and Bolivia in coal. Trading coal for manufactured goods and vice versa increases the total quantity of good exchanged and the best use of resources is made. As Rees notes (1990, p. 146), this view of international trade in minerals is by no means uninfluential and informs some of the negotiations on trade liberalisation undertaken in the GATT rounds.

Thus market processes on a domestic and international scale will result in the optimal allocation of investment in minerals exploitation, encourage innovation to earn profits and thereby overcome scarcity and ensure the maximum level of consumption given limited resources. In such a situation planning has little role to play beyond protecting local amenities at the site of exploitation. Strategic issues concerning the amount and location of minerals mined are best left to the decision making of the minerals industry.

▌ Market failure: imperfect competition in the minerals industry

The minerals market is characterised by extensive supply concentration – that is, a relatively small percentage of the firms in the market supply a relatively large proportion of the overall quantity demanded. In the case of certain minerals there is also substantial demand concentration (or monopsony) with a handful of consumers comprising the entire market. In addition, vertical integration, with the different elements of a production process contained within one firm, means that the consumer and producer of a mineral are often merely separate divisions within a large enterprise. These forms of market distortion render an efficient outcome in minerals markets unlikely.

Rees (1990, p. 115) has analysed the degree of supply concentration and its impact on market functioning. In the case of copper, the four largest producers were majority owners of 19 per cent of the non-socialist world's output: the 10 largest companies accounted for 35 per cent. Within the single country of the USA, three companies were responsible for 55 per cent of national output: eight companies for 88 per cent. Taking the case of bauxite and aluminium, six producers were whole or partial owners of over 70 per cent of the non-socialist mining and smelting capacity in 1985. While for steel, in 1981 20 firms produced over 52 per cent of the non-socialist world's output: eight firms produced 29 per cent. The inclusion of state owned companies in socialist countries introduces a further element of concentration, since these organisations face no national competition. In 1980 the four state owned copper producers accounted for 42 per cent of world output. And in 1981, the output of the Soviet Union's steel industry comprised 21 per cent of world output. While the degree of concentration has reduced somewhat over recent decades, the degree of concentration of economic power is still substantial.

The reasons for such concentration lie in a number of different factors. First, there is the extent of scale economies in minerals production, due to the large amount of capital investment needed. The minimum viable scale of operation acts as a high threshold, preventing firms from readily entering the industry. In the US steel market, a 5 per cent market share is a minimum necessity (Rees, 1990, p. 117). Second, there are also economies of vertical integration, which arise when different stages of a production process are combined in one organisation. In part these are technical, as with the energy saving in combining smelting and refining. In part these are commercial, associated with the certainty of overall planning of the organisation if the flow of mineral from one stage to another of production is known. In part these are political, in that the tax regimes of different countries can be played off against each other if the corporation has control over the location of the complete product stream.

A third factor which also inhibits entrants into the market is the scale of venture capital necessary for undertaking search activities for new minerals deposits. Fourth, the costs of acquisition of technical knowledge in this field can be high and, in some cases, patents and commercial secrecy may limit access to this knowledge, regardless of cost. Finally, there are the aggressive actions of established market leaders in keeping competitors out by underpricing sufficiently to drive them out of the market, and then restoring prices to their higher level. Collusion between a number of market leaders to maintain their joint position is not unknown.

The effects of supply concentration in an industry has been analysed by neo-classical economics as a move away from the perfect market scenario and towards the limiting case of a pure monopoly – only one supplier (Lipsey, 1989). In a monopoly, the firm is the industry and influences price by adjusting the amount of produce allowed onto the market. It is most profitable for such a monopolist to restrict output and thus drive up price. In this way excess profits above the normal costs of production (which include the average rate of return to entrepreneurs) can be earned.

This strategy of restricting output is particularly effective if the demand schedule facing the firm is inelastic, so that consumers do not substantially adjust their consumption in response to price rises. The classic example of this is the fourfold increase in the price of oil achieved by OPEC producers in 1973 by relatively small cuts in production, given the inelastic nature of demand for oil at that time. In the event of such market manipulation, the efficient point of production, where marginal cost equals marginal benefit, will not be achieved.

To this basic strategy of any firm with a degree of market power can be added other possible strategies: reducing the scope for substitution; splitting the market into segments; adopting specific pricing strategies; and collusion with other firms. These strategies take one so far from consideration of market operations and towards a broader discussion of the decision making process of economic institutions that these points are better covered in the institutionalist analysis below.

The existence of imperfect competition poses a problem for planning policy. Inefficient outcomes are inevitable in such circumstances but the market failure can be adequately dealt with only at the level of industrial structure through economic restructuring. Local planning policy can seek to regulate the activities of a mining operator in one area, but the very size of such operators will allow them to play one local authority off against another.

The marxist model: dependency and restructuring

The marxist model begins from an analysis of the relationship between capital accumulation and minerals exploitation. In doing so, it is capable of treating both the flow of such resources from underdeveloped to developed countries and the detail of resource exploitation in specific locations.

At the international level, the issue of trade in minerals is not seen in terms of comparative advantage (as in the ideal market model) but in terms of the dependent relations between developed and underdeveloped countries. Under advanced capitalism, this relationship is imperialist in nature (see Chapter 14 for further discussion of imperialism). This means that capitals within developed countries use less developed countries as a pool of cheap and pliable labour, a source of raw materials (particularly natural resources) and a forced market. Thus the geographical distribution of natural resource production is, in many ways, a map of imperialist activity in controlling raw materials. The conditions under which such production occurs is determined by the capital accumulation needs of owners of the resources and the needs of capitalist enterprises within developed countries for those resources. Depletion is likely to occur at an excessive rate, with little thought for worker health or safety, conservation or the local environment. If an area becomes exhausted, then capitalist interests can expand their imperialist activities, moving on to exploit another region.

As Kakönen (1988, p. 222) argues, addressing the issue of the scarcity of non-renewable natural resources:

> The answer is: it all depends on the capitalist mode of production and its relation to nature. So far the imperialist system has been able to solve the problem through expansion, by opening new mineral deposits in remote areas. The problem is not whether natural resources will suffice, the crucial question is: who will get control over new deposits?

Kakönen goes on to argue further that maintaining control over resources creates a political problem which necessitates the development of means of controlling underdeveloped countries by economic, political or military means. The centrality of cheap resources from the Third World in reducing the cost of reproducing capital, and thus countering the tendency of the rate of profit to fall, renders this political problem ever more urgent.

A further dimension of this can be seen in the way that the Third World debt crisis has been handled to encourage natural resource trade on terms favourable to developed countries. Third World debt preexisted the 1973–4 oil crisis, but the oil crisis both increased the amount of money available on world finance markets, from the surpluses of oil exporters deposited in financial institutions, and created deficits in developing countries due to the greatly increased bill for imports of oil and oil derivatives. As a result, from 1975 to 1979 the credits granted to developing countries increased by 25 per cent. Private credits to developing countries increased 6.5 times from 1970 to 1978 and represented two-thirds of all their debts. Such private loans had few strings attached, but interest rates were high and repayment periods short. By 1979 the total debt of developing countries was $400 billion, foreign debt increasing by 20 per cent p.a.

From 1982 onwards the banks and representatives of world capitalism have used the debt crisis to impose free-market policies on developing countries. The 1985 Baker Plan had an aim of economic adjustment to encourage the private sector and allow market forces a larger role in the allocation of resources. To quote Hall (1988, p. 8) the plan had the aims 'on the one hand, of promoting the indigenous – usually comprador – capitalist class, and on the other, of integrating the industry and agriculture of the countries concerned firmly into the international circuitry of capital'. This meant that, to meet debt repayments, developing countries were encouraged, or more realistically forced, to concentrate on those sectors that could generate export earnings in response to the needs of world markets. There was a policy of encouraging increased levels of trade so that exports could pay for the debt. This meant narrowing economic development onto the natural resource sector. This proved an endless downward spiral. Commodity prices fell, while the value of the debt increased; more and more income went to service the debt. In 1986 25 per cent of all (not net) export earnings went on servicing debt. In Latin America the figure rose as high as 50 per cent and it was even worse in sub-Saharan Africa. This meant increased rates of resource exploitation at any cost. The international organisation of capital accumulation is thus the determining factor in patterns of minerals exploitation.

The marxist approach can also be used to examine more localised minerals exploitation, for example coal mining in Britain. Again the focus is on demonstrating a link between the imperatives of capitalist accumulation and environmental degradation (Beynon, *et al.* 1990; Fine, 1984, 1990).

British Coal has been the target for major restructuring. Both of its main customers, British Steel and the electricity supply industry, have been privatised and the early recognition of this prospect prompted the 1985 *New Strategy for Coal* replacing the 1974 *Plan for Coal*. As a result of the implementation of this strategy the number of workers in the industry has fallen from 207 000 in 1983 to 87 791 in 1989; the number of collieries has fallen from 191 to 93 with the majority of those remaining vulnerable to closure. The stated goals of the strategy were to phase out the subsidy to coal, to sell coal at a competitive price and to abandon fixed production targets in favour of more flexible output. The under-lying motive was to produce low-cost coal which would compete with cheap imports, such as those from Poland. This meant closing down deep pits, introducing more technology and expanding the opencast mines.

There has already been considerable technological change in the coal industry, focusing on a shift from power loading of the mined coal to introducing new face-based cutting technology which would allow continuous cutting. Using larger faces, with self-advancing steel pit props and steel roof supports, together with multiple shifts of miners, productivity can be considerably enhanced. New methods of working, known as retreat mining, have been introduced and there has been considerable investment in computerisation of the mining process. Overall within British Coal, output has increased by 94 per cent over 1982/3–1989 with an increase in output per man shift of 85 per cent. Average capital employed in deep-mined operations rose from £3633 million in 1982/3 to £4824 million in 1988/9.

But a second, key element of the strategy for restructuring the coal industry has been the shift to opencast mining (Hudson and Sadler, 1990). This shift has not been related to the search for new deposits in the context of scarcity, proven reserves outpace extraction, and in 1983 the Chairman announced that exploration was adding five years' output to reserves each year. Rather it concerns the quest for cheaper coal. The operating profit on opencast sites rose from £192 million in 1982/3 to £272 million in 1988/9, with a fall in the average capital employed from £277 million to £173 million and a return on capital rising to 158 per cent in 1988/9 (Hudson and Sadler, 1990, p. 444). The average production costs for opencast mines was £1.04/GJ (Giga Joule – a measure of energy) in 1988/9 compared to £1.54/GJ for deep mines. It also represents a desire to broaden the nature of the labour force, challenging the predominance of the National Union of Mineworkers (NUM).

Opencast mining had generally been considered a temporary and emergency measure, for use in wartime. For this reason the NUM did not always recruit in opencast mines; existing mines were not fully unionised and, in the recent expansion, the TGWU rather than the NUM or Union of Democratic Mineworkers has been recruiting. In addition to completely non-unionised sites, it is common to find labour-only sub-contracting where self-employed miners offer their services. This can provide flexibility for British Coal in their relations with the labour force.

While opencast mining may be a cheap and flexible source of coal, it carries significant local environmental consequences (Roberts, 1989; Walsh *et al.*, 1991). It generates noise and dust, local roads have to bear significant extra traffic, and there is a loss of considerable surface landscape. The result adversely affects local amenities, wildlife habitats and agricultural activities. To enable the expansion of opencast mining has, therefore, involved a considerable change in planning policies.

In 1981 the Flowers Report on *Coal and Environment* had suggested that opencast coalmining would be reduced because of its environmental impact. But by 1983 it was apparent that market criteria should play a larger part in minerals planning decisions. DoE Circular 3/84 stated in para. 15: 'each project should be considered in terms of the market requirement for its planned output'. This paralleled changes in British Coal's strategy towards opencast mining. By 1988, the shift in planning policy had become clear. The Minerals Planning Guidance Note No. 3 (1988) said in para. 5: 'because opencast coal is one of the cheapest forms of energy available to this country it is in the national interest to maximise production where that can be done in an environmentally acceptable way.'

From a marxist perspective this is a clear example of the dynamics of capital accumulation driving developments in minerals exploitation and the state acting in the interests of capital through facilitating production and encouraging the provision of cheap resources. Any role of planning in protecting the environment and local amenities is a minimal one and, indeed, any scope for effective planning is tightly constrained by the powerful economic forces of capitalism.

■ Institutionalist economic analysis: monopolies and mediation

As emphasised in Chapter 11, much institutional work starts from the neo-classical model and develops through a thorough critique of it. Judith Rees' seminal work on natural resources is in this vein (1990). Her careful analysis of the monopolistic nature of the minerals industry and, in particular, of the details of decision making within supplying firms, together with her critique of conventional economics, places her firmly, if implicitly, within the institutionalist approach.

Minerals markets exhibit a high degree of supply concentration as already outlined in the section on market failure above. However, while that analysis concentrates on the effect concentration has in pushing up price by restricting output, Rees points to a much broader range of consequences (1990, pp. 114–22). These emphasise the ways in which decision making by these large firms helps to structure the minerals market.

For example, firms may control access to substitutes through ownership of substitute suppliers or they may tie consumers to a particular technology which limits the scope for substitution. They may control the product range and structure consumer demand for products through advertising. Market segmentation may be encouraged, with slightly differentiated products being supplied to separated groups of consumers. This allows price movements in one segment to occur independently of movements in others. Pricing policy may play a part in creating such segmentation. Some consumers may be offered contract pricing with a reduced price for large, long-term buying commitments while other consumers will be on a cost-insurance-freight basis which offers the same price to a group of consumers within a region. In either case there is not the freedom of price movement assumed by the market model. In extreme but not uncommon cases, there may be extensive collusion between suppliers to divide up the market between major firms.

Of particular importance is the attitude of firms in the minerals market to risk. Minerals producers are very risk averse. Output stability, volume and market share are the most important goals for minerals producers. Production decisions are taken to maximise flexibility in order to minimise potential disruption to profit flows. This will influence the location of mining and the speed of exploitation of a particular resource. Risk aversion itself leads to further concentration within the industry as firms seek to take over substitutes and competitors and, thereby, prevent disruption to supply patterns.

The overriding importance of risk avoidance means that costs are unlikely to be minimised since continuity will be preferred over reduced costs. In addition the barriers to entry, natural, technological and artificial, that are encouraged by large, already established firms generate further costs. Control over the market by these large firms and such pressures towards higher costs clearly has implications for economic development. As Rees concludes, the minerals sector does not conform to any of the conditions needed to ensure that market forces will created economic efficiency. Therefore (1990, p. 129) 'the whole idea of correction [for market failure] becomes untenable when the entire system is made up of inefficient conditions; when inefficiency is not the exception but the rule.'

Thus in the institutionalist approach, the extent to which the minerals industry diverges from the neo-classical model renders the concept of market failure unhelpful. Like marxism, the resulting analysis of the strategies of minerals operators emphasises their control of market outcomes, but the focus is on a diversity of strategies and not on the inevitable result of capital accumulation processes. These similarities and differences with the marxist approach are also apparent in local-level analyses. Institutionalism, is well adapted to considering the interrelation of structural influences, such as those arising from a highly concentrated mining industry, and the activities of agents in a particular locality. Spatially-specific case studies are a hallmark of this approach in contrast to the sectoral case studies of marxism.

Healey *et al.* (1988) provide case studies of open cast coal production in Greater Manchester and South Staffordshire which contrast nicely with the marxist approach to this issue. The institutional case studies focus on the role that local planning can play in response to and anticipation of the environmental impact of opencast mining: that is, noise, dust, visual intrusion, landscape degradation, and loss of habitat. It emphasises the power of economic actors, the minerals operators, but suggests a variety of ways in which planning could ameliorate the effects of extraction through a process of mediation and negotiation with the operator. This process would be enhanced, from the local planning authority's point of view, if they had more property rights at their disposal.

The case studies tell of lengthy negotiation between local planners and the Open Cast Executive over a variety of issues: identifying the sites for mining, determining the precise boundaries of activities, pinpointing the location of disposal points for crushing and storing the coal, and agreeing a Code of Practice for controlling day-to-day operations. All this negotiation between production interests and the local state over the use of land for mining activity occurs in the context of local residents who wish to preserve their own use interests in the local environment and the value of their dwellings, their investment interests. The outcomes, therefore, reflect the conflicts between producer use interests and residents' use and investment interests in the context of, on the one hand, strong pressures towards opencast mining in the coal industry and, on the other hand, the representation of residents by the local state.

Planners were shown to be relatively weak in these negotiations. In part this was because of the rapidly changing structural context and the difficulty that local authorities were finding in developing strategies to deal with the unexpected expansion of opencast mining. As the researchers conclude: 'local authorities have an increasingly tenuous hold on powers to guide significantly the process of exploitation of natural resources in open land' (Healey *et al.*, 1988, p. 150). This lack of local authority powers existed in the context of central government policies advocating more open-cast mining, the aggressive pursuit of profit by the British Coal Corporation, and the shift of land out of agricultural use following reform of the CAP. In particular, the fact that central government was more favourably disposed to such production interests underpinned the predominance of production interests in minerals exploitation and restricted the scope for effective local planning activity.

This analysis is borne out by Roberts (1989), who argues that local authorities face difficulties in dealing with coalmining as they are given the unenviable task of both reacting positively to the industry-led changes promoting productivity and managing the consequences on local environments. Added to this is contribution of coalmining to local employment and role of local planning as promoting local economic development. Caught between local concerns and central government 'advice' to promote mining in the national interests, local planners (Roberts, 1989, p. 1287):

> can justifiably claim that their powers to control and manage the activities of the coal industry are severely limited, and that planning applications which are based upon the 'national interest' are, in reality, often an attempt to divert attention away from the more undesirable local impacts of proposed coalmining developments.

Further reading

Rees' book (1990) provides an excellent account of alternative analyses of minerals exploitation, encompassing the ideal market, market failure and institutional approaches. Kakönen (1988) provides an interesting attempt to apply marxist ideas. More detail on the coal industry in particular is given in: Hudson and Sadler (1990) which provides a wealth of empirical material; Fine (1990) which gives a historical and marxist perspective (including a discussion of rent theory not covered here); and Healey *et al.* (1988) which includes the case study on opencast mining in its analysis of the mediating role played by the land use planning system.

■ Chapter 14 ■

Pollution: Emission and Control

Pollution control has become a much more salient planning issue in the 1990s, with an emphasis on a greater variety of pollutants: not just smoke and toxic emissions but also those which cause acid rain and contribute to global warming. At the same time, there has been a resurgence of interest in fiscal instruments, such as pollution taxes, to replace or at least supplement pollution standards. Accepting the case for such taxes involves a commitment to a particular economic approach, based on the concept of market failure. As this chapter sets out, this is only one way to approach the environmental problem of pollution.

■ The ideal market model: green consumerism

Recent years have seen a 'green' revolution in retailing and the emergence of the eco-consumer (Cairncross, 1991; Rhys, 1991; Smith, 1992). This has affected goods as diverse as washing up liquid and motor cars. To the adherent of the market model, these are examples of the responsiveness of suppliers to consumer pressure. Sustainability Ltd, the environmental consultancy who have pioneered environmental auditing, describe the chain of events in their 1989 publicity material as follows. Environmental pressure groups influence consumers who act as 'green purchasers' and generate change within retailing organisations. The retailers then put pressure on manufacturers to alter production processes, encouraging the trend towards environmental auditing within commercial organisations. Investment funds will follow consumer preference, as investors identify 'green' producers as a future growth sector.

The neo-classical perspective extends this analysis of the change. Such 'green' products have very high costs of production so that, initially, less expensive products and production processes are preferred in the competitive drive to maintain profits and minimise costs. However, dissemination of knowledge on the environmental effects of products such as aerosols, CFC-based refrigerators, and phosphate-based washing powders affects consumers' demand schedules. Demand for such products falls back and consumers indicate their willingness to pay more for 'environmentally friendly' products. Suppliers react to these changing patterns of demand by shifting investment into these new lines.

The exemplar of the 'green' retailer and producer is probably the Body Shop. Started as a single outlet in Brighton in 1976, by 1990 the chain comprised 488 shops, 338 of these abroad. The shops sell beauty products with the emphasis on no-animal testing, natural ingredients, biodegradable products, minimum packaging, recycling waste and reusable containers. The profitability of the company is indicated by pre-tax profits in the year to February 1990 of £14.5 million (a 29 per cent increase on the previous year), out of an annual turnover of £84.5 million (a 53 per cent increase on the previous year). When the company went public in 1984, shares rose from the placing price of 95p to 142p on the first day. The Body Shop's founder, Anita Roddick, is quoted in their publicity material as saying: 'I think you can trade ethically; be committed to social responsibility, global responsibility . . . I think you can rewrite the book on business.'

Impressive though the Body Shop may be as a 'green' company, of more significance is the shift in the major supermarket chains towards 'green' products. In 1989 Tesco, Sainsbury, Co-op, Asda, Marks & Spencer and Safeway all took steps towards more environmentally conscious retailing. These included: stocking organic produce, biodegradable washing products, recycled and unbleached paper products or their own-label 'green' housecare products; converting their fleet cars to unleaded petrol; and raising the profile of environmental issues in store layout, shelf labelling and publicity material. Many have also made space for recycling banks and bins in car parks and encouraged the re-use of carrier bags. The launch of Green Grocer Awards and the publication of *The Green Consumer's Supermarket Shopping Guide* have further spurred these initiatives.

To take Sainsbury as an example, they have appointed an Environmental Affairs Manager and established an Environment Affairs Committee to inform corporate policy. Its objective is : 'to conduct our affairs with real consideration for the environment, both in the products we sell and in all operational practices throughout the business' (*Press Notice*, April 1990). This involves changes in business practice in a range of areas: in site acquisition, architecture and store development; in sponsoring the Building Research Establishment's environmental assessment scheme for commercial buildings; in promoting energy efficiency; in altering refrigeration procedures; in promoting 'green' products, reducing packaging and encouraging recycling.

Proponents of the market model would argue that such examples are increasingly common. They would point not just to retail outlets, but many production processes. Here the costs of altering processes to be less environmentally damaging can be costly and involve a long lead-time. One example of this is the motor car industry. There has been concern over a variety of pollutants from car exhausts, including lead, potentially carcinogenic hydrocarbons, sulphur dioxide which contributes to acid rain, and carbon dioxide and monoxide which form greenhouse gases. Increasing consumer knowledge of the adverse effects of some of these emissions and the likelihood of government policy to enforce reductions, particularly in order to achieve promised reductions in carbon dioxide emissions, have prompted manufacturers to fund substantial research and development into environmental aspects of their product.

Volkswagen/Audi have put great emphasis on this in an attempt to beat competitors in marketing a 'greener' car. This involved early incorporation of catalytic converters into their new cars as well as ongoing research into alternative means of propulsion: diesel engines and hybrid diesel/ electric engines. Micro-computers are being incorporated into driving controls to enable the driver to achieve steady speeds, thereby reducing fuel consumption and carbon dioxide emissions. In the 'Wolfsburg Wave', information technology within the car processes information from traffic signals indicating the optimal speed for the car to minimise stops and starts. In the production process itself, consideration is being given to reducing minimise harmful emissions, as from paint spraying, and to reduce waste production. This can mean new technologies, which minimise the waste generated, or ways of re-using the waste, as with drying and reprocessing paint coagulates. Water and other waste products are also recycled and there is R&D into recycling car parts themselves back into the production process in the future. At the company's showcase, the Wolfsburg factory, waste heat fuels a community heating scheme and water reservoirs are linked into local amenity areas. The company argue in their publicity material that:

> As environmental awareness has always been encouraged, consistent environmental protection is a matter of internal conviction for the people at Volkswagen AG and has concrete aims: to guarantee prosperity and quality of life for us and future generations; to maintain the innovative lead vis-a-vis competitors in the international market; part of entrepreneurial responsibility and company culture.

The market model highlights the point that only a successful, profitable and expanding company can afford the investments in R&D that environmentally aware production requires. Only such companies can bear the risk that such changes to production and marketing strategies involve. In short, environmental protection requires healthy profits. In the longer term, as 'green' production expands, the costs will fall, with economies of scale being exploited and the of early high R&D expenses spread over more units of output. This will lead to even greater consumption of less environmentally damaging goods, now at lower prices. In this analysis, emphasis should be placed on supporting market processes, rather than using regulations, to encourage 'green' production.

■ Market failure: pollution taxes and permits

The emission of pollution is a key example of an externality, often associated with the use of the global commons as public goods in the form of pollution sinks. Assuming that the net gain from pollution is not so large as to potentially compensate for the externality, then a situation of pollution results in an inefficient allocation of resources (Pearce and Turner, 1990; Sandbach, 1982).

The disparity between social and private costs in the two markets, for products with less adverse environmental impact and their more damaging counterparts, means that the former are undersupplied while the latter are oversupplied. A move towards a more efficient equilibrium would raise the price of more polluting products and lower those of less polluting products. Welfare economists thus emphasise the barriers to the development of 'green' products while proponents of the market model optimistically see the existence of any 'green' producers as a signal of future change.

The generation of externalities through pollution is associated with the use of public good aspects of the environment. With a public good there is no disincentive to use, or overuse, of the good. Thus the global commons, of the air and waters, may be used as waste sinks for many emissions by polluters without cost. The lack of any private property rights to ration access means that pollution will occur, possibly up to the point of irreversible damage. The emission of CO_2 into the atmosphere can be analysed as a modern example of this 'tragedy of the commons' to use Hardin's (1968), emotive phrase .

The discussion of public goods is clearly closely akin to the argument of the market model that the absence of market processes can create environmental problems. However, the market failure argument is more fully developed, with different types of public good proposed depending on whether the producer or the consumer is able to exclude others

(Willis, 1980). Also the market model case rarely goes beyond the bald statement that allowing free markets to establish themselves will solve the problem, while the welfare economist recognises that government intervention will be needed to create quasi-markets. However, unlike the institutionalist approach, the detail of the marketable right to be created is not a focus.

Missing markets are a further factor in the slow development of 'green' products. Such products may involve a considerable risk on the part of the supplier. In some cases a substantial R&D effort is needed to produce even a prototype of the good. In others, presenting a new good to the market involves the risk of the consumer not accepting the replacement good. Unless competitors are producing such goods and attracting market share, there is little incentive for producers to devote resources to such product development. What is required is a market which will allow this risk to be traded at a price so that potential risk-bearers can participate in providing the finance for risky 'green' products.

Welfare economics, therefore, identifies 'failures' in market processes which allow continued pollution and inhibit environmentally responsible production, but it rests on the assumption that, nevertheless, market processes are a useful allocative mechanism. Policy prescriptions from welfare economists tend to favour market-based instruments which use the market to achieve social goals, rather than trying to replace it with centralised planning. A pollution tax is the exemplar of a market-based instrument which could inhibit environmentally damaging production and encourage the transfer of resources into 'greener' areas. It is primarily useful where it is the act of consumption that is environmentally damaging, though this applies to the consumption of intermediate as well as final goods (see Figure 14.1).

The pollution tax shifts the supply curve of a producer upwards to take into account the full social costs of production, including the impact on the environment. This means that the consumer pays a higher price for the product, sharing the burden of the tax with the producer, and overall quantity consumed is reduced. As pollution is assumed to be directly related to output, the fallback in consumption reduces emissions and the impact of the tax on profits means that firms have an incentive to find less polluting methods of production.

Pollution taxes are also a flexible policy tool since they take account of the economic circumstances of each firm. If each firm is charged the same price or tax for a marginal unit of pollution, then each firm will pollute up to the point where the marginal cost of reducing pollution will equal the price of pollution, that is the tax. Beyond this point it will be cheaper to abate the pollution, through new technology or produc-

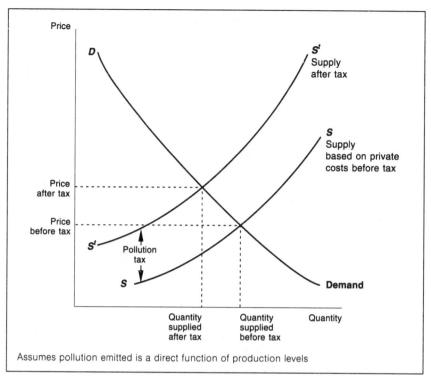

Figure 14.1 *Market failure: achieving efficiency with a pollution tax*

tion cutbacks, than pollute and pay the tax. If firms have different marginal costs of reducing pollution, then firms with low marginal cost will reduce emissions more and firms with high marginal cost will reduce them less.

This responsiveness to the cost situation of each firm is a great advantage over pollution standards, that is setting a fixed level of emissions which each and every firm must not exceed. Standards are inflexible policy instruments which apply to each firm regardless of the ease with which a particular firm can avoid pollution. It is very difficult to set the standard so as to balance social costs and benefits in the market, thus achieving the goal of efficiency in the welfare economist's eyes. Standards make no use of the allocative mechanisms of the market and the incentives to changed production behaviour that price signals can give. By contrast, the use of a pollution tax will lead to a greater level of pollution control than the use of a standard. This is because it encourages each firm to reduce pollution in line with its marginal cost of pollution abatement.

In the 1990 White Paper on the environment, *This Common Inheritance*, the government argued (p. 275) that: 'Taxes can be the most effective means of tackling environmental problems, and so merit serious examination'. In particular (p. 69), the case of a tax to reduce carbon dioxide emissions was discussed:

> In deciding on measures to restrain CO_2 emissions, the Government will need to take into account the argument that market-based instruments will often be more efficient and less expensive than regulation in reducing emissions because they allow producers and consumers, rather than regulators, to decide how energy can est and most economically be used.

And again (p. 275):

> From an environmental point of view there would be advantages in relating any taxation to the quantity of CO_2 emitted, so as to encourage producers to move to less environmentally harmful patterns of production and consumers to move to less environmentally harmful choices of goods and services.

There are problems associated with a tax. Strictly speaking, it requires the continuous monitoring of pollution generated by each firm in order to assess the tax. In practice, there is likely to be an assumption that pollution emissions are proportional to production levels, and the level of output will be used as a proxy for tax assessment (as in Figure 14.1). To achieve economic efficiency, policy makers would further need to know the costs and benefits of marginal changes in pollution to set the tax. This will be highly difficult to assess as it involves both technical data on pollution abatement and estimates of future, altered behaviour by firms and consumers. It will therefore be necessary to adjust the tax in the process of its operation, to find the appropriate tax rate and draw up the rules of incidence. In the meantime, setting the wrong tax rate could produce unexpectedly high levels of pollution, which could affect the political acceptability of the tax, or severely reduce output and profits, provoking a reaction from firms.

A third alternative to both taxes and standards is the issue of pollution permits. The state issues permits which, in aggregate, allow a set amount of pollution. These permits can then be traded in a market and pass between firms as a market price. Permits may carry permanent, fixed period or annual rights to pollute. Permits are already used in North America to control local air pollution. They have the advantages of pollution taxes with the added benefit that the market sets the price of pollution, not the tax authority. Such policy tools are likely to be more widely used – their effectiveness in controlling pollution is yet to be tested.

The marxist model: capitalism and the environment

The marxist discussion of 'green' aspects of production focuses on the ways in which capital accumulation inevitably entails environmental degradation. It is not simply that the development of 'environmentally friendly' products would involve higher costs and reduce the rate of capital accumulation. Rather, current patterns of capital accumulation rely on exploitation of the environment. Such exploitation is integral to capitalist production (Pepper, 1984, p. 169).

At the centre of capitalist treatment of the environment is the nature of relations between developed and underdeveloped countries. It is imperialism, not just capitalism, and the environment that is at issue. Imperialism is a stage of advanced capitalism based on world markets in goods, an international division of labour and a high level of mono-polisation of national economies. The international character of production under imperialism implies a particular form of relation between developed and underdeveloped countries, which can at best be characterised as exploitative, at worst as the locked-in relation of dependency.

Underdeveloped countries can act as markets for production from developed countries, an important strategy in periods of overproduction. But increasingly, with the growing importance of transnational corporations, they are used as production sites. Capitalist enterprises move into underdeveloped locations for a variety of reasons: cheap labour pool; labour with no experience of organising against capital; low overall production costs, particularly where natural resources are involved (see Chapter 13); and a policy stance by the host government which maximises financial incentives and minimises regulation. The environmental impact of such location strategies can be considerable, particularly when industrial disasters occur as in Bhopal, India in 1984 when up to 2500 people were killed and some 300 000 affected by a chemical explosion in an under-maintained, American owned plant.

Production activities in a situation of lax environmental protection can result in direct localised damage with pollution to ground, air and water systems. The underdeveloped world can also act as a pollution sink for production activities in developed countries with hazardous waste stored in unsafe conditions, putting local populations and natural habitats at risk (Moyars, 1984). Because transnational corporations have no long-term commitment to location at any one site, they will regard resource stocks in a particular country as an expendable asset. When those stocks are depleted, then strategic relocation will occur:

there is no reason for conservation of resources or careful management of their method of extraction.

But environmental harm arises not just from the relation of the capitalist enterprise to the local environment, but also from its relation to local communities in underdeveloped countries. The entry of such an enterprise is often premised on, and results in, the transformation of the local population into a wage labour force. This entails breaking the link between people and the land and making them dependent on wage-labour for any income. The balance that existed between local community and the environment, in terms of providing for basic needs of food and shelter in a sustainable manner, is broken. Land becomes subject to capitalist imperatives regarding its use (such as cattle ranching for hamburger-beef markets), making a profit on a relatively short timescale, rather than providing for community requirements, generation after generation. Furthermore, the separation of land and population and the latter's reliance on wages creates poverty rather than wealth in local communities. The level of poverty induces people to change their practices in relation to such land as they have access to. The result is unsustainable use of the local environment by the local population (such as the clearance of tropical forests for firewood), as a direct result of the introduction of capitalist production processes.

The marxist model thus emphasises that environmental quality in the developed world is bought at the expense of the rest of the world and its peoples (Redclift, 1987; de la Court, 1990). In the developed world itself, maintaining environmental quality is dependent on economic growth. Recession can result in attempts by national capitals to trade off environmental standards for inward investment. Furthermore the end-less search for profit can result in technological development which poses new environmental threats. An example of this is the subjection of agriculture to the agro-industry. The impact of an increasingly large scale agro-industry in developed countries is well known: the soil erosion from agricultural practices; the loss of local biodiversity; the pollution from pesticides and herbicides; the loss of natural habitats (Pepper, 1984, p. 171). The latest episode in the story is the use of biotechnology by capitalist enterprises: that is, the ability to undertake genetic engineering to replicate or modify natural organisms (Barlow, 1988a). The legal possibility of patenting genetically modified organisms turns them into another form of capital, a means of production. As Seabrook (*New Statesman and Society*, 10 May 1991, p. 19) says: 'Creation thus becomes the equivalent of manufacturing; life itself can be owned.'

This does not mean simply that profits can be made from nature. Rather, modified nature can be used to enhance profits through restructuring relations between producer and consumer, capitalist competitors, and developed and underdeveloped countries. Petrochemical and pharmaceutical companies have been buying up seed companies and there is the prospect of seeds being genetically modified to resist pesticides and herbicides, rather than diseases and pests, in order to maintain pesticide and herbicide sales. Food processors are developing laboratory-based means of producing foodstuffs, until now the mainstay of underdeveloped countries' production output. Just as artificial sweeteners have depressed sugar markets, so other products, such as vanilla, cocoa butter or palm oil, may be produced outside underdeveloped countries, lowering price by expanding output and undercutting their natural competitors. The ultimate environmental risk of this production strategy by capitalists is the unknown effect of 'accidents' whereby genetically modified organisms are released into the wider environment.

Does this emphasis on the environmentally destructive aspects of capitalist production mean that there is no prospect of 'green production'? Marxists see change arising from two quite distinct sources.

There is the fact that the risks to capitalism itself posed by the environmental crisis are severe and increasingly apparent. As the data on this crisis becomes more readily understood and accepted, the contradiction between the short-term needs of individual capitals and the long-term needs of capitalism become more apparent. This is one area where marxism points to a role for the capitalist state, since it is inevitably charged with the responsibility of maintaining the long-term existence of the capitalist order. This can involve overriding the interests of one capital in the interests of all capital; constraining the actions of capital in the short run in the long-run interests of all capital; or conceding to limited demands from non-capitalist interests in order to maintain social order and the legitimacy of capitalism (Redclift, 1987).

The actions of national states to deal with the environmental consequences of production within their borders can be interpreted in this light. Proposals to increase regulation of water and air pollution by capitalists may be seen as a capitalist state acting against individual capitals in pursuit of their joint interests. However, increasingly neither production processes nor environmental impacts are national in nature. The exporting of environmental effects and the role of transnational corporations requires supranational action in order to safeguard capitalism. Hence the role of international conventions in proposing reductions in the use of CFCs and CO_2 emissions.

An alternative analysis is possible, still within a marxist framework, which focuses on class more than on capital. This involves recognising that some state actions arise from responses to popular demands, from class-based organisations. Such responses are necessary to maintain the legitimacy of capitalism and prevent its collapse from class-centred political struggle. However, marxists face a problem with claiming environmental politics as a working class success story. Environmental demands from political groupings are rarely presented as from the proletariat; environmentalism does not appear as the face of the working class acting for itself. This leaves the analysis of environmental planning as a response either to a crisis of capitalism in general or to the demands of the middle class in developed countries, seeking to maintain their own quality of life (Castells, 1978).

▌ Institutionalist economic analysis: sustainable decision making and property rights

The term that has most often been used to express the hopes of environmentalists is 'sustainable development'. Sustainable development refers to patterns of production and consumption by the current generation which do not disadvantage future generations. The aim is for each generation to pass on to the next an undiminished stock of man-made and natural assets and this means abating pollution which may do irreversible damage. This concept has been publicised in the Brundtland report (WCED, 1987) and the recent Pearce reports (Pearce *et al.*, 1989 and Pearce, 1991). However, while environmental economists espouse a welfare economics viewpoint and advocate pollution taxes and other market-based instruments, the notion of sustainability implies changed decision making in pursuit of a new goal through institutional reform. As such, institutionalists would argue that their approach is more appropriate to a discussion of sustainable development, particularly where property regimes are considered as part of the policy approach.

From an institutional perspective, unsustainable production processes arise from the decision making of manufacturers operating within the context of the structure of industrial production. Three elements of these decision making processes are particularly relevant.

Of first importance is the timescale adopted by companies. Berge (1990, p. 70) has pointed out that one necessary (but not sufficient) condition for a private property regime to be compatible with sustainable development is that the interests of the owners of the resource must be long term. Many of the environmental consequences of production activities occur in the future and are redistributed to other generations. The timescale of commercial activities is usually shorter than this and therefore most consequences are simply not relevant to actors' decision making. Furthermore, if adverse consequences become apparent within their operating timescale, then the firm can often move away and begin elsewhere.

Two factors are changing this. Corporate timescales are getting longer, partly because of short-term financial problems during repeated periods of recession and partly because of the increased concentrated of capital which allows greater market control and has introduced more strategic-level planning into corporate decisions. In addition, there is growing public concern about the long-term environmental impact of current production processes and this appears to be affecting consumer demand. In a recession, in particular, firms become more sensitive to consumer pressure and may seek to achieve competitive edge through green marketing.

However, as institutionalists emphasise, market demand can be created through the marketing activities of firms themselves. Apparent moves to satisfy 'green' consumers will therefore relate to the marketing strategies of oligopolistic firms, the need to maintain market share and the use of environmental issues in advertising to do so. Greening is essentially a marketing ploy rather than a substantive transformation of the timescale of corporate decision making. It is a means of manipulating consumers in to preferring one firm's products and, more generally, into desiring green products. This does not necessarily mean patterns of consumption which are environmentally friendly. Many products are labelled as green are not at all conservationist in environmental pressure groups' eyes: for example, aerosols labelled as ozone-friendly when all aerosols are deplored for their longevity and lack of recyclability. Furthermore green advertising continues to encourage consumption while sustainable development may imply less consumption to conserve resources and establish sustainable levels of development.

Even if firms appear to be adopting longer, and hence more environmentally aware timescales, in relation to their production planning, two other aspects of their decision making will maintain unsustainability.

On the one hand, there is the attitude to uncertainty, to the inability to forecast events even within the timescale of decision making. In commercial organisations, uncertainty (complete unpredictability) is translated into risk (the probability of an event occurring). Risk will be included in commercial decision making provided that it occurs within the adopted timescale, the risk affects the corporation or another property owner and it is measurable in size and probability. However, many environmental impacts are ill suited to such assessment. They are uncertain rather than risky and cannot be measured. The non-substitutability of the environmental goods affected means that the impact cannot be traded off as commercial decision making will assume. Finally such effects are often irreversible and therefore require a different form of assessment than trading off risk against benefits.

On the other hand, there is the widespread use of discounting in commercial decision making. This is the process by which the value of costs and benefits which arise in the future are systematically reduced to a value in present day terms. Discount factors are used which reduce the value of any cost or benefit arising in the more distant future. The theoretical basis for discounting depends on the concept of the opportunity cost of money. Any money that an agent holds today may be invested at current interest rates and will earn interest over time, accumulating to a larger sum in the future. If that sum of money is received years hence instead of today, the opportunity of earning that interest is lost. Hence, £1 received in the future is worth less than £1 received now (Pearce and Turner, 1990).

Environmentalists are concerned that this practice of discounting downgrades many environmental impacts which occur in the future. Inter-generational equity is threatened by discounting. Yet the above explanation makes it clear that the use of discounting for evaluating investment decisions is linked to the earning of interest on deposits, and hence to the very fundamental nature of a capitalist economy. Finding new decision making methods to replace or supplement discounting will therefore rapidly come up against structural constraints.

One way of developing sustainable forms of production is to change the underlying property regime. This can be a radical proposal as capitalist production presumes individual, private property over all factors of production. In particular, institutionalists suggest that forms of common property over key environmental assets may be the best way of achieving sustainability (Bromley, 1991; Berkes, 1989). This is in clear opposition to the 'tragedy of the commons' view put forward by welfare economists, and the argument put by proponents of the market model that lack of private property is the source of environmental degradation.

Berge (1990, p. 62) reviewing the debate on Hardin's (1968) tragedy of the commons thesis, points out that this tragedy is not an inevitable law, rather it describes the result of a particular set of rules governing resource utilisation. Although Hardin referred to 'common property', in fact his examples concern open access property, which has been defined in Chapter 11. As Bromley (1991, p. 35) convincingly argues:

> The Hardin analysis is not only socially and culturally naive, it is historically false. In practice, to emphasise the 'tragedy of the commons' is to deflect analytical attention away from one class of social arrangements with a potential to overcome resource degradation. Those with incomplete knowledge of tenurial differences and systems of customary rights, encouraged by

those confused about the differences between open access regimes and common property regimes, may well attribute resource degradation to an assumed (but non-existent) regime of 'common property'.

Bromley also points out that when private property regimes are demonstrably unsustainable, the property regime is not identified as the cause but blame is pointed at externalities, etc. Thus 'the egregious erosion that accompanied the Dust Bowl years of the depression has never, to my knowledge, been blamed on the private ownership of land' (Bromley, 1991, p. 35).

This analysis suggests that a carefully defined common property regime could in fact be a policy solution for environmental degradation, a policy option which has been undermined by the widespread misapplication of the Hardin thesis. Common property would here refer to a regime 'in which resource users act together and institute checks and balances – rules and sanctions – for their own interaction within a given environment' (Bromley, 1991, p. 35). Berkes' work (1989) has demonstrated the range of situations in which such regimes already operate sustainably.

The institutionalist approach therefore sees the barriers to reducing pollution and other aspects of unsustainable development in terms of the decision making of market actors, but sees the scope for rectifying that in negotiating common property regimes for the use of environmental public goods. The cautious optimism of the approach is summed up in the phrase 'sustainable development' itself which, unlike the marxist view, suggests that economic activities and environmental protection are potentially compatible. Planning has a role to play in negotiating that compromise.

Further reading

The arguments of free-marketeers in relation to environmental protection can be found in Schmidheiny (1992) or Roddick (1992), with a survey in Cairncross (1991) and Marshall and Roberts (1992). Pearce and Turner is an up-to-date textbook of conventional environmental economics, while Redclift (1987) is an excellent account based on marxist principles. The best way of tackling the institutional approach is to read and counterpose the Brundtland Report (WCED, 1987) and the Pearce Report (Pearce *et al.*, 1989). Bromley (1991) provides a more formal analysis, which at times is close to the welfare economics approach.

■ *Chapter 15* ■

The Inner City Problem

Recent experience of urban planning has again emphasised the need to stimulate as well as control development, to attract resources to certain areas as well as divert them from overdeveloped locations. Planners have adopted new entrepreneurial skills and personae to undertake this task of 'creating' markets in areas abandoned by market forces. Directly engaging with the economic processes that have caused the prevailing pattern of investment and disinvestment highlights the need for a thorough understanding of these processes. Again there are alternative analyses which have to be debated and weighted against each other in any analysis of local urban planning.

■ The ideal market model: decentralisation as a market adjustment

Part 1 indicated that one of the key features of the 1960s through to the 1980s has been the decentralisation of population and employment from metropolitan areas to suburban and rural areas. This has given rise to concern about the future of inner city locations as well as the pressures placed on the destinations of such migratory flows. The market model provides an analysis of these trends and suggests future market adaptations to the ensuing urban problems.

From the point of view of urban planning, the relevant markets are those for inner city (see Figure 15.1 (a)) and suburban or rural land (see Figure 15.1 (b)). Assuming a start from equilibrium positions in both markets, decentralisation should be explicable in terms of shifts in supply and demand schedules.

Beginning with the inner city land market, economic growth pushes the demand for land up and increases its price. This effect is accentuated due to the inelasticity of the supply schedule. This means that the quantity supplied is not very responsive to changes in price. In the case of Figure 15.1 the supply is fixed (elasticity equals zero) so that price changes have no effect on the quantity of land supplied. Such an analysis is true only if inner city land in aggregate is discussed: with specific, identified uses, the supply schedule is more elastic as land can transfer

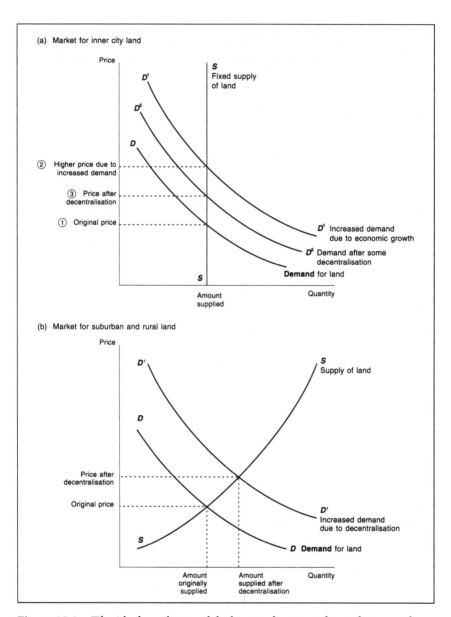

Figure 15.1   *The ideal market model: decentralisation of population and employment*

from one use to another. The effect of inelastic supply means that a small upward shift in the demand schedule prompts a relatively large increase in land prices. This price rise for inner city land prompts a reaction from firms and households. They can adjust the quantity of land they consume so that densities increase. Or they can decentralise, thus increasing demand in the suburban and rural land market. On the ground this may be seen as high value uses, such as offices and retailing, replacing lower value industrial and residential uses.

Other factors may encourage the shift in the demand schedule and thus decentralisation. For example, improvements in transportation due to car ownership or faster public transport networks may ease the process of migration while the quality of the environment in suburban and rural locations, lower priced labour, room for expansion, lower local property taxes (in the days before the Uniform Business Rate) and local planning policies may all be positive attractions.

This type of analysis often informs the research and publications of property market professionals. Thus a 1989 report by chartered surveyors, Healey & Baker, on industrial land values (*Chartered Surveyor Weekly*, 9 February 1989, pp. 68–9) stated:

> Land in the south-east [of England] is in short-supply and a growing population puts pressure on the infrastructure, especially transport, which makes industry inefficient. Additional pressure on industrial land in southern England comes from retail warehousing, food store operators and even residential developers as well as the new B1 use-class . . . A higher level of relocation out of the south-east will occur among the most labour-intensive industries as staff costs and staff turnover rise and labour shortages occur due to lack of cheap housing and amenities in core areas. We expect therefore to see rising land values and rent for standard, traditional 'sheds' in areas on the periphery of the south-east market core.

The fact of employment decentralisation means that urban locations and those in suburban and rural areas are good substitutes for each other. This gives the demand schedules in both markets a flatter shape, denoting greater elasticity of demand or price responsiveness by consumers. Thus in the suburban and rural land markets, a more elastic supply schedule interacts with an outward shift in a fairly elastic demand schedule. The result is a fairly modest rise in price and a relatively larger rise in the quantity of such land supplied and consumed. Initially the land may be used at fairly low densities, though eventually price rises in suburban and rural locations will encourage more economical use of sites (Richardson, 1971; O'Sullivan, 1981).

Urban decentralisation can thus be analysed in terms of shifts in demand schedules in the two land markets. The ensuing problems arising from decentralisation, the selective migration of population leaving an increasingly poor and dependent urban community, the urban dereliction, the unemployment arising from the movement of firms, are seen as only short term. If decentralisation progresses to such an extent that such problems become serious, then the demand schedule for inner city land will shift back again. In this case the price will fall and, once it has fallen to a sufficient extent, households and investors will be attracted back into the inner city again. The problems will persist only while the adjustments to a new equilibrium occur. One major source of delay in such a readjustment is government action. Planning policies actively promoting decentralisation, such as the new towns programme, the policies of inner city local authorities in raising local rates (before the Uniform Business Rate) and diverting funds from business support, and the effect of restrictive development control decisions have all been cited as causes of the continued decline of employment in urban areas (Balchin and Bull, 1987, p. 104).

However, businesses have been active in seeking to reverse inner city decline. For example, Business in the Community (BIC) was formed in 1982 with the aim of 'making involvement in the community a natural part of successful business practice'. By 1989 they had a membership of 445, including 54 per cent of the top 200 firms identified by *The Times*, producing an annual income of £3.2 million. Its president is the Prince of Wales who has forcefully put the case for community involvement by business (BIC publicity material):

> Companies will benefit in the long-term from being active in the local community by working in partnership to improve educational standards, the economic prospects of inner cities, and through contributing to making towns and cities more safe, healthy and enterprising .

As the banner headline in their publicity material proclaims: 'Community involvement is good for business.'

The same point is emphasised by Stanhope Properties PLC, a developer promoting the concept of 'collaborative development' in its publicity literature: 'Stanhope's involvement in employment and training stems from commercial self-interest to support the development of areas around their investment.' To expand on this:

> An assured labour supply is a key concern for any company considering relocation, especially to a new and large development site, where similar businesses are either non-existent or very thin on the ground. Correctly targeted local training will ensure that tenants will have a skilled workforce on the scene, when they arrive and set up operations. Assurance of available staff may be major incentive for a company to move to a development . . . In the longer term, an investment in local economic and social well being must

augur well for the future success of any project. Boosting the development of the local area, making a successful place where people will want to live, work, locate their businesses, or place their investments, will inevitably enhance the developer's scheme and help to market his space.

Thus market processes are, fundamentally seen as a positive factor in the changing inner city. Planning has tended to inhibit the market in redressing urban decay and should be reoriented to a role in which is it subservient to the market and facilitates the private sector.

■ Market failure: inefficient urban land markets

The market model stressed the way in which the operation of the price mechanism could explain the shift of firms from the inner city to less urban locations and bring land markets into a new equilibrium. From this point of view decentralisation of jobs is not a problem, simply a response to changing market pressures. The end result will be a better allocation of resources. This is somewhat at odds with the actual experience of decentralisation with its resulting urban dereliction and apparent waste of resources, both physical and human. The market failure viewpoint seeks to explain this in terms of imperfections in land markets which render the adjustment towards a new equilibrium very prolonged (Harvey, 1981; Fraser, 1984). It is inner city land markets, rather than with their suburban and rural counterparts, which are particularly prone to market failure.

First, it is clear that information is far from perfect in such situations. Knowledge about key features of inner city sites, such as their land-ownership and precise boundaries, is not readily accessible. Further investigation, often costly, is needed to establish other features, such as the physical condition of the building and the ground and the precise nature of the obligations and benefits conferred by the legal right on offer. Most important, a veil of secrecy covers the pattern of prices agreed for land and property recently traded. This means that price signals can have little direct effect on buyers' or sellers' behaviour.

Second, spatial externalities are important in inner city locations. The activities occurring on one site will probably have significant impacts on adjoining users, whether in terms of direct pollution, traffic generation, nature of clientele, or state of repair of the local built environment. Where the local environment has deteriorated, the existence of such externalities can hinder movement in the market to improve the situation. Everyone will wait for others to begin improvement works, before they either improve their own properties or sell in a rising market. The generation of a positive externality then becomes a prerequisite for market trading. Without it, the level of trading falls and the local environment continues to deteriorate. Yet without some subsidy or compensation, it is in no one property owner's interest to generate that externality.

The discussion of externalities highlights the risk involved in undertaking inner city development to improve the environment in normal market conditions. A third relevant concept of market failure is then the missing markets in risk, the absence of those willing to underwrite the risk involved in anticipating change in such locations. Thus, in stating that '[o]ver much, but not all, of the inner city the key problem is one of market failure', Goodchild and Munton (1985, p. 175) are referring to the relative perceived risk of inner city development. Drawing on their research in inner London, they state that:

> The study of Tower Hamlets shows that in places, on the edge of the City of London, for example, land values are sufficient to encourage commercial and residential re-development without government subsidy. The same cannot be said for most of the borough. This is not so say that demand is non-existent, or that land values are always negative, but the costs of site rehabilitation and the perceived risk surrounding residential re-development make the development of greenfield sites a safer commercial venture.

Goodchild and Munton go on to argue that government must underwrite the risk of such development through subsidy and grant, since the private market will not step in to do so.

Goodchild and Munton also identify a fourth source of market failure, the monopolistic nature of land supply in many inner city markets. In this case, the main monopoly landowners are in the public sector. To quote them again:

> A significant proportion of property in the inner city is held in public ownership and public owners have to meet a range of social, environmental and statutory obligations as well as being concerned with the economically optimal use of public assets. Some public owners have been slow to market land surplus to their current need, often having to be cajoled into doing so by government actions, whilst others are fully cognisant of the market value of their land but have no incentive to sell it.

While the analysis of market failure is most fruitfully applied to the inner city locations, it can be relevant to the more prosperous suburban and rural markets. Here the existence of positive spatial externalities, creating public goods available to newly locating firms and households, is a major advantage of these markets. In expanding the concept of public good, Willis (1980, p. 40) identifies various interesting and relevant cases. Parks and other public open space are a form of public good in which exclusion could be practised by the producer and consumer but there is no opportunity cost attached to consumption. Willis argues that this also describes uncongested roads, another attraction of suburban and rural locations. The amenity of pleasant locations, such as green belt villages or conservation areas, fits the case of a public good where exclusion cannot be practised by consumers. Another example of this case put forward by Willis is road noise, a public 'bad' readily found in urban locations. Thus the pattern of spatial externalities, both positive and negative, and associated public goods and bads can be used to explain a significant element of spatial patterns of migration.

The analysis of decentralisation in terms of market failure provides an argument for planning to rectify it: for land use planning to improve the balance of positive to negative externalities in the inner city; for strategic planning to provide information about inner city property markets; for undertaking pump-priming development projects to alter the private sector's perception of associated risks; for occasional use of compulsory purchase powers to break the deadlock of monopoly private landowners or transferring land from reluctant public landowners. The scope for urban planning is substantial.

▪ The marxist model: the flight from the urban labour force

While both the market model and welfare economics looked to the land and property markets and to industrial enterprises' demand for premises to explain urban decentralisation, marxists turn to the production process occurring within those premises. The cause of decentralisation lies in the relative merits of inner city and suburban or rural locations for capital accumulation. Urban geography is thus recast in terms of the labour process underpinning capital accumulation and the role of space vis-à-vis that labour process.

Firms are decentralising because the requirements of the capital accumulation process are changing as capitalism matures into advanced forms. There is a shift from Fordist forms of organising the labour process to other forms, labelled as post-Fordist or flexible specialisation. This means a shift from large scale factories based around conveyor-belt production systems to greater use of sub-contractors, short-term orders and adjustable production plans. Meanwhile, the social relations of the inner city have developed so that capital in urban locations is increasingly running up against the constraints of a well-established, organised and unionised labour force. This makes it difficult to adapt to the requirements of advanced capitalism and to respond to the crises endemic in economic change by introducing new working practices (extracting absolute surplus value) or new technology (extracting relative surplus value).

By contrast, less urbanised locations offer the opportunity to tap new labour forces, such as part-time women workers who are more docile in the face of the new working requirements of capitalists. Thus the urban–rural shift has been accompanied by, and can be explained in terms of, a new spatial division of labour. The term 'spatial division of labour' is a central one in marxist explanations of urban decline. It refers to the ways in which the labour force is distributed, created and exploited over space on the basis of 'the spatial structuring of the organisation of relations of production' (Massey,1988). This spatial division of labour is currently typified by the shedding of full-time male workers in areas of traditional industrial employment and the recruitment of part-time women workers in areas previously little industrialised.

In addition the growing importance of the service sector within advanced capitalism in developed countries places its own requirements on the spatial division of labour. The need is for a professionalised, white collar workforce, quite distinct from the industrial workforce of 'traditional' industries. Residential and employment segregation, spatially as well as socially, is an important part of establishing a distinct class identity for this service workforce. Service firms are increasingly found in rural locations where both the housing and offices are seen to be 'high amenity' in quality. Massey (1988, p. 268) has argued that the definition of such locations as high amenity is central to the self-assertion of the service labour force as upwardly mobile from the industrial labour force. The urban–rural shift is therefore part of the manufacturing–service shift within advanced capitalism and the changing class identity of labour. 'Everything points to the importance of class dynamics in a social sense as a factor in the emerging location patterns of the currently dominant sectors and strata in the UK economy' (Massey, 1988 p. 269).

From the point of view of landed capital, this shift in industrial activity has the effect of devaluing the capital tied up in the inner city built environment, with the potential for profitable redevelopment when sufficient devaluation has occurred. However, while this process of devaluation prior to a renewed cycle of capital accumulation may have echoes of the price movements in situations of a relative surplus of inner city property identified by the neo-classical model, the endpoint of each model is very different. In the neo-classical model, the result would eventually be an equilibrium in which resources would be re-used once the price adjustment had occurred. In the marxist model, uneven development of space is an inherent feature of capitalism. More than that it is a necessary feature in that it provides pockets of devalued capital and areas of unemployed labour which enable capitalism to continue functioning. Inner city decline is a functional necessity for capitalism, not a temporary adjustment problem (Holland, 1976; Harvey, 1982). Urban planning can seek to help locationally-trapped capitals in the inner city, often in the name of aiding the local working class, but such a task is doomed to marginal improvements at best and is totally dependent on the underlying patterns of capital flows in and out of localities.

Marxism is also interested in the class dimension of the inner city problems. While the experience of urban decline may politicise sections of the community, it also poses a problem for trades unionism, the political movement by which labour has traditionally defended itself against capital. Industrial trades unionism was based on urban areas and drew its strength from this location in a number of ways: the mass of workers; the close location of work and home which increased the political saliency of workplace disputes; the invisibility of industrial activists within a large, heterogeneous urban population. With urban decentralisation of industrial employment, urban trades unionism becomes more and more a public sector phenomenon, a sector in which traditional forms of industrial action have less force. In rural and small town locations, there is no tradition of militant unionism, the workforce is residentially dispersed and, in many cases, restrictive agreements are imposed from above before production begins.

However, the spatial restructuring of labour relations is never simply functional for capital. New forms of political resistance to capital develop, many focused around the activities of the local state; the New Left urban boroughs are an expression of this. In addition, the problem of inner city unemployment and poverty create an alienated population, often bound by ethnic ties, which can challenge the very nature of the political and economic system. The most dramatic evidence of this is the repeated occurrence of inner city riots, some termed 'race riots', which vehemently express the limitations of capitalism in containing the problems arising from a new spatial division of labour.

State planning is more of a problem than a solution in such a marxist analysis, an attempt by the state to contain the crisis tendencies of capitalism and, as such, a focus for political challenge. Only where the representatives of the working class take over the state, as in some local authorities, can urban planning be used to challenge capital.

▌ Institutionalist economic analysis: urban property interests

In an early institutionalist analysis of uneven development, Myrdal (1957) suggests the implausibility of market forces attracting private investment back to depressed areas such as the inner city. Myrdal's analysis uses the concepts of 'spread' and 'backwash' effects. Once investment has been attracted to an area, then the benefits of that investment will spread in a multiplier-like effect to other enterprises in that area. Agglomeration economies will develop whereby the presence of a number of enterprises reduces the average costs of each organisation. The public sector will also benefit from enhanced tax revenues and reduced social burdens, enabling further expenditure on infrastructure and other services to encourage further inward investment. By contrast backwash effects indicate the process whereby the economic development of one area contributes to the decline of other areas, effectively sucking further investment from already depressed areas. In this way prosperous areas enter a virtuous circle while depressed areas enter a vicious circle. The two regions move further away from each other in terms of level of economic development rather than approaching a balance. More recent institutionalist work has looked at the details of the process whereby urban areas enter a cycle of decline.

Starting from a critique of the neo-classical ideal, work by Adams (1990), Adams *et al.* (1985) and Fothergill *et al.* (1987) has investigated the industrial property markets in inner cities. Substantial mismatches exist between the industrialists' demand for premises and the supply of such premises from developers and existing owners. Referring to his own work in Manchester and Salford, Adams (1990, p. 123) points to the growing role of financial institutions as investors backing urban development and (p. 9) argues that:

> urban development pressures by the late 1980s have become highly centralised and standardised and far too attuned to the needs of investors rather than those of users . . . The very real variety in demand for industrial space is not being satisfied by the rigid nature of supply.

This is a point echoed by Hennebury (1988).

Premises that are available to firms fail to meet their operational needs in terms of: location with many small firms having a tightly circumscribed areas of possible operation; quantity of floorspace; specification in terms of size and layout; appropriate tenure, with preference varying between freehold, long leasehold and shorter lets; and, of course, affordable rents. Firms wishing to expand in situ are faced with particular problems in inner city locations because of the difficulties of obtaining adjacent premises. Fothergill *et al.* (1987) argue that these mismatches can have severe impacts on the efficiency of inner city enterprises, thus acting as a factor in generating decentralisation and urban unemployment. Adams (1990) uses the analogy of a 'ladder' of available premises and sites which should match the ladder of business development, with many small firms at the bottom, some failing and some expanding, and fewer larger firms at the top. Again, if the property ladder is not fully available then the process of business development may be hindered, adversely affecting the urban economy.

Within this analysis particular emphasis is placed on the role of the owners of industrial property and potential development sites. Many landowners in the inner city are passive, not actively marketing their holdings. They frequently hold their assets in anticipation of asking a price above a specific threshold and will not consider selling below the threshold. This threshold, based on very limited comparative evidence, is usually above the price a developer would be willing to bid, based on residual valuations. Evidence suggests that many physical problems of inner city sites are not allowed for in the asking prices of landowners (Adams *et al.*, 1985). Furthermore where an industrialist wants to sell existing premises for relocation, the asking price may be held high in order to finance the relocation itself. All these strategies by landowners create a ratchet effect whereby prices rise but rarely fall sufficiently to enable rapid exchange and redevelopment of inner city sites.

Some analysts, reviewing this evidence, have felt that the term 'market' is an inadequate description of the processes of exchange of land and buildings in the inner city. Such markets are very small, lacking breadth in terms of the numbers of active buyers and sellers, and depth in terms of the number of transactions per period. Furthermore, the heterogeneous nature of sites, in terms of age, size, location, tenure, etc. means that the already shallow, narrow inner city land market is more accurately described as a number of even smaller sub-markets. The low overall level of transactions in land in many inner city locations has caused Adams (1990, p. 121) to argue that 'the term "market" is hardly applicable', preferring to use the term only in a colloquial and not strictly economic sense.

Thus change in the urban environment is influenced by inner city property owners with their particular dynamic of decision making. Urban planning for these areas has to deal with these owners alongside the other pressure for use of the inner city. Healey *et al.* (1988, p. 77) describe these interests as follows:

The interests most frequently voiced in the inner city relate to the principle concerns of land *users*, especially industrialists, retailers and householders. There is little pressure from developers or land speculators in such areas and only occasional (though possibly increasing) interventions by conservationist groups.

Local planning has to mediate this group of interests, but what it can positively achieve depends on the balance of interests and, given the context of disinvestment, the resources it can control. Where public sector funds are flowing into a location then Healey *et al.* (1988, p. 97) found that:

> In the inner city then, local planning authorities are not mediating between local 'consumer' interests and those of private sector investors, as in city centres or the urban fringe . . . but between local interests and the sectoral nature of service provision by the rest of the public sector.

Again Healey's research in urban North East England (1992a) stresses the central role of government revenues supporting local production interests, while criticising marxist models for their overemphasis on financial circuits of capital.

But in a climate of declining public investment and a growing reliance on attracting private sector funds, Healey's other research (1990, p. 97) points to a further role: 'Government involvement thus offers a way of securing risk and supporting land and property markets. In doing so, it created new forms of dependency in the development industry.' This suggests a role for local planning beyond mediating between interests to actually structuring urban development processes. This structuring (Healey and Barrett, 1990, p. 97) can occur through the impact of policies on:

> the constitution of the development industry, the organisation of the development process, the economic, social and environmental effects of the development process, and the product of development in terms of cultural and environmental outcomes as well as economic ones.

This structuring effect of planning may have substantial effects, but ones which have been given relatively little consideration to date compared with more obvious direct effects.

Further reading

Balchin and Bull (1987) provide an account which encompasses both the ideal market model and the application of the concept of market failure. Massey (1984) provides an instructive marxist study which can be usefully counterposed to Fothergill and Gudgins' work (1982). For an institutional approach, Adams' work (Adams *et al.*, 1985; Adams, 1990) and that of Hennebury (1988) combine analysis and empirical detail.

■ PART 5 ■

ASSESSING PLANNING

Part 5 ends the book with an assessment of the British planning system. Chapter 16 makes use of published research and statistics to assess the effects that the planning system has had in practice. This draws on the understanding of the operation of the planning system provided by the discussions of actors and institutions in Part 3 and the relation between planning and the market in Part 4. The different elements of the planning system are assessed under the headings used in Part 2: land use planning and conservation; countryside policy; environmental planning; urban policy and transport. The Conclusion in Chapter 17 then asks the question 'why plan?'. It argues that there are strong rationales for a planning system, even given the weaknesses of the current one. It calls for a greater emphasis on the redistributive potential of planning and for continued vigorous debate amongst opposing theoretical positions.

■ *Chapter 16* ■

The Impacts of British Planning

■ Land use planning and conservation

Land use planning is a difficult policy area to assess and, as Reade (1987) notes, such an assessment has rarely been systematically undertaken: one of the sources of this difficulty lies in the nature of land use planning as a set of procedures with goal-setting as one of the tasks. The objectives which planning seeks to achieve are defined *within* the planning process and, therefore, there are no externally determined goals against which to judge land use planning activities. This means that an analysis of land use planning can take two distinct courses. First, the activities of local planning authorities can be viewed as a form of decision making or administrative procedure, and the rigour of the stages and strength of the links between stages can be assessed. Second, the effects of planning in terms of an altered pattern of land uses can be judged from a variety of standpoints, standpoints which are personal to the analyst rather than intrinsic to the planning system. These two approaches will be taken in turn.

The goal of land use planning as a form of decision making or administration is the effective management of environmental change and the control of urban development. The rhetoric stresses the strengths of planning, its power to control and manage. However research, which begins from this standpoint, has consistently found land use planning to be a weak administrative system. For example, most analyses of the development plan system emphasise its weaknesses as a strategic planning tool, weakness which has rendered the continued downgrading and even abolition of the strategic planning tier as inevitable. Considering the planning of the south-east region, Breheny and Congden (1989) point to the absence of regional plans, the abolition of metropolitan government, the lack of any satisfactory planning replacement and the resulting inability to deal with a succession of major strategic issues: European integration, the Channel Tunnel, London airport development. After a mock inquest into the causes of the final death of strategic planning during the 1980s, they record a verdict of 'death by manslaughter' on 'a rather sickly strategic planning system' (1989, p. 18).

The main weak link within strategic planning has often been pinpointed as the structure plan. Originally conceived in ambitious terms as a comprehensive and integrating planning tool, structure plans were intended to take on board the range of available resources and associated constraints, and devise strategies for using them to meet sets of politically identified goals. They were to be socioeconomic in focus, operating on the spatial scale. This ideal proved to be unobtainable. Whether or not structure planning in these terms was a philosophically flawed idea, it certainly proved to be beyond the administrative and political realities of the existing system. Jowell and Noble (1981, p. 480) point to the way in which central government, through case law and DoE powers reduced the scope of structure plans:

> The begetters of the structure plan system must surely be disappointed. Attempts at 'positive planning' have been defeated. And the alternative vision of planning revolving around social and economic need has not only been dashed by recent judicial interpretation of development control decisions or conditions attached to planning permissions, but by the Secretary of State's strict attitude to structure plans that dared to stray from strictly land-use concerns.

But, although central government may have ended the dream of integrated socioeconomic structure planning leading resources, the dream was already turning sour in many local authorities. Structure planning turned out to be very costly and time-consuming. In the absence of available public sector resources it was ultimately power-less. And the integration of the various social and economic dimensions to an area's problems had to deal with the realities of a local authority divided into departments where professionals guarded their power and there were conflicts between local authorities and budget-holding public sector organisations beyond the local authority. This conclusion on structure plans has meant that the search for effective planning has focused more and more on detailed local planning and the link to development control.

Bruton and Nicholson's research on local plans (1987) updates Healey's earlier work (1983). They found that local plans were quite a flexible planning instrument which could reflect local planning issues and operating environments while at the same time being constrained by central government policy operating through statute, regulation and advise. The result was great variety in local plan content (1987, p. 178). However, like the structure plan, local plans had weaknesses. They too took time to prepare, on average three years to complete a plan up to deposit with a further 16 months on a public local inquiry and modification up to final adoption. Small wonder that, as at 1985 – seven years after the relevant legislation for local plans – local authorities had completed only 38 per cent of their intended local plans (1987, p. 135).

Bruton and Nicholson's criticisms of local plans echo those made of structure plans (1987, p. 178): 'The commitment to the statutory system that current progress on local plan deposit and adoption represents, however, cannot hide the basic weakness of the local plan as a land use policy vehicle.' This is analysed as: its inability to deal directly with local socioeconomic policies, having to deal indirectly with the land use implications of such policies; its lack of effective control over the local activities of public agencies; the lack of control over the resources necessary to implement the development proposals of local plans which are based outside the planning department or outside the local authority altogether; the difficulty of integrating local plans with other area-based policies and plans; and the problems in implementing local plans through development control.

In particular, integration of policy documents has always been a problem. Ever since the creation of a two-tier local government system in 1974 undercut the principles of structure and local plans embodied in the 1968 legislation, conflicts have arisen between county and district councils over development planning. In addition, there has been a divorce between development plans and expenditure based plans, such as HIPs and TPPs, which the corporate planning idea of the late 1960s and 1970s never resolved and which continues to this day (Carter *et al.*, 1991).

These problems with development planning led to more attention (and hope) being focused on development control. After all, the one real resource that land use planning controlled was the power to grant or deny planning permission. But the debate about development control also echoes the familiar theme of the weakness of land use planning (Kirk, 1980). Development control is a negative, reactive policy tool, responding to development pressures emanating from elsewhere in the private and public sectors. It is limited in terms of the development proposals that come before the development control planner, limited in terms of the factors it can take into account in making planning decisions, limited in terms of the conditions and agreements that can be attached to a permission. Changes such as the recent revision of the Use Classes Order serve only to weaken development control further. As Oatley points out (1991), the creation of the B1 class, intended to facilitate high tech development, has actually allowed the conversion of high tech space into offices.

In addition to these basic criticisms, research has suggested that the link between development plans and development control is not strong. Research undertaken in 1979 by Poutney and Kingsbury (1983) in seven local plan areas found that a relatively large proportion of planning applications (24–65 per cent) were not covered by any specific reference in a local plan map or text. 45–65 per cent of planning decisions were in accordance with plan policies. In a DoE study undertaken during 1982, Davies *et al.* (1986) used a checklist of planning considerations to assess policy documents and planning applications in 12 districts and six planning agencies. They concluded that 'taking all the planning considerations together, the degree of overlap between policy and control is small' (p. 207).

In their analysis of a random 10 per cent sample of appeal decision letters for 1982 in England and Wales, Davies *et al.* (1986) found that in almost a third of all appeals there was no reference in the decision letter of any policy, national or local. Central government policy was mentioned in 35 per cent of cases. A Polytechnic of East London study (Rydin *et al.*, 1990) of 942 appeal decisions in 24 districts in 1988 found that about two-thirds of the cases involved some discussion of local policy and central government policy was discussed in about 40 per cent of cases, DoE circulars being the most common source (27 per cent cases).

Generally the conclusion is that many development control decisions are not based on development plans. A common finding across the research studies is that where local policy is discussed in development control it is given more emphasis if plans are statutory, up-to-date and adopted. (Davies *et al.*, 1986; Bruton and Nicholson, 1987; Rydin *et al.*, 1990). But much of the minor and householder development which dominates the average development control officer's workload of 156 planning applications a year (Audit Commission, 1992) lies largely outside the concerns of development plans. A large proportion of development control deals with issues of importance mainly to neighbours. Admittedly the aggregate effect of many minor changes can be significant, but the planning system finds this kind of incremental change very difficult to handle in terms of its strategic impact.

This lack of overlap between development planning and control does not necessarily mean that planning decisions actually conflict with development plans; the conflict between development control and developments was variously estimated at 7 per cent (Poutney and Kingsbury, 1983); 10 per cent (Kendrick, 1987); 19 per cent (Rydin *et al.*, 1990). Rather policy and control concern a different set of issues: for example, the impact of a development on the immediate surroundings of the site are not always spelt out in detail in plans. As Whitehand (1989,

p. 412) points out, local planning authorities have rarely considered in detail what the development of a particular site should be like before the planning application is received.

To summarise, Davies *et al.* (1986) pinpointed the problems of low overlap between plans and development control as resulting from: the partial nature of local plan coverage across districts; policies which are not geared to development control situations; policies in plans which require interpretations; and a difficulty in identifying which individual planning applications are significant from the point of view of plan policies. These problems are likely to be overcome only slowly as plan coverage spreads and policies are revised to take note of problems encountered in appeals. Furthermore, there is no systematic monitoring in most local authorities to inform the plan review process of how previous policies have fared during development control.

If development plans and development control are weak planning tools and there is a lack of overlap between development plans and development control, how does the planning system impact in terms of physical development? The Audit Commission, in their 1992 review of the development control system, again emphasised (p. 40) the lack of monitoring that occurs within local authorities:

> In practice most authorities lack systems to ensure that their decisions are faithfully implemented . . . most planning departments, having given attention to the decision-making process, do little to monitor and thereby demonstrate the success of development and their achievements in the quality of the outcomes.

Patsy Healey's work provides an important analysis of the links between development and the planning system. Drawing on the institutional approach discussed in Parts 3 and 4, Healey, Davis, Wood and Elson (1982) emphasise the mutual interaction between planning and development processes. Development plans are not simply a framework for guiding development control. They perform two distinct functions depending on the scale of developer involved. For the smaller developers, plans act as a framework for organising their activities; for larger developers, they are a baseline for negotiation with planners. This means that development control is a much more interactive process into which development plans are just one input. As a result, the larger and more sophisticated development interests have a considerable role in influencing patterns of development. The circumstances in which planning policies are able to exert the dominant influence are identified as follows (Healey, Davis, Wood and Elson, 1982, para. 1.17):

The policies investigated here have been effectively implemented because they relate to the central planning power of controlling the release of land in areas of high market demand, and because there has been considerable policy stability over time and consistency between levels of government about policy directions.

Thus in case studies of High Wycombe, Wokingham and Banbury, studied over 1974–80, Healey *et al.* found that local planning authorities had been successful in directing a fairly buoyant development sector to build housing and commercial property in certain locations but had found difficulties with controlling the level of employment afforded by development in particular sites, ensuring new housing was made available for local needs, phasing development in accordance with a timetable, and matching development with infrastructure provision.

In the face of such development pressure it is clear that local planning marginally adjusts market pressures, containing them and limiting the local impact. In commenting on Peter Hall and his teams' finding that planning had contained urban England (1973), Healey (1983, p. 41) says: 'We might conclude that the planning system has organised the process of suburbanisation but has not resisted it.' This conclusion continues to hold true although, perhaps, over the 1980s restrictive planning has bitten a little more sharply. Government statistics show that between 1985 and 1990, an average of 68.3 km^2 of countryside was lost to urban development each year. However, in areas where more positive planning is required, where constraining private sector development is not enough, it is more difficult to identify the distinctive contribution of planning. For example in inner city areas outside the central business core, land use planning is very dependent on the availability of public sector monies (Healey *et al.*, 1988, pp. 16–17). Again in open land beyond the urban areas, the lack of land assembly and land management powers severely restricts the ability of local planners to influence change in the environment (Healey *et al.*, 1988, pp. 150–1).

For this reason the *removal* of planning constraints within SPZs is proving an inappropriate method of urban renewal in all but the most buoyant of local development markets. Since the enabling legislation in 1986, only four SPZs have been designated in Britain with a few more in the pipeline. Research suggests that it was the financial incentives that attracted development to their predecessors, EZs (see section below on urban policy), and the absence of such incentives seriously undermines SPZs as a planning tool. Rowan-Robinson and Lloyd (1986, p. 63) argued in 1986 that: 'The ideological significance to the government of SPZs would seem likely to be greater than their political impact where the concept is adopted.' This appears to have been borne out by events.

Who then benefits and who loses out as a result of this type of planning system? Hall *et al.*'s 1973 study argued strongly that planning was benefiting: those with property interests in rural areas protected by restrictive planning; young, mobile skilled workers who would enter owner-occupation in the new suburban estates; and firms seeking large well-serviced sites. This has been at the expense of public sector tenants and those in the private rented sector who have faced less choice in housing and become increasingly trapped in inner city locations with poor amenities and limited employment opportunities.

Healey and her co-researchers argue that developers have also been served by the planning system (1982 and 1988). Land assembly and infrastructure have been facilitated and restrictive planning waived in return for limited planning gain to encourage urban renewal and city centre redevelopment. Ambrose (1986, p. 258) notes that planning collates information with a commercial value and can prevent the oversupply of new development space that would arise from unfettered competition. He adds that the planning system can also act as a handy support for the development industry, since the planning authority's (overambitious) claim to be guiding urban change also brings with it responsibility for adverse outcomes. In addition larger landowning interests have found planning beneficial. It is these interests who are most likely to desire that new development is coordinated, concentrated and reasonably predictable in location (Healey, 1983, p. 208). Furthermore, without rehearsing the debate on land prices covered in Chapter 12, it seems likely that planning has sustained certain land values, benefiting existing landowners. Such landowners are also more likely to receive planning permission unlocking the development value of their assets (Simmie, 1981).

In such a planning system, focused on negotiating with developers and landowners, certain interests can be forgotten. Recent feminist work on planning has shown how the needs of women are ignored by a patriarchal form of planning (Foulsham, 1987; Little, forthcoming). Much of this work has focused on the problems that women as carers face in the built environment and the physical threat posed to women by urban areas where safety has not been 'planned in' (Valentine, 1992; Trench, 1991; Oc, 1991). The specific needs of ethnic minorities have also been left out of planning policy and decision making, an issue which the Royal Town Planning Institute is now trying to address.

The overall conclusion on land use planning seems to be that it is weak in relation to its aspirations and regressive in many of the impacts it does have. Marginal improvements to private sector development proposals can be achieved and local pressure groups are sometimes successful in obtaining desired changes in the built environment. But as the discussion in Part 3 has shown, pressure group politics is itself inequitable and many planning procedures are ill suited to public participation on an open and equitable basis. These points can particularly be seen at work in conservation policies.

Preservation of urban and rural areas of heritage has interacted with local property markets to benefit middle and upper class owners of property. Indeed conservation policy is dependent, to a large extent, on these property market effects. English Heritage's 1992 study based on a survey of 43 000 listed buildings argued that 7.3 per cent of listed buildings in England were 'at risk' and 14.6 per cent were 'vulnerable' (a less serious category of decay). They found that the condition of buildings was related to the existence of an appropriate and profitable use: affluence protects buildings (1992, p. 4). 10 per cent of surveyed buildings in less affluent areas were at risk, compared to 4 per cent in affluent areas. Pressure group politics reinforced these tendencies (see Chapter 10 above). Threats to amenity, such as through traffic, have been diverted to 'less valued' areas, often working class residential areas.

The vociferous pressure groups of conservation areas have reinforced the heritage protection policies of local authorities to render conservation policies one of the success stories of postwar planning in terms of the objectives of preserving the built environment (Bruton and Nicholson, 1987, p. 376; Ambrose, 1986, pp. 257–8). But it is a success which illustrates the dependence of land use planning on market processes and the potential for regressive impacts reinforced by pressure group politics.

■ Countryside policy

As was explained in the discussion of land use planning, assessing the impacts of policy depends on the objectives of that policy. Countryside policy has had a fairly clear set of objectives to date and now appears to be in the process of slowly shifting priorities. For most of the modern postwar period of countryside policy, security of primary production has dominated that policy's operation. Ensuring supplies of food, timber and minerals for the country's needs has driven countryside planning. This has been clear in the system of agricultural financial support, the corporate mission of the Forestry Commission, the basic assumptions of minerals planning and the access that primary producers have had to central government policy makers.

In terms of this overriding objective countryside planning can be said to have been successful. Agricultural production has risen to such an extent that indigenous needs are satisfied, foodstuffs are exported and surpluses mount in EC stores. For example, the European Commission's 1985 estimates were for cereal production to rise by 5.1 million tonnes over 1984/5–1990/1, an annual surplus over consumption of 43.5 million tonnes (Bowers, 1990, p. 24). The Forestry Commission has achieved its own 1943 target of three year supply of timber in siege conditions or 5 million acres of afforested land in 1984 (Mather, 1991). A Treasury study in 1972 concluded that no further afforestation was justified on the basis of the economics of timber production. And there have been adequate supplies of minerals for energy production and construction needs.

The prevention of development in pursuit of such countryside protection has also had some effect. Recent research has begun to show the extent to which settlement boundaries may have been influenced by the application of green belt policy (Longley *et al.*, 1992), though the link between the stated goals of green belt policy and its actual impact can be questioned (Rydin and Myerson, 1990). Nevertheless, the application of land use planning policies to rural areas has reinforced the general conclusion on the land use planning system given above, that is has to a degree contained urban development.

However, it has been increasingly recognised that the primacy given to agricultural production objectives has created problems in terms of the other, subsidiary goods of countryside policy (Lowe *et al.*, 1986, p. 38). As Chapter 5 outlined, countryside policy encompasses public access and recreation, nature conservation and rural economic development. These goals have existed alongside the production goal but rarely been accorded equal status. Even in selected areas, such as National Parks, AONBs or SSSIs, the underlying thrust of production support has often overshadowed these other concerns. Analysts are broadly agreed that the result is a series of environmental and socio-economic problems in rural areas.

Public access to the countryside remains limited by the adherence to a system of selected exemptions to the power of private landowners to exclude people from their land. Even in cases of public landownership, such as the estates of the Forestry Commission, the former water authorities or Ministry of Defence, public access can be severely curtailed in the interests of the public agency's operating activities. Supporters of greater public freedom to wander in the countryside contrast this with systems, such as that in Sweden, where the right to walk across land dominates provided no harm is done to crops and animals. Again British national parks involve no transfer of landowner-ship rights so that public access is not automatically extended upon designation, as is the case with North American national parks. Rather, there is a heavy reliance on groups such as the National Trust to buy land and either make it available for public use or, in the case of tenanted farmland, encourage the farmer to tolerate public traverse of the land. It could be argued that these restrictions on general public access to the countryside are counterproductive since they channel people towards honeypot areas where they detract from the 'quiet enjoyment' of the countryside and can generate environmental damage due to sheer numbers. The Lake District has to handle 12 million visitor days p.a.; the Peak District 20 million (Crabtree, 1991).

Marion Shoard has been a rigorous critic of the British limitations on public access. She points to the problems that exist with the current network of footpaths, with frequent cases of obstruction and poor maintenance of paths, stiles, gates and signposts (1987, p. 342). She places the source of these problems with the continuation of the tradition whereby footpath maintenance is given to local interests. This may have been appropriate in the days when local people were the main users of the footpaths, but not so today when the use of the network by urban residents is resented by the local farmers and landowners who often dominate rural district and parish councils (Shoard, 1987, p. 352). After all, 74 per cent of the population walk in the countryside at least once a year, 54 per cent at least once a month (Lowe *et al.*, 1986, p. 60)

Turning to nature conservation, the record of minerals and agricultural industries has not been a good one. The disruption of mining activities to local environment is both apparent and spatially contained. The relative success of increasingly stringent conditions on mining operations and improved aftercare can be seen in the fact that dereliction from mining is roughly static (Kivell, 1987) despite continuing growth in output; recent changes in mineral planning are likely to continue improvements in this area. However, the environmental effects of agriculture seem more intractable. This is because they affect a much larger area of the country, technological change has been rapid and environmentally harmful, and the effects become apparent only when considered over time and at a broader spatial scale.

Bowers (1990, p. 2) provides a comprehensive account of the adverse environmental effects of postwar agricultural practice that have been confirmed since the publication of Rachel Carson's *Silent Spring* in 1962:

> The list of environmental 'bads' of modern agriculture is extensive: destruction and damage of natural and semi-natural habitats with attendant losses of plant and animal species; landscape damage; pesticide residues in food-chains and foodstuffs, nitrate pollution of water courses and water supplies . . . ; serious problems with the use and disposal of wastes from

intensive livestock systems; soil degradation and erosion, health risks from crop spraying and use of agricultural chemicals.

The causes of this situation are three-fold (Andrews, 1990). First, farming and forestry have become much more intensive relatively suddenly, using more capital in the form of machinery and buildings and more chemical applications to land, livestock and crops at the same time as expanding output and the turnover of agricultural production. Second, mechanisation has encouraged specialisation within units, enlarging fields and estates and restricting the diversity of habitats in any one area (Lowe *et al.*, 1986, p. 64). It is also more difficult to protect flora and fauna within remaining habitats by altering operating practices given the use of large semi-automatic machinery. Third, the historic process of the destruction of semi-natural habitats has reached a critical stage in ecological terms as many become very restricted or fragmented. For example, 22 per cent of the hedgerows existing in 1947 had been lost by 1985. 95 per cent of flower-rich meadows, 40 per cent of lowland heaths, 80 per cent of chalk grasslands and 30–50 per cent of ancient woodlands have been destroyed. Half of the lowland marshes have been drained (Blowers, 1987; Lowe *et al.*, 1986, pp. 63–72). Government statistics list some 2830 species, 15 per cent of all native species, as either at risk or already extinct. In addition to these technological causes, Andrews points to the current tendency for farmers to equate tidiness with good husbandry (1990, p. 63). Carr and Tait (1990) have shown that farmers equate stewardship of the rural environment with just the kind of tidy land management which many environmentalists see as causing ecological harm.

Buckwell (1990) has argued that although the system of agricultural support has contributed to such environmental damage, its reform or even removal (FoE, 1992) would not halt or rectify the damage. Indeed, a rapid fall in farm subsidies may lead to more environmentally damaging agricultural practices (Lowe *et al.*, 1986, p. 4). Buckwell argues that environmental protection in rural areas needs an environmental policy. The recent policy innovations of set-aside and environmentally sensitive areas (ESAs) have the potential to encourage environmental protection, but their detailed operation is the key. First, the level of compensation payments relative to farm profits will determine the take up of the schemes and the nature of the land on which take up occurs. In 1988–9 only 1.3 per cent of the total cereal acreage in the UK had been set-aside, just above the EC average of 1 per cent (*Planning*, 20 September 1991, p. 15). Coincidentally, 1.3 per cent is also the percentage of the UK's agricultural land that is subject to an ESA management agreement (FoE, 1992, p. 21). The current decline in farm incomes will not automatically encourage a shift towards conservation as compensation payments will fall also, although the general uncertainty in farming may mean that management agreements are seen as a way of reducing risk (Bowers, 1990, p. 32).

Second, the detail of the management agreement will determine the actual environmental benefits to arise from the policy. FoE (1992) found that ESA designation had slowed the decline in environmental quality but had yet to result in positive enhancement. The policy has changed farmers' attitudes within ESAs so that they accept the need to undertake environmental care and management, but achieving that remains dependent on the structure of financial compensation, and its relation to the financial incentives for agricultural 'business as usual'. In forestry new grant schemes have begun to have an effect. In 1983/4, 91 per cent of planting and restocking in the private estate and 98 per cent in the public estate consisted of conifers. By 1990/1 the figures had fallen to 54 per cent in the private sector but remained high at 93 per cent in the public sector. Much of this shift in planting has occurred in England not the vast afforested areas of Scotland, and the schemes are also weakened by the fact that there is no ongoing involvement in the management of estates (Lowe *et al.*, 1986, p. 49). In any case the total expenditure on supporting broadleaved planting was less than 10 per cent of all grant aid in 1986/7 (Crabtree, 1991) and operated in a context in which broadleaved forestry had declined by a quarter since 1947 (Blowers, 1987). Any significant effect on the overall stock will take decades to become apparent.

It is clear that environmental protection will depend on this balance between compensation and profits (Lowe *et al.*, 1986, p. 3), and the negotiation of more environmentally aware management practices between farmers and conservationists. The system of regulation is unlikely to be strengthened sufficiently to take over this role. Availability of resources will be a central issue in how far compensation and negotiation can work. Although the grant to the NCC increased from £9 million in 1981 to £32 million in 1986/7, this is dwarfed by the £2 billion still spent supporting agricultural production. It is also estimated that the cost of implementing management agreements on all SSSIs alone would substantially exceed the NCC's total budget (Lowe *et al.*, 1986, p. 162).

This remains a fairly fragile basis for environmental policy as the evidence on damage to SSSIs shows (Shoard, 1987, p. 440). Of the 13 614 SSSIs notified in 1981, only 0.2 per cent were subject to the voluntary management agreements. This had increased to 5.5 per cent out of 17,785 SSSIs by 1991. Yet in 1990/1 damage affecting 273 SSSIs was reported: this is 1.5 per cent of all SSSIs notified under the 1981 legislation. Agricultural activities were listed as the main cause in 44 per cent of cases, far outstripping any other cause.

Surprisingly perhaps, the commitment to primary production in rural areas has not ensured a strong socioeconomic base for such areas. The underlying substitution of capital for labour has meant a decline in agricultural employment and in agriculture's role in the rural economy (Bowers, 1990, p. 2). Between 1960 and 1979 the number of agricultural workers halved. Similarly technological change, although offset by the maturing of forestry estates into more labour-intensive stages, means that forestry remains a poor source of rural employment (Whitby, 1990). The system of agricultural support has failed to maintain the incomes of smaller and poorer farmers or even to maintain the gap between average industrial and agricultural incomes. Tenanted farmers have found that the financial benefits of agricultural support have almost entirely seeped through into rental increases, fuelling a shift from the rented to owner-occupied tenure in farming (Bowers, 1990, p. 29). Farming has polarised into the capitalist sector employing agricultural labour and the smaller family farm relying largely on self-labour (Symes, 1990, p. 105).

The decline in agricultural employment in rural areas has been aggravated by the decline in local rural services and has not been offset by the shift in manufacturing jobs into the countryside. As Symes puts it (1990, p. 111): 'rural areas are gaining an increasing share of jobs in a declining manufacturing sector! They are getting hardly any share of the expanding non-local service sector.' The result of this is a profound change in social structure in rural areas. The rural working class are becoming more attenuated. Symes identifies a process of 'accumulative causation of rural deprivation' (1990, pp. 112–13). This is made worse by central government policies on public transport and primary education in rural areas. As a result it is estimated that 25 per cent of rural households exist close to or within the margins of poverty, including many elderly people.

At the same time there has been a shift in population. Depopulation of remoter rural areas continues, unstemmed by agricultural support mechanisms (Bowers, 1990, p. 2) and more accessible rural communities have acquired new populations: commuters, ex-urbanites and second-home owners. The immigration of these groups has put considerable pressure on rural housing markets, pressure which land use planning policies have been unable to deal with to ensure affordable housing for local needs (Shucksmith, 1990). Furthermore, Symes argues (1990, p. 113) that the immigrating groups have entered into political alliance with landowning farmers and other landowners to stifle debate on rural employment and low-income housing. Neither are these vital planning issues promoted by local authority officers who have tended to listen to environmental pressure groups in developing policy which benefits the 'amenity fraternity' but disadvantages the rural working class.

Certainly in the future it seems more than likely that the concerns of the rural working class will remain low in the countryside planning agenda. It is clear that the dominance of production interests has been challenged by the recognition of current agricultural support mechanisms as 'wasteful, inefficient, regressive and regionally biased' (Buckwell, 1990, p. 18) and it seems that environmental concerns are tentatively gaining a new ascendancy (Lowe *et al.*, 1986, p. 2). As Mowle and Evans (1990, p. 129) conclude:

> The various current initiatives are showing a greater sensitivity to conservation lobby pressures, but in an uncoordinated and ad hoc way. It seems likely that this will continue until agriculture establishes a new set of objectives and a new consensus in the place of agriculture within which rural development emerges. Until then, progress for conservation interests is likely to be fitful and uncertain. However, it is at least possible that out of the present confusion of diverse interests a balance between conservation and development can be struck.

Where this places the needs of rural communities or the access rights of urban dweller is unclear.

■ Environmental planning

Environmental planning has one overriding policy objective – environmental protection – which can be judged in technical terms through the collection of scientific data. However, the operation of that policy remains a matter of institutional relations between public and private sector organisations, as the discussion of IPC and the 'greening' of land use planning emphasises.

There is no shortage of scientific-based material which emphasises Britain's poor record in environmental protection. Rose (1990) collates much of this work in support his argument that Britain remains 'The Dirty Man of Europe'. All media show evidence of contamination: air, water and land. Government statistics show declines in many measured air pollutants, particularly as measured per unit of GDP (see Table 16.1). But this cannot be read as a success story for pollution control. Much of the reduction in emissions is accounted for by restructuring of British industry towards high tech and service sectors and the introduction of new technology. Many emissions are not represented in these statistics and new industrial processes are continually producing new compounds with unknown polluting consequences. (This is also a major problem for water pollution control.)

Table 16.1   *Emissions to air (UK)*

	1980		1990	
	million tonnes	*million tonnes/ unit GDP*	*million tonnes*	*million tonnes/ unit GDP*
SO_2	4.9	15.1	3.8	9.1
Smoke	0.56	1.7	0.45	1.1
NOx	2.3	7.1	2.7	6.6
VOC	2.3	7.1	2.4	5.7
CO	5.0	15.6	6.7	16.0
CO_2	165.0	510.0	160.0	383.0
Methane	4.5	14.0	4.4	10.5

Source: Digest of Environmental Protection and Water Statistics

In addition, reductions in emissions are not a success if the absolute level remains too high. And average levels may conceal 'hot spots' of pollution. Environmental pressure groups repeatedly point to instances of breaches of international recommended limits on particular pollutants (see *Earth Matters*, the Friends of the Earth magazine). The debate about the thresholds for global environmental change, whether global warming or ozone depletion, provide other criteria against which emissions may be judged too high.

In the case of water pollution, the situation is more clear cut since government statistics show declining environmental standards since 1980. The main source on the quality of rivers, canals and estuaries is the quinquennial survey undertaken since 1970, by DoE and now by NRA. These surveys classify stretches of water into four classes. Interpretation of these surveys is complicated by the poor methodological base, with a variety of methods used in the former water authority areas (NRA, 1991b, p. 68). Other problems are that the surveys assess the length of rivers of different quality regardless of width, that lengths of river are added between surveys and weather conditions greatly influence the outcomes, as do other conditions at the point of sampling. Thus there is a 20–30 per cent chance of a stretch of water being declared to have changed from one quality class to another when there has been no real change in water quality. A new methodology is being developed by NRA to prevent some of these problems in the future. This will reduce the chance of error to 10 per cent (see Table 16.2).

Existing surveys indicate an increase in water quality up to 1980, with the percentage of unpolluted non-tidal rivers and canals rising from 72 per cent in 1958 to 75 per cent in 1980, and for tidal rivers from 41 per

Table 16.2   *Changes in water quality (England and Wales)*

	Improving in quality km (%)	Declining in quality km (%)	Net change km (%)
1980–5	4873 (12)	5729 (14)	−856 (−2.0)
1985–90	4641 (10)	6340 (13)	−1699 (−3.6)

Source: DoE and NRA, Water Quality Survey

cent to 50 per cent. Thereafter it is clear that, whatever the methodological problems, there has been a net downgrading of water quality in each survey (NRA, 1991a, p. 45). As at 1990, 63 per cent of freshwater rivers and canals were classified as good and 66 per cent of estuaries (see Table 16.3).

Table 16.3   *Classification of water quality (England and Wales)*

	% water length			
	Freshwater rivers and canals		Estuaries	
	1990 (%)	1980 (%)	1990 (%)	1980 (%)
Good	63	(69)	68	(66)
Fair	25	(21)	23	(24)
Poor	9	(8)	5	(7)
Bad	2	(2)	4	(3)

Source: DoE and NRA, *Water Quality Surveys*

Any improvements in water quality are the result of new investment by the water authorities/companies and other industry. Deterioration, principally due to pollution from sewage works and agricultural sources, has however run ahead of such investment. The 1990 survey (NRA, 1991a, p. 46) argued that progress was needed in relation to farm waste production and storage, leakage from contaminated land and the control of permitted discharges into water 'in order to reverse the deterioration of some of the country's best rivers and to accelerate the necessary improvement of those rivers which have long been abused'. Great emphasis is being placed on the proposed scheme of water quality objectives in retrieving this situation (NRA, 1991b).

In a situation where polluting activities have outreached investment in abatement technology, the effectiveness of the regulatory system must be called into question. It is clear that control by water pollution is only slowly being brought into line with the demands placed on it. The 1951 Rivers (Prevention of Pollution) Act hardly scratched the surface as it dealt only with new discharges. The 1961 Rivers (Prevention of Pollution) Act extended control to existing effluent but the rush of applications meant that many were never dealt with, to potentially become deemed consents under the 1974 Control of Pollution Act (COPA) (Beck, 1989). COPA itself was considered sufficient in theory to deal with routine direct discharges but could not control diffuse discharge such as nitrate leaching. In practice its operation was compromised by the influence of those it sought to control (Hallett *et al.*, 1991). For example Section 31 (2)(c) of COPA allowed farmers to use 'good agricultural practice' as a sufficient defence against polluting activities on the farm. The important section on water quality (Part II of COPA) was implemented in a reduced form only after 16 years and the public disclosure requirements took 10 years to be enacted! The introduction of IPC is supposed to remedy the weaknesses of COPA.

IPC involves the consideration of the full range of environmental impacts from a process on all media (land, water and air) with the aim of mitigating the overall impact – achieving the Best Practicable Environmental Option (BPEO). While long advocated from an environmental policy perspective, IPC goes against the medium-specific tendency of pollution control policy in the past (Weale *et al.*, 1991, p. 61) and raises considerable problems of implementation. Owens (1989) points to a number of limitations in the proposed IPC system: its focus on industrial pollution; the control over pesticides remaining within MAFF; the separate control over radioactive waste; the treatment of non-scheduled processes on a single media basis; the control over Red List substances being based on quality of receiving water rather than on best attainable abatement technology to prevent emission at source; the location-specific nature of much BPEO assessment. A pilot BPEO audit showed that it is possible to achieve, but it is expensive in terms of time and staff (Weale *et al.*, 1991).

There are clearly conceptual and administrative problems in integrating cross-media expertise and, further, reconciling integration across media with geographical integration. Similar considerations lead Weale *et al.* to question whether IPC, as conceived in terms of BPEO, will ever operate (1991, p. 94): 'Conditions for the successful integration of policy are daunting in their demands, and . . . there are powerful intellectual, organisational and political reasons why the move towards IPC might fail,' and, again (p. 158): 'BPEO may never be more than an imaginative statement of pollution control philosophy.'

Instead Weale *et al.* see IPC being largely based on BATNEEC (Best Available Technology Not Entailing Excessive Cost). This is in line with continental pollution control practice which is being imported in EC directives. A technology-led approach to regulation is more readily defined and enforced, and lends itself to an administratively accountable form of regulation (Weale *et al.*, 1991, p. 160). However, they emphasise that sector-by-sector BATNEEC, while an improvement on the discretionary, flexible and ineffective British system of the postwar years, will not bring the environmental benefits of BPEO.

Change is also likely to result from the growing influence of the EC in directing pollution control measures (Blowers, 1987). For example, the EC directive on large combustion plants (No.88/609) has already had a considerable effect, bringing emissions of SO_2 from power plants down to 82 per cent of their 1980 levels by 1990, only just above the 1993 target set in the directive. The directive is also responsible for some reduction in NOx emissions from power plants. Again, following action by the EC there has been some improvement in the quality of bathing waters. Whereas in 1988 only 66 per cent of identified bathing water complied with the EC directive (and there was some controversy over the beaches which had been so identified – Blackpool was excluded), in 1990 and 1991, 76–77 per cent of such beaches complied. The number of beaches awarded the EC Blue Flag rose from 22 in 1989 to 35 in 1991 but fell back to only 17 in 1992 (*Guardian*, 5 June 1992).

Whatever the regulatory system, adequate enforcement is the key to environmental protection. There have been considerable doubts about this from the point of view of both financial resources and administrative or political will. HMIP began its life seriously understaffed; indeed, there was a strong rationalisation and efficiency saving motive for setting up HMIP (Weale *et al.*, 1991). New salaries and an increase in staff complement mean that it now employs 313 staff; another 100 may be needed by 1995 (HMIP, 1991). It should be noted, though, that the increase in professional staff is much less than the total figures indicated (see Table 16.4). Staffing clearly constrains inspections and the demands of restructuring HMIP for IPC have been acknowledged to have this effect (HMIP, 1991). In 1990/1 HMIP undertook 3876 visits covering 2092 scheduled works (or 3079 processes). In practice most sites were visited just once a year with more frequent visits to larger works. Some 843 emission tests were made, indicating a reliance on in-house monitoring.

In addition there is concern over the will to enforce. It has been argued that the ethos of HMIP (and its predecessors, see Chapter 8) acts against

Table 16.4   *Her Majesty's Inspectorate of Pollution staff complement*

	Professional (%)	Administrative	Total
1988	120 (66)	63	183
1991	134 (54)	114	248
1992	176 (56)	137	313

Source: Digest of Environmental Protection and Water Statistics

vigorous enforcement (Spooner *et al.*, 1992, p. 110). Despite moves to make HMIP more accountable, public participation remains limited to the publication of registers, insulating HMIP from public pressure for enforcement (see Table 16.5). As a result the 28 143 water pollution incidents reported in 1990, including 658 major incidents, resulted in 282 persecutions. And HMIP found 16 injunctions of control relating to scheduled processes in 1990/1 resulting in one prosecution. This attitude has been reinforced by central government attitudes, particularly in the case of pollution from sewage works. In 1986, 23 per cent of sewage treatment works tested in England and Wales were found to be in breach of approved standards. The Government legalised much of this pollution by granting several water authorities 'relaxations' so that the new water companies would not be liable for prosecution for breaches after privatisation. With such a precedent it is not surprising that pollution control enforcement remains lax.

Similar concerns over the laxity of past legislation, principally COPA, and the lack of adequate enforcement have been voiced over waste management practice. Reports by HMIP and, before that by the

Table 16.5   *Enforcement of water pollution control 1990*

	Water pollution incidents (%)	Major incidents (%)	Prosecutions (%)
Agriculture	11	36	44
Industry	10	17	27
Oil	21	13	7
Sewage	21	20	10
Other	37	14	12

Source: Digest of Environmental Protection and Water Statistics

Hazardous Waste Inspectorate, point to considerable variability in waste disposal practices, with unacceptable standards at the lower end. Site licences did not prove not effective in ensuring environmental protection and the ability, removed by EPA, to surrender a licence and walk away from a site led to highly contaminated and contaminating sites being left as problems without anyone responsible for the solution. Leakages from landfill sites and methane generation at domestic landfill sites are two particular problems arising from poor past waste management. And the British strategy of codisposing industrial and domestic waste has created further problems, as it is difficult to know the precise contents of sites. The Hazardous Waste Inspectorate's findings (1988, pp. 50–83), that the strength of that regulation had been subordinated to a market-led industry, could apply to the whole waste management area: 'The Inspectorate believes that the market will not sustain more realistic prices until uniformly high standards are insisted upon and achieved; until then, price cutting will deter the necessary investment in site improvements.'

One area where there has been a clear and complete failure to establish a credible waste management policy is in the case of nuclear waste (Blowers *et al.*, 1991). Blowers and his coresearchers tell of how apparently easy options were found, one by one, to be politically or technically not feasible leading to a situation where adequate provision has clearly not been made for the varieties of waste that are arising and will increasingly arise in the future (for example, upon decommissioning a nuclear power plant). In 1976 the RCEP said that it found insufficient appreciation of the long-term requirements either by government departments or other organisations involved. In 1991 Blowers *et al.* repeat this finding. They argue that public support for a coherent strategy has been frustrated by institutional centralisation, obsessive secrecy and a lack of openness. As in much pollution control and other waste management, nuclear waste management has been too closely linked with and dependent on the industry it has sought to regulate, so that economic imperatives (here of the civil and military nuclear industry) have driven environmental performance, instead of the other way round.

Finally there is the growing role of land use planning in achieving environmental policy goals (Tromans and Clarkson; 1991; Miller; 1990; Marshall, 1992). As a mechanism for integrating a variety of environmental concerns with location-specific land use decisions, 'green' planning has much to offer. There are a number of mechanisms by which this can achieved: environmental impact assessment (EIA), waste disposal plans, pollution control concerns within development control, local authority environmental assessment of policies and programmes.

Some of these are innovations in local authority practice and cannot yet be fully judged. For example, while there was concern originally over the quality of environmental statements (Jones *et al.* 1991; Wood and Jones, 1991), this situation seems to be improving. The lack of experience of many local authorities in EIA is being eroded over time or county councils are stepping in to provide bridging expertise. Problems remain as to the role of EIA in outline planning applications and the availability and interpretation of data, often technical in nature. On the other hand, recent research by Oxford Polytechnic and ERL (1992) has indicated the extent to which pollution control and waste management concerns are already integrated into development planning and development control. Indeed there is a suggestion that the greater openness of local authorities to public pressure when compared to environmental quangos has encouraged pollution control, in particular, to become a material consideration in local land use planning. Development control has also been used to deal with perceived inadequacies in environmental policy such as protection of ground-water, post-closure pollution control for waste disposal sites and protection of the aquatic environment upon development (that is, flood prevention, land drainage and nature conservation). The research emphasised that the key problems implicit in the current situation are the lack of confidence of the public in the process and problems in consultation between environmental agencies and local authorities. This is also true of EIA. Integrating environmental and land use planning is not a matter of applying technical environmental data to existing planning decisions. It involves a whole new array of consultations and interactions in decision making. It brings new interests into the mediation process that planning engages in. The prospect that green land use planning offers is the incorporation of environmental concerns in an arena potentially open to public participation and democratic control. This contrasts with the way in which environmental quangos have operated in the past (see Chapter 8). However, the discussion of land use planning has indicated substantial weaknesses and inequities in that system, suggesting that achieving environmental protection through this route may also be problematic.

■ Urban policy

Urban policy faces one of the greatest challenges in urban and environmental planning, for it seeks to alter entrenched processes of economic restructuring. Population decentralisation, the urban–rural shift in industrial employment, the switch from a manufacturing- to a service-based economy, and increased concentration in the retail sector have all had their effects on urban areas. Some areas have faced disinvestment, others have had to cope with substantial redevelopment. It is the social consequences of these processes that have given rise to 'the urban problem': the poor housing conditions, the high levels of unemployment, the large numbers of households in poverty. Clearly many aspects of the welfare state exist to deal with such problems, but urban policy has been seen as a distinctive local-level, often area-based approach to urban deprivation. Urban policy has taken three different angles on such deprivation: dealing with the social dimension; seeking to foster business activity; and altering the built environment.

The traditional form of urban policy has been the channelling of funds from central to local government through the Urban Programme, with funds going as grants to local community groups or projects of local government investment, such as industrial and residential estate improvement (see Table 16.6). Most of this expenditure was social in nature, trying to ameliorate the effects of urban change on depressed groups or foster self-help within those groups. This Urban Programme has been steadily declining in real terms from a peak in 1982–3 as more and more money has been sliced off its budget to fund other urban initiatives. For example, £75 million was taken from the Urban Programme to fund the first year of City Challenge.

As Urban Programme expenditure declined, community-based organisations have maintained their budgets so that by 1986–7 voluntary sector projects took 35 per cent of such expenditure, compared to 15 per

Table 16.6   *Urban Programme expenditure*

(at constant prices)	£ million
1979–80	348
1980–1	321
1981–2	312
1982–3	399
1983–4	391
1984–5	376
1985–6	344
1986–7	325
1987–8	319
1988–9	284
1989–90	157

Source: Brownill (1990) p. 11

cent in 1978–9 (Bailey, 1991). They have also had a 10 per cent share of the admittedly small Task Force budgets and been involved in City Challenge bids, which come from the local authority but require •evidence of networking with the local voluntary sector. This means that community groups are now significant actors in urban policy. The National Council for Voluntary Organisation estimated that in 1988 the annual turnover of voluntary organisations in the 57 inner area programme authorities was £400 million, part grant and part trading income. As much again could be being earned in fees and payment for contract work.

Bailey (1991) locates the causes of this growth in importance of community groups in the decline in local authority spending, the shift in policy towards ad hoc initiatives and the effects of community mobilisation over the past three decades. The move may hold benefits in terms of the empowerment of local communities and the generation of social facilities but such activity cannot, nor is it intended to, counter the underlying economic forces affecting urban areas. Such community-based policies can, in the current context, only mitigate the worst impacts of economic change. For example, the urban housing problem remains serious: urban homelessness increased 60 per cent between 1981 and 1988; and it is estimated that £36 billion is required to repair the housing stock in poor repair. Furthermore the reliance on community groups in urban social policy can be seen as reflecting the low priority given to urban poverty compared to economic goals (Lawless, 1991, p. 21).

The second angle on urban change has argued that fostering local enterprise, usually in the form of small business, can alter the economic situation of urban areas. During the 1980s this took the form of local enterprise agencies (LEAs). There are 300 LEAs in the UK with funding of £34 million in 1988 of which 41 per cent came from the private sector, 35 per cent from central government and 24 per cent from local authorities (Smallbone, 1991). In the early 1980s local authorities took the lead, creating arm's length LEAs to generate local employment, focus assistance to ethnic minorities and, more ambitiously, to restructure local economies. In practice local authority-led LEAs never lived up to this goal of restructuring from below that some left wing labour urban authorities espoused. Commenting on London, Buck *et al.* (1986, p. 188) points to a lack of capability within local authorities: 'the boroughs have sometimes seemed out of their depth when it comes to both industrial assistance and tackling employment disadvantage.'

As from 1991 core funding of the agencies is being phased out so that they have to get central government funding from project-based grants, contracts from the TECs or increased private sponsorship. The evidence seems to be that the private sectors are becoming much more discriminating in providing funds to LEAs as the demands on them increase and they are seen as the major funders. Cooke (1989, p. 299) argues that LEAs have not been effective because they have largely sought to rescue ailing companies. He contrasts them with the SDA (now Scottish Enterprise) and WDA who have probably 'been generating between 2000 and 3000 jobs per annum since 1976' (p. 299) or 50 000 jobs in all. But these major regional agencies have 'succeeded' on this rather modest scale by strategically identifying growth sectors which locally-based LEAs are not able to do with the possible exception of LENTA in London. Furthermore the funding going into SDA and WDA dwarfs that available to LEAs: £60 million p.a. to WDA and £100 million p.a. to SDA by the mid-1980s (Cooke, 1989, p. 300). Each LEA is a small-budget organisation with an average budget of £108 000 in 1988 and only three full-time staff (see also Bovaird, 1992).

Whether such agencies can effectively work against prevailing economic trends when the private sector is actually driving them seems doubtful. The economic impact can, at best, be marginal, resolving market failures regarding information and advice. Task Forces, another form of urban economic development agency, have also had a fairly small impact. Government figures claim total funding of £193.5 million over 1986–91, of which 43 per cent is public funding (30 per cent spent, 13 per cent committed). This has generated 12 593 jobs with another 11 546 forecast: a public sector cost per job of £6600.

Finally, there are the batch of property-led policies: EZs; UDCs; city grant and its predecessor UDG; and derelict land grant. EZs were intended to comprise a package of incentives: a less regulated form of land use control; other reductions in bureaucracy; and the incentives, principally capital allowances and the 10 years' holiday from paying local business rates. However, all assessors have agreed that it is the financial incentives that have proved the attraction to developers moving into EZs. The financial costs in terms of taxes foregone has been considerable while, as Wood and Hooper (1988) argue, a significant degree of land use control is exercised in EZs albeit through different channels than the development control system. Indeed the mixture of landlord powers, planning agreements and prior negotiation in the context of an EZ can prove more effective than the 'normal' planning system. Furthermore the later rounds of EZs seem to demonstrate more intervention of this nature by local authorities than the first round (Barnes and Preston, 1985).

The outputs of the EZs experiment did not meet the government's hopes. Their own figures, from *Enterprise Zone Information* annual bulletins, suggested that substantial development had occurred in the zones: 27 per cent of land was developed at designation, 70 per cent by 1987/8. But then the second round EZs were selected on the basis of developability (Bruton and Nicholson, 1987, p. 206). Employment in the zones between designation and 1987 was claimed to have tripled by 59 000 with a 3:2 bias towards industry rather than services. But the cost has been £354 million up to March 1987 at 1986/7 prices, 65 per cent in capital allowances and 35 per cent in lost rate revenue. In addition there had been public sector investment in the zones of £197m, 82 per cent on infrastructure and the rest on land acquisition. Some £99m of this would have occurred anyway, leaving a total cost of £452m or £7661 per job. Furthermore these figures exclude the substantial public investment that had already occurred in many first round EZs before designation (Bruton and Nicholson, 1987, p. 206). The National Audit Office's report on EZs, which ended the experiment, argued that the full cost of EZs was not known, and that their effectiveness as a policy tool could not be known with any certainty. In addition it seemed that many of the jobs counted as arising from the EZ policy had probably been directed from elsewhere and the increase in land values in EZs were often at the expense of surrounding land. It is also clear that the most successful zones were those where other public sector programmes had invested resources. As Bruton and Nicholson conclude (1987, p. 209):

> Paradoxically despite the free market ideology of the EZ measure, active public sector involvement appears to be a key factor in the successful development of the zones, although this activity may bear little relation to EZ concessions and will probably use resources diverted from elsewhere.

Indeed Lloyd and Botham (1985) argue that local authorities were positively using EZs as an element within existing local interventionist economic strategies. The concept has not been applied to areas where development pressures are being resisted by planning policies (Bruton and Nicholson, 1987, p. 211). Given that EZs were not an exemplar of free-market non-planning but an unfocused, costly and interventionist policy tool, it is perhaps not surprising that the quality of development has not proved sub-standard compared to other sites. This is because of a number of factors: the fairly effective control of new development noted above; some development in EZs had already gone through normal planning procedure; building regulations continued to apply; standardised designs, materials and construction methods were being used by developers; and owners wished their properties to maintain their investment value (Thornley, 1991, p. 197).

If the EZ experiment is generally seen as a failure, UDCs seem to be regarded by government as sufficiently successful for continuing rounds of designation (see Table 16.7). Expenditure on UDCs has grown eight-

Table 16.7 *UDC expenditure and leverage ratios*

Urban Development Corporations	Public funding £ per acre p.a.	Leverage ratio
London Dockland Development Corporation	11 400 to 1988	11:1
Merseyside	23 100 to 1988	0.14–0.45
Black Country	3 400 ⎫	7:1
Cardiff Bay	9 600 ⎪	4:1
Teesside	2 200 ⎪ for 5 years	7:1
Trafford Park	8 700 ⎬	7:1
Tyne and Wear	4 300 ⎪	2:1
Central Manchester	17 100 ⎭	
Leeds	2 900 for 9 months	
Sheffield	3 600 for 7 years	
Bristol	4 800 for 9 months	

Source: Stoker (1989b) p. 160

fold in real terms from 1981/2–1989/90 (Brownill, 1990, p. 11). The success of UDCs is measured, in the government's eyes, by leverage ratio, the amount of private sector money brought in per unit by public sector investment. In essentially social programmes, a low leverage ratio is acceptable: the task forces were reporting ratios of 0.5:1 in their inner city areas. However the ratio of 1:1 or 2:1 found by the National Audit Office for EZs was considered inappropriate given their rationale and, indeed, name. As can be seen from Table 16.7 the leverage ratios for UDCs have varied widely.

It is clear that is the state of the local property market that determines the leverage ratio. The London Docklands must be taken as a special success case; it is likely that the substantial sums proposed for the 100 hectare UDC in Central Manchester could also draw in huge amounts of private capital in the right economic circumstances. As emphasised in Brindley *et al.* (1989), leverage policies follow market rationality and basically magnify existing disparities between areas. Thus when a recession in the property market occurs, as in 1991/2, UDCs cannot generate development and the cost of their support may seem excessive. Declines in land values in their areas also undermine their financing and rationale during a property market downturn.

Other relevant factors in determining a UDC's impact are the character of the relationship between the corporation and the pre-existing local authorities and the approach taken by key board members and corporation officials (Stoker, 1989b). This influences the character of the development that occurs and its relation to local community needs and established local authority policy.

The LDDC is the prime example of a corporation at conflict with local authorities for most of its life and led by officers highly attuned to the requirements of the development industry. The scale of development has been substantial: 5.2 million ft^2 of industrial and commercial floorspace as at 1989 with a further 5.9 million under construction and 8.8 million ft^2 proposed in Canary Wharf (now in process of construction but suspended due to the financial problems of the developer); and 15 000 dwelling starts. Developers have benefited from land sold on highly favourable terms (Brownill, 1990, p. 44) and the extensive investment in infrastructure and site servicing that occurred before and after designation. By March 1989 the LDDC had received £547 million in grants with an additional £909 million planned for 1989–93; and over 1981–9 was spending 84 per cent of all income on pump-priming development; the DoTr had committed £600 million on transport; the EZ concessions were worth £130 million to 1987; and the utilities and Dockland Joint Committee (of local authorities) had invested in the area in the past. In addition by 1988/9 the LDDC was receiving 50 per cent of its income in the form of enhanced land values upon sale (Brownill, 1990, pp. 45–6).

In London's property market during the 1980s such investment was bound to generate development. However critics have consistently argued that the development did little for the employment, housing and community facilities needs of the local population. Many of Brownill's conclusions on the LDDC (1990, p. 173) hold true for all UDCs:

> The most immediate tension is how the operation of market forces and inner city policy geared to promoting the physical rebuilding of areas leads to unequal distribution of benefits, leading to the spatial exclusion of those groups who cannot afford to pay, in particular the low-paid, the working class, black people and women.

Brownhill finds that landowners, property developers and some owner-occupiers were the principal beneficiaries of UDC policy. Stoker (1989b) states that UDCs produce 'a pattern of urban renewal which is broadly beneficial to the top three quarters of the income distribution' (p. 165). This is an urban policy which offers little to the urban poor.

UDG, now city grant, and the Scottish equivalent LEG-UP, are a project-specific form of leverage which seeks to generate net addition private investment while addressing some special social need in urban areas. The impacts of UDG have been assessed and they provide further evidence of the problems of urban policy over the last decade or so. Over September 1982–April 1984, 446 UDG bids were submitted, 32 per cent approved and 81 per cent of these were taken up resulting in 116 projects (Jacobs, 1985). To December 1983 some £54 million was expended on grants resulting in £221 million of private investment, a leverage ratio of 4:1. 40 per cent grants are supporting industrial development, 35 per cent commercial and 23 per cent housing. An HRF study (1986) estimated that UDG projects were generating 129 dwellings per £1m grant or £7750 per dwelling, with higher costs where special social needs were being addressed. In Scotland, up to October 1984, £11 million of LEG-UP had levered in £46 million of private monies, a ratio of 4:1 also (Zeiger, 1985). The Scottish analysis suggests that, allowing for other relevant public monies, LEG-UP created 1717 permanent jobs at £6600 per job and housing at £4700 per dwelling over September 1982–October 1984. However, various innovative funding schemes in use in Scotland means that much of the grant will be repaid to SDA, reducing the cost per job and dwelling substantially.

What UDG and LEG-UP does is classic leverage: it is 'a market oriented scheme designed to cater for private sector needs with a pay-off to the public sector in terms of inner city revival' (Jacobs, 1985, p. 199). However that revival is measured in physical development, not the socioeconomic benefits which are often spuriously claimed in grant applications (Matson and Whitney, 1985). It is difficult to prove 'additionality', that projects are being funded which would not otherwise have occurred, but Jacobs argues (1988, p. 198) that: 'Indications are that the nature and size of the projects coming forward would simply not have come about through the mechanism of the normal Urban Programme had it not been for the introduction of UDG,' but it is a marginal effect (1988, p. 199): 'Experience shows that things have worked best when UDG has been asked to do things that the private sector actually wants to do, rather than to revive large comprehensive development plans initiated by the public sector.'

This does not mean that the public sector is not involved; on the contrary, Matson and Whitney (1985) found that 67 per cent of the UDGs in their survey were public sector-led, but the public sector is edging the private sector to conform to a policy framework which is largely in line with market trends. Again the effect of such an urban policy in shaping urban change cannot be substantial. A recent report has assessed the range of urban policy initiatives and concluded that the gap between deprived areas and the rest of the country remains as wide as it was 15 years ago (Willmott and Hutchinson, 1992).

So if these policies can only marginally alter the social and economic impact of urban change, have they at least accelerated physical development processes to reduce urban dereliction if not urban deprivation? Kivell (1987, p. 269) argues that: 'After 20 years of reclamation, the problem of derelict land remains as large and intractable as ever.' He argues that relying public sector monies to pump-prime the private sector has resulted in an overemphasis on reclaiming for hard uses (65 per cent approved reclamation up to 1984/5), insufficient funds being put into the problem and a short-term approach which stores up maintenance problems for the future. From 1974 to 1982 derelict land increased from 43 300 to 45 700 ha despite major programmes which reclaimed 17 000 ha. Inner city areas are increasingly the location for derelict land: 32.4 per cent in 1982. At reclamation rates of £44 000 per ha, current expenditure will take 26 years to clear the existing stock, ignoring any additions. A recent assessment from within central government (DoE, 1992) has been more optimistic. It pointed to an increase in derelict land grant (DLG) expenditure to £106 million in 1992. 1500 acres was reclaimed each year between 1988 and 1992. But this has to be matched against the 1988 survey figure of 40 500 hectares of derelict land and a cost of £50 000 p.a. for recent DLG schemes. Even in purely physical terms it seems that pump-priming is an inadequate policy for urban areas.

As Lawless (1988, p. 540) states:

> Yet any overall assessment of the policy must remain critical. In many respects it has simply not made that mush difference to the inner cities and those living in them . . . the programme as a whole cannot be seen as a comprehensive strategy to address the problems of urban decline. It remains as it always has been a pragmatic *ad hoc* response to a complex series of constraints operating on the cities.

Lawless argues that any change in policy is likely to require substantial additional resources, requiring both economic growth and a change in government (1991, p. 28).

■ Transport policy

In the final section I deal, admittedly very briefly, with transport policy. The current state of British transport is defined as a problem by almost all sectors of society. The dominant trend in transport has been the growth in road traffic from 272 billion vehicle km (b.v.km) in 1980 to 408 b.v.km in 1990 in Britain. Energy consumption by the UK transport sector rose by 19 per cent over 1986–1990, while total consumption rose by less than 3 per cent. Local communities see traffic in their areas as the main local problem. In a Civic Trust Survey (1991) of 650 local amenity societies, 75 per cent of inner city societies and 50 per cent of societies in towns and villages placed traffic at the top of their list of problems. Business interests are counting the cost of congestion in financial terms; the CBI estimated in 1989 that congestion cost British business £15 billion per annum.

Meanwhile public transport is found wanting in terms of cost, frequency, reliability and comfort, and its inadequacies disadvantage groups without access to a car who are therefore dependent on buses and trains: that is the elderly, the poor and women. In 1985 38 per cent households did not have access to a car, 83 per cent did not have access to two cars, usually leaving the women car-less. In addition, women find the organisation of roads, car parks and public transport threatening to their personal safety (Trench, 1991; Oc, 1991).

Finally, environmentalists point to the costs in terms of pollution of unrestricted reliance on personal and freight road traffic, leading to ill health, acid rain and global warming (FoE, 1991). The single major contributor to many actual increases in emissions has been road transport which is not, of course, covered by air pollution legislation in the same way as industrial processes. Nitrous oxides from road transport increased from 0.8 million tonnes (mt) to 1.4 mt over 1980–90 and now account for 51 per cent of total NOx emissions. Road transport amounts for 41 per cent of volatile organic compounds (VOC) emissions and these increased from 0.86 mt to 0.97 mt over 1980–90, while the other main contributor, industry, managed to keep absolute VOC emissions stable. 90 per cent of all carbon monoxide emissions are attributable to road transport and this contribution went up form 4.1 mt to 6.0 mt over 1980–90. Similarly for carbon dioxide, road transport's current share of 19 per cent represents an increase from 21 mt in 1980 to 30 mt in 1990.

The verdict on the current state of transport is clear: that it has emphasised road provision at the expense of all other considerations in the belief that this met individualist aspirations on freedom of travel and sustained economic growth.

Transport policy of the past decade has only exacerbated this situation with continued roadbuilding, reductions in subsidy to public transport, privatisation and deregulation of public transport. For example deregulation of the buses under the 1985 Transport Act is argued to have led to: a loss of services geared to need; a loss of timetable integration and coordination; local private monopolies following price wars and a shake out of companies; reduction in number and quality of services supported by cross-subsidisation; and problems in integrating bus with other transport services (SEEDS, 1987).

There is also an inherent bias against public transport in assessment methods. The cost benefit analysis for roadbuilding includes a figure for the benefits of relieving congestion; the assessments of rail schemes do not. Furthermore, the policy on emissions from road transport vehicles is currently limited to improving the performance of existing vehicles through MOT test and requiring new technology in new cars. These are clearly marginal policies which have to be set in the context of overall transport policy.

Many of these consequences of current transport policy arise from a lack of integration both within the transport sector and with other forms of policy. Road planning is isolated from public transport planning and, in many areas, bus and train services are not integrated with each other. Neither is traffic management operated with the needs of public transport in mind. Transport planning, in all its constituent and isolated parts, is not integrated with land use planning with the result, as Herington (1984) has argued, that roadbuilding programmes have led land use change often, in challenge to strategic planning policies. Emissions from transport policy are not within the major schemes for pollution control and, certainly, social policy only marginally affects transport provision.

There are signs that this is altering in some respects. The environmental impact of transport both local and global, is being recognised and it seems as if a new consensus on transport policy is being reached (Goodwin, 1990). On the one hand this arises from a recognition of the variety of costs associated with continued growth in car use. On the other it is associated with a long overdue recognition that roadbuilding cannot solve congestion as new roads merely increase car use to a new point of saturation (Mogridge, 1990). This is reshaping aspects of transport policy. Curbs on road traffic are being sought, with a vigorous debate over road pricing and parking controls (LBA, 1990; CIoTr, 1991), more investment in public transport being sought. Local land use planning is taking on board the concept of road-calming and research is investigating the broader links between strategic land use planning and transport patterns. The diffuse nature of environmental impacts is putting integration of transport policy back on the agenda.

Further reading

It is difficult to provide selected references which cover a full assessment of the planning system. For consideration of the land use planning system, the reader is directed to Bruton and Nicholson (1987), Healey *et al.* (1988) and Ambrose (1986). These provide perspectives from liberal political economy, institutional and marxist approaches respectively. Lowe *et al.* (1986) is an excellent critique of countryside policy, Rose (1990) gathers a mass of information on environmental planning and Lawless (1991) is a brief overview of urban policy. The latter can be supplemented with Bovaird (1992) and Parkinson (1989).

■ *Chapter 17* ■

Conclusion: Why Plan?

Chapter 16 may have left the reader a bit depressed! Certainly British planning has had its successes but the chapter catalogues profound criticisms of the planning system: its weaknesses; its lack of desired effects; its tendency to generate unintended and inappropriate outcomes. This discussion may leave the reader wondering 'why bother to have a planning system at all?'. This chapter concludes the assessment of the British planning system by addressing the question of 'why plan?'.

■ The necessity of planning

Without adopting a tightly functionalist approach, it can be argued that planning is a necessary state activity. Economic and social circumstances prompt a degree of state action in managing our physical environment and trying to influence our use of that environment. There are several senses in which this is the case.

First, planning, in its most general sense, is a means of avoiding anarchy and disorder. There are strong tendencies towards such disorder in our economic system. The interaction of competitive forces in the market place does not automatically lead along a smooth path to the public interest. Instead competition can generate the anarchy of the market, with periodic oversupply of goods, mismatch of needs and supply (or even demand and supply), underutilisation of some resources (such as labour) and overexploitation of others (such as environmental goods and services). The cycles of boom and slump, of crisis and temporary recovery have shaped our economy and society during the 20th century, and will continue to do so in the foreseeable future.

These outcomes of a market system have particular consequences in the case of the natural and built environment, as change often has long-term consequences. In urban areas, the cycles of property development can leave cities scarred for many years, whether by the disruption of large scale development activity, the dereliction of abandoned sites or the apparent irrationality of empty new buildings. The London Dock-lands area has seen all these stages over the last two decades: docks left to decay for years as the Port of London Authority pulled out to newer, more profitable locations; the decade of massive redevelopment and disruption for local communities under the UDC in the 1980s; and the now-empty tower of Canary Wharf standing as testimony to the collapse of yet another property boom. In the case of the natural environment, the effects of market decision making are similarly long-term and unstable. Mining activity can change the face of a rural area completely for decades. Cessation of that activity only creates new problems of dereliction, equally persistent. Pollution flows may alter over the short term with levels of industrial output and technological change, but the impact on ecosystems of receiving media can be long term. They take time to adjust, assimilate and recover, or, more pessimistically, to adjust, alter and change irreversibly for the worse.

Planning has a role in reacting to and, more important, trying to prevent the worst excesses of this inherent instability (Hobbs, 1992). The use of knowledge about economic, social and physical environmental systems, combined with a future oriented approach could at least suggest scenarios for the future and propose some mechanisms for movement towards a more acceptable pattern of use of our built and natural environment. Even if it is accepted that these mechanisms for controlling the anarchy of the market are weak, the existence of the planning system represents a strong statement that the worst excesses of a market system need not be tolerated. And, in between the extremes of planning as effectively controlling instability and planning as a statement of hope, there is the prospect of a planning system limiting some of the effects without necessarily ensuring a smooth path in environmental change in urban or rural areas, economic, social or ecological systems.

Another role for the planning system in relation to economic and social change is in terms of accommodating long-terms shifts in structure. There has been much debate on the transition from a Fordist to post-Fordist system of production in Britain and other developed countries, and within the global economic system as a whole (Harvey, 1989; Lash and Urry, 1987; Graham, 1992). For some this is associated with a shift from modernity to postmodernity, as a distinct era in social and cultural organisation. To quote Harvey on Fordism (1989, p. 135):

> Postwar Fordism has to be seen, therefore, less as a mere system of mass production and more as a total way of life. Mass production meant standardization of product as well as mass consumption ... Fordism also built upon and contributed to the aesthetic of modernism − particularly the latter's penchant for functionality and efficiency − in very explicit ways.

and on post-Fordism (or flexible accumulation, as he prefers to term it) (p. 147):

> It rests on flexibility with respect to labour processes, labour markets, products and patterns of consumption. It is characterized by the emergence

of entirely new sectors of production, new ways of providing financial services, new markets, and above all, greatly intensified rates of commercial, technological, and organisational innovation. It has entrained rapid shifts in the patterning of uneven development, both between sectors and between geographical regions, giving rise , for example, to a vast surge in so-called 'service-sector' employment as well as to entirely new industrial ensembles in hitherto underdeveloped regions.

These broader, longer-term changes raise the question of whether the planning system is implicated in smoothing the transition to post-Fordism and postmodernism and, in the process, is reshaping itself in a post-Fordist and postmodern form. If post-Fordism involves a greater emphasis on flexible patterns of production and service delivery, with more specialised, non-standard products, then existing regimes of state influence over product and service delivery also need to adopt the flexible specialisation approach. Current changes in the management of the planning system can be seen in this light (Stoker, 1989a; Gyford, 1991, p. 122): the creation of arm's length organisations for a variety of tasks from hearing planning appeals to disposing of waste; the emphasis on responsiveness and flexibility in all planning decisions; the attack on planning as an activity under professional control operating within a state bureaucracy.

Some already discern a postmodern form of planning developing (Harvey, 1989; Goodchild, 1990). Modernist planning was concerned with comprehensive management of the environment, conceived as a totality, and with developing master plans for planning action. Post-modern planning perceives economic processes as chaotic and un-controllable, with change as endemic and indeed attractive. Talking specifically about urban design, Harvey (1989, p. 66) says:

> I take postmodernism broadly to signify a break with the modernist idea that planning and development should focus on large-scale, metropolitan-wide, technologically ration and efficient urban plans, backed by absolutely no-frills architecture (the austere 'functionalist' surfaces of 'international style' modernism). Postmodernism cultivates, instead, a conception of the urban fabric as necessarily fragmented, a 'palimpsest' of past forms superimposed upon each other, and a 'collage' of current uses, many of which may be ephemeral. Since the metropolis is impossible to command except in bits and pieces, urban *design* (and note that postmodernists design rather than plan) simply aims to be sensitive to vernacular traditions, local histories, particular wants, needs, and fancies, thus generating specialized, even highly custo-mized architectural forms that may range from intimate, personalized spaces, through traditional monumentality, to the gaiety of spectacle.

In this way, planning can ease society onto the path towards a new pattern of organisation. It can also play a part in dealing with the inevitable side effects of the transition process, making the process less disruptive and painful. If this seems an overly functional view of planning and its relation to economic and social change, it must be remembered that such change will generate political pressures from a broad spectrum within society looking to the state to deal with the unpleasant consequences of restructuring. It is not just in the interests of post-Fordist entrepreneurs to plan the transition, including its environmental dimension. Structural change hurts many in society, both because of the uncertainty generated and the reallocation of resources involved (but see below for further discussion of planning and distributional impacts).

Beyond these rationales for planning, in dealing with first, periods of instability in economic activity and second, transition during periods of restructuring, there is a third reason why planning is necessary. In relation to both the built and natural environment there is a system maintenance function for planning. This means that planning can play a part in ensuring that economic, social and ecological systems do not irreparably break down. The anarchy of market competition can threaten to undermine the basic dynamics of economic processes. The social consequences of unfettered competition can undermine the legitimacy of existing patterns of political organisation. And the unrestrained use of environmental goods and services can cause irreversible ecological damage, including damage to the life support systems of our planet. Planning is necessary to prevent such damage to the broad structures within which we live, work and exist.

At different times, different aspects of the system maintenance function of planning are apparent. In periods of profound slump, the state puts its efforts into local and national economic development to promote growth, recently in a quasi-entrepreneurial style. When social movements challenge existing political structures, then the state has to put resources into meeting, or appearing to meet, demand for change (O'Connor, 1973): more extensive public consultation and participation procedures over nuclear power developments in the face of campaigns by the Campaign for Nuclear Disarmament and environmental groups; creating community programmes and encouraging business to be involved in local training and social programmes in the wake of inner city riots. Currently the growing evidence on global environmental change, particularly an enhanced greenhouse effect, is pushing governments into stepping up their environmental programmes (DoE, 1990).

Success in any of these three tasks for planning is not assured. Planning, of the environment or more directly of the economy, has not been able to sustain a steady path of growth. The process of restructuring is not frictionless, problems of adjustment occur and some sections of society lose out in the change that does occur. While Britain and other western developed countries have managed to avoid economic and social collapse, we do not yet know if ecological crisis has been averted or whether our current changes in behaviour will result in a level of climatic change to which we can adjust. But planning for the built and natural environment has an important role to play at each level of periodic, structural and systemic change.

■ The potential of planning

While these processes of change provide a strong rationale for planning, there is a further, progressive argument for planning. All the processes discussed so far – the ups and downs of market-led patterns of investment, the change in mode of production, and the potential for irreparable damage to economic, social and ecological systems – have distributional consequences. The existence of these consequences can result in a broad-based support within society for planning. But planning also has the potential for dealing with the distributional impacts of change in a more equitable and democratic manner. Many of the distributional consequences take the form of spatial and environmental externalities, and planning is particularly well suited to dealing with such externalities, regulating to prevent negative externalities, and coordinating activities to maximise positive externalities. Dealing with externalities and other distributional consequences of market activity is a primary way in which planning can encourage redistribution in society. Preventing the full impact of urban redevelopment being felt by local communities, controlling pollution which is affecting local residents in an industrial area, supporting employment opportunities for rural residents in a situation of agricultural decline, are all examples of the way in which the planning system can manage change in the pursuit of a fairer distribution of resources. But planning can play a more positive role than just reacting to the adverse consequences of market outcomes. It can actively try to redistribute resources through patterns of land use, provision of urban and transport facilities, ensuring access to leisure and beauty spots, and promoting the quality of local environments.

Planning, therefore, has a reactive and proactive role in relation to the distribution of resources, of the costs and benefits of change in the built and natural environments. This is not just to suggest that the planning system has to manage distributional consequences. It is not just a matter of professional management, of planners deciding to adopt a more egalitarian approach to their work. The distributional consequences of planning is one key reason why planning is a political activity. The potential for planning to redistribute is also a political issue and therefore closely related to the view of the planning system as an arena for democratic action. The planning system can be an arena where a broad range of interests organise around conflicts over the effects of economic and social change and, further, where those processes of change can be challenged.

Enhancing the potential for planning to redistribute resources in society means opening up planning to democratic pressures. Planners may pay lip service to local pluralism, but a democratic planning system would seek to make this a reality. This does not mean that redistribution will be easily achieved through a more open planning system. Increasing public involvement in planning brings more conflicts within the planning system and raises hard questions. Any planning decision is taken in the context of particular constraints. Participation in the planning process often exposes those constraints, which frequently arise from the decisions of a higher tier of government: say, over the need for a road proposal, or extent of a grant scheme, or the allocation of residential development for demographic change. These decisions, taken at the higher level, may sometimes represent a balance between or compromise between competing local interests, or resource constraints in a situation of a legitimately tight budget. However, the higher-tier decisions can represent the power of vested interests, the outcomes of a crass bureaucracy or a total disregard of the needs and wishes of a local community. A more participatory planning system can allow the nature of higher-tier decisions to be at least challenged. It rarely leads to consensus nor readily achieves the shift of resources towards the least well-off. What it can do is give more of a voice to those who routinely bear the costs of environmental change. This may help protect those groups in the face of economic and social change.

Of course, participation carries burdens. Those with the most to gain financially and politically have already, by and large, ensured their place in the participatory processes of planning. Extending participation to the less powerful, in the pursuit of a fairer distribution, does try to redress this but it also places a burden on those participating. Public participation exercises which do not genuinely involve communities in decision making are likely to be rejected because of the high opportunity costs involved in what is essentially a 'sham' participation. Empowerment may be a more meaningful form of participation for communities, but may also be rejected by those who seek a more passive form of citizenship.

The least the planning system should offer in these cases is the right to challenge the state when decisions are judged unequitable and undesirable by the community affected. And this will be a benchmark even where a fully participatory system already operates. For not every group can be included within a participatory schema and the right of an excluded group (even if excluded by their own choice for passivity) to challenge planning decisions remains an important principle of open planning.

While these potentialities for an open and redistributive planning system exist, they have not been realised to date. Vested interests inside and outside the state have resisted both elements: the redistributive and democratic programmes. Economic processes have continually frustrated moves towards a more equitable distribution in practice. These processes create inequality, and political pressures arising from powerful economic interests continue to prevent redistribution. The economic and political barriers to the planning system achieving its potential in this respect are strong.

There are those who see the shifts towards postmodern planning as potentially bringing more voices within the planning system (Goodchild, 1990). Criticising modernist planning for the arrogant way in which it has dealt with many groups – ethnic minorities, women, the disabled – postmodern planning emphasises the virtues of diversity and the collage of alternative viewpoints that comprises current culture. However, there is an opposing view that postmodernism is 'shamelessly market-oriented' (Harvey, 1989, p. 77) and, therefore, is bound to favour the affluence and the private sector, rather than the poor and public needs. The emphasis on community action is not really a matter of choice, but results from the disintegration of broader narratives, more comprehensive claims to explanation and faith in general strategies. Political action is necessarily reduced to local action and specific communities and becomes meaningless when it moves outside these boundaries. The scope for social change this offers is clearly limited. Postmodern planning can then be seen as inherently reactionary and must be resisted in order to achieve change. The extent to which faith can be placed in local movements and initiatives in the new era is a major question for progressive planning in the 1990s.

■ Debating planning

Planning has not in practice been able to overcome the barriers towards achieving its progressive potential. As Healey (1992a, p. 43) says: 'the weakness of the system lies in the limited powers available to citizens, and all those economic, environmental and social interests which do not have a property interest in a specific site, to challenge political and administrative decisions'. Yet planners continue to make statements which emphasise both their ability to manage many aspects of built and natural environmental change and the intention to do so in the name of the public interest, balancing interests and protecting the least powerful groups. Thus many activities within the planning system are diversionary, appearing to promote social change but making only limited moves in practice. The language of apparent commitment is at least as important to the analyst of planning as the substantive outcomes on social groups. Indeed the diversionary nature of much planning activity is a contributory factor in preventing further movement towards redistribution and openness.

There are good reasons why planning should contain may elements which are essentially diversionary. The planning system has characteristics of a bureaucracy and bureaucrats do seek to extend their arenas of influence. Given the weaknesses of many planning tools and hence the problems in achieving stated planning goals, there are incentives to extend planning activity in other directions. Vested interests will usually exist who benefit from an area of planning activity and will lend support to its maintenance and even extension.

This means that a critique of planning and planners is an essential part of a move towards an alternative planning system, which fulfils its redistributive potential. Complacency is perhaps the most dangerous feature of a planning system in this respect. It is not the ambition or scope of the planning system which necessarily needs to be questioned. Rather, the operation of planning in all its facets needs to be criticised from outside *and* inside. Indeed robust internal criticism is likely to render the planning system more able to stand up to external criticism, a problem it has faced in the past. Self-criticism will raise questions of performance in the various sectors of the planning system and, more important, of priorities. The essential and diversionary elements of the planning system can then be disentangled. Such self-criticism is being institutionalised in the form of audits and assessments of planning activity. While such activities can themselves be criticised for the time and resources they consume, they may offer the scope to an internal reassessment of planning which identifies the diversionary elements and prepares the way for a change of emphasis within planning. This assumes, of course, that the goal against which planning is audited and assessed includes redistributive and democratic aims.

For such an assessment not to degenerate into another futile, bureaucratic procedure, it needs to operate in the context of debate. Such debate may occur in many different arenas: community, professional, political, and academic. Implicit in all such debate, as this book has tried to argue, is one or more theoretical views on planning, the role of the state, professionals and the public, and the relation between planning and the market. Even if not explicitly stated, a theoretical stance stands behind statements and views. This is, I believe, to be welcomed not deprecated. Theories help us organise our ideas and relate them one to another. They link general issues about our society to specific issues of concern within a particular planning situation. Most important, theories exist in opposition to each other and holding one theoretical viewpoint inevitably involves conflict with others. Debate is intrinsic to theoretical discussion and theoretical debate should underpin the ongoing assessment of planning.

■ So, to conclude . . .

Planning is a necessary activity, managing short- and long-term change in our economic system, preventing system breakdown and managing conflicts that arise. It has potential for redistributing resources, and for becoming a democratic arena for decision making over resource allocation. However, it has not achieved that potential to date and instead many aspects of planning have become the diversionary activities of a bureaucracy supported by vested interests. To overcome this, continued critique of the planning system is essential, internal and external. And theory has a vital role to play in maintaining a critical debate which could foster progressive change in British planning. In this hope, the interaction of theory, policy, procedure and data in this book is offered to the reader, with a view to stimulating debate and argument about the British planning system.

Bibliography

The place of publication is London unless otherwise stated.

Adams, D. (1990) 'Meeting the needs of industry? The performance of industrial land and property markets in Inner Manchester and Salford', in P. Healey and R. Nabarro (eds), *Land and Property Development in a Changing Context* (Aldershot: Gower) pp. 113–27.

Adams, D., Baum, A. and MacGregor, B. (1985) 'The influence of valuation practices on the price of inner city vacant land', *Land Development Studies*, 2 (3) pp. 137–57.

Alterman, R. (1990) 'Developer obligations for public services in the USA', in P. Healey and R. Nabarro (eds), *Land and Property Development in a Changing Context* (Aldershot: Gower) pp. 162–74.

Ambrose, P. (1986) *Whatever happened to planning?* (Methuen).

Ambrose, P. and Colenutt, B. (1975) *The Property Machine* (Penguin).

Andrews, J. (1990) 'The relationship between agriculture and wildlife', in J. Bowers (ed.), *Agriculture and Rural Land Use: in the the 1990s* (Swindon: ESRC) pp. 58–69.

Armstrong, J. (1985) *The Sizewell Report: a new approach for major public inquiries* (TCPA).

Ashworth, W. (1954) *The Genesis of Modern British Town Planning* (Routledge & Kegan Paul).

Audit Commission (1992) *Building in Quality: a study of development control* (HMSO).

Bailey, N. (1991) 'Community Development Trusts: an essential component of urban regeneration strategies', paper presented to AESOP Congress, Oxford Polytechnic (June).

Balchin, P. and Bull, G. (1987) *Regional and Urban Economics* (Harper & Row).

Ball, M. (1984) *Housing Policy and Economic Power* (Methuen).

Ball, M. (1988) *Rebuilding Construction* (Routledge).

Barlow, J. (1988a) 'A note on biotechnology and the food production chain: some social and spatial implications of changing production technology', *International Journal of Urban and Regional Research*, 12 (2) pp. 229–46.

Barlow, J. (1988b) 'The politics of land into the 1990s: landowners, developers and farmers in lowland Britain', *Policy and Politics*, 16 (2) pp. 111–21.

Barnes, I. and Preston, J. (1985) 'The Scunthorpe Enterprise Zone: an example of muddled interventionism', *Public Administration*, 63, pp. 171–81.

Barrett, S. and Fudge, C. (eds), (1981) *Policy and Action* (Methuen).

Baumol, W. and Oates, W. (1975) *The Theory of Environmental Policy* (New Jersey: Prentice-Hall).

Beck, L. (1989) 'Farm waste pollution' in Institute of Water Engineers and Managers, *Agriculture and the Environment*, Technical Papers of Annual Symposium, University of York (IWEM) pp. 5.1–5.24.

Begg, D., Fischer, S. and Dornbusch, R. (1991) *Economics* (New York: McGraw-Hill).

Bennett, R. (1991) *Attaining Quality: the agenda for local business services in the 1990s*, Research Paper (London School of Economics, Department of Geography).

Bennett, R., Wicks, P. and McCoshan, A. (1992) *TECs and LECs: early development*, Research Paper (London School of Economics, Department of Geography).

Benyon, H., Hudson, R. and Cox, A. (1990) 'Opencast coalmining and the politics of coal production', *Capital and Class*, 40, pp. 849–114.

Berge, E. (1990) 'Some notes towards a property rights perspective on institutional change in the welfare state', INAS–NOTAT 1990:0 (Institutt for Socialforsking, Oslo).

Berkes, F. (1989) *Common Property Resources* (Belhaven).

Blackman, T. (1991) 'People-sensitive planning: communication, property and social action', *Planning Practice and Research*, 6 (3) pp. 11–15.

Blowers, A. (1987) 'Transition or transformation? Environmental policy under Thatcher', *Public Administration*, 65, pp. 277–94.

Blowers, A., Lowry, D. and Solomon, B. D. (1991) *The International Politics of Nuclear Waste* (Macmillan).

Blunkett, D. and Jackson, K. (1987) *Democracy in Crisis: the town halls respond* (Hogarth Press).

Boddy, M. and Fudge, C. (eds), (1984) Local Socialism? Labour Councils and New Left Alternatives (Macmillan).

Bovaird, T. (1992) 'Local economic development and the city', *Urban Studies*, 29 (3/4) pp. 343–68.

Bowers, J. (1990) 'The consequences of declining support for agriculture', in J. Bowers (ed.), *Agriculture and Rural Land Use: in the the 1990s* (Swindon: ESRC) pp. 23–34.

Braybrooke, D. and Lindblom, C. (1963) *A Strategy of Decision: policy evaluation as a social process* (Collier-Macmillan).

Breheny, M. and Congdon, P. (eds), (1989) *Growth and Change in a Core Region* (Pion).

Brindley, T., Rydin, Y. and Stoker, G. (1989) *Remaking Planning* (Unwin Hyman).

Broadbent, T. A. (1977) *Planning and Profit in the Urban Economy* (Methuen).

Bromley, D. (1991) *Environment and Economy* (Oxford: Basil Blackwell).

Brownill, S. (1990) *Developing London's Dockland* (Paul Chapman).

Bruton, M. and Nicholson, D. (1987) *Local Planning in Practice* (Hutchinson).

Buck, N., Gordon, I., Young, K. with Ermish, J. and Mills L. (1986) *The London Employment Problem* (Oxford: Oxford University Press).

Buckwell, A. (1990) 'Economic signals, farmers' response and environmental change' in J. Bowers (ed.), *Agriculture and Rural Land Use: in the the 1990s* (Swindon: ESRC) pp. 7–22.

Burkitt, B. (1984) *Radical Political Economy* (Brighton: Wheatsheaf).

Burns, D. (1988) 'The decentralisation of local authority planning', paper to Radical Planning Initiatives Conference, Polytechnic of Central London (8 January).

Byrne, T. (1986) *Local Government in Britain* (Penguin).

Cairncross, F. (1991) *Costing the Earth* (Business Books).

Carson, R. (1962) *Silent Spring* (New York: Fawcett Crest).

Carr, S. and Tait, J. (1990) 'Farmers' attitude to consumption', *Built Environment*, 16 (3) pp. 218–31.

Carter, N., Brown, T. and Abbott, T. (1991) *The Relationship between Expenditure-based Plans and Development Plans*, Final Report (Leicester Polytechnic, School of the Built Environment).

Castells, M. (1977) *The Urban Question*, English edn (Edward Arnold).

—— (1978) *City, Class and Power* (Macmillan).

—— (1983) *The City and the Grass Roots: a cross-cultural theory of urban social movements* (Edward Arnold).

Chapman, R. A. (1984) *Leadership in the British Civil Service* (Croom Helm).

Cherry, G. (1972) *Urban Change and Planning* (Henley on Thames: Foulis).

—— (1974) *The Evolution of British Town Planning (1914–74)* (Lawrence Hill).

Cheshire, P. and Sheppard, S. (1989) 'British Planning Policy and Access to Housing: some empirical estimates', *Urban Studies*, 26, pp. 469–85.

Child, J. (1977) *Organization: a guide to problems and practice* (Harper & Row).

Christensen, T. (1979) *Neighbourhood Survival* (Prism).

CIoTr (1990) *Paying for Progress* (CIoTr).

Civic Trust (1991) *Audit of the Environment* (Civic Trust).

Clark, M. and Herington, J. (1988) *The Role of EIA in the Planning Process* (Mansell).

Clifford Chance (1992) *European Environmental Law Guide* (Clifford Chance).

Cloke, P. and Goodwin, M. (1992) 'Conceptualizing countryside change: from post-Fordism to rural structured coherence' *Transactions of the Institute of British Geographers*, 17 (3) pp. 321–36.

Collins, R. (1990) 'Changing conceptions in the sociology of the professions', in R. Torstendahl and M. Burrage (eds), *The Formation of Professions: knowledge, state and strategy* (Sage), pp. 11–23.

Commission of the European Communities (1992) *European Community Environmental Legislation Vol. 1 General Policy* (Brussels: CEC).

Confederation of British Industry (1989) *Roads to Growth* (CBI).

Cooke, P. (1983) *Theories of Planning and Spatial Development* (Hutchinson).

—— (1989) 'The Local Question – Revival or Survival?', in P. Cooke (ed.), *Localities* (Unwin Hyman) pp. 296–306.

Cox, A. (1984) *Adversary Politics and Land* (Cambridge: Cambridge University Press).

Cox, G., Lowe, P. and Winter, M. (1990) 'Private rights and public responsibilities: the prospects for agriculture and environmental controls', in J.

Bowers (ed.), *Agriculture and Rural Land Use: into the 1990s* (Swindon: ESRC) pp. 70–90.

Crabtree, J. R. (1991) 'National Park designation in Scotland', *Land Use Policy*, 8 (3) pp. 241–52.

Cullingworth, J. B. (1975a) *Environmental Planning Vol.1 Reconstruction and Land Use Planning 1939–47* (HMSO).

—— (1975b) *Environmental Planning Vol.2 National Parks and Recreation in the Countryside* (HMSO).

—— (1979) *Environmental Planning Vol.3 New Town Policies* (HMSO).

—— (1980) *Environmental Planning Vol.4 Land Values, Compensation and Betterment* (HMSO).

—— (1988) *Town and Country Planning* (Unwin Hyman).

Dargie, T. and Briggs, D. (1991) *State of the Scottish Environment* (Perth: Scottish Wildlife and Countryside Link).

Davies, H., Edwards, D., Roberts, C., Rosborough, L. and Sales, R. (1986) *The Relationship between Development Plans and Development Control and Appeals*, Working Papers in Land Management and Development, Nos 10, 11, 12 (University of Reading, Department of Land Management).

Davies, J. (1972) *The Evangelistic Bureaucrat* (Tavistock).

Dearlove, J. (1973) *The Politics of Policy in Local Government* (Cambridge: Cambridge University Press).

de la Court, T. (1990) *Beyond Brundtland* (Zed).

Dennis, N. (1972) *Public Participation and Planner's Blight* (Faber).

DoE/Welsh Office (1986) *River Quality in England and Wales 1985* (HMSO).

DoE (1988) *Enterprise Zones Information 1987/8* (HMSO).

DoE (1991a) *Policy Appraisal and the Environment* (HMSO).

DoE (1991b) *Environmental Assessment: a guide to the procedures* (HMSO).

DoE (1992) *Derelict Land Grant – Developments and Achievements Report 1988–92* (DoE).

Desai, M. (1979) *Marxian Economics* (Oxford: Basil Blackwell).

Dobson, A. (1990) *Green Political Thought* (Unwin Hyman).

Donnison, D. and Middleton, A. (1987) *Regenerating the Inner City: Glasgow's experience* (Routledge & Kegan Paul).

Downs, A. (1992) *Stuck in Traffic* (Washington: The Brookings Institute with The Lincoln Institute of Land Policy).

Duncan, S. (1989) 'Development gains and housing provision in Britain and Sweden', *Transactions of the Institute of British Geographers*, 14, pp. 157–72.

Duncan, S. and Goodwin, M. (1988) *The Local State and Uneven Development: behind the local government crisis* (Cambridge: Polity Press).

Dunleavy, P. (1980) *Urban Political Analysis* (Macmillan).

Dunleavy, P. and O'Leary, B. (1987) *Theories of the State: the politics of liberal democracy* (Macmillan).

Dwyer, J. (1991) *The County Wildlife Trusts*, Discussion Paper, No. 30 (University of Cambridge, Department of Land Economy).

Eggertsson, T. (1990) *Economic Behaviour and Institutions* (Cambridge: Cambridge University Press).

Elkin, S. (1974) *Politics and Land Use Planning: the London experience* (Cambridge: Cambridge University Press).

Elkington, J. (1987) *The Green Capitalists: how industry can make money and protect the environment* (Gollancz).

—— (1989) *The Environmental Audit* (World Wildlife Fund).

Ekins, P., and Max-Neef, M. (eds), (1992) *Real-life Economics: understanding wealth creation* (Routledge).

Elson, M. (1986) *Green Belts* (Heinemann).

English Heritage (1992) *Buildings at Risk: a sample survey* (English Heritage).

English Historic Towns Forum (EHTF) (1992) *Townscape in Trouble* (Butterworths).

Engwicht, D. (1992) *Towards an Eco-city* (Oxford: Jon Carpenter).

Evans, A. (1973) *The Economics of Residential Location* (Macmillan).

—— (1987) *House Prices and Land Prices in the South East – a review*, paper prepared for the HouseBuilders Federation, HD87.308 (HBF).

—— (1988) 'South-east England in the eighties: explanations for a house price explosion', in M. Breheny and P. Congdon (eds), *Growth and Change in a Core Region* (Pion) pp. 130–49.

Fairley, J. (1992) 'Scottish local authorities and local enterprise companies: a developing relationship?', *Regional Studies*, 26 (2) pp. 193–207.

Faludi, A. (1973) *Planning Theory* (Oxford: Pergamon).

Faludi, A. (ed.) (1973) *A Reader in Planning Theory* (Oxford: Pergamon).

Faulks, J. (1991) 'The changing attitude towards liability for damage to the environment under European Community law', *European Environment*, 1, 3, pp. 17–20.

Fennell, R. (1990) 'Socio-structural initiatives under the CAP', in J. Bowers (ed.), *Agriculture and Rural Land Use: in the 1990s* (Swindon: ESRC) pp. 91–102.

Fine, B. (1984) 'The future of British coal', *Capital and Class*, 23, pp. 67–82.

—— (1990) *The Coal Question* (Routledge).

Foley, D. (1960) 'British town planning: one ideology or three?', British Journal of Sociology, 11 (3) pp. 211–31.

Forester, J. (1989) *Planning in the Face of Power* (Berkeley: University of California Press).

Forrest, R. and Murie, A. (1990) *Residualisation and council housing: a statistical update*, Working Paper, No. 91 (University of Bristol, School of Advanced Urban Studies).

Fortlage, C. (1990) *Environmental Assessment: or practical guide* (Aldershot: Gower).

Fothergill, S. and Gudgin, G. (1982) *Unequal Growth: urban and regional employment change in the UK* (Heinemann).

Fothergill, S., Monk, S. and Perry, M. (1987) *Property and Industrial Development* (Hutchinson).

Foulsham, J. (1987) 'Women's needs and planning practice: a critical evaluation of recent local authority practice', paper to Radical Planning Initiatives Workshop, Polytechnic of Central London (January 8).

Franklin, M. with Wilke, M. (1990) *Britain in the European Community* (Pinter).

Fraser, W. (1984) *Principles of Property Investment and Pricing* (Macmillan).

Friends of the Earth (FoE) (1991) *Traffic Free Towns* (FoE).

—— (1992) *Environmentally Sensitive Areas: assessment and recommendations* (FoE).

Galbraith, J. (1981) *The Galbraith Reader*, selected by the editors of *Gambit* (Penguin).

Gerald Eve and Department of Land Economy, Cambridge University (1992) *The Relationship between House Prices and Land Supply*, DoE Research Report (HMSO).

Giddens, A. (1984) *The Constitution of Society* (Cambridge: Polity Press).

Gilg, A. (ed.), (1992) *Restructuring the Countryside: environmental policy in practice* (Aldershot: Avebury Press).

Gillet, E. (1983) *Investment in the Environment: recent housing, planning and transport policies in Scotland* (Aberdeen: Aberdeen University Press).

Godschalk, D. (1991) 'Negotiating Intergovernmental development policy conflicts: practice-based guidelines', paper to AESOP Conference, Oxford Polytechnic (July).

Goodchild, B. (1990) 'Planning and the modern/postmodern debate', *Town Planning Review* 61 (2) pp. 119–37.

Goodchild, R. and Munton, R. (1985) *Development and the Landowner* (Allen & Unwin).

Goodwin, P. (1990) 'Towards a Consensus in UK Transport Policy', paper to PTRC Summer Annual Meeting (Brighton) TSV Ref.548.

Graham, J. (1992) 'Post-Fordism as politics; the political consequences of narratives on the left', *Environment and Planning D: Society and Space*, 10, pp. 393–410.

Granovetter, M. and Swedberg, R. (1992) *The Sociology of Economic Life* (Colorado: Westview Press).

Greed, C., (1991) *Surveying Sisters* (Routledge).

Grimley, J.R. Eve in association with Thames Polytechnic and Alsop Wilkinson (1992) *The Use of Planning Agreements* (HMSO).

Guardian (1992) 'Britain's beaches fail Blue Flag test' (5 June, p. 7).

Gyford, J. (1985) *The Politics of Local Socialism* (Allen & Unwin).

—— (1991) *Citizens, Consumers and Councils* (Macmillan).

Hague, C. (1984) *The Development of Planning Thought: a critical perspective* (Hutchinson).

Haigh, N. (1989) *EEC Environmental Policy and Britain* (2nd ed. rev.) (Longman).

Hall, M. (1988) 'The international debt crisis: recent developments', *Capital and Class*, 35, pp. 7–17.

Hall, P., Gracey, H., Drewett, R., and Thomas, R. (1973) *The Containment of Urban England* (Allen & Unwin).

Hall, S. (1988) *The Hard Road to Renewal: Thatcherism and the crisis of the Left* (Verso).

Hallett, S., Hanley, N., Moffatt, I. and Taylor-Duncan, K. (1991) 'UK Water Pollution Control: a review of legislation and practice', *European Environment*, 1 (3) pp. 7–13.

Hambleton, R. and Hogget, P. (eds), (1984) *The Politics of Decentralisation*, Working Paper, No. 46 (University of Bristol, School of Advanced Urban Studies).

Hardin, G. (1968) 'The tragedy of the commons', *Science*, 162, pp. 1243–8.

Harding, A. (1990) 'Property interests and urban growth coalitions in the UK: a brief encounter', paper to Property-led Urban Regeneration Seminar, University of Newcastle (29–30 March).

Harrison, A. (1977) *Economics and Land Use Planning* (Newbury: Policy Journals).

Hart, H. (1961) *The Concept of Law* (Oxford: Clarendon Press).

Harvey, D. (1973) *Social Justice and the City* (Edward Arnold).

—— (1982) *Limits to Capital* (Oxford: Basil Blackwell).

—— (1985) *The Urbanisation of Capital* (Oxford: Basil Blackwell).

—— (1989) *The Condition of Postmodernity* (Oxford: Basil Blackwell).

Harvey, J. (1981) *The Economics of Real Property* (Macmillan).

Hazardous Waste Inspectorate (1988) *Third Report* (HMSO).

Healey, P. (1983) *Local Plans in British Land Use Planning* (Oxford: Pergamon).

Healey, P. (1990) 'Policy processes in planning', *Policy and Politics*, 18 (1) pp. 91–103.

Healey, P. (1992a) 'An institutional model of the development process', *Journal of Property Research*, 9 (1) pp. 33–44.

Healey, P. (1992b) 'A planner's day; knowledge and action in communicative practice' *American Planning Association Journal* Winter, pp. 9–20.

Healey, P. and Barrett, S. (1990) 'Structure and agency in land and property development processes: some ideas for research', *Urban Studies*, 27 (1) pp. 89–104.

Healey, P. and Gilroy, R. (1990) 'Towards a people-sensitive planning', *Planning Practice and Research*, 5 (2) pp. 21–29.

Healey, P. and Nabarro, R. (eds), (1990) *Land and Property Development in a Changing Context* (Aldershot: Gower).

Healey, P., Ennis F. and Purdue, M. (1992) 'Planning gain and the "new" local plans', *Town and Country Planning*, February, pp. 39–43.

Healey, P., McDougall, G. and Thomas, M. (1982) *Planning Theory: prospects for the 1980s* (Oxford: Pergamon).

Healey, P., Davis, J., Wood, M. and Elson, M. (1982) *The Implementation of Development Plans*, Report of an exploratory study for DoE (Oxford Polytechnic, Department of Town Planning).

Healey, P., McNamara, P., Elson, M. and Doak, A. (1988) *Land Use Planning and the Mediation of Urban Change* (Cambridge: Cambridge University Press).

Heilbronner, R. (1983) *The Worldly Philosphers* (Penguin).

Hennebury, J. (1988) 'Conflict in the industrial property market', *Town Planning Review*, 59 (3) pp. 241–62.

Her Majesty's Inspectorate of Pollution (HMIP) (1988) *The Licensing of Waste Facilities*, Waste Management Paper, No. 4 (HMSO).
—— (1991) *Fourth Annual Report* (1990–91) (HMSO).
Herington, J. (1984) *The Outer City* (Harper & Row).
—— (1989) *The Future of Green Belts*, Discussion Paper (Regional Studies Association).
Hobbs, P. (1992) 'The economic determinants of post-war British town planning' *Progress in Planning*, 38, (3) pp. 180–300.
Holland, S. (1976) *Capital versus the Regions* (Macmillan).
Housing Research Foundation (HRF) (1986) *Impact of UDG/DLG on Urban Dwelling and Greenfield Development*, Report by Coopers & Lybrand Association (HRF).
Hoyle, B. S. and Knowles, R. D. (1992) *Modern Transport Georgraphy* (Belhaven).
Hudson, R. and Sadler, D. (1990) 'State policies and the changing geography of the coal industry in the UK in the 1980s and 1990s', *Transactions of the Institute of British Geographers*, 15, pp. 435–54.
Institute of Water Engineers and Managers (1989) *Agriculture and the Environment*, Technical Papers of Annual Symposium, University of York (IWEM).
Jacobs, J. (1985) 'The Urban Development Grant', *Policy and Politics*, 13 (2) pp. 191–9.
Jessop, B. (1982) *The Capitalist State* (Oxford: Martin Robertson).
Johnson, S. (1973) *The Politics of the Environment* (Tom Stacey).
Johnson, T. (1972) *Professions and Power* (Macmillan).
Johnston, R. (1989) *Environmental Problems: nature, economy and state* (Belhaven).
Jones, C., Lee, N. and Wood, C. (1991) *UK Environmental Statements 1988–1900*, Occasional Paper, 29 (University of Manchester, Department of Planning and Landscape).
Jowell, J. and Noble, D. (1981) 'Structure Plans as Instruments of Social and Economic Policy', *Journal of Planning and Environmental Law* (July) pp. 466–80.
Kakönen, J. (1988) *Natural Resources and Conflicts in the Changing International System* (Aldershot: Gower).
Kendrick, M. (1987), 'Planning Appeals in Northamptonshire 1979–86', paper prepared in the Planning Department, Northampton County Council.
Kimber, R. and Richardson, J. (1974) *Pressure Groups in Britain: a reader* (Dent).
Kirk, G. (1980) *Urban Planning in a Capitalist Society* (Croom Helm).
Kivell, P. (1987) 'Derelict land in England: policy responses to a continuing problem', *Regional Studies*, 21 (3) pp. 265–9.
Laffin, M. and Young, K. (1990) *Professionalism in Local Government: change and challenge* (Longman).
Lash, S. and Urry, J. (1987) *The End of Organised Capitalism* (Cambridge: Polity).

Lawless, P. (1988) 'British Inner Urban Policy: a review', *Regional Studies*, 22 (6) pp. 531–40.

—— (1991) 'Urban policy in the Thatcher decade: English inner city policy 1979–90', *Environment and Planning*, 9, pp. 15–30.

LBA (1990) *Road Pricing for London* (LBA).

Leach, S. (1989) 'Strengthening local democracy? The government's response to Widdicombe', in Stewart and G. Stoker (eds) (1989), *The Future of Local Government* (Macmillan) pp. 101–22.

Leyland, D. (1986) 'Town planning and business strategy', in K. G. Willis (ed.), *Contemporary Issues in Town Planning* (Aldershot: Gower) pp. 31–43.

Lindblom, C. (1977) *Politics and Markets* (New York: Basic Books).

Lipsey, R. (1989) *An Introduction to Positive Economics* (Weidenfeld and Nicholson).

Little, J. (forthcoming) *Gender, Planning and the Policy Process* (Oxford: Pergamon).

Livingstone, K. (1987) *If Voting Changed Anything They'd Abolish It* (William Collins).

Lloyd, M. and Botham, R. (1985) 'The ideology and implementation of Enterprise Zones in Britain', *Urban Law and Policy*, 7 (1) pp. 33–55.

Longley, P., Batty, M., Shepherd, J. and Sadler, G. (1992) 'Do green belts change the shape of urban areas? A preliminary analysis of the settlement geography of south east England', *Regional Studies*, 26 (5) pp. 437–52.

Lowe, P. (1986) *Urban Social Movements: the city after Castells* (Macmillan).

Lowe, P., Cox, G., MacEwan, M., Winter, T. and Winter, M. (1986) *Countryside Conflicts: the politics of farming, forestry and conservation* (Temple Smith/Gower).

Lowe, P. and Goyder, J. (1983) *Environmental Groups in Politics* (George Allen & Unwin).

MacEwan, A. and MacEwan, M. (1987) *Greenprints for the countryside?: the story of Britain's National Parks* (Allen & Unwin).

Macpherson, C. B. (1978) *Property: mainstream and critical positions* (Oxford: Basil Blackwell).

Maitland, R. and Newman, P. (1989) 'Meet the new management of planning', *Planning*, 846, pp. 32–3.

Mallalieu, K. and Townroe, P. (1991) 'Entrepreneurship and the development of small business: skill, competence and training needs', paper to AESOP Congress, Oxford Polytechnic (June).

March, J. and Olsen, J. (1989) *Rediscovering Institutions: the organisational basis of politics* (New York: Free Press).

Marriott, O. (1969) *The Property Boom* (Pan).

Marshall, T. (1992) *Environmental sustainability: London's Unitary Development Plans and strategic planning*, Occasional Paper, No. 4/1992 (South Bank University, Faculty of the Built Environment).

Marshall, T. and Roberts, P. (1992) 'Business and the environment', *Planning Practice and Research*, 7 (2) pp. 25–8.

Masser, I. (ed.), (1983) *Evaluating urban planning efforts: approaches to policy analysis* (Aldershot: Gower).

Massey, D. (1984) *Spatial Divisions of Labour* (Macmillan).

Massey, D. (1988) 'Uneven development: social change and spatial divisions of labour', in D. Massey and J. Allen (eds), *Uneven Re-Development* (Milton Keynes: Open University Press).

Massey, D. and Catalano, A. (1978) *Capital and Land* (Edward Arnold).

Mather, A. S. (1991) 'Pressures on British forest policy: prologue to the post-industrial forest?', *Area*, 23 (3) pp. 245–53.

Matson, M. and Whitney, D. (1985) 'Urban Development Grants: evaluation of practice in Yorkshire and Humberside', paper to Research in Local Land Use Planning, Oxford Polytechnic (31 May/1 June).

McCormick, J. (1991) *British Politics and the Environment* (Earthscan).

Mertz, S. (1989) 'The European Economic Community Directive on Environmental Assessments: how will it affect United Kingdom developers?', *Journal of Planning and Environment Law* (July) pp. 483–97.

Midwinter, A., Keating, M. and Mitchell, J. (1991) *Politics and Public Policy in Scotland* (Macmillan).

Miller, C. (1990) 'Development Control as an instrument of environmental management', *Town Planning Review*, 61 (3) pp. 231–45.

Mishan, E. J. (1982) *Introduction to Political Economy* (Hutchinson).

Mogridge, M. (1990) *Travel in Towns - jam yesterday, jam today, jam tomorrow?* (Macmillan).

Monk, S. (1991a) *Planning, Land Supply and House Prices: a literature review* Monograph, No. 21 (Cambridge University, Department of Land Economy/Property Research Unit).

—— (1991b) *The Speculative Housebuilder*, Monograph, No. 31 (Cambridge University, Department of Land Economy/Property Research Unit).

—— (1991c) *Planning, Land Supply and House Prices: the national and regional picture*, Monograph, No. 33 (Cambridge University, Department of Land Economy/Property Research Unit).

Montgomery, J. and Thornley, A. (1990) *Radical Planning Initiatives* (Aldershot: Gower).

Morphet, J. (1992a) 'Continental doors open to mobile professionals', *Planning*, 900, pp. 26–7.

—— (1992b) 'A question of control over professional entry routes', *Planning*, 955, p.17.

Mowle, A. and Evans, S. (1990) 'Conserving the rural environment – reconciling farmer and nature in the less favoured areas', in J. Bowers (ed.), *Agriculture and Rural Land Use: in the the 1990s* (Swindon: ESRC) pp. 118–31.

Moyars, B. (1984) *Global Dumping Ground* (Lutterworth).

Munton, R. (1983) *London's Green Belt: containment in practice* (Allen & Unwin).

Myerson, G. and Rydin, Y. (1991) 'Language and argument in people-sensitive planning', *Planning Practice and Research*, 6 (1) pp. 31–3.

Myrdal, G. (1957) *Economic Theory and Under-developed Regions* (Duckworth).

National Audit Office (1986) *Enterprise Zones* (HMSO).

National Rivers Authority (NRA) (1991a) *The Quality of Rivers, Canals and Estuaries in England and Wales* (NRA).

—— (1991b) *Statutory Water Quality Objectives Scheme* (NRA).

Newell, M. (1977) *An Introduction to the Economics of Urban Land Use* (Estates Gazette).

Newman, P. (1991) 'Quality, democracy and directions for local government', *Planning Practice and Research*, 6, pp. 29–30.

Oatley, N. (1991) 'Streamlining the system: implications of the B1 business class for planning policy', *Planning Practice and Research*, 6 (1) pp. 19–28.

Oc, T. (1991) 'Planning natural surveillance back into city centres', *Town and Country Planning* (September) pp. 237–9.

O'Connor, J. (1973) *The Fiscal Crisis of the State* (New York: St Martin's Press).

Office of Water Services (1991) *Paying for water: a time for decisions* (Offwat).

O'Riordan, T., Kemp, R. and Purdue, M. (1988) *Sizewell B: an anatomy of the inquiry* (Macmillan).

O'Riordan, T., and Turner, K. (eds), (1983) *An Annotated Reader in Environmental Planning and Management* (Oxford: Pergamon).

O'Sullivan, P. (1981) *Geographical Economics* (Penguin).

Outer Circle Policy Unit, with Justice and Council for Science and Society (1979) *The Big Public Inquiry* (Outer Circle Policy Unit).

Owens, S. (1989) 'Integrated pollution control in the United Kingdom: prospects and problems', *Environment and Planning C: Government and Policy*, 7, pp. 81–91.

—— (1992) *Land Use Planning and Climate Change*, DoE Research Report (HMSO).

Oxford Polytechnic and ERL Consultants (1992) *Planning, Pollution and Waste Management*, DoE Research Report (HMSO).

Pacione, M. (1990) 'The site selection process of speculative residential developers in an urban area', *Housing Studies*, 5 (4) pp. 219–28.

Pahl, R. (1975) *Whose City* (Penguin).

Parkinson, M. (1989) 'The Thatcher Government's urban policy, 1979–89', *Town Planning Review*, 60 (4) pp. 421–40.

Pearce, D. (ed.) (1991) *Blueprint 2: Greening the World Economy* (Earthscan).

Pearce, D., Markanya, A. and Barbier, E. (1989) *Blueprint for a Green Economy* (Penguin).

Pearce, D. and Turner, R. K. (1990) *Economics of Natural Resources and the Environment* (Hemel Hempstead: Harvester-Wheatsheaf).

Pearce, F. (1982) *Watershed* (Junction Books).

Peet, R. (1992) 'Some critical questions for anti-essentialism', *Antipode*, 24 (2) pp. 113–30.

Pepper, D. (1984) *The Roots of Modern Environmentalism* (Croom Helm).

Pickvance, C. (ed.), (1976) *Urban Sociology: critical essays* (Tavistock).

Planning (1991) 'Singling out the impact of environmental policy', (20 September, p. 15).

Pollit, C., Lewis, L., Negro, J. and Patten, J. (eds), (1979) *Public Policy in Theory and Practice* (Hodder & Stoughton).

Pountney, M. and Kingsbury, P. (1983) 'Aspects of development control', *Town Planning Review*, 54 (2) pp. 138–54 and (3) pp. 285–303.

Ranson, S., Jones, G. and Walsh K. (eds), (1985) *Between Centre and Locality* (Allen & Unwin).

Reade, E. (1987) *British Town and Country Planning* (Milton Keynes: Open University Press).

Redclift, M. (1987) *Sustainable Development* (Methuen).

Rees, J. (1989) Water Privatisation and the Environment, Research Paper (London School of Economics, Department of Geography).

—— (1990) *Natural Resources* (Methuen).

Reeve, A. (1986) *Property* (Macmillan).

Rhodes, R. (1981) *Control and Power in Central–Local Relations* (Aldershot: Gower).

Rhys, A. D. (1991) *The Greening of Business* (Aldershot: Gower).

Richards, B. (1990) *Transport in Cities* (ADT Press).

Richardson, H. (1971) *Urban Economics* (Penguin).

Roberts, J., Elliott, D. and Houghton, T. (1991) *Privatising Electricity: the politics of power* (Belhaven).

Roberts, P. (1989) 'Coal and the environment: planning and management issues for the future of the coalfields', *Environment and Planning A* 21 (12) pp. 85–96.

Robinson, M. (1992) *The Greening of British Party Politics* (Manchester: Manchester University Press).

Roddick, A. (1992) *Body and Soul* (Century Hutchinson).

Rose, C. (1990) *The Dirty Man of Europe* (Simon & Schuster).

Rowan-Robinson, J. and Lloyd, M. G. (1986) 'Lifting the Burden: a means or an end?', *Local Government Studies*, 12 (3) pp. 51–64.

—— (1991) 'National Planning Guidelines: a strategic opportunity wasting away?', *Planning Practice and Research*, 6 (3) pp. 16–19.

Rowlands, I. (1992) 'Environmental issues in world politics', in N. Rengger and J. Daylis (eds), *Dilemmas of World Politics* (Oxford: Oxford University Press) pp. 287–309.

Rydin, Y. (1986) *Housing Land Policy* (Aldershot: Gower).

—— (1988) 'Joint Housing Studies: housebuilders, planners and the availability of land', *Local Government Studies*, 14 (2) pp. 69–80.

—— (1992) 'Environmental Impacts and the Property Market', in M. Breheny (ed.), *Urban Form and Sustainable Development* (Pion).

Rydin, Y., Home, R. and Taylor, K. (1990) *The Policy Implications of the Planning Appeals System*, Report to Association of District Councils (February).

Rydin, Y. and Myerson, G. (1990) 'Explaining and interpreting ideological effects: a rhetorical approach to 'green belts', *Environment and Planning D: Society and Space*, 7, pp. 463–79.

Samuelson, P. and Nordhaus, W. (1989) *Economics* (New York: McGraw-Hill).

Sandbach, F. (1982) *Principles of Pollution Control* (Longman).

Saunders, P. (1979) *Urban Politics: a sociological interpretation* (Hutchinson).

—— (1985) 'The forgotten dimension of central–local relations: theorising the "regional state"', *Environment and Planning C: Government and Policy*, 3, pp. 149–62.

Sayer, A. (1991) *Radical Geography and the Crisis of Marxist Political Economy*, Working Paper, No. 81 (University of Sussex, Centre for Urban and Regional Research).

Schmidheiny, S. (1992) *Changing Course* (Cambridge, Mass.: MIT Press).

SLABS Research Unit (1985) *Housing Land in Urban Areas*, Final Report (Leicester Polytechnic, School of Land and Building Studies).

Self, P. and Storing, H. (1962) *The State and the Farmer* (Allen & Unwin).

Selman, P. (ed.) (1988) *Countryside Planning in Practice: the Scottish experience* (Stirling: Stirling University Press).

Shaw, K. (1990) 'The lost world of local politics revisited: in search of the non-elected local state', *Regional Studies*, 24 (2) pp. 180–4.

Sheail, J. (1981) *Rural Conservation in Inter-war Britain* (Oxford: Clarendon).

Sherlock, H. (1990) *Cities are Good For Us* (Transport 2000).

Shoard, M. (1987) *This Land is our Land* (Paladin).

Short, J. (1984) *The Urban Arena: capital, state and community in contemporary Britain* (Macmillan).

Short, J., Fleming, S. and Witt, S. (1986) *Housebuilding, Planning and Community Action* (Routledge & Kegan Paul).

Shucksmith, M. (1988) 'Policy aspects of housebuilding on farmland in Britain', *Land Development Studies*, 5 (2) pp. 129–38.

—— (1990) *Housebuilding in Britain's Countryside* (Routledge).

Simmie, J. (1981) *Power, Property and Corporatism* (Macmillan).

Smallbone, D. (1991) *Enterprise agencies in local economic development: some policy issues*, paper to AESOP Congress, Oxford Polytechnic (June).

Smith, D. (ed.) (1992) *Business and the Environment* (Paul Chapman).

Smith, N. and Williams, P. (1986) *Gentrification of the City* (Allen & Unwin).

Smyth, H. (1985) *Property Companies and the Construction Industry in Britain* (Cambridge: Cambridge University Press).

South East Economic Development Strategy (SEEDS) (1987) *Changing Buses: a study of bus transport planning, deregulation and privatisation in seven towns*, SEEDS Strategy Study, No. 4 (SEEDS).

Spencer, K. (1989) 'Local government and the housing reforms', in J. Stewart and G. Stoker (eds), *The Future of Local Government* (Macmillan).

Spooner, D., Arnett, R. and Justice, M. (1992) 'Building a geographical base for integrated pollution control: some problems', *Area*, 24 (2) pp. 105–12.

Spretnak, C. and Capra, F. (1985) *Green Politics: the global promise* (Paladin).

Stewart, J. and Stoker, G. (eds), (1989) *The Future of Local Government* (Macmillan).

Stoker, G. (1989a) 'Creating a local government for a post-fordist society: the Thatcherite project?', in G. Stoker and J. Stewart (eds), *The Future of Local Government* (Macmillan).

—— (1989b) 'Urban Development Corporations: a review', *Regional Studies*, 23 (2) pp. 159–67.

—— (1991) *The Politics of Local Government* (2nd edn) (Macmillan).

Stoker, G. and Wilson, D. (1991) 'The lost world of British local pressure groups', *Public Policy and Administration*, 6 (2) pp. 20–34.

Suddards, R. (1988) *Listed Buildings: the law and practice of historic buildings, ancient monuments and conservation areas* (Sweet & Maxwell).

Sutcliffe, A. (1981) *British Town Planning: the formative years* (Leicester: Leicester University Press).

Swedberg, R. (1990) *Economics and Sociology: redefining their boundaries* (Oxford: Princeton University Press).

Symes, D. (1990) 'The rural community in lowland Britain: counting the garden gnomes', in J. Bowers (ed.), *Agriculture and Rural Land Use: in the the 1990s* (Swindon: ESRC) pp. 103–17.

Thornley, A. (1991) *Urban Planning under Thatcherism: the challenge of the market* (Routledge).

Trench, S. (1991) 'Reclaiming the night', *Town and Country Planning* (September) pp. 235–7.

Tromans, S. and Clarkson, M. (1991) 'The Environmental Protection Act 1990: its relevance to planning controls', *Journal of Planning and Environmental Law*, pp. 507–15.

Underwood, J. (1980) *Town Planners in Search of a Role*, Occasional Paper, No. 6, (University of Bristol, School of Advanced Urban Studies).

Valentine, G. (1992) 'Images of danger: women's sources of information about the spatial distribution of male violence', *Area*, 24 (1) pp. 22–9.

Veblen, T. (1976) *The Portable Veblen*, edited and with an introduction by M. Lerner (Penguin).

Vincent, S. and Marshall, R. (1991) 'The role of local planning authorities in urban nature conservation', *Planning Practice and Research* 6 (3) pp. 5–10.

Wainwright, H. (1987) *Labour: a tale of two cities* (Hogarth Press).

Walsh, F., Lee, N. and Wood, C. (1991) *The Environmental Assessment of Opencast Coal Mines*, Occasional Paper 28, EIA Centre, University of Manchester.

Wannop, U. (1985) 'Introduction to symposium on "leveraging" urban development: a comparison of urban policy directions and programme impact in the United States and Britain', *Policy and Politics*, 13 (2) pp. 176–219.

Wates, N. (1976) *The Battle for Tolmers Square* (Routledge & Kegan Paul).

Wathern, P. (ed.) (1988) *Environmental Impact Assessment: theory and practice* (Unwin Hyman).

Weale, A., O'Riordan, T. and Kramme, L. (1991) *Controlling Pollution in the Round* (Anglo-German Foundation).

Westbrook, D. (1991) 'Environmental Policy in the European Community: observations on the European Environmental Agency', *The Harvard Environmental Law Review*, 15 (1) pp. 257–273.

Whitby, M. (1990) 'Ex-post and ex-ante view of forest employment: to the future with the wisdom of hindsight?', in J. Bowers (ed.), *Agriculture and Rural Land Use: in the 1990s* (Swindon: ESRC) pp. 50–7.

Whitehand, J. (1989) 'Development pressure, development control and suburban townscape change', *Town Planning Review*, 60 (4) pp. 403–20.

—— (1990) 'Makers of the residential landscape: conflict and change in outer London', *Transactions of the Institute of British Geographers*, 15, pp. 87–101.

Whitehand, J. and Larkham, P. (1991a) 'Suburban cramming and development control', *Journal of Property Research*, 8, pp. 147–59.

—— (1991b) 'Housebuilding in the back garden: reshaping suburban townscapes in the Midlands and South East England', *Area*, 23 (1) pp. 57–65.

Wilder, C. L. and Plant, G. (1992) *What Environmental Institutions does the UK need?*, Background Paper, 2nd Round Table Conference, London School of Economics, Centre for Environmental Law and Policy (13 July).

Williamson, D. (1975) *Markets and Hierarchies: analysis and anti-trust implications* (New York: Free Press).

Willis, K. (1980) *The Economics of Town and Country Planning* (Granada).

Willmott, P. and Hutchinson, R. (eds), (1992) *Urban Trends 1* (Policy Studies Institute).

Wood, C. and Hooper, P. (1988) 'The effects of the relaxation of planning controls in enterprise zones on industrial pollution', paper to Planning Practice and Research Conference, Polytechnic of Central London (January).

Wood, C. and Jones, C. (1991) *Monitoring Environmental Assessment and Planning*, Report of Department of the Environment Research Project (HMSO).

World Commission on Environment and Development (WCED) (1987) *Our Common Future* (Oxford: Oxford University Press).

Yearley, S. and Milton, K. (1990) 'Environmentalism and direct rule', *Built Environment*, 16 (3) pp. 192–202.

Zeiger, H. (1985) 'LEG-UP: Local Enterprise Grants for Urban Projects', *Policy and Politics*, 13 (2) pp. 199–210.

Zukin, S. (1988) *Loft Living* (Radius).

Index